LIVING A POLITICAL LIFE

Madeleine Kunin

LIVING A POLITICAL LIFE

ALFRED A. KNOPF NEW YORK 1994

THIS IS A BORZOI BOOK
PUBLISHED BY ALFRED A. KNOPF, INC.

Library of Congress Cataloging-in-Publication Data
Kunin, Madeleine.
Living a political life / Madeleine May Kunin.—1st ed.
p.   cm.
ISBN 0-679-41181-X
1. Kunin, Madeleine.   2. Governors—Vermont—Biography.
3. Vermont—Politics and government—1865–   I. Title.
F55.22.K86A3   1994
974.3′04′092—dc20
[B]   93-11084   CIP

Manufactured in the United States of America
FIRST EDITION

To my mother, Renée, and my aunt Berthe

"Power is the ability to take one's place in whatever discourse is essential to action and the right to have one's part matter. This is true in the Pentagon, in marriage, in friendship, and in politics."

—Carolyn G. Heilbrun, *Writing a Woman's Life*

Preface

"Women must turn to one another for stories; they must share the stories of their lives and their hopes and their unacceptable fantasies."
—Carolyn G. Heilbrun, *Writing a Woman's Life*

"Most [women writing autobiographies], needing an appreciative audience for their causes to prosper, had to present themselves as the embodiments of romantic femininity, women to whom things happened rather than people who shaped events."
—Jill Ker Conway, *Written by Herself*

This book was written to tell the story of my political life so that I might better define it for myself, and in doing so, provide some useful material for others.

I am grateful to Carolyn Heilbrun and Jill Conway, who expressed the need for women to write forthright autobiographies so that we may learn from one another. Only if we resist the temptation to attribute success to luck or chance can we help other women articulate their ambitions and shape their destinies, as men have often done.

We all borrow bits and pieces of role modeling clay from one another to build our composite selves. I am grateful to those who were generous to me by revealing fragments of themselves which I could rearrange to suit my needs. Writing this memoir gives me the chance to reciprocate. Only by writing our stories can we pass the political DNA from one generation to another, a transference that is still less common for women than for men.

I suspect that is why I continue to be asked, "How did you get into politics?"

This book is the long answer to that question, the one that I never had the time or courage to explore until now.

In the self-searching exercise of writing a memoir I tried to portray the many sides of political life, holding it up like a crystal, capable of revealing a new light pattern with every turn. The public is well tutored in the dark side of politics, but is less acquainted with its brightness, the many facets that make it so attractive.

I confess to feeling continued ambivalence about political life, aware of its shortcomings and disappointments, but drawn back to it again and again because of its infinite promise. Justice can triumph, wrongs can be righted, and pain can be alleviated, if the right fix is found. The optimistic illusion that one can change the world is difficult to resist, especially when from time to time that illusion is sustained by even a hint of reality. Change does happen in the political process. When a political decision affects a life, the result is extraordinarily satisfying. And I am seduced once again into believing—for the moment—that political engagement is the only way to lead a meaningful life.

It is also fun. It is exciting to be at the center of things, something I suspect men have long known, and women are just beginning to find out.

We cannot leave the responsibility of self-government to a select few whom precedent seems to have destined for the task. Democracy depends on fresh recruits for its vitality. Our political system is far more accessible than it appears to be, but not everyone knows or believes that. If we can restore that belief ever so slightly, we enhance our ability to govern ourselves fairly and well.

Acknowledgments

I would like to thank the three people who read the early drafts of my manuscript and gave me important feedback and encouragement: Carolyn Heilbrun, Dale Brown, and Liz Bankowski.

My editor, Elisabeth Sifton, gave me the best advice by simply telling me to keep on writing. Her subsequent editorial advice was invaluable. I thank my other editor, Jane Garrett, who was there both at the very beginning of this undertaking and in the final stages.

I am very grateful to the academic institutions that gave me the time and space to acquire the discipline of writing: Dartmouth College, where I was a Montgomery Fellow in the winter and spring of 1991, and the Rockefeller Center for the Social Sciences, where I was a Visiting Fellow in Public Policy in the fall of 1992.

The Bunting Institute at Radcliffe College, where I was the first Distinguished Visitor in public policy in the 1991–92 academic year, gave me the warmth of sisterhood and the discipline of other women's intellectual achievement, strengthening my resolve to write and easing my loneliness.

I thank the students at both Dartmouth and Harvard who informed me through their questions and comments.

I was able to complete my book thanks to the MacDowell Colony in New Hampshire, which provided the greatest period of isolation and concentration I had ever known, permitting me to further transform myself into a writer. I am grateful to my fellow artists, who gave me encouragement, both by their words and by their example.

I thank those who helped with research and support services, including Betty Lou Marple, Elizabeth Caputo, Leslie Farrar, Louis Berney, and my good friend Marilyn Stout.

I am very grateful to my family for bearing with me—even when it was difficult for them—during those times when I could not tear myself away from my word processor.

And I thank the people of the state of Vermont, who provided most of the material for this book.

LIVING A POLITICAL LIFE

1

DON'T CRY, I TOLD MYSELF FIERCELY, STAY IN CONTROL. STANDING AT the top of the curved stairway across from my executive office in the state-house, I concentrated on the announcement I was about to make at the press conference scheduled for 10:00 a.m.—just a few minutes from now—one floor below, in room 11. It was April 3, 1990.

I eyed the stairs with trepidation and steadied myself by grasping the dark-brown railing and feeling its smooth contours filling the cave of my hand. I let the hardness of the wooden railing extend into my fingers, my arm, and up through my backbone, until I was firmly braced, ready to make my descent.

Breathe deeply, exhale slowly, once again, I told myself, to establish the normal rhythm of my heart.

Coming up the stairs toward me was the familiar face of a legislator; my eyes met his. What did he see in my face? Pity? Fear?

He knew.

I was exposed. The geyser of tears, which I had securely capped with a firm twist, was undone. I fought the eruption until my facial muscles ached.

I smiled to relieve the pressure. Grinning, I stood mute, unable to speak.

The legislator nodded and, kindly, moved on. I extended my foot, tentatively reaching for the next step, hoping to catch the tempo of the stairs to lead me down.

I knew what I had to say, but I simply did not know if I could say it. I was about to announce that I would not run for reelection to a fourth term as governor of the state of Vermont. I did not need to cling to power; I was ready to let go and move on to new challenges. I was grateful that I could use the familiar phrase "new challenges." It gave me exactly what I needed to make my exit. Like all good clichés, it said everything, and it said nothing.

Why, then, the tears? I no longer could trust my body to obey the commands it had learned by rote, to be calm, be strong, and smile. As I had gone over my speech a few moments before, in midsentence, like a hot flash, I had been betrayed, and red blotches rouged my face in erratic patterns, bleeding down into my neck. A terrible sadness had overcome me; I felt as if I were mourning my own death.

Why this upsurge of emotion? I was a seasoned political warrior, the survivor of three campaigns for the state legislature, two for lieutenant governor, and four for governor. I had known both victory and defeat. I had disciplined myself to become who I wanted to be, a strong and confident woman.

And I had long ago become familiar with my political demons: fear, self-doubt, and paranoia. Through practice, I had gained the capacity to keep them under control. Each time I got the upper hand, I felt a sense of accomplishment; I had triumphed over myself once again. After a particularly grueling press conference or tough debate, I would experience a rush of adrenaline, as my stronger self flaunted its prowess over my weaker twin, forcing it to beat a retreat. And each time, I was certain, it would be the last time I would have to fight. I was wrong. My skills improved, and I amazed myself with my daring, but the battle continued. With each step I took toward greater political responsibility, I felt a heightened sense of vulnerability, which, in turn, intensified my need to overcome it.

Today's challenge fit into the familiar pattern of terror followed by triumph. The danger was timing; would I be able to rescue myself in time, before my vulnerability was exposed?

Controlled emotion is essential on the political stage, and this is what I strived for. At times I questioned whether my self-control was too successful, making me seem too distant or aloof. The political audience is always searching for the genuine person who they suspect is hidden under the political facade, and a sudden show of anger, joy, or grief gives us all a rare and furtive look into what we take to be the reality of the man or woman who accidentally left the door ajar. But there is no public tolerance for a show of sloppy emotion that overcomes the speaker and reveals that the struggle for self-control has been lost.

In theory, women and men should be allowed to cry in public, but rarely have they been permitted to reveal such human frailty. Strong men, such as Ronald Reagan and George Bush, whose tough credentials are not debated, have more leeway. A tear in the corner of the eye at a poignant moment is a welcome sign of compassion in them, but a woman crying prompts mixed reactions, the depths of which are difficult to comprehend. Men may experience remorse and discomfort when they see a woman crying in public, and women often cringe with embarrassment at the sight of other women's tears, fearing that they—that all women—will be held responsible for such behavior. Seeking an idol, a woman whose life is under control, they may have little tolerance for disappointment.

Most women cannot risk revealing public emotion; they are asked to take the toughness test each time they appear in public. A silent assessment is made by the audience as a woman approaches the podium: Can this woman be as strong as a man?

If I cried, my tears would be taken as a sign of defeat, proof that I had not been tough enough to handle the strains of political life. Worse yet, they would reveal regret.

The rhythm of my political life, like that of all political lives, had been punctuated by a series of tests: the day I first announced that I would run for lieutenant governor, my first statewide race, the night I conceded defeat when I lost my first race for governor, and, two years later, the morning I was elected governor for the first time. These experiences taught me that a grand exit is as important as a great entrance. First words and last words are recorded; my legacy as well as my future depended on how effectively I would now explain my decision to leave public life.

I was concerned with more than outward appearance; I wanted to be in control not only for my audience, but also for myself. I had made a voluntary, rational decision not to seek a fourth term as governor. So this was not a concession speech, and I reminded myself I was not giving up in the face of defeat. This press conference was taking place on the morning of a bright spring day in the Vermont statehouse. It was not taking place in dark November, on election night; I was not being forced to walk into a floodlit hotel ballroom, steadying myself at the podium, eyes smarting from cigarette smoke hovering overhead. I had chosen the date, the time, the place, and the text. It was not foisted on me. I had not taken my cue from the ring of the telephone, from election returns spewed into my ear.

Yet I could not totally dispel the smell of defeat. Leaving office voluntarily to return to private life is such an unusual decision for a politician that there is a public presumption that one is being pushed out the door. If no apparent election struggle is taking place, the decision to leave a highly competitive position of power is seen as an act of submission and, ultimately, weakness. The meek walk away; the strong stay and fight. All the more important to keep my head high.

I envisioned myself a few minutes from now—standing in front of the jam-packed crowd of legislators, press, and lobbyists, surrounded by the flotsam and jetsam that washes up at political gatherings—saying the words: "I have decided not to seek a fourth term as governor of the state of Vermont."

I imagined headlines appearing the minute the words were out of my mouth: "Kunin Bows Out, Gives Up, Quits."

I hated it. Each time I had announced that I was running for office, I had experienced exhilaration at the words "Yes, I will run"; I had felt the audience cheer, embrace, and support me in the great escapade of a political campaign.

I now saw myself in room 11, the same room in which I had announced twelve years before that I would run for lieutenant governor and where, eight years before, that I would be a candidate for the governorship of the state of Vermont.

When I had entered that room, I felt a mixture of terror and elation, knowing that what I said and how I said it would set a course for the rest of my life. Striding into room 11 to declare that I was ready for battle was, in retrospect, a simple task, easily understood, regardless of the odds. Our advance work had consisted of making sure that the microphone was in the right place, that there were enough seats, but not too many. I recall how astute I thought Steve Kimbell, my first professional campaign manager, was when he asked the sergeant at arms to remove three rows of chairs so there would be no risk of empty seats. Repeated phone calls were made to make certain that there was a crowd, that the right people were there, and, most important, that all the right members of the press would show up. Organizing an announcement was a production that would be interpreted as a sign of whether we could organize a government.

This time, everything was different. There was no advance notice; none of us worried about the seating, the press, or the audience. The room was jammed, not because we had taken the time to place calls, but because that morning the news of the announcement had whipped through the statehouse by word of mouth.

I had known that the only way I could make an exit from politics was to leave by my timetable. I had recoiled at the thought of being backed into an explanation, being badgered by a reporter's unanticipated call at eleven o'clock at night, being asked to admit that I was not running. Denials, hedges, evasions—I dreaded those responses, knowing they would blur my message and raise questions about my motives. On this day, I had to have the first word, and the last.

The night before, three of my closest advisers—they were also my friends—had planned the event: Liz Bankowski, my former chief of staff and campaign manager; Kathy Hoyt, my present chief of staff; and Kathy Stankevich, who had managed my office from the time I had been elected lieutenant governor in 1978. The three women, to avoid suspicion, had stayed at the La Gue Inn in Berlin, a few miles beyond Montpelier, under assumed names. Liz used her husband's name and became Elizabeth London, and Kathy Hoyt went back to her unmarried name, Kathy Clark. It worked. No one had advance notice of the press conference. I had made a few key calls—to my brother, who was a state senator; a few close friends; Tom Menson, my secretary of administration; and Judy Stephany, my legislative liaison. I swore them to secrecy.

But earlier that morning, when I had stepped off the elevator on the fifth floor of the Pavilion Office Building, I knew my world had changed. Karen O'Hagen, my secretary; Janel Johnson, my scheduler; and Marilyn Johnson, the receptionist, had just received word of "the decision." They began to cry. We instinctively clutched one another in a tight embrace. It was as if we had been told that a close friend had just died. And when I called the staff together, I knew by the look in their eyes that despite some internal warnings my decision came as a shock.

An hour later, the extended cabinet, composed of agency secretaries, commissioners, and their deputies—a group of forty people—had gathered in my conference room. The usual chatter was missing. They knew.

I reached out for Joe Patrissi, commissioner of corrections, because I knew I could get a laugh when I asked him the usual question: "Is everyone tucked safely in their beds, Joe?"

"Yes, Governor," he would reply, wringing his hands, and we would both chuckle at the familiar exchange.

Despite my efforts to lighten up the room, when I stood at the front of the rows of chairs, facing the people I had worked with every day for the last six years or more, I hadn't been able to hold back the tears, and then, in frustration, I had burst out with, "Oh, shit."

That did it. I was so glad I could make them laugh, and that here, among my extended family, I could tell them how hard it was to let go. I previewed lines from my prepared speech, alternately laughing and crying. The women expressed the most open emotion, in part because this announcement meant for them that their experience as women working in a male environment was coming to an end; we had been part of an unusual experiment, a matriarchy; now it was over, and we might not experience something like it again for a very long time.

Endings, with all their pain, place the past in focus. In that room, at that moment, I had begun to put a frame around the last six years. A bittersweet feeling took over, sadness that our turn was brief, and happiness that we had had the chance to do it at all. Then I had walked the short distance from my office in the Pavilion Office Building to my state-house executive chamber, surrounded by a protective phalanx of staff, achieving the visible mass of power I had always envied when I observed other governors in motion: they never walked alone.

Standing at the first-floor window of the Appropriations Committee room was my brother, waving his arms wildly. I laughed uproariously. When Edgar met me in the hallway, shouting, "Free at last!" I successfully concealed that I felt I was going to the hangman.

When I stepped into the executive chamber with its enormous brass Victorian chandelier and red velvet chairs, there, sitting in the royal-looking governor's chair behind my desk, was Ralph Wright, Democratic Speaker of the House, wearing a big grin. Goldilocks himself.

Was I imagining it, or was his shirt crisper than ever, his suit better fitting, his tie in astounding good taste? And where did he get that after-shave lotion? Was it only a jest, or was this how he brandished his ambition—not waiting for the body to be cold, already celebrating my wake?

"What are you doing there? Get out!" I shouted, breaking into laughter and grabbing his arm. The physical act of pulling him out of my chair released mock anger and provided comic relief. Our tussle ended in a long hug.

I forgave him.

This caricature of a Boston-Irish politician from Somerville gloried in following a tough political script. With equal relish, he loved to depart from it, if only to surprise his enemies. Better than anyone, he understood power: how it is won and how it is lost. Today, his finely tuned political instinct was telling him I needed him; he knew what had to happen at this moment of reckoning. I had to express fury and beat against his chest, even as I let myself be comforted by his embrace.

Despite myself, he had made me laugh. I was grateful.

I could not tell whether he thought I was courageous not to run again, to leave of my own free will on my terms, without a rout, or whether he thought, according to his marine training, it was an act of cowardice.

Ralph, I had no doubt, would have punched his way out the door. My battleground was in my head.

I rehearsed my part: how I would enter the room, stand at the podium, plant my feet firmly on the floor, keep my voice at a low, steady pitch, no cracks, no hesitant pauses, no wavers. Eye contact: I would focus on the ugly swollen lens of the camera, never glancing downward in thought or inward in doubt.

Lying in bed in the early hours of the morning, I had begun to mouth the words: "I have reached the conclusion that I will not seek a fourth term—" and then I had stopped. There, in the shelter of my own womb-like bed, warm, drippy tears had spotted the wrinkled sheets.

"Crying time, we have to schedule crying time," Liz Bankowski had announced several days before. Liz had returned to Montpelier from her home in Brattleboro to be present for my announcement; just as she helped bring me into the political world, she now arrived to help lead me out. She and the "two Kathys" acted like nurses tending a patient; I succumbed to their loving care.

They soothed me with their calm voices, administered cool liquids to bring down my fever, and supported my arms to help me walk. Most significant, they diagnosed my illness correctly and provided the right prescriptions, enabling me to break the fever and assure my recovery. They knew precisely how I felt.

"Get it out of your system," Kathy Hoyt said, and I obliged like a good girl, blowing my nose into a Kleenex.

"We built crying time into the schedule," Liz announced seriously. "It's okay." And we had giggled ourselves into a liberating, raucous mood, seeing ourselves as we were: a bunch of silly women gushing out emotion. If we were the generation that wore girdles, we now would be taking them off with a great sigh of relief, exulting in our freedom. We felt fantastically good. Even as we instinctively understood the need for such emotional release, with equal clarity we saw the need to contain it when the time came, when we would be on display again in the men's world.

Any political administration becomes a family and develops a special and enduring camaraderie. The unrelenting pace—one crisis following on another, day after day—weaves a tough fabric. You come to know the same jokes, the same stories; you experience the same moments of terror and glory in shared bursts of triumph. As with brothers and sisters who have eaten so many meals at the family table, you can speak in gestures, looks, and incomplete sentences and remain confident that someone will indeed pass the ketchup, even though you didn't exactly ask for it.

In a woman-governed administration, such as mine in Vermont, this traditional political bonding was magnified by the knowledge that we women were doing it differently; we were inventing ourselves, gazing out on a vast political landscape with the curiosity of explorers. Always, in the backs of our minds, we were sobered by knowing that, whatever we did, our deeds would be silhouetted up against the wall of history, and our shadows would outline the shape of things to come for other women.

Women were present in significant numbers during my governorship, and in positions where they did not have to accommodate themselves to the existing power structure but could, in fact, establish a new tone, new values and priorities, because women themselves were at the center.

An inevitable comparison was made between my administration and a traditional male-led administration. This was not because of male chauvinism, but because of the inescapable truth that all Vermont governors before me had been men. Two questions were raised by the visible notoriety of unprecedented female leadership: How were we like our predecessors, and how were we different? Of course, we were expected to be both.

The historic male model, while no longer idealized, has nonetheless become synonymous with a universally accepted definition of "leadership." Both women and men are accustomed to it, because until now no alternatives existed. When we women scanned the names and faces of those men who had governed before us, we could not help but follow their examples, yet simultaneously we resisted precedent. And that is where the excitement was—in finding ways to veer off, to reinvent, to throw out, to start afresh. And, in the process, to boldly, brazenly, expose our womanhood whenever we dared to do so.

The tension between surviving under the old rules and inventing our new rules made for a continuous subtext beneath all our official words and actions. Sometimes we swung in one direction, needing the solace of tradition, needing to be noncontroversial and easily understood, and at other times we relied on our female instincts and let them surface, realizing that this was why we were there, to be different. Sometimes we faked it, acting like proper schoolgirls, while underneath we harbored outrageous thoughts of rebellion. Often, we simply blended traditional male ways with our newly emerging female political styles.

We came to realize all this slowly, over a period of years, because at the beginning we felt compelled to follow tradition. Our teachers were men, and we were eager students. Gradually, as we grew in experience and in numbers, we began to trust ourselves. Our inventiveness grew, and something akin to a woman's political culture emerged.

I soon learned that not only did my female cohorts need me, but I needed them. The presence of women in key places at critical times made me feel less alone, alien, and bizarre in male political terrain. I discovered that we could communicate as women in a secret and often silent language that was easily understood and created among us a feeling of shared conspiracy.

I now understand that this could only have happened with a woman in a leadership position. The power of a governor to set the tone and define the values of a state administration is enormous. But even with this well-defined and clearly understood power, I had to learn how to redefine it on my terms. That learning process never really stopped; just when it became clear that I and my colleagues had, in fact, created a different political culture, I realized it had come to a close.

The search for an appropriate and effective expression of my womanhood in a male-defined position of power was constant. Often I felt my feminine perspective might sabotage me, make me critical of the very system I was trying to master. Gender gave me a certain degree of political naïveté, an insider-outsider dual perspective, which at times was valuable and at other times damaging, when it impeded my wholehearted participation in the political system. I was the dignitary marching in the parade going down the middle of the street, but part of me was drawn to the sidelines when I identified with the crowd watching, since that was where I had been for so long and, on some level, still felt I belonged.

It was shocking to me to see how susceptible I continued to be to that most chronic symptom of female insecurity: feeling like a fraud.

At times, the dual perspective of participant-observer was entertaining and informative. I felt I could see things that more seasoned male politicians could not. I knew the thrill of being in two worlds at once, having the unusually rich experience of looking at the crowd through a politician's eyes and returning the gaze from the public's vantage point. I could empathize with the parade-watching crowd and feel how they felt looking at me. This made it harder to take myself seriously but also permitted me to serve as an interpreter from time to time, translating messages from one country to another.

Once, as governor, I was invited to a national Democratic party cocktail party in Washington and observed the glittering personalities in the crowd, surrounded by a throng of press who probed and circled the room with television lights and cameras, settling briefly on the faces of Senators Ted Kennedy, Joseph Biden, Gary Hart, and Governor Michael Dukakis. For some time, I stood at the periphery, caught beyond the outer ring of camera-clicking press. I was fascinated, watching the dramas unfold. Then, with a start, I reminded myself, Get into the inner circle, Madeleine. Have your picture taken. Talk to those people. You are one of them.

In some ways, keeping my distance was a protective strategy: if I did not become too engaged in this dangerous game of politics, I could always tell myself that I am not like the men who have always done this, whose sense of self is so dependent on their power positions. I could say, I can go back to private life because that's fundamentally where I have always been and still belong. Did it take a special energy to step into that inner circle, a predominantly male crowd, to present myself as the politician I knew I was but suspected I wasn't? Yes, I had to force myself to plunge in. But once I caught the rhythm, I, too, was lost in the dance.

As I CONTEMPLATED the prospect of leaving the governorship, I began to understand, perhaps for the first time, the seductive nature of power. I had always known about power, I thought, and had prepared myself for relinquishing it by keeping a distance, by maintaining an inner life, by not taking myself too seriously. But in truth there is no assured protection against the seductions of power. Now that I had made my decision, I experienced in a new way the truth that it is more exciting to be in the center of the ring than on the sidelines, watching.

That theatrical aspect of power—the excitement, the lights, the action—is well understood. What is less obvious is that the pressure of being onstage forces one into a continuous state of becoming, and that *that* is where the adventure is.

To govern is to live in the future tense. "The governor will," "the governor is considering," "the governor may"—this gives you the most potent power of all, the power of what *might* happen. Politics creates an almost endless time horizon into the future.

This was the hopeful world I lived in, filled with invention, optimism, and creativity. Dreams were articulated and programs planned to make those dreams come true. As governor I had the incredible luxury of being able to dream on a grand scale. And this sense of infinite possibility gives politics its romance. The announcement that I would not run again collapsed the dream; my political future became finite.

Now the tidying-up process would begin. So many months and days left in the term. All the loose ends to be tied up, projects to be concluded, reports to be signed. My task was to leave in good shape for the next occupant the house that I and my colleagues had built. But the quest itself—the quest to govern well, to govern differently as a woman—had ended. My announcement did mean that I was giving up, not power as commonly interpreted, but the dream of governing differently, of creating change indefinitely.

Two weeks after I left the statehouse, on vacation in Mexico, I began to record the loss. I wrote in my diary:

> *Walking on the beach yesterday in the late afternoon, alone, singing to myself, swinging my arms, stretching, I felt a sort of exorcism, the stirring of a physical relief from emotional pain. My first language reappeared, and I enunciated the German word for pain,* Schmerzen. *All that accumulated pain covered up by layers of self-control began to reveal itself here, by the sea. I don't understand it, and I am afraid to confront it, but as I began to breathe deeply, I felt a weight begin to lift from my chest.*

I was mourning the loss of the quest. Ironically, it was the quest to govern differently, as a woman, that had given me the courage to enter the political world, and, ultimately, it was my womanhood that helped to alienate me from that world. But I did not abandon it completely, and with time, I retrieved it in new forms.

But now, on the day of my announcement, I resented the ticking of the political clock, so ruthlessly inconsiderate of my need for more time. Ready or not, the clock forced me to make a decision before the next election cycle. Only after it was over was I glad for the clean separation of this part of my life from the next.

I could now see my name chalked in white on the blackboard of history: three gubernatorial terms, six years, Madeleine M. Kunin, 1985–1991, an epitaph. I feared I would be incomplete without my title appended to my name, like a weighty anchor, grounding me in status, telling me who I was each time my name was spoken. When the title preceded me, it heralded my entrance, as when the Vermont state trooper at the wheel announced to the uniformed White House guard at the Southwest Gate, "The governor of Vermont," and our car was waved through with a white-gloved hand. How much would I miss the grand prefix that swept me into such places? Did it, in fact, explain who I was, not only to the White House guard, but also to myself? Public life provided ceremony and status and gave constant reassurance that one's life had purpose and meaning. Only when I contemplated its loss did I fully understand power's grip. Now I know why dictators fight to the death. I, too, was capable of wanting never to let go.

I reminded myself of the importance of looking for new meaning elsewhere, beyond the structured world of politics. In the previous weeks I had reached what I believed to be a sensible, logical conclusion: that it was time to test myself in new ways, and I eagerly looked forward to a postpolitical life. Yet at other times, I rebelled against my own argument. Politics was my life; how could I give it up?

My ambivalence was reflected in my dreams. I was taking an exam but hadn't taken the course and wondered how I could have gotten myself into such a situation. I was unprepared. My dreams switched to a different scene: large, red, bear-shaped Maurice Sendak creatures made of clay were stomping through the house, breaking off pieces of clay as they walked. I was buffeted around by them, pushed, shoved, and terrorized. Perhaps they were the wild things, representing the raw, rough, unpredictable nature of politics, for which I was also unprepared. Perhaps they were the political thugs of defensive paranoia, pushing me around, pushing me out.

The morning before my announcement, I went swimming, a ritual I maintained two or three times a week both for the physical exercise and for the mental release. I concentrated on the sensation of my body moving through the water, stroke after stroke, buoyed by the weightlessness of this altered state. As I swam, I wondered, Am I entering a different state of life? I'll be free of the staccato pressures of a campaign, the murderous suspense of its outcome; I won't be on call in continuous twenty-four-hour shifts, no instant anxiety in my chest each time the telephone rings.

What will that be like?

Better or worse?

Will time itself be different, dragging lazily through a day, rather than marching through an organized grid of fifteen-minute segments, commandeered by my daily schedule? Will I miss that feeling of being intensely alive, generated by each day's new maze of connections with people and ideas? Will I lose my electricity, the current that lights up the aura of power, the energy to leap to my feet to respond to a tough question, linking the synapses of my brain at amazing speed? Is this what made me flash a warm smile, take a long stride, and thrust out my hand in greeting, "Wonderful to meet you!"?

I had been living on the precipice of my own competence, touching a fine line between courage and terror for six years. Each time I extended myself further, closer to the edge of the cliff, and succeeded in subduing my demons, I was shocked by a surge of energy. Under pressure, I had mined new sources of competence, enabling me to survive and even to triumph. Would the loss of that hot flush of success leave me anemic? Once the current was shut off, would I be deflated, as in some science-fiction movie, when the body is separated from the soul and a crumpled dark blob is left lifeless on the floor?

"Yesterday's mashed potatoes," Liz had called it. "Be prepared. The minute after you announce, you'll be just like yesterday's mashed potatoes."

Arthur, my husband, preferred the ravioli metaphor, gleaned from a magazine article suggesting that one should use yesterday's leftover meat to stuff today's ravioli, just as Italian grandmothers did. Me, ravioli?

I laughed at both of them, happy to be served these culinary metaphors, delighted to have a reason to express my disgust.

What I really saw was the disappearance of the future tense and the transformation into the past tense. The clear sound of "governor" would be cluttered by an "ex" or a "former" placed in front of my name. Instead of the future, there would be that leaden word "legacy." I felt it pulling me to the ocean floor. After my announcement reporters would ask me to define my legacy, with kind but persistent questions: "What is your greatest accomplishment? How do you wish to be remembered? What do you most regret? Well, then, what would you do differently? There must be something that you would do differently if you could."

This was perhaps the only opportunity I would have to be the prime author of my posterity. As I watched the reporters' pencils moving across their notepads, I returned to my record: Vermont was recently ranked the number-one state for environmental policy, for children's services, for mental health. This was the scorecard I held out, listing the source for each accolade, glad to be armed with such heavy ammunition. As I mentioned that I had been listed in a recent issue of *Fortune* magazine as one of the nation's ten top education governors, I realized my reply sounded like a recitation. How long would the record last? How long would it be before a new crop of governors was ranked?

When our turn was over and the new team took charge, would we be erased? Will this woman-led administration be like a sand castle, fun to build and freely admired, standing in that brief space between high tide and low that would disappear when the inevitable, moon-drawn tide moved in, nothing remaining but smooth, glistening sand, and our spot indistinguishable from any other?

Or was I only objecting to the loss of immortality, as all public figures are prone to do? Did I want to leave some imprint to verify my existence? Or was there more at stake? Did I fear that as a woman I would, once again, not only be relegated to observer status, but be stuck high up in the balcony, hardly visible from the floor, where the speakers held forth and the votes were cast? Did I think that in bringing this brief period of woman rule to a close, I would rejoin generations of silent, invisible women, that once again I would become peripheral, that biting my tongue and turning my cheek would again be my lot? This has been the pattern of women's history, laced with empty spaces indicating where we might have been had we been seen and heard.

THE BEAUTY of our woman-centered administration in Vermont was that it assured our place in history; we lived lives of daily record, situated precisely at the apex of power, where everything we said and did was transcribed, impossible to be stricken. Unlike earlier generations of women, who had to find the courage to raise voices in reaction to men in positions of authority, it was we women who spoke first, an amazing reversal of the usual sequence. No longer pleaders at the bench, asking for men to intervene on our behalf, we stood at the podium and ourselves exerted control.

When I juxtaposed our experience against the past, I saw how remarkable it was for us women to spend our days being keepers of the castle, instead of climbing to the highest tower and peering out at the world below from a narrow slit, hoping to be rescued by a prince. That had been the yearning of countless generations of women in history who told their stories in songs and poetry, diary jottings, and ribbon-bound letters, their names rarely, if ever, encased in the heavy and dark volumes that recorded the history of humankind.

I felt the thrill of breaking precedent when I signed my first executive order with my woman's hand and woman's name, and Elizabeth Bankowski, my newly appointed secretary of civil and military affairs, signed hers. We both suspended our pens in the air for a moment, awed by the sight of our names on this official document, weighted by the gold seal of the state of Vermont.

"Will people fifty years from now look back and speculate about what happened here in the state of Vermont, when two women's signatures appeared for the very first time on such a document?" Liz and I asked each other as we enjoyed a secret moment of celebration. The bold appearance of "Madeleine" and "Elizabeth" was our homage to "Anonymous," to those women who, through the ages, dared not use their names. We felt the lineage of male succession had broken.

Today, as our rule was ending, I feared that the avalanche of history would bury our barely perceptible tracks. Perhaps we had been only an aberration from tradition, accidental tourists on the political landscape. In the context of "geological-political" time, my administration in Vermont was but a thin blue line wedged between thick layers of male rule, piled on one another. Just a spasm, that was what we were, shifting the layers ever so slightly, but they would soon align themselves again, and everything would go back to normal.

What did I expect? A golden glow emanating from our age, the women's age? A time people would reminisce about. Would some janitor, interviewed in the year 2021, say, "Yeah, it was different then, a woman governor and lots of women working here."

"Tell me how they were different," the reporter would ask the aged statehouse custodian.

"Kinda pretty. Didn't bang on the table like those fellers did, talked more softly. No cigarette butts to clean up. Just lipstick on the glasses. Lots of meetings, yeah, lots of meetings, had to open up first thing in the morning, keep the lights burning late at night. Talked about a place they called consensus. Lots of laughing and giggling."

It was true, in a way, that we had played house, pretended we lived in the governor's suite, had a wonderful time trying on oversize clothes, imitating the guys, aping their gestures in front of the mirror, laughing hysterically when we saw our fun-house reflections.

"Daddy's coming back," Kathy Hoyt, my chief of staff, joked, about the return of Governor Richard Snelling, who had preceded me, in 1985, and might succeed me, having recently announced his bid for another term.

"That's it!" I exclaimed, "Daddy." It had been a great six years of make-believe, but now the real daddy-governor was coming back, and he wouldn't like what he saw.

"What a mess," he would shout when he came in the door. "The place isn't how I left it! You've dumped your stuff all over the living room floor, dishes in the sink, and what's this? Makeup, lipstick, hairspray, and Tampax in my bathroom?"

The first time I had gone into the governor's executive bathroom, I thought I had stepped into a men's room by mistake. I opened the medicine cabinet, like a guest snooping on the owner's belongings. I discovered a slightly used, large cake of soap with a large letter *S* carved on it. I opened the shower door, sniffing the musty smell. Would I ever dare take my clothes off and step inside? I put the toilet seat down. I washed my hands.

We had taken possession of the fifth-floor executive suite at precisely the hour I was sworn in. Kathy Stankevich remembered the governor's large brown leather executive chair being wheeled down the hall by an aide and pushed into the elevator. The doors closed.

Years before, as a legislator visiting the governor, I had mentally re-arranged the furniture in his office, torn down the dark paneling, and opened the narrow windows wide. I don't think I had begun to envision myself as governor, and yet, as I sat before him in silence with a group of legislators, looking at his Harvard football team picture on the shelf, I was busily imagining how I would do things differently. I had had a negative reaction to being seated in front of his desk, and while trying to concentrate on the governor's uninterrupted barrage of words, I had in-vented a room of my own and dreamed of how I would behave, and what I would say, if I had the chance to usher people into my executive office. These are the daydreams from which new visions of leadership take shape.

Women have been inspired to renovate the trappings of power because we have been imprisoned in the old ones. If female leadership is different from male leadership, it is for this reason: we know what it means to be demeaned, to be intimidated, to be talked at by generations of men who ensconce themselves behind fortress-desks. So when I won the credentials to sit behind the desk, a woman decorator who volunteered her services helped me to open the room to light, to tear down the paneling and replace it with textured ivory-colored wallpaper, to put a bright hand-woven rug on the floor, hang sun-dappled paintings on the walls, borrow a graceful handcrafted cherry rocking chair made in Vermont. I soon learned to abandon my desk and sit instead in the rocking chair when I conducted meetings, seeking the lightness of touch that President John F. Kennedy, too, enjoyed in a rocking chair.

The day I moved in, I found a uniformed trooper seated at the recep-tion desk, a guard dog resting at his feet. Not my idea of a friendly wel-come to the governor's office. I told the trooper to hang up his uniform and wear plain clothes; the dog was ordered back to the kennel. My staff removed the newly bought brown Naugahyde couches and ordered fur-niture upholstered in rosy-colored fabric, framed in maple. I thought the office should be a hospitable and comfortable space for the people of Vermont, putting visitors at ease, like a home.

Every leader, man or woman, has the irrepressible desire to remodel the office—not because the rug is worn-out or the furniture falling apart, but because the old order must be exorcised, and the new one inaugurated. Women have concentrated—unduly, perhaps—on creating new and comfortable private spaces, focusing on those features that were within the traditional female domain, kitchens, living rooms, entryways, seeing them as extensions of ourselves. Make yourself comfortable, this is who I am. We are relatively new occupants of the public spaces, where people come and go, where decisions are made, where the chairs are hard and the backs are straight. As women, we had been the backstairs maids to history, catching power on the fly. Now we found ourselves inside the rooms we once glimpsed as visitors from afar.

At the beginning of my third term of office, I designed a new executive suite, abandoning the rooms under the slanting mansard roof for ones with huge, straight, square glass windows that framed the distant hills, the sky, and the brilliant golden dome of the statehouse. Light streamed in on the white walls and fell on the azure carpeting. This space was mine. It had taken four years to make it my own.

THAT IS WHY, now, on the day of this announcement, I found it hard to leave.

"The room's packed, they're all piling in there," Liz said to me, encouraging me to go downstairs. It was time. My husband, my closest staff members, and my twenty-five-year-old son, Adam, formed a protective phalanx around me.

I was glad Adam could be there, representing his two brothers and older sister. I knew this was a lesson, even if the subject was undefined. Would he learn about courage? About grace under pressure? I only knew it was important for him to see me meet the test to which I would submit myself. I couldn't let him down. We walked down the stairs, and the electricity in the air was palpable.

There are two climaxes in political life: rising to power, and falling from it. Because all political life hovers around these opposing possibilities—power won and power lost—when the definitive moment arrives, it almost does not matter for most onlookers which it is; victory or defeat, the suspense is the same, generated by the thrill of being privy to such raw emotion. We know what power looks like in these transforming moments when we focus on the face of the speaker, her hands gripping the podium, her every word and gesture. Would they be able to read my innermost thoughts? I wondered.

We walked down the stairs, and I happily shook each hand thrust out to me, accepted a hug here and a kiss there, and avoided direct exchanges of glances. "Congratulations," people said, and I wondered why, but I smiled and said, "Thank you."

We pushed our way through the throng that lined the hallway, past the marble statue of Abraham Lincoln. I needed a minute to compose myself and ducked into the doorway of a room across from where the crowd was waiting. Arthur and Adam stepped inside with me. Whatever emotional control I had stitched together was coming undone, like the buttons on the back of a dress that popped when I turned my head. I took out some Kleenex, blew my nose, put on a new layer of powder, and felt a warm hug from my husband.

"You can do it, you'll be great," he said.

I did my best to believe him, trying not to discount his words because I knew they were said out of fierce loyalty.

Should I take a Kleenex with me or not? I knew if I used it, that is how I would be photographed. I feared that if I cried and my nose ran and there was no Kleenex, the picture would look even worse. I flattened a Kleenex carefully inside my jacket pocket, not to reveal a bulge, and opened the door.

It was a short few steps from room 9 across the hall to room 11. These rooms were pleasantly familiar: room 9, the smaller of the two, was where the Democrats used to caucus, until they achieved a slim majority in the Vermont legislature and graduated to the more spacious room 11. It was a space whose walls radiated history. I gratefully inhaled its familiar air.

Applause. I had forgotten how healing its sound was. I scanned the packed room of legislators, press, friends, administrators, and staff, recognizing all but one or two of the faces. The applause began to ebb and then resumed with new vigor. It was impossible for me to measure whether it lasted one minute or five, but with each crescendo, I felt happier, stronger, lighter, letting the space inside me fill with sound.

The Speaker of the House whispered in my ear, "They love you, Governor."

At other times, I would have parsed those words, trying to decide if he was being jealous or kind; now I succumbed to the verbal embrace, like a teenager, eager to believe anything.

They could only clap that way because they knew how hard this decision had been. The audience knows what I feel, what I will say. I am not alone. I will be forgiven.

I had to become who they expected me to be: the person who could make a perfect exit.

I placed the Kleenex on a shelf underneath the podium and began to speak.

"This is the hardest speech I have given," I ad-libbed and smiled, immediately revealing the inner turmoil I had wanted both to hide and to share. Despite my mental self-control, I seemed to have a streak of self-sabotage: I could not help myself; I wanted them to know how I really felt. In part, it was a confession made in self-defense; they were being warned that I might not be able to carry it off. By exposing my vulnerability at the outset, I was also acting in animal self-defense, rolling over on my back, as if to say, Don't hit me.

I went on. "I would like to tell you about my future plans. Over the last several months I have had an internal debate about which path to take at this fork in the road—whether to seek reelection or to embark on a new and less certain course."

I took the Kleenex out of its hiding place and wiped my nose.

Snap!

They got me.

Sure enough, that was the picture on the Associated Press wire that afternoon.

"I have reached the conclusion that I will not seek a fourth term as governor of the state of Vermont. It is time for me to move on to new challenges."

New applause.

I began to feel a transformation. The political taint of public life was washing off my body. I was beginning to feel cleansed, scrubbed clean, an ordinary person once again.

> As your governor, I have experienced extraordinary times of elation and achievement, as well as some difficult hours. But at all times, I am so very proud to serve as the head of this great and special state.
>
> One thing I look forward to is having the time to reflect, to write, to share the details of this unique experience, and to inspire others—particularly women—to participate in public life.
>
> We have made history here in Vermont. We have shown that women are strong and capable leaders.

The applause exploded.

They agreed; they understood.

The secret was out. My feminism, which had formed the subtext of my administration, like the hard-to-read English subtitles in a foreign film, was now appearing in bold print on the screen.

My womanhood and its relationship to my capacity to govern were the central issues of my political life, but I had kept them hidden, sometimes even from myself and, more frequently, from public view. In order to govern, I had to behave as if being a woman was not an issue, because otherwise the "woman thing" would take on monstrous proportions and devour whatever else I hoped to accomplish. I couldn't have afforded to expend the emotional energy required to analyze the huge number of subtle but frequent gender questions, which could have either weakened my capacity to govern or given it fresh resolve.

The only standard available to me and to the people of Vermont of what constituted acceptable governing behavior, leadership, and success was set by men. I had to meet it, and more. As I governed like the men who had governed before me, I had to be what I undeniably and unambiguously enjoyed being—a woman.

Governing in the male tradition while being true to myself as a woman meant I had not, in fact, governed like a man. I had invented a new person, and neither I nor anyone else knew precisely what form she was taking. Internally, I had found myself in a tug-of-war, pulled in one direction by my male role model and in the other by my female experience.

In room 11, when I heard the crowd happily applaud the achievements of women, the tensions all dissolved. I felt whole. The new woman who had the strength to govern and the courage to be true to her feminine self had been recognized as one. The term "woman governor" no longer connoted a contradiction in terms, a curious deviation from the customary governor.

The applause seemed to be telling me that when I had expanded the definition of women and power I had also enlarged everyone's sense of possibility. This is what being a role model means: giving clues to those who watch you and enabling them to extract what they need for themselves. Being such a role model also relieved me of the burden of ambition, which weighed on me with accusatory discomfort. I could construe my political ambitions differently: rather than separating myself from my family in order to promote myself, I could be seen to be adhering to the female tradition of self-sacrifice, not in the capacity of a daughter, wife, or mother caring for children and men, but as a woman in service to other women and men. To further their lives, not my own, I had chosen this course. That is how I was justifying my political life.

*   *   *

THE DAY AFTER my announcement a surprise lunch was given for me
by a group of women: members of my administration, a few close friends,
and legislators. We let ourselves go with girlish silliness, letting out hoots
and cheers as I unwrapped my gifts: a mobile of tiny suspended naked
women made of lavender clay, each bearing the name tag of a female
member of the administration. Here, in the private room of this restaurant, with the doors shut, we could shriek with laughter. This is how the
women extended their embrace and told me that I was back in the folds
of sisterhood.

But the most powerful communications among women occurred when
we found ourselves in formal political settings where none of us could
speak but, through a glance, could share our subversive thoughts. The
subtle and instinctive manner in which women communicate such mutual understanding was made wonderfully clear to me when I was seated
in the Roosevelt Room of the White House on June 12, 1989, with seven
other governors, President George Bush, Chief of Staff John Sununu, and
Roger Porter, the president's chief domestic policy adviser, and other
White House and gubernatorial staff members. As I surveyed the room, I
made eye contact with the only other woman there, seated away from the
table, against the wall, a Republican White House staff person in charge
of state and local government relations. She sat straight in her chair,
notebook and pencil poised for action. We smiled at each other, and I
could feel a current of communication pass between us. I could read the
message in her eyes: "I'm proud you are there, sitting at the table. You'll
do great, don't worry."

I silently said to her, "I'm glad you're there, so that I'm not the only
woman in the room. Isn't it terrific that we're both here in the White
House? I'd like to cheer, but we have to pretend this is perfectly normal
for both of us."*

The same message of reinforcement could be sensed among women at
meetings of the National Governors' Association. A staff member would
smile at me from the sidelines, where she dutifully sat behind her gover-

* In February, 1993, I was invited back to the Roosevelt Room in the White House for a meeting
with newly elected President Bill Clinton and members of his staff. Everything was different than
I had remembered it from the last time.

The numbers of women and men in the room were about equal, the President sat relaxed in his
chair, one arm draped over the back of it, his legs crossed in front of him. The conversation was
lively; no one waited very long for anyone else to finish a sentence. The portraits on the walls
seemed to have lost their macho tint. How could I ever have thought this was a masculine space?

The next time I was back in the Roosevelt Room, I smiled. Someone had placed a portrait of
Eleanor on the mantelpiece.

nor, just beyond the reach of the hot television lights. When a woman complimented me after I spoke at a session, I would realize again how important it was for me to be there, not only for myself and for Vermont, but for other women.

In this almost exclusively male environment, I would often be my most severe critic and chastise myself. Why didn't I have the courage to speak up on that question? Or, after I did speak, I would second-guess my effectiveness. Why hadn't I made my point more forcefully? Did I sound too pushy and angry, or was I being too tentative? Communication with women in such settings gave me important feedback and reaffirmed my right to be in this ornate hotel ballroom with the male governors of this country.

The encouragement that I received from women and men contained an implicit acknowledgment: that no woman gained entry into these political rooms without being tough and, sometimes, afraid. It can be argued that all politicians, men and women, must meet those criteria. But then, what makes the political experience different for women? Women are newcomers, newly arrived immigrants, learning both the customs and the language of this new place. Men's political citizenship is unquestioned; many have held it for two or three generations. When they look around the table, they see themselves mirrored everywhere, other men wearing dark suits, red ties, and white shirts. When they walk into the ceremonial rooms of statehouses, courthouses, and the Capitol, the portraits on the walls tell them, "Welcome, we've been waiting for you; take your seat."

But when I took my seat at that antique table in the elegant Roosevelt Room in the White House, I looked up at portraits of Teddy Roosevelt and Franklin Roosevelt. This was their room. Women had not been expected.

And when I first stepped euphorically into the red-carpeted executive chamber of the Vermont statehouse, the day after my election to the governorship, I had found the walls lined with somber dark portraits of governors, each one a man.

What are they thinking? I asked myself as I stepped lightly and kept my voice low. This was a political cathedral, and I was a heretic.

"I'll be damned," I thought I heard a voice say. It seemed to come from a portrait that had suddenly tilted to the left.

"We'll get used to one another, I'm sure," I replied.

A woman visiting my office a few days later looked at me, looked at the walls, and looked at me again with a nod: "You're good for them."

In time, they were also good for me. At least they had held the job too and understood. And they *seemed* to listen. Once or twice I detected smiles crease the corners of their mouths.

After a few months of working in the office, I asked the statehouse curator to find a portrait of a woman to hang in the executive office. And he did. She was Eliza Hoyt, the little-known wife of the man who had built the portrait painter's house. Not a governor or even related to one, but she nevertheless succeeded in changing the chemistry of the room. With two of us there, I felt less alone.

(There were two other portraits of women in the statehouse: one the first Vermont woman legislator, Edna Beard, elected in 1921, and the other, the first Vermont woman lieutenant governor, Consuelo Northrop Bailey, elected in 1955. Whenever I welcomed schoolchildren to my office, I would point out the portraits of these women, sensitive to the visual impressions they made, particularly on little girls, who may have wondered, as I once did, whether they belonged here.)

Because women's portraits are so rarely hung in the high-ceilinged rooms where governmental decisions are made, women look elsewhere to find themselves reflected. They often find their likenesses in the unframed faces of other women, seated quietly in the room waiting for things to happen. This poignant expectation, from legions of silent women past and present, poised to catch each word we say, propels women like myself into these historic rooms and compels us to take our seats.

During my time in office—indeed throughout my years in politics—I have continually rediscovered the power I receive from women and give back in return. During a speech at the end of one of my gubernatorial campaigns, I was describing the need for a family-leave law before a chamber of commerce audience, a group on record in opposition to such legislation. One man, directly in my line of vision, kept looking at his hands and shaking his head from side to side as I spoke. As I read his hostile body language, my voice became weaker and my words more tentative. In my frustration, I felt myself getting angry with the audience. Why didn't they understand the importance of this issue? I began to question my political acumen.

In desperation, I looked around the room, and my gaze fell on a woman leaning forward in her seat, nodding vigorously, smiling directly at me. "Yes, yes," she was saying, "go on, go on." I was rescued, and I hammered away once again at my theme, forging the connection between family-leave laws and increased worker productivity. I could convert this audience after all.

A week later I received a letter, and I knew immediately from whom. She wrote, "I am so glad you said what you did. I had a baby three months ago and had to beg my boss to get time off to be with my baby. I never, never, want to go through that again."

So my words had strengthened her resolve to avoid future humiliation, had given her back the power she had lost in "begging her boss" for time off, and she, in turn, had restored my confidence, enabling me to face a tough audience. Each of us, in different but related ways, had brought our female experiences into a male environment and strengthened each other when we were in danger of being misunderstood or ridiculed.

As the governor of Vermont, I was given a larger stage to play out the conflict that many women feel between their desire to retain a traditional female identity and their wish to become full equals in society. Even as I was thought to be showing the way, I was continuing to explore the unknown. Would I overstep the bounds in one direction or another, be either too weak or too aggressive? Always, I felt the need to steer my feminism carefully through this uncharted course.

NOT UNTIL I announced that I would not seek reelection and the applause reverberated around me did I feel that I had struck the right balance. Then both my feminism and my ability to govern had been miraculously understood. I stood there in happy amazement.

My voice boomed out the next lines of my prepared text: "I am so proud of the record number of women who have led—and lead—this team."

More applause.

I had scored many firsts, including naming a woman to the Vermont Supreme Court and placing women in key positions in the administration. Sometimes I had sensed a backlash because of the number of women I had appointed in the executive, judicial, and legislative branches of Vermont's government. Here, in this room, now, there was only approval.

"We are tough, we are compassionate, and we are fine managers of the public trust." I conceded nothing. I claimed it all. Everything that I had been striving for, which had seemed just out of reach, was now in my grasp.

But I also wanted to acknowledge my debts, including my gratitude to the men in my administration. "And I am proud of the men we work with, who have understood this so well."

They had helped me to create a different agenda and govern in a new way, inspired by the reform possibilities presented by a new, woman-led administration. That they understood us as women and applauded our efforts had made for unusual camaraderie.

At times, men like John Dooley, my first secretary of administration and, later, a state supreme court justice, and Tom Menson, who succeeded him, and my press secretary, Michael Wilson, seemed bemused to find themselves surrounded by so many women, and with good humor they defended their male turf. They were proud to be working for and with women, and they contributed generously to Vermont's newly emerging political culture.

The most difficult task I had was to explain precisely why I was not seeking reelection and to make it clear, in both words and spirit, that I was not leaving office either in anger or in fear.

"I think our democratic political system is kept alive and vital when people like me understand that public service in the form of holding political office is not a lifetime occupation."

A rational statement, but it did not tell the whole story. A part of me wanted to stay in office, and I admitted as much when I continued, "As I turned this decision over in my mind, like some multiangled prism, reflecting different rays of light, I confess that for a time, I simply wanted to hold on.

"Power is difficult to release.

"Voluntarily.

"It is also difficult to walk away from a fight."

There it was. I was putting fear of cowardice on the podium and, in doing so, transforming it into courage. Like a man, I was declaring myself strong enough to be weak.

What I did not say, but everyone knew, was how difficult the political fight could be. The Vermont economy, like the rest of the New England economy, was deteriorating daily, and every incumbent New England governor was shouldering much of the blame. Governor John ("Jock") McKernan of Maine faced a tough race. In Rhode Island, Governor Edward Di Prete was in deep trouble. When Governor William O'Neill of Connecticut had announced a few weeks earlier that he would not seek reelection, I began to wonder how I could explain my own decision without being placed in the same class of ailing governors. As I watched Michael Dukakis struggling to get out of the black hole he had fallen into after running for president in 1988, and saw him sinking deeper into a political quagmire in Massachusetts, I was thankful I was not in his shoes.

The Vermont economy was in better condition than that of either Massachusetts or New Hampshire, and my political problems did not compare with those of Dukakis or the others, but I faced real difficulties if I ran for reelection. There were negative factors to overcome: the decline in the economy had forced me to make budget cuts and enact a fifty-million-dollar tax increase. My strong support for environmental legislation—including Act 200, a comprehensive planning law—had provoked a vigorous attack from a small, but highly vocal, constituency on the right. And increasingly I had become a national spokesperson on reproductive rights, which I was confident expressed the majority view in Vermont, but which elicited outrage from the opposition.

I understood the cyclical nature of politics, and I was sure that I could mount a strong campaign to prevail over these difficulties and win reelection, but after three gubernatorial terms and eighteen years in public life, I had difficulty in putting this disgruntled public mood into a long-term perspective. The poor economy had created a new anxiety in the electorate, and I sensed, on some gut level, that what the people wanted now was not the kind of government activism that had been characteristic of my administration. I was proud of having managed a series of budget cuts and achieving legislative support for a tax package, thereby avoiding an economic crisis, but fiscal management was not what I would be remembered for. The fear of defeat, which every candidate lodges in her or his heart and takes pains to suppress, had begun to make itself known. I had felt the onset of fear with each election cycle, but this time, it was harder to isolate, control, and conquer.

There had been days when the bravado needed for a campaign returned, when I felt that I had to continue in office and—most important—that I would win. I knew that the issues I espoused, education and the environment, were the issues Vermonters cared about most. I'd go through all the reasons for running again: eight years had more symmetry than six; there were achievements I wanted to protect; there was a need to prove I could ride out the economic storm, and then there was the administration, an extended family to whom I felt extremely loyal—I hated the thought of letting them down. On one level, I felt I had just hit my stride, only begun to establish a strong and professional team. What a pity to let go.

But another list of reasons for not running had begun to take shape. I felt a certain rebellion against the job itself for forcing me into a mold that fit less and less well. I began to feel that I was being held captive by the schedule that was laid out for me each morning and followed, step by step, through the day and into the night. For years, I had been willing to make the trade-off: in return for leading a governor's life, with all its demands and restrictions, I enjoyed the glorious freedom of being able to articulate a state agenda and experienced the satisfaction of seeing much of it transformed into policy, changing people's lives. These successes generated enormous excitement. I was leading a meaningful life, attached to the center of things. I had become whole: my inner values were being expressed in external action, and that was an extraordinary reward for public life.

It was this sense of wholeness that was coming apart. The person I appeared to be in public and the person I was in private were no longer the same. In an effort to connect the two, I had emptied myself out, like a box turned upside down. It was time for replenishment. By the spring of 1990, I felt I was neglecting my inner life. I knew that I could still go through the motions of governing, say and do the proper things, but I feared that I might do so by rote rather than conviction. I did not want simply to hang on.

I did not want to become a political figure whose sense of self-worth depended on looking in the mirror each morning and saying, "You are the governor." Having felt the seductive nature of power, I wanted to free myself of it and prove that I could live without it once again.

Political life by its nature is uncompromising. Some men and women have mastered a balancing act between their private and public selves, but few can do so for prolonged periods. The tempo and scope of the work are merciless. It is almost impossible to draw a circumference around a private life.

I felt the yearning to return to a more personal existence, to listen to the voice within, rather than to react. I felt the need for renewal, both spiritual and intellectual.

Political life is satisfying only when there is a connection between one's inner life and the outer persona. One adds intensity to the other and keeps them both at a high synchronized pitch. And the inner life has another, less-acknowledged purpose: it gives the public person that most critical ingredient—courage. It was an inner fire that had warmed and comforted me whenever I felt besieged and isolated in public. And it temporarily blinded me to what everyone else could see clearly: that the political life is brutal.

I could withstand repeated physical and emotional assaults—including lack of food, sleep, family, and friends—when I was able to draw upon a reservoir of idealism and conviction. But I now began to fear that this private stockpile had run low. I wanted the opportunity to be alone, to read, to write, to observe, and to create ties with a few individuals, one at a time, instead of reaching out to a hundred hands in the crowd. The luxury of an unscheduled day, of a meandering conversation with no agenda, of a walk that had no destination, these are the things I yearned for.

The thought of another political campaign filled me with dread. Everything extraneous would be shut out of my life, and I would have to focus exclusively, with an intensity hinging on madness, on the election. Early each morning and late every night, I would lie in my bed confronting the private terror—the possibility of defeat. Did I have the strength to push it away, relegate it to a circumscribed, dark place, and then get up, get on the road, plunge into the crowd, with a bright smile and a firm, extended hand? Yes, I could do it; I had done it before.

But whenever I looked at the choice between running again and not running, I realized that I felt refreshed and rejuvenated at the thought of living a more flexible, private life. I wanted to try to reinvent myself once more, but I knew that could happen only after a period of quiet incubation. My decision, which might seem like a withdrawal from risk, was in fact the opposite; I was rejecting the near certainty of a known identity in order to discover who else I might become.

STILL, I felt a painful ambivalence about abandoning one course and embarking on another. I acknowledged it now in room 11, when I told the crowd, in mock-macho language: "It is also difficult to walk away from a fight. Let me reassure you," I said as I was reassuring myself, "that I would have relished another bout in the ring with Richard Snelling or anyone else."

Applause greeted my male metaphor. I had instinctively reached for it, knowing it would be most easily understood. "But I do not have to prove my fighting mettle.

"But neither the desire to maintain a position of power nor the temptation to engage in battle is a valid reason for asking the people of Vermont to give me their confidence once again.

"Not even the knowledge that I could win is good cause to embark on this path.

"What was most difficult about this decision, I confess, was the fear that it would be interpreted as an abandonment of the issues that first stirred my political blood.

"What enabled me to arrive at this decision with a new sense of purpose was the realization that there are other ways to create change. Holding the highest office in this state is one route, a highly visible and effective one.

"But there are others."

I described my metamorphosis from private to public to private person once again.

"Innocent as it may sound," I told the crowd, "I think the decision I have made is made on two levels which are closely connected. One is highly personal—namely, how do I want to live my own life for the next several years?

"The pace of the governorship is so intense, demanding eighty to ninety hours a week, it is so fast-paced, that yes, it is tantalizing to dwell on the luxury of using some of one's time in a different way, with family, friends, alone. But that is only part of the equation. There is a second part, and it is, frankly, more important, and that is posed by the question: How can I lead a meaningful life? My personal life has been so intertwined with my public life that I know myself well enough to realize that a retreat from public life would, in fact, cause me personal unhappiness."

This is the drive I never understood; why could I not be content, as most people seemed to be, with a smaller circumference to my life? At times, I envied people whose lives were more self-contained, who did not need outside approval to affirm their personal validity. From this perspective, those of us who lived public lives were not more courageous, only more fearful of confronting ourselves, turning to others for confirmation of who we are. This assurance and reassurance becomes increasingly necessary, because a public figure is constantly in a state of becoming, learning to play new roles on strange turf, needing feedback in order to stay on course. The process of self-invention is creative but also dangerous. Mistakes are made. Then delight of new discovery gets the upper hand and sets caution aside once again. This cycle of risk taking, followed by fear, followed by euphoria, followed by new risk taking, must be akin to what a gambler experiences each time he rolls the dice. There was a part of me that thrilled to the game, but another part felt trapped by the addiction.

By the time I reached the end of my speech, I knew I had stopped the cycle. I felt light-headed. I had visibly shed one identity for another. Suddenly I was not a politician, but simply a human being, and all the protective political gear that I had been wearing for eighteen years fell in a pile on the floor. I was in a state of weightlessness that made me want to leap into the air. My mind did somersaults. Part of me cautioned the other part to get off the stage before I said or did something foolish.

I looked at Tim Lewis for a signal—he was the television reporter who, by virtue of his seniority, had always closed my press conferences. This time I laughed and said, "Hey, I don't need to wait for you anymore, Tim," and then I walked away from the podium and into the crowd.

As I looked into people's eyes, I knew they were seeing a different person than the one who had stepped into the room a half hour earlier. A friend volunteered a few moments later, "Madeleine, you've come home, you're one of us once again."

I wanted to say, "But I am exactly the same person I was ten minutes ago!" Yet I could not get the words out of my mouth. For, in fact, I was *not* the same person; I had shed part of my persona, a part I had not known existed until I cast it off.

I was always happy that I had taken the step to enter public life. But now I was also happy to step to the other side. How delightful it would be to engage in the ridiculing of other politicians! I felt a comic release and wanted to break into a private giggle. Simultaneously I realized that the warmth of my welcome back into the fold of humanity revealed the vast degree of separation between the public and its leaders and just how deeply suspect I had become as a politician.

Politician: that was a label that had locked me in a mold. The very fact that I had joined "them," the politicians, had placed me in alien territory. Everything I said or did in my official capacity was viewed through a political lens.

Remarkably, once I announced my intention to go, the agenda I had fought to achieve for six years came into focus. Everything I had said and done now seemed to be understood.

The praise and affection I received in the next few days made me feel as if I was present at my own wake and had been reborn.

"I never dared to say this to you before," the usually noncommunicative head of the Vermont Sugarmakers Association said to me, "because it might have been considered political, but you're the best governor we maple people ever had. Sure appreciated that you came to the maple-tree-tapping ceremony every single year."

Newspaper editorials summed up my three-term record with an accuracy usually reserved for obituaries; certainly I never saw such assessments while I was a political contender. I marveled at this: it was like reliving my political honeymoon.

The *Burlington Free Press* wrote: "She's led the most energetic state government since Gov. Philip Hoff in the 1960's, compiling a record rivaled by few men. In the past six months she's demonstrated the macho virtue of grace under pressure—the torrent of personal and political abuse over her planning law, Act 200. . . . If Kunin's decision is understandable in human terms, it's too bad for Vermont politics. Kunin sees government as a benevolent force. Under her prodding, lawmakers increased spending on child care and education and enacted broad environmental protections. . . ."

The *Rutland Herald* editorial of April 5, 1990, concluded: "Vermont has never had a governor whose motives, objectives and principles were more honorable than hers."

That very night, I was interviewed live on WCAX-TV by Marcelis Parsons, who had been the anchorman for six years. As I sat there, perched on the high stool next to his, hands folded quietly on the edge of the anchor desk, my knees under the rough wood of the phony, hollow set, I noticed for the first time how fragile it was, in contrast to the solid appearance the structure gave on the screen. I could see the lines of Marcelis's makeup, and I watched him push his hand through his hair and straighten his tie three times as he cleared his throat. Marcelis could not have been more deferential: "Thank you so much, Governor, for appearing on our show this evening." I was lulled into a relaxed state of trust by his kindness, until I realized that I was politically dead in his eyes, and I found myself making a few twitching motions to prove I was not ready to be buried.

My mind went back to the last big story he had done on me, several months earlier, when he accused me of the worst political sin—exploiting tragedy for my own political gain.

Two young women had been brutally assaulted in a massage center in downtown Burlington—it was a vicious crime that had shaken the community. The assailant had come to town on a bus and headed straight for the massage center, not knowing whom or what he would find.

A few days later, on a Saturday afternoon, I decided at the last minute to go to the hospital and visit the victims. I got a call from my press secretary, Peter Freyne, on another matter and then told him of my plans. He sensed a human-interest story and suggested some press calls. I hesitated, but then agreed, believing it was appropriate to let the press know of a change in my schedule. I did not take sufficient time to consider the possible consequences.

I will never know precisely how Peter Freyne conveyed the news of my hospital visit to the press, but Marcelis concluded I was putting on a show for the cameras. In any case, a television crew showed up at the hospital, and I asked it to stay in the lobby because I did not want to impose publicity on the patients. I had called the nursing staff to ask if a visit would be advisable, and we had agreed that one of the women would be pleased to see me and that we would keep it low-key. When I got to the room, the woman's family was there, too, and we had a quiet conversation, and I handed her flowers.

That night and the next, Marcelis Parsons gave stinging accounts of the intent of my visit, blasting my press secretary and me for self-promotion.

I was devastated. What I had thought of as an act of kindness, an opportunity to express concern about the growing number of incidents of violence against women, turned into a macabre portrayal of crass political opportunism. Helpless rage about being grotesquely misunderstood sent shudders through me. I didn't know how to fight back, and the more I tried, the worse it got.

Although I had made telephone calls and paid many similar visits in times of tragedy before, and my sincerity had never been questioned, I now began to analyze my motives with self-accusatory diligence. I must have done something to bring this on. Had I given any hint to Peter Freyne that this was a good press opportunity, and, if so, was I in fact overly eager for press coverage? Why hadn't I said a flat no when he suggested it? I suddenly felt endangered, afraid that I had momentarily lost my instinctive ethical compass, which had usually guided me well. Perhaps I had become a desperate politician, the kind I abhorred.

Tonight, though, here at the studio, on the night of my announced departure from politics, whatever lust for power he had attributed to me was fully forgiven. I had just rendered myself harmless and was therefore impervious to attack. No dark motives could be assigned to me. He treated me gently, like someone who just learned she has a terminal illness. Not once did he interrupt me; he gave me the pleasure of saying whatever I wished. My last words.

I had arrived in political heaven.

The day I had dreaded became a day I celebrated. I had obtained what every politician so desperately wants to receive: love and understanding. Ironically, those gifts could be given to me only at the precise moment that I renounced all ambition.

2

THE FIRST TIME I RAN FOR OFFICE, IN 1972, IT WAS BY MISTAKE.

This is how it happened. I was the mother of four children: Daniel, two and a half; Adam, six; Peter, nine; and Julia, the oldest, eleven. We were living in Burlington, Vermont, where my husband, Arthur, was an assistant professor of medicine at the University of Vermont. I had held various full-time and part-time jobs in journalism and teaching and had been actively involved in the community, but I identified myself as a homemaker.

On January 27, I recruited four or five neighbors to come with me to the local Democratic ward caucus, where I planned to make a short speech pointing out that there had never been a woman elected to the Burlington Board of Aldermen. I was inspired to do this—at my first Democratic caucus—because I had recently joined the Vermont chapter of a new organization called the Women's Political Caucus, whose purpose was to recruit women into politics and lobby for the Equal Rights Amendment.

When our group first discussed the upcoming aldermanic caucuses, I considered challenging the incumbent alderman, Clarence Meunier: that, we agreed, would clearly convey the message that it was time for women to get into politics. When I tested out this idea on several party regulars, they warned that I would make enemies if I tried to win the nomination in a surprise raid on the nominating caucus, usually a routine affair with only a handful of people present. The small attendance leaves open the possibility for a challenger, armed with a group of supporters, to "take over" the caucus, since whoever gets a majority of the votes of those present wins the nomination. But not wanting to alienate the party at my political debut, I abandoned the idea. Instead, I decided on a brief statement saying it was time for a woman to serve on the Burlington Board of Aldermen. I was following the teachings of the League of Women Voters, a school that believes that information equals power: once educated, politicians are expected to do the right thing.

The moment I entered the room, I knew that just being there was a political statement. The ten or fifteen people all knew one another, and most were relatives of the incumbent, Clarence Meunier. I was sure they were asking, as they turned to one another, "What is she doing here?"

Then they looked at the four friends who had come with me. We were all outsiders from Red Rocks, a new, upper-income development that, I later learned, was called the Gold Coast by some of the French Canadians who made up the largest ethnic group in the ward; an area that included several distinct neighborhoods: Lakeside, where factory workers lived in the houses and tenements constructed long ago for textile workers; the Cherry Lane area, a step up from Lakeside; and Southcrest, a step up from Cherry Lane. This whole part of town was referred to as the South End, and its center was St. Anthony's Church, a Catholic parish. Not everyone, however, sent their children to St. Anthony's school. Champlain Elementary School was the meeting ground for children and their parents from all the neighborhoods, and this is where the caucus was being held.

My friends and I filled up half a row of chairs and waited for the chairman to begin. I listened as Clarence Meunier was nominated. There was a pause. I looked around me and decided, If you're going to do this, now is the time. So I stood up and spoke briefly about the importance of women serving in public life. I noted that Vermont was the first state to outlaw slavery, and it would be appropriate for Burlington to be the first city to elect a woman to the Board of Aldermen. Then I sat down.

Henry Frankel, a community-minded IBM engineer who published a local newsletter called the *South End News*, assumed that this was a signal to place my name in nomination. The message that I did not want to be nominated had not gotten to him. So with surprising enthusiasm, he stood up, carried through on the theme of "it's time for a woman," and announced that I, too, would be a candidate.

It is hard to reconstruct precisely what I felt at that moment. With hindsight I realize that of course I could have asked to have my name withdrawn. The fact that I didn't makes it clear to me that on one level I must have welcomed Henry's "mistake." It may also have been the only way that I could step over the threshold into public life—being carried over it by someone else.

Henry's action created confusion. The chairman, Michael McGarry, a tall, pink-faced young man who had inherited the dubious mantle of caucus chairman from his recently deceased father, had not been prepared for such a complication, having thought Meunier's nomination would be a short, routine formality. Abruptly, he called for a voice vote, and before I knew it, I was declared the loser. I offered no protest, despite the fact that the ayes and nays seemed to be considerably closer in volume than McGarry's hearing may have allowed him to acknowledge.

Later, I had a good laugh with Henry Frankel about the misunderstanding. I was happy with the way things worked out; I had successfully raised the women's issue, and I had surfaced as a potential political challenger. Fortunately, by losing I had been spared a real power struggle.

The following day, the *Burlington Free Press* reported the event, including the voice vote. Our local state representative, Brian Burns, who never missed an opportunity to enjoy a political fight, immediately announced that the caucus had been illegal: when there is a contested election at a caucus, the vote must be by secret ballot, he said, citing chapter and verse from Vermont election law.

The embarrassed caucus chairman scheduled a new meeting for a week later. Meunier's immediate response in the press to this turn of events was that he didn't think "Mrs. Kunin was a serious candidate."

Having had this slight brush with elective politics, I bristled. "I am serious," I said, and that is how I launched my first campaign for public office. Challenged by Clarence and cheered by the Vermont Women's Political Caucus, I jumped in.

I now see that the Women's Caucus was a support group, but in 1972, that language had not yet been invented. I simply knew it as a small group of women, led by Caryl Stewart, who started the Vermont chapter. The person among us who became most influential was Esther Hartigan Sorrell, mother of all Vermont Democrats. Politics had been as much a part of her life as her family and the church. All the Hartigan sisters were political; their mother had worked in the mills, Esther explained, and that is where she learned to fight for justice. At the age of forty-one Esther bore her fifth child, but this hardly broke her energetic stride. Whenever a Democrat ran for office in Vermont, Esther's blessing was sought. For more than twenty years, she had worked to elect a handful of Democrats to the Board of Aldermen and the state legislature. In the weeks before an election, the traffic flow in and out of Esther's house turned her modest living room into a bustling command center—everybody was put to work, women, children, and old men. Esther, her neighbors, and friends, coffee cups and cigarettes in hand, would spend hours poring over voter checklists and telephone books piled high on the cluttered dining room table. Their job was to make sure the right people were called to go to the polls.

For one hundred years, Vermont had had the reputation of being the most rock-ribbed Republican state in the nation. What the South signified for Democrats, Vermont did for Republicans. An elegant portrait of one Charles N. Davenport hangs in the Rockingham, Vermont, meeting house, with a large brass plaque attached to the frame that lists all of Mr. Davenport's impressive accomplishments and concludes, "He was a Democrat in politics and consequently did not hold public offices." Democrats like Davenport, with serious political aspirations, ran under the Republican rubric if they did not wish to be sacrificial lambs. But year after year, Vermont Democrats inched their way toward numerical respectability, gradually outgrowing the proverbial phone booth that once had been commodious enough to include them all. Esther knew each benchmark. In 1952, when Robert Larrow was the Democratic candidate for governor, he received 39 percent of the vote, a close contest, by Democratic standards, against Republican Lee Emerson. In 1958 Bernard Leddy was the Democrats' standard bearer; the narrowness of that race was said to lay the groundwork for the next. A bitterly disputed recount revealed a winning margin of 716 votes. Democrats suspected they were stolen.

Four years later, they themselves were incredulous when Philip H. Hoff, a thirty-eight-year-old legislator from Burlington, became the first Democratic governor to be elected in more than a century. Spontaneous motorcades tooted jubilantly through the dark streets, rousing Republicans from their sleep to see what on earth had happened.

By 1972, there were sixty Democrats and one hundred and seventeen Republicans in the Vermont legislature. That year, Esther became a feminist. One afternoon when we were talking about how to get more women to run for public office, Esther and I looked at each other, laughed, and exclaimed, "Why don't *we* do it?"

That November, she was elected to the Vermont Senate and I was elected to the Vermont House.

Esther taught me to love politics. As I sat at her dining room table, I would listen to the conversation that matched the rhythm of stamps being licked and envelopes being stuffed.

"Did you hear that Mrs. McSweeney's husband just died, isn't it a shame?"

"Can you believe what the president said last night on the news?"

"Did Joe pick up those petitions? Be sure he gets them, we need at least five hundred names, and they have to be good ones."

"Like the cookies? I baked them this morning. I made Michaela the cutest dress last night, red corduroy."

"When did you have time for that, Esther?"

"Oh, it was easy, nothing to it."

"We've got to find another candidate for Burlington, what about—?"

"No, his wife just had a baby, and besides, she hates politics. Never comes to the polls. Maybe his brother will. Ask him."

Every few minutes, one of the names would remind Esther of a story; she would pause and ask, "Would you believe?" We'd stop what we were doing and listen.

One afternoon after Esther had launched her campaign, she announced, "Hey, girls, will you listen to this?"

Our stamp-licking tongues were happy for a rest, and we shuffled the damp envelopes into neat stacks.

"They asked me the other night when I was handing out my brochures after church, 'What do we call you if you get elected? Do we call you Madam Senator, Mrs. Senator, or Senatress?' " Esther roared, then paused, sat up straight, looked at each one of us with mock seriousness, and slowly said, "I told him, just call me Senator!"

She repeated, "Just call me Senator," and we clapped and cheered.

Esther was a great teacher. She understood politics, down to the last detail, but more important, she had an unshakable faith in the system. There was no question in her mind that the way to help people was through the political process.

On the Friday before Easter Sunday she made a speech on the floor of the Vermont Senate in defense of the poor. Single-handedly she got a majority of conservative Republicans to vote for an unprecedented 24 percent increase in welfare benefits. She had no doubt about what was right and what was wrong. She was doing God's work.

In her school of politics, people had fun, and money didn't matter; passionately held beliefs did, and she expressed them. As I look back, I was fortunate to receive my political baptism at Esther's hand. I became part of an extended political family with many cousins and uncles and aunts who cleared a space for me at the table.

The first meetings of the Women's Political Caucus at Esther's house were the female equivalent of the smoke-filled room. This is where we plotted strategy, gave one another courage, and practiced saying, "Just call me Senator." Without the approval, advice, and laughter of these women, I could not have gone into politics.

For generations men have had such initiation rites at the club, the bar, or the office. That's where they could practice the roles they would play and be indoctrinated in masculine lore. They could learn their lines by listening to stories of political feats and fiascoes. Politics was another genre of war story.

Women had been absent from these places, sometimes by accident, sometimes on purpose. The result was the same: there was no one to weave the political myths for them, to construct a sense of their destiny, to make footprints that women could follow. In the Women's Political Caucus, we learned to take one another's hands and form a chain.

DURING the early days of my first political campaign against Clarence Meunier, I would come home each night and speak into a tape recorder, cognizant that I was exploring a new world. Two days before the second Democratic Ward 5 caucus, in recollecting the events of the prior day, I concluded it was "one of my most action-packed days."

> *Arthur had the news on, as he usually does when he's shaving, and we heard Jack Barry giving the local news, announcing that a second woman had entered a contest for alderman, this time in Ward 2. Unlike me, however, or perhaps she wished to be contrasted with me, she said she was not "a women's libber." She said, "I'm not for that."*
>
> *That kind of amused me because I felt that indirectly she was "a women's libber" whether she realized it or not, by the very fact that she was running. I also felt that I had probably spurred her on and I found myself saying, "Great, more power to her."*
>
> *Next, I tried to get along with the usual household chores, which was difficult. I was fairly confused, between fatigue and excitement. Arthur had gone off early to work. But I managed to get lunches made and give the kids some kind of breakfast, and got Daniel ready for nursery school. I was about to leave the house when the phone rang. It turned out to be Bill Daniels, who, I think, is State Democratic Chairman. He is considered to be the intellect behind the Democratic party and is also a professor of history. I respect Bill Daniels's opinion.*
>
> *He had a tentative proposition for me. He said there was a rumor that Wilfred Thabault, the school commissioner from this ward, might be resigning because he's also an obstetrician and does not have enough time to devote to the school board, which is a "very, very demanding job." In that case, Daniels thought, there was a good possibility I might be nominated as a candidate for school commissioner. He thought it would be a good thing to do*

because I would be starting out with an assured victory. I would remain friends with everyone and avoid the bloody battle of alienating Clarence Meunier and alderman Robert Blanchard, all they stood for, and all the people they worked with.

Well, I told him I didn't know if I could turn everything off, and that I had an appointment for two o'clock that afternoon with Martha Canfield of the Burlington Free Press *to do a story on the race. He suggested I wait because once that story was in the paper it would be difficult for me to withdraw from the aldermanic race and run for school commissioner. I said I'd have to think about it.*

He said, "Well, you know, politics does sometimes involve making split-second decisions."

I said, "I realize that, but I have to have time to adjust to political life."

I knew that there was no guarantee that Thabault would resign and suspected that he was working with the mayor on this.

I left home and went to Esther Sorrell's house. I desperately needed advice. I did not know what to do. Should I do the political thing of making friends with everybody and maybe even being more effective in the long run in the city by being on the school board? But the school board frankly does not tempt me as much because it's more limited, and I think you don't go far on the school board politically because you never get popular serving on it. But I also feel a sense of mission because the schools in Burlington are very demoralized.

So, I went to a meeting of the newly formed Women's Political Caucus at Esther's house, walked in, opened my arms, and said, "Boy, do I need advice!" We had lunch at the same time, and sat around the table, and it was all very cozy and comfortable.

I placed my cards squarely on the table with the women who were there. There was Esther Cohen, a member of the legislature; Mary Taylor, who worked in the Democratic party for several years; and Esther. Also, Caryl Stewart, who organized the caucus, and Faire Edwards, very sharp, she worked with the Bread and Law task force. Another woman by the name of Jean Popecki is trying to get on the Police Commission. It seems that everything is happening at the same time. We are breaking into male ranks, and we feel a common bond.

Everybody talked at once at first, but what came out of the chaos was: "Don't give up now; if you do lose, Thabault may still resign, and you will have asserted your power." Caryl Stewart felt very strongly that I would be copping out, that it would obviously be a deal. Esther was the most politically astute and experienced. She had the same advice, which I was delighted to hear. I embraced her.

It was a terrific release of tension for me to be able to have these women to talk to. How lucky I was and how timely that I could

*talk to them. I saw, too, that in politics, you cannot make decisions
alone. I think I'm learning this—you have to seek various pieces of
advice from many sides and then form your decision. You have to
figure out who you can trust and whose opinion is valuable.*

Next I went down to the Free Press, *and after the interview I
called home to check on the kids, told them to get ready for Hebrew school. The juxtaposition of everyday life is difficult. It still
goes on and I'm still responsible for it.*

*Then I went back to Esther's house, and she told me that Clar-
ence had called her. Clarence was really hurt that Esther was trying
to help me, and he could not understand it. He felt it was a personal
attack, which is unfortunate. I hope he doesn't continue to feel that
way. I felt badly that perhaps I had jeopardized Esther's position,
but she tossed it off.*

As I look back on that conversation, I see that Esther's support for me
against a longtime Democrat marked the beginning of the Old Girls'
network. Clarence couldn't understand it, but I did; Esther had given me
the courage to plunge ahead with my new life. Already it was beginning
to present some conflicts.

*After I left Esther I went and bought grinders for supper for every-
body, and then I went to pick up Daniel and the baby-sitter. Daniel
was overtired, thirsty, and in a crabby mood. I don't think he was
happy about being taken from nursery school and then being left
with a baby-sitter, and I can't blame him. I felt guilty about doing
that, and I hope I won't have to do it too often, that it won't be the
price of being in this political game, but I suspect at times it will be.*

Typically for a busy housewife of the early 1970s, my life was further
complicated by a dinner-party engagement.

I felt an obligation to go, because I promised to bring bread.

Meanwhile, my political education continued. Earlier in the same day,
I had begun to build what I now recognize to be a political network.

*I went to see George Little at the George Little Press to pick up my
flyers. Arthur and I debated about having them printed or using the
purple ditto process: Arthur convinced me to have them printed.
They will look more professional.*

*George spent a lot of time with me, considering he is a very busy
man; he spends one day of the week in his office and the rest in
Montpelier, where he is the legislator from this district. He is the
president of this large printing company, influential, and a Republican. He drew the ward lines for me on a map, and said he hap-*

pened to be on the committee that had helped redistrict the wards in 1967.

Even though I feel unknown and anonymous, I realized that just by being in this city for fourteen years and being involved in various activities Arthur and I have gotten to know a lot of people. These things suddenly became more significant. When you step into public life, you realize you need everybody. Everybody you happen to know may be able to help you.

After that I went to the city clerk's office to get the checklist. There was no charge for it. Somehow, I thought, you had to prove something or be somebody to get the list of registered voters in the ward, but anyone can get it. At the city clerk's office I spent time running upstairs and downstairs—downstairs to the registrar's office for the names of new people registered since the checklist was printed, upstairs again to check with the city clerk, Wallie Henry, who was nice to me.

Then I thought I'd gather up my courage and stop in and just say hello to the mayor. There's no harm in making a friendly gesture.

I stepped in the office and there was his secretary, who knew me, which was gratifying. She gave me a little pep talk. "I'm so glad you're running," she said, "I told the mayor I knew you. If anybody can do it in that ward, Madeleine Kunin can. She's smart and she'll learn."

You know, my ego just expanded 95 percent. Why, I was really thrilled.

I now realize that she was a person who had done a great deal of work for the mayors of this city and had been very political in her own way but she had always worked behind the scenes, until now.

As I was going back to the car, leaving city hall, I ran into someone who looked familiar, and it turned out to be Bernard Sanders. Now that I was becoming more aggressive as I got further into the campaign, I did not hesitate to approach people. Sanders was the Liberty Union candidate for U.S. Senator, and I had heard him speak at Ohavi Zedek Synagogue, so I latched on to him for a moment and asked, "Do you know anybody in this area who could come to the caucus?" I outlined the ward boundaries for him. He was noncommittal, but he might do something.*

That evening, as I was getting dressed to go out to dinner, there was a telephone call from a man with a French accent who refused to give his name. He only asked, "What are your plans, Mrs. Kunin, for Thursday?" My immediate reaction was that this might be a threat, so I was very cautious. I said, "Please tell me your name.

---

* Sanders was elected Burlington's mayor in 1981, became my opponent for governor in 1986, and was elected to Congress in 1990.

I don't like to talk over the telephone to people whom I don't know."

He finally gave me his name, said he's from Lakeside. "You know, Mrs. Kunin, there are a lot of people who are dissatisfied here with the way things have been going with Meunier. They usually call us to come out for a caucus, but this time they didn't. We think a change would be good."

I was amazed and overjoyed to hear this. I even said, "Merci milles fois, Monsieur."

He added, "Come over and see us."

I think I will. I will make an effort to see this man in Lakeside. I was surprised to discover that there are people whom I don't even know about who are going to come to the caucus to vote against my opponent.

Well, I did go to the party, homemade bread in one hand and checklist in the other. (I was going to go over the checklist with my friend Nicky Roth.) It turned out to be an exciting reception. There were the Leopolds, the Welshes, the Roths, the Blands, and the Masseneaus. I felt the electricity—that people were enjoying this adventure with me and for me. Everybody talked about it.

Later that evening, Ed Miller called me. He had run against Meunier at a caucus two years ago, lost, and then ran as an independent, causing considerable hard feeling. It was a very confusing conversation because I didn't realize that you could be a state representative, which he is, and also run for alderman. At the beginning, he said he wanted to run for the Democratic nomination; at the end he said he might withdraw if he was nominated and then support me. He sounded very bitter toward Meunier.

I don't know if I want to get mixed up with him. But if he got elected to the legislature, he must have some people who will support him. This is something I have to find out more about.

Then we had a meeting of about ten volunteers from the neighborhood at our house. We went over the checklist and everyone picked names to call to tell them to come to the caucus. This is our essential task, because whoever gets the most people to the caucus will get the nomination.

We talked about who should nominate me. It was agreed that we needed somebody outside this neighborhood, a respected member of the community and the parish. My neighbor Sonny Corman suggested Dick Ziemba, who is an independent. I called him; he says he would do it but he has to be out of town.

The other thing we talked about was the doorbell strategy, who would come with me and when. We talked about the flyer, the publicity. I was pleased by people's dedication, by their willingness to give up time, to make calls. It was a good evening.

I recorded a conversation between me and my husband Arthur, a few days before the caucus.

ARTHUR: *This is Monday, or is it Tuesday?*
MADELEINE: *It's Tuesday.*
ARTHUR: *It's Tuesday, February 1, and it is now exactly ten o'clock in the evening and our candidate has just returned from town glowing, excuse me, from her day's labors.*
MADELEINE: *Glowing but tired and, I might add, slightly hoarse. I've been doing a lot of talking all day, but this has been a great day. I had trouble getting started this morning. I thought I'd never wake up, maybe because I went to bed so late, and as usual I woke up about six and couldn't get back to sleep. I mean, as usual since last week, since I've somehow been turned on to politics.*
ARTHUR: *Slow down.*
MADELEINE: *Okay, I'll try to slow down.*

I did get a call from Bill Daniels this morning. He wanted to know the answer to his question. He had an appointment with the mayor at ten and wanted to tell him where I stood.

I explained to Bill that in good conscience I couldn't withdraw at this point from the aldermanic race because too much was at stake. I had involved too many other people, and besides, it was the principle of the thing. I didn't want to run just because I was a woman, but because I felt I could do more for the city. The more involved I get, the more I realize there are a lot of people who are unhappy with Meunier, which is a great revelation to me.

I made another phone call to Mary Pat Kehoe, who is on the school board and whose husband, Vernon, is a public official. She was very sweet. She too said, "Go ahead and do it," even though she felt I'd get hurt and I wouldn't make it.
ARTHUR: *What ward is she in?*
MADELEINE: *This ward. She's been at the game for a while. It was a pleasant conversation, mostly a courtesy call. Since she's a woman and she is in politics and is in this ward, I felt I should consult her. I'm learning that everything gets around and people are easily offended, and I've got to learn how to be diplomatic and approach people.*

Afterward, I had a big debate whether I should do the breakfast dishes and make the beds, which I somehow haven't gotten to in the last two mornings, or whether I should just leave and get on my way. So I decided to leave, obviously a difficult, heartrending decision. I packed up Daniel and we went off to nursery school, which, thankfully, he is glad to go to.

Then I had a very relaxing and pleasant morning with Nicky. I give one piece of campaign advice: If you're going to get into this business, find a friend with two phones, because we could both keep calling simultaneously, and this was great.

I made a telephone call to the newspaper, which had not printed my interview because I had talked to the wrong reporter who didn't cover the city beat. First, I tried to make my announcement once again to a different reporter over the phone, but I found it very difficult to give the story over the phone, so we decided I would type it out and bring it over later in the afternoon. This was a very wise decision, because I worked at the typewriter and ended up with something strong and neat, whereas the interview I had had yesterday was rambling and casual. It might not have come out so well.

Sometimes I think this whole political career of mine is a series of happy accidents. It's just fortunate that the article didn't appear today, and that the one that appears tomorrow will be a serious statement of my intentions to run.

Then I made phone calls for the Women's Political Caucus, and Nicky made a lot of phone calls—she really sounded great on the phone. We had a very nice lunch, which was what I needed because I do get too tense. We had meatloaf sandwiches and pimento, and we sat and looked at the lake. She's a very good influence on me, and if I had to choose a campaign manager again, I couldn't have a better one.

We decided to make a couple of posters to put up at the health-food store, and Legal Aid, and the Coffee House.
ARTHUR: *All the places that don't count.*
MADELEINE: *But I hope there may be one or two people who will see them. It turns out I couldn't put them at Legal Aid because they can't be involved with partisan politics, but I did leave them at the Coffee House and the health-food store. I don't know about going into Red's.*

Red Roberts is Republican ward chairman. Earlier today I was scared about doing that, but now I'm not scared anymore.

Red Roberts was where we got the Sunday paper; it was open all the time—in the evening until ten o'clock—and was a focal point in this part of town, opposite St. Anthony's Church, and very conveniently located next to Champlain School. Everybody went there at least once a week for some reason or other, the kids more often for candy.

After lunch, and talking some more, which we always seem to do now, constantly, I left Nicky to go down to the Free Press *to hand in my article and had a nice chat with Elizabeth Kirkness. Elizabeth and I started out at just about the same time to work at the* Free Press. *How many years ago? 1957. She looks just about the same. I don't know about me.*

Then I went around with posters, and I next stopped at Marie

Moulton's house to leave the checklist with her for a couple of hours so she could look it over and call people in the Birchcliff area because she had lived there.

She was nice about it, but not revved up. When I came back later to pick up the checklist, she was very excited. "I'm getting all kinds of responses and lots of people are interested. I tell them, 'Well, you better go if you're interested,' " as only Marie can say it. She was turned on and is obviously going to go to the caucus!

That made me feel good—that she was getting a reaction from people who don't know me but who are really voting against my opponent rather than for me. But that's all right as a beginning. Later, I'll try to prove that I am worth voting <u>for.</u>

I went home and saw the kids and saw what a mess the house was. I rapidly tried to clean up the kitchen and called Pat Dunn to give her some names to call. Oh, I left out one thing, I stopped off at a little store on St. Paul Street and thought, Well, I've got this other poster here that Legal Aid didn't take, let me see if I can hang it up here. And the man let me.

Then, Arthur, you called and said, "I'll be home late. I've got this very sick patient and I'm on service."

I said, "Well, I wanted to go knocking on doors with Nicky," so I scurried around looking for a sitter.

ARTHUR: *Well, it's obvious that I've been playing only a supportive and minor role, picking up little bits of this and little bits of that, furnishing grist to the mill, as it were. But there were a number of people in politics whom I knew by accident or through some type of medical contacts, and one was H. Clifford Dubie, a native-born Burlingtonian, a street commissioner whom I saw as a patient over a number of years. I did call him at home where he is convalescing from a heart attack. The reason I mention this is that he was immediately enthusiastic about your race.*

While you were out campaigning and I was in the house putting the children to bed and washing the dishes and being the good wife at home—I mean, what can you do?—I had a conversation with Julia. She sat down on the stairs beside me and she said, "Daddy, what do you think of Mommy running?" And I said, "Well, when she's happy, I'm happy. If she's unhappy, it spills over on me and I don't have so good a time. So if this pleases her, it's okay with me."

"Well," she said, "is that really all you feel?"

I said, "Yes, I feel positively about it and I don't feel threatened in any way."

She asked would this mean that Mommy would be spending more time away from home and be making lots of telephone calls.

I said yes, that would be so, but that was part of it, and perhaps Julia was a little unhappy about this.

After they were all in bed, the telephone rang, and Bill Daniels called. He told me that he had spoken to Mayor Paquette earlier today and I was to deliver the following message to you: that Mayor Paquette did not object to your running.

While you were out, Mr. Miller also called. He wanted to speak to Madeleine, and when told she was not here, asked me to deliver two messages. One, that it was going to come out in the Free Press *tomorrow that he would declare himself a candidate for alderman. However, he told me he was a sick man. He had just come back from the VA hospital in White River Junction. His doctor had told him that the seat in the state legislature was enough for him, but perhaps for his own personal reasons, he wanted to make a statement at the caucus, citing all the difficulties in this ward which had been brought about by misrule and misrepresentation.*

He said he would ask the person nominating him to make a few statements castigating Meunier, and then he would ask everyone who came to cast their votes for you.

In trying to understand what this man's motivation was, the conclusion that I came to was that he had his own personal grudges to settle, and that perhaps he could be of some help, but if he was trying to earn a political gift from you for throwing votes your way, this certainly was not going to help. I made no promises. I was exceedingly polite, complimentary, solicitous about his health, and was looking forward to meeting him in person at the caucus.

In other words, it was a snow job on both our parts.
MADELEINE: *I'm sure you both enjoyed it, which is what is funny in this game.*

As I LOOK back at these notes, I see how I began to build a political network, and how quickly we learned to distinguish friend from foe, or left some room for doubt, as in the case of Mr. Miller. With each new step I took, I overcame one more hurdle.

A major one was campaigning. I had never asked anyone to vote for me before. Nicky and I decided to go into friendly territory first. I'd almost never done this doorbell-ringing routine, except ages ago when I went with an alderman from another ward to get more Democrats to register, and we took someone along who could administer the Freeman's Oath. I remembered enjoying it and being surprised how pleasant people were when you knocked on their doors.

We went to Cherry Lane. First, we were going to pick out names from the checklist and find their addresses, but then I figured, what the heck, we'll just ring the doorbell wherever there's a light on and see what happens.

Well, the first one we rang was Dr. Foley's.

ARTHUR: *Dr. Foley?*

MADELEINE: *Yes, and Mrs. Foley was there and she was very nice and we chatted with her for a while. She asked a good question, "How are you different from Meunier?" and I had to answer quickly. I don't think I did it all that well. I tried to emphasize that I would represent the whole ward and the interests of various people in different sections of it.*

At least we started out with a positive reception. I think we might have influenced her to come to the caucus. She said that her husband had told her she should, which is interesting.

Then we knocked on more doors. There was an old man who said he'd been a Democrat for eighty years. Most places people were watching TV. And they were friendly. They said, "Oh, I think we're going to come."

We handed everyone a flyer, so they have something printed in their hands with details. We didn't have to do much explaining about why we were there and what was happening. They seemed to know I was a candidate. Everybody was extremely nice. I just couldn't believe it.

One funny thing was that we were following a bridge game. The Girouxes, whose daughter used to baby-sit for us, were very pleased to see us and we had a nice chat with them but then Mrs. Giroux said she had to go to a bridge game.

At the next house we came to we looked through the window and saw two little tables set up. We hesitated but rang the bell anyway, and it turned out this was the bridge game. There were the Michauds, whose daughter had also baby-sat for us. Then we went to another house where the woman was going to the bridge game. So we got all the bridge partners that night.

ARTHUR: *Guess who they're talking about.*

MADELEINE: *Right! We met one woman who said, "I don't know if I can get out of the house. I just had a baby." I don't think she'll come. I don't think all or even a third, or a quarter, will come, but some will.*

Then we went to another house on Bittersweet Lane, I think their names are McGarry. They knew me from the PTA meetings, and one of their kids went to school with Peter. You find all these connections. You also find that everybody knows everybody else. It's a very small, tight-knit town, not this impersonal place I once thought Burlington was.

We must have gone to about fifteen or twenty houses, and I'd say about ten of those were extremely positive. The only thing that made us stop was that I ran out of flyers.

Later that evening, I had followed up on the conversation with Mr.
Achille Therrien, the man with the French accent who had called me the
day before.

*Nicky and I went over to Lakeside. It was very dark on the street,
and we didn't know which door to go in, and I thought, My God,
what if it's a trap? Then we walked into a warm and cozy kitchen
and there was Mr. Therrien and Mrs. Therrien and two of his
daughters and a son-in-law, all sitting around the table playing
Parcheesi and having drinks. A big coffeepot was percolating on
the stove. Immaculate, very simple, nothing fancy. Mr. Therrien
said, "Now, pull up a chair, sit down, and take your coats off, have
a cup of coffee." He's probably a man in his midseventies and
speaks English with a strong French accent, but there's no problem
understanding him.*

*Well, the conversation that ensued made me wish I had the
tape recorder. First of all, he used to be the political boss of Lakeside, and I think he feels like a dethroned king. The upshot is that
these people really do not like Meunier. They are angry because the
Meunier people did not let them know about the caucus. They feel
that this was not an accident. Discontent has been brewing for
some time, and they feel he hasn't done a thing for them in the two
years he's been an alderman.*

*On the other hand, they feel very positive toward Blanchard, the
other alderman from the district. They always call him first if
there's a problem. He's right there when there's an oil leak—the oil
tanks are just a few feet from the houses.*

*Meunier's mother had called up one of the women there and
asked her, "Are you a women's libber?" And she had said, "Well,
I don't know. I don't know what you mean." She kidded around
with me about it, but it seems that they are trying to say, "If you're
involved with Mrs. Kunin, you're a women's libber."*

*Finally I asked them, "What really bothers you? What are your
complaints?"*

*The big thing is the entrance to Lakeside. When there is a lot of
rain, the road is flooded, and they believe they couldn't get out in
case of an emergency. And another thing is the oil leaks: those
tanks smell, and there is soot when they burn off stuff. The beach
is polluted and they say there's an open sewer going into the lake
there. They have many complaints. I can see that they feel that their
needs have not been taken seriously.*

*Therrien also gave me advice: "Be sure to have a checklist there so
you check off the people as they come in and then count up the number of people marked on the list, so when the vote is taken you know
exactly how many people were eligible." He doesn't trust them. He
said, "We must be on guard, we must play it very carefully."*

He spent quite a bit of time talking about how he used to orga-nize this ward, how he'd work three months in advance calling up people. And I thought to myself, This is a man to whom politics has been very important. It's true for many of these people. It's the exciting thing in their lives. This is what they sit around and talk about. Therrien had been the party boss and had been slighted and his people had been slighted. He'd been working hard all his life, and now they shunted him aside. That is what really got me into Lakeside.

ARTHUR: *Politics is part of their lives.*

MADELEINE: *That's right. There is so much to talk about because you can go back so many generations and through so many fami-lies. Midway through our conversation, Therrien said, "Why don't I call up my daughter-in-law who lives down the street and have her come over? Her son could take these flyers and put them in the newspaper. He has a paper route. Or better yet, she might even work for you."*

She came over a little while later, a young woman named Ro-chelle who works at General Electric and has a child at Champlain School.

Therrien asked her, "Would you be willing to go around with them tomorrow night? They've only got one night left to go to the homes. Do you think they'd get a good reception?"

She said, "Sure."

So we're going to meet Rochelle tomorrow night at seven o'clock and she's going to take us around Lakeside. We're meeting the enemy on his home territory.

ARTHUR: *Where does Meunier live?*

MADELEINE: *Meunier grew up across the street from the Therriens, but now he lives in Southcrest and his mother does too. If nothing else, I am learning something about the development of this city and the various economic and ethnic groups in it.*

This really is a special bit of Americana. I felt I was getting in on something that under no other circumstances would I have been included in. Except for politics I would never have gotten into that kitchen and seen those people playing Parcheesi and talking about those families, and saying it was time for a change.

And they said, "It would be good to have a woman." Like it or not, the women's issue is an issue in this campaign. Many women, consciously or unconsciously, are very receptive to this idea.

The next night, I recorded the following conversation:

ARTHUR: *This is Wednesday evening, February 2, 1972. The time is five minutes after ten. The candidate has just returned from a tour through Lakeside with Nicky and the daughter-in-law of*

Achille Therrien. She's eating the remains of some leek soup and a scrambled egg. She'll be speaking for herself very soon.

We who have been holding the fort have diapered babies, have rubbed salve on their chafed legs, and have helped little children get into pajamas. All in all, the cooperation has been, I would say, better than might be expected.

As long as I have the stage and the tape recorder, I might as well say that this is the second evening that I have washed these fuckin' dishes. The first night I got done at five after nine, and tonight I got done at five minutes to ten.

MADELEINE: *What have you been doing all this time, Arthur?*

ARTHUR: *And if this pattern continues, there'll be no husband to take care of this establishment.*

MADELEINE: *I don't think you really mean that, Arthur. I mean, after all, it's only been two nights. I realize I left you with every-body hollering. I felt very guilty—*

ARTHUR: *Yeah.*

MADELEINE: *—But the minute I pulled out of the driveway, I forgot about it.*

ARTHUR: *You forgot about it, yeah.*

MADELEINE: I realize you've really been sensational but—

ARTHUR: *Don't give me any of these political words. "Sensational." You never used that word until you started campaigning.*

Second of all, I had to curry special favor with Julia tonight. The reason you're eating leek soup is that she didn't want to eat any of the things that had been prepared. So she had a grilled-cheese sand-wich and some of this soup. But she really came through. She helped diaper Daniel when I was putting him to bed and taking care of Adam. She and Peter did a lot to clean up the kitchen. While I was cleaning up the dishes a number of telephone calls came. Sonny Corman called and had a very interesting story. She called a friend of one of her sons who lives on Morse Street to tell her that you were running in the caucus.

The woman said, "Oh yes, yes. I know all about it. Of course I can't vote because I'm a Canadian citizen, but my husband might." And in Sonny's hearing she hollered, "Dear, would you vote for a woman for the Board of Aldermen?"

He said, "Sure."

And when she heard that, she said, "If he would vote for a woman, anybody would vote for a woman, and I'm going to go all up and down Morse Street and get some votes for you."

How was your trip tonight?

MADELEINE: *Rochelle Therrien is very spunky and energetic.*

ARTHUR: *How old is she?*

MADELEINE: *She's a little younger than I am, but she's got a sixteen-year-old son. She's worked at GE for fifteen years. As she put it, "All the women here work, both of us have to hold down jobs." Her husband drives a truck, an oil truck, to Montreal. He makes that trip twice a night.*

I could see why she was for women's lib in her own way. It strikes a responsive chord with these working women.

When we went from door to door, they were almost embarrassed to mention women's lib, but it always came up. It came up with the men and the women, and everybody chuckled, but was good-natured.

Everyplace we went Rochelle would say, "This is Mrs. Kunin. She's running for alderman, you know. Don't you think it's about time we had a woman on the Board of Aldermen?"

Then she'd launch into something personal with each person. She did it so well. She'd say, "How's Joey?" or "How's your mother?" or "I see, you're expecting a baby." She was perfect. She paved the way.

When people see strange people at the door, they sometimes don't know what to say, but the minute they saw her face, they knew her, so it was okay. We went trooping in everywhere.

ARTHUR: *You think you're going to be envious of regular people once you get elected?*

MADELEINE: *Um-hm [finishing my scrambled eggs].*

ARTHUR: *People who go home at night and sit down comfortably and don't have anything to do.*

MADELEINE: *That's right.*

ARTHUR: *You're going to be bothered reading reports and all that sort of thing.*

MADELEINE: *Maybe. But you know every house we went in tonight had a color TV, and every house had the TV going. I will never again underestimate TV as a medium.*

ARTHUR: *No kidding? Did anybody see you on television?*

MADELEINE: *They'd seen me, yes.*

ARTHUR: *What did they think of that?*

MADELEINE: *They just were thrilled.*

ARTHUR: *No kidding?*

MADELEINE: *Yeah.*

ARTHUR: *In other words, you're a celebrity because you were on TV?*

MADELEINE: *Yes, I felt like I was cast in a movie. But what I learned most was not to listen to what other people say about things but to explore them for myself. You know, that neighborhood has a reputation for being run-down, but what we saw with Rochelle, which was mostly her family and friends, was very different. Every house was kept up; many were remodeled with new kitchens and new carpeting. You felt that these people had a sense of pride. Most of them were born there.*

ARTHUR: *How many houses do you think you visited?*

MADELEINE: *Oh, we must have visited about twenty-five. We went zip, zip, zip. We didn't stay and have coffee anywhere. I'd say hello, and stay just a few minutes. She only took me to people who have always turned out for caucuses. She didn't bother with the others. I had the feeling that if you didn't go to the caucus, you were missing out on the biggest social event of the year.*

She also took me to people whom she said were the "fighters," who fought for things like the hockey rink in the middle of that park. It is really beautiful, perfectly planned. It's an intimate kind of place, a little island. All the boys were out playing hockey, and they maintain it themselves. It's well lit, and it's a central focus of the neighborhood.

They also have a local social club, the St. John's Club, a VFW kind of club. That's where the men go. As Rochelle said, some of the wives would like to bomb it sometimes.

The solidarity of this place got to me. It's not at all a slum; people care about it. These people have jobs and are hard-working.

ARTHUR: *What would you say is your conclusion about tonight?*

MADELEINE: *I learned something important. People talk about enemies and say that you can't go into their territory. That's what I had been warned about in Meunier's old neighborhood. We build up fears about people that aren't really so. Then you meet them face-to-face and and you feel at ease with them, and if you show that you're at ease, they are too.*

ARTHUR: *That's right. Never show you're afraid of a dog because he'll bark. But I have some advice for you. You know, I'm your great adviser. If you do get elected, aside from the nomination, get down there and be visible.*

MADELEINE: *I will.*

ARTHUR: *Be visible all the time, because the time may come when you need them for something bigger. It's your power base.*

MADELEINE: *Exactly. I know that. Afterward we sat around in the Therriens' living room and had coffee and talked. I've learned a lot listening to people talk, and I learned what they expect of an alderman. They expect to read about him in the newspaper, for one thing. "Whether he wins or not, he should make some noise," Therrien said.*

ARTHUR: *If you do win, just keep that smile.*

MADELEINE: *I smile too much, don't I?*

ARTHUR: *Yeah, don't get too uppity, baby. You're not in yet.*

MADELEINE: *I know. Another thing, I spoke to Vince Naramore. He's a political pundit, and longtime adviser to Democrats, and he told me it would be good to make a two-minute statement beforehand.*

ARTHUR: *Before what?*

MADELEINE: *Before the voting. It would be good to reaffirm my allegiance to the party, to say that I am a Democrat and that if I lose, I would not run as an independent, and that it is basically a choice among friends and that I don't want divisiveness to result. You do have to say that, and I believe it.*

ARTHUR: *Whom are you going to have nominate you?*

MADELEINE: *Mike Dunn. I talked to him.*

ARTHUR: *When was this?*

MADELEINE: *This morning.*

ARTHUR: *You didn't tell me.*

MADELEINE: *I didn't tell you? Well, I discussed this problem of the nomination with Vincent and he thinks the significance of who nominates you is overrated. He said, "Don't waste your time scrounging around." And I mentioned Mike Dunn to him and he thought it was a good idea.*

ARTHUR: *You didn't tell me!*

MADELEINE: *He said you had approached him about it. Connie Kite will second me.*

ARTHUR: *Good.*

MADELEINE: *I had to take care of these little details. She'll also have a checklist there to check off people as they come in. We'll have our checker and they'll have their checker.*

Then this evening I also talked to Brian Burns. He said a caucus has absolutely no rules. They don't even have to follow Robert's Rules of Order. *But you can contest any decisions that are made, and say, "This should be voted on." I'm glad to know that, in case anything comes up.*

ARTHUR: *What about after the caucus? We better buy some whiskey for tomorrow, win or lose.*

MADELEINE: *Yes. We should buy something. We've got to buy something. Soda and chips and stuff.*

ARTHUR: *Yeah, and I'll buy some scotch and I'll buy a big bottle of gin.*

MADELEINE: *Why don't you turn on the ice maker now so we'll remember it?*

Oh, I stopped at Marchand's store; is it Alphonse and Marie?

ARTHUR: *Yes, that wonderful store.*

MADELEINE: *Yes, well I figured I'd give them a flyer. You know the smell in there of kerosene? I ended up calling it the Tootsie Roll campaign, because I bought ten Tootsie Rolls and an old bag of potato chips. Those right here.*

ARTHUR: *Humpty Dumpty?*

MADELEINE: *Yeah.*

ARTHUR: *They are the lousiest potato chips, really. I'm going to throw them away.*

MADELEINE: *Consider it part of my campaign expenses.*
ARTHUR: *All right, but really . . .*
MADELEINE: *I went too far. I went too far buying the potato chips. I could have just stopped with the Tootsie Rolls. I made the grand gesture.*
ARTHUR: *You could have bought some cream of mushroom soup. Julia was looking all over for soup tonight. She said, "Mommy went shopping and didn't buy a goddamn thing."*
MADELEINE: *She didn't say "goddamn." Anyway, another place I stopped was at Camille's, the barbershop. Have you seen that place?*
ARTHUR: *Right next door. Is he a good barber? I'll go to him.*
MADELEINE: *I'd like you to go. I told him I have three sons.*
ARTHUR: *Oh, boy, anything for a vote.*
MADELEINE: *Well, he was at the last caucus. Camille is a party regular. He said it was one of the best caucuses he'd been to, so Camille may be with us.*
ARTHUR: *Oh, Mrs. What's-her-name came down for the petitions for the railroad-crossing light.*
MADELEINE: *Oh, did you find them?*
ARTHUR: *Yeah, I found them, luckily. But she saw this house. Spoons all over the floor, Daniel had a snotty nose, pots and pans all over, and not only that but I didn't recognize her. She knocked on the door. I said, "I'm Arthur Kunin." She said, "I know."*
MADELEINE: *Oh, God, Mrs. Lauritzen! Isn't that awful? She's a good Republican, and I'm certain she has a spotless kitchen.*
ARTHUR: *She said, "I'm Mrs. Lauritzen and I've come for the things." I finally found them for her, but I was ashamed of the snotty nose and said to Adam, "Pick up those spoons," and he said, "I don't wanna," but he finally picked them up.*

Arthur made our final recording the night of the caucus, February 3, 1972.

It is about six o'clock, and we're home getting ready for supper before going to the Democratic caucus in the Fifth Ward. . . . Now this afternoon Madeleine was interviewed by Jack Barry over WVMT, and I listened to it in the laboratory with Pat and with Karen [lab technicians], with Mike Dunn, who is going to nominate Madeleine this evening. Madeleine's delivery was excellent. Her voice sounded good; she was fluent and authoritative in her answers. The questions were obviously delivered in an extremely friendly manner, and Mr. Meunier lost support because he wasn't there. The time of the caucus was announced at least five or six times.

One of the very best answers that Madeleine gave was in answer to the question: "Since you are a mother with young children, how do you think you will be able to do this job?"

Madeleine answered that most of the men who are on the Board of Aldermen have full-time jobs, and do it as a second job. She has a full-time job as well, raising a family, and the Board of Aldermen would be her second job. I thought that was a very slick answer.

I wrote in my diary that night:

The caucus was held in the gymnasium of the Champlain Elementary School at 7:00 p.m. The moment the clock struck seven, Alderman Bob Blanchard stopped people from coming in to be checked off. I was dismayed when some of my supporters who arrived late were barred from voting, and I told myself that next time I must be prepared for this. I was glad the children were there, sitting beside us. The turnout was huge. I was surprised to see how few people I recognized. My heart sank; they must all be Meunier people.

Caucus chairman Michael McGarry opened the meeting with the announcement that the purpose of the caucus was "the nomination of the aldermanic candidate for Ward Five."

Bob Blanchard rose to nominate Clarence, first observing, "I haven't seen this many people at a caucus since 1967. Then we had two hundred forty-four." Later I learned our count was 245.

Blanchard explained that Clarence had done "one heck of a job" in his two years on the board and had attended 106 out of a total of 107 Board of Aldermen meetings, "the best record on the Board of Aldermen." He was a "hardworking man" and a "dedicated individual."

Now it was Mike Dunn's turn to nominate me. I wondered how he would equal Blanchard.

"I'd like to place the name of Madeleine Kunin before this caucus for the position of alderwoman for the Fifth Ward. I think Mrs. Kunin is a superb candidate, and I'm going to recommend her to you on the basis of her background. She has experience as an educator, in the League of Women Voters, and on the Governor's Commission on the Status of Women, and she is a longtime resident of the city of Burlington."

Dunn noted that this would be a full-time job for me, that I would be available "continuously" and had an "ongoing interest in the welfare of the citizens of the ward." I sounded considerably better than I had expected; Mike had done a terrific job.

Next Ed Miller was nominated and, as he had indicated, announced that he would not accept the nomination but instead would vote for me.

Nominations were closed, and Clarence and I were asked to stand behind the ballot boxes in front of the gymnasium as people lined up to drop their ballots into a large brown cardboard box placed on a gray metal folding chair. Clarence stood on one side, and I on the other. As people approached the box, they would do one of two things: wink at Clarence or smile at me.

No future election would equal the embarrassment of that face-to-face appraisal. This was judgment day.

While the ballots were being counted, I felt as if I had labor pains. No matter what the outcome, I just wanted the baby to be born. I didn't know whom to talk to or what to say, where to stand or where to sit. I had tried to prepare the children beforehand by telling them that there was a strong possibility that I wouldn't make it. At the same time, I kept thinking—you know—what if I do?

I turned around and saw a thick line of dark-coated, middle-aged, rotund men standing in the rear of the gymnasium. They had formed a spectators' gallery: the mayor, several aldermen from other wards, and sundry political hangers-on. Their presence confirmed what I had begun to suspect: this caucus was rife with drama.

I looked up; Mike Dunn and Bob Blanchard had stopped counting ballots and were returning to their seats. I scanned their faces for clues, but they revealed nothing.

The chairman approached the podium. "It is now official. The winner with one hundred thirty-eight votes is Clarence Meunier. Mrs. Kunin obtained one hundred seven votes."

I turned to Arthur, and we hugged. I tried to keep my head on his shoulder as long as possible to allow my face to relax. While the ballots were being counted, I kept telling myself, You're going to lose, you're going to lose; but still, I wasn't prepared. Clarence's acceptance speech drifted in and out of my mind as I registered the numbers in my head.

"I pledge to you that I will continue to work as I have in the past for all of the residents of Ward Five and for the city as well," he said.

I had been certain I would win. How could I have lost?

Clarence went on, "I feel the next two years are going to be real challenging and very exciting for the city of Burlington, and I'm going to be proud to be a part of it and do what I can for all of us. I have a very deep faith that God will guide me in whatever decisions I make in the next two years."

I hoped no one would notice my tears as I kept my eyes focused on my lap. Ed Miller came up to me, took my arm, and said, "I think we better go congratulate Clarence."

The next day over breakfast, I listened to the local radio station give the results: "The special Ward Five caucus was held last night and nominated incumbent alderman Clarence Meunier to run for another term. Old-line party politicians, however, got a real shock in the amount of support generated for political newcomer Mrs. Madeleine Kunin. Only thirty-one votes separated the two."

Afterward, I went through all the what ifs. What if I had done this or that or the other thing? I tortured myself. I wished that I had introduced myself at the beginning of the caucus and that I'd made a statement afterward, though neither would have changed anything. I don't think I lost for any reasons related to gender. Anybody trying to break into the power structure would have had a very difficult time. I don't feel I was discriminated against as a woman at all. I was treated equally in the political game. Of course, you have to learn not to be too ladylike. You have to appear like a lady, but you've got to fight like a man. "Worse than a man," Arthur said, but I don't think there could be much worse.

When I talked to Esther Sorrell the next day, she saw the whole caucus in a much broader perspective. She felt it was a tremendous victory to get those 107 votes. It indicated a change in the political climate for the whole state. She said, "Nothing like this has happened since Phil Hoff ran. The power of the old order has been broken."

I wasn't sure Esther's analysis was correct, but I took courage from it. And the phone had not stopped ringing. One alderman told me, "You really put up a good fight, and you did yourself proud."

Several people called suggesting that I run as an independent in the general election, but after consulting with Vincent Naramore, I decided against it. If I was ever going to run for public office again, I would want the support of the Democratic party.

To demonstrate that I was serious about city politics, I attended a Board of Aldermen meeting a few weeks later. After the routine meeting, Alderman Bob Blanchard pulled me aside and asked, "Tell me, what do you want?"

I didn't know what to say.

"What do you want to *be*?" he said more slowly, as if to a child. "Do you want to be on a commission? Do you want to be alderman? Do you want to be mayor?"

Finally, I said, "What do you mean?"

"Well, you tell me, and I'll get it for you."

I told him, as politely as I could, that whatever I wanted I would get on my own. But as I left the meeting, I said to myself, My God, what kind of a ball game am I getting into? At the same time, I was amused. I had become a contender, a political force to be reckoned with. I began to ask,

Where do I go next? For the first time, I thought it might be interesting to be in the legislature.

I vowed to pay attention to everything that was going on in the city and in the state. These had been a fantastic few days for me. And I had learned a great deal. And whether by accident or intent, I knew that I was no longer the same person I had been when all this began.

3

As I look back, my transformation from private citizen to public person did not occur by chance. During my nonpolitical years, I had experienced a quiet apprenticeship, and long before I dared call myself a politician, I had become one. During those meandering years when my children were young and I had not yet defined my career, I realize now that I was unknowingly preparing myself for a political life. For one thing, I was beginning to listen to my inner voice and learning how to express it as a member of my community. In the familiarity of my street and neighborhood in Burlington, Vermont, I could test myself in small ways without fear of failure.

Making the shift from private to public person, as I had done with the aldermanic race, meant, I realized, that I would have to learn to speak in public. At first, the thought was terrifying. Better to squelch the impulse to "do something" about a problem than to risk sounding foolish or making a mistake in front of others. In the privacy of my daydream world, I could say anything, and the words would sound heroic. But in public I feared that the phrases would stretch across the sky as if they were being pulled by a little plane—people would crane their necks, point, and say, "Look at what she's saying." So much easier to harbor private thoughts—funny, outrageous, and rebellious—than to expose them to the open air.

I am told that I suffered from unusual shyness as a child. My aunt had worried whether I would be able to cope. I arrived in the United States with my mother and brother at the age of six and a half, not speaking English. It was 1940, war was spreading over Europe, and my mother feared that Switzerland, too, would be overrun by Hitler. My first day in public school was traumatic: I was placed in the second grade and asked to read the five-digit numbers chalked on the blackboard. I could say nothing, so the teacher put me back in first grade. My strongest memory is of Joyce Pugliese, a sweet-faced little girl who astonished me when she recited the entire alphabet by heart on the second day of school.

During most of my school days, it was easier to be a silent observer than to risk being a misfit participant. By the time I was in college, though, I had begun to express myself by writing for the college newspaper. In my senior year I became editorial-page editor. Rarely, however, did I have to face an audience. I ask myself what was it that enabled me to learn to speak in public. Speech is more than a tool of politics; it is essential to the political life. Without articulating a view of the world, political action is impossible. I had no choice: I had to learn how to project my inner self onto the public stage. The constriction in my throat that once silenced me is as difficult to diagnose as it is to say what cured me. Now that I look back at it, it was not skill that I lacked, but courage. Silence was safe. Speech was not. Being the courteous listener for so long, I became adept at keeping the other person's flow of words moving, interjecting a nod here, a word there, to make my presence known but not heard. How could I reverse roles?

I feared speaking, not because I had nothing to say, but because I worried that my articulated words would come out wrong, too angry, too passive, or be misunderstood. I didn't trust the spontaneous expression of my ideas or emotions. Could I rely on them? Or would they embarrass me? How could I filter out what I didn't want to say? How could I say precisely what I *did* want to say?

I learned how to speak because, after a time, keeping silent became more disturbing than the fear of public exposure. I lost self-consciousness when I focused less on how I was saying something and more on what I was saying. As I learned to trust my beliefs, I learned to speak. I discovered courage because cowardice became unbearable. I could no longer bear the chastisement I inflicted on myself for not speaking the lines I had rehearsed. At first I spoke in spurts, as if releasing pressure, like a faucet suddenly turned on after having been long shut off. I spoke as if possessed. The sudden stimulus of an idea temporarily anesthetized the part of my brain that had been the censor, hushing me into silence.

When I stood up at the Democratic caucus in Burlington, I abandoned my customary caution because I had something I had to say. I felt compelled to tell this roomful of Democratic party regulars about the revolution that was about to begin: women were going to enter politics. What a surprise to discover that when fired up by conviction, I could speak spontaneously! Public dialogue was not like a spelling bee; every question did not have only one correct answer, printed on a cue card closely held in someone else's hand. Still I would wonder as I heard myself, Who is that speaking? My microphoned voice seemed to come from another body in an adjoining room. I was tempted to pause and listen to what this other woman was saying.

With time, I felt less awkward. Repetition gave me grace. Like a runner who carries the memory of past victories in her head as she visualizes herself leaping over the finish line, with each new foray into the public arena I accumulated another trophy for my small triumph. And as I continued to move further into public life, I got what I needed most: practice. That was how I overcame my classic nightmare of finding myself standing before a crowd only to discover that I was wearing pajamas. Or that I was giving a speech and suddenly my teeth loosened, fell out, and knocked against one another in my mouth like so many marbles in a jar; I was afraid I would swallow them. My cheeks swelled into terrified silence.

The fearful idea that by speaking out I would no longer be a good girl, that my words might antagonize those who heard me, was deeply rooted. If I said the wrong thing at the wrong time, I risked punishment: I might not be liked. Worse yet, I would not be loved.

I was certain that if I found the correct way to express myself, all this could be avoided, and I could make everybody happy. The "right" answer would be one that was factually correct and politically pleasing. If I found the appropriate way to be both considerate and persuasive, there would be no price to pay. I scanned the list of male politicians whom I admired and they seemed to know the formula. What did they know that I did not? Whatever it was, I had to learn it. A successful political life was like a play, filled with hidden cues and set lines, which, if I studied hard and paid close attention, I could master.

It took time for me to understand that no matter how politically skillful one became, controversy could not be avoided, and I would have to trust myself to improvise. Often there was no right answer. Speaking out always carried a price. What I had to learn was that it was worth the risk. When governor, I crammed for weekly press conferences; the scramble to find the right answers to every hypothetical question drove me and my staff into a frenzy of research every week. I wanted to be able to step up to the podium, armed with facts and figures at my fingertips, and face a bouquet of microphones with equanimity, telling myself, I know everything.

As the first woman governor of Vermont, I felt I had a special obligation to master the facts. A man in my position might be able to slide over what he did not know. As a woman, I continued to feel the need to prove that I was qualified for the job. If I said the words "I don't know," the aura of power might fade under the hot lights. Not informed? How can she govern?

My instincts were correct. Information is power. Without it, one cannot lead. I could not risk being unprepared. But I had to learn that mastery of the facts is not sufficient proof of leadership ability. One has to learn how to defend the facts when they come under attack. The art of public speaking requires more than recitation. I had to learn to argue for what I believed. I had to learn to trust not only my ideas but also my emotions. This was what I had been taught to fear: the release of uncontrolled female emotion. When I learned how to meld information with conviction *and* emotion I discovered my true public voice.

Sometimes my old anxieties staged a relapse, long after I had become a comfortable public speaker accustomed to the give-and-take of debate. After an unrehearsed outburst, I would feel the weight of public judgment pushing me into my seat. I blushed as I told myself, You shouldn't have said that; it sounded stupid. I'd feel mute, my body hunched into invisibility. It was hard to surmount the fear that speaking out would prompt unexpected interrogation, that my ugly ignorance would be laid bare. Safety in silence was deeply ingrained in my psyche, like shimmering threads in a black taffeta dress. I had stayed seated for so long, like Whistler's mother, her face silhouetted in profile, waiting, hands folded in her lap, absorbing like a dark blotter all her tragedies within herself.

As I recognized my outline in hers, her portrait also told me who I did not want to be. Her stoic figure made me both sad and angry. Why had she been content to wait, when I was not? Something within me rebelled against this portrait of patient passivity, long considered noble. It is from these black negatives that positive images are developed. Her figure moved me to rise from my chair and step out of her prisonlike space. I wanted to face front and look directly at the world. I wanted to function in it, to observe how others did it.

One such apprenticeship took place in the 1960s, at a New England regional meeting of the League of Women Voters at Tufts University near Boston. I sat in a darkened auditorium, observing serious-minded women, one after another, walk in great sensible strides down the center aisle, right up to the microphone. No quaver in their voices. No pauses between their words. Could I ever be capable of such forthright speech, putting my opinion forward as if it were a shoe?

I did not think so. When my words fell out, I wanted to stuff them back into my mouth before anybody noticed what had dribbled down my chin.

Several years later, I learned to forge the spontaneous connection between my thoughts and words. I accepted a job in 1969 at Trinity College in Burlington, to be a part-time instructor in freshman English. My assignment was to teach three classes of fifty students each.

The first day, I delayed my entrance into class as long as possible, hiding in the ladies' room. It was a safe refuge where I could look in the mirror and comb my hair while rehearsing my first words: "Good morning, class, welcome to freshman English. . . ." I had taken a furtive glance into my classroom, where the students, seated in parallel rows, looked like a tidy army. How would they attack? At four minutes past the appointed hour, I marched into class, eyeing the students who were eyeing me. I unloaded my armload of books and papers on the desk; this was my defense. But immediately the tottering pile sagged, an unsteady fortress.

After staying with my notes for a while, as faithfully as a dog on a leash, I made a surprising discovery. I could be turned loose. To my delight, I found that once I learned to let my intellectual excitement carry me forward, I could speak on my feet. Unexpected questions demanded new answers, and finding them was surprisingly easy. There was no time to be self-conscious. When I defined a point for a student, I simultaneously illuminated it for myself. Now I understood the pleasure of teaching! I had not known what I knew until I had expressed it. Ideas prompted a fresh flow of words, which in turn provoked new ideas.

In the process of teaching Mailer's *Miami and the Siege of Chicago*, I also further defined my political values. As I lectured on Friedan's *Feminine Mystique*, my feminism came into better focus. Teaching taught me to clarify my ideas, a helpful prerequisite for public life.

Through teaching I also discovered the excitement that comes from connecting with an audience. When I lectured, I sometimes would spot a pair of eyes in the crowd responding with recognition. This was one of the joys of public life, I discovered: being understood. The isolation of the speaker standing apart from the crowd could be replaced by its opposite: connection. The energy that sometimes radiated from a receptive audience gave my words momentum. I felt that a good audience would tolerate anything: my jokes, my mistakes, and my foolishness. My formula was simple then: the more I spoke, the easier it became. I came to know that the strength of my political voice was directly related to the strength of my political beliefs.

In time, it became impossible to remain silent, as I discovered when the debate on ratification of the Equal Rights Amendment in the Vermont General Assembly brought me to my feet for the first time as a newly elected state legislator, on January 12, 1973, only a few days after I had taken the oath of office. The unwritten rule for freshman legislators was not to speak until Town Meeting Day, the first Tuesday after the first Monday in March. But the resolution to ratify the federal Equal Rights Amendment was on the floor. Should I keep quiet? This was the issue that had motivated me to run for the General Assembly. I had lobbied for it as a citizen, now I had the opportunity to speak on it as an elected official. How could I stay in my seat?

I sought advice from a seasoned legislator across the aisle from me: Representative Lew Kedroff, a committee chairman who spoke with impressive authority (notwithstanding his thick Czechoslovakian accent).

"Do you think it's okay for me to get up and speak?" I whispered to him. As a fellow immigrant, I thought he might be sympathetic.

"Go ahead, if you feel you have to. But keep it short."

I took that to be encouragement. But wait, the debate seemed to be coming to a close. Perhaps I would be spared.

The Speaker of the House, Walter ("Peanut") Kennedy, was saying, "Listen to the third reading of the bill . . . ," when Kenalene Collins, the conservative Republican member from Readsboro, stood up to be recognized. It was not over! I knew Collins by reputation as a vehement opponent of the Equal Rights Amendment, and she wasted no time in making her position clear. Gravely, she warned that passage of the ERA would force women to be drafted, which would lead to "rape and incest in the barracks." The breakdown of the family would be next.

I could contain myself no longer. The possibility that a woman opposed to the Equal Rights Amendment would have the last word made me stand up. I pulled the small microphone out from the corner of my desk and held it to my lips, uncertain of the correct distance between it and my mouth. Would I sound too soft or too loud? Would the Speaker see me?

"Member from Burlington, Mrs. Kunin."

I had been recognized. His words granted me permission to speak.

"Mr. Speaker," I replied.

"Proceed." The Speaker nodded.

So far, so good. I had remembered to use the proper form. Rows of chairs swiveled in my direction. This would be known as my maiden speech. These were my peers; they would judge me.

I looked at my notes one last time and proceeded to counter each point Kenalene Collins had made. Then I appealed to the gentlemen of the House.

"The Equal Rights Amendment will not stop anyone from being a gentleman or a lady, nor will it create new gentlemen or ladies. We will continue to regard each other with respect and courtesy on an equal basis," I said, assuming a level of gentility to which I hoped my audience would rise.

I noted that the Equal Rights Amendment had been called a "women's liberation amendment" by its opponents. "This is not a term I find objectionable," I said, "but it is not accurate to apply it here. This amendment was conceived by our mothers and grandmothers, long before the phrase 'women's liberation' was invented. Perhaps you feel your wives and daughters don't need this amendment, but you were elected to serve the people of Vermont, and fifty-two percent of them are women. Many of them are not cared for by men and have to support their families."

I appealed to the Vermont tradition of respect for individual rights and opposition to slavery. "Today we can follow the path taken by our forefathers and foremothers, and reaffirm the Vermont belief in equality for all our citizens.

"Speaking of foremothers," I said, "we have one: Clarina Howard Nichols, of Townshend, Vermont," the editor of a weekly newspaper, the *Windham County Democrat*, and the first woman to appear "before this house on behalf of a bill which would have allowed women to vote in school district meetings in 1852." Her request to speak had been labeled a "scramble for the breeches," and I quoted her reply: "I will not appeal to the gallantry of this House or to its manliness, if such a taunt [about breeches] does not come with an ill grace from gentlemen who have legislated our skirts into their possession. And will it not be quite enough time for them to taunt us with being after their wardrobes, when they shall have restored to us the legal right to our own?"

I concluded, "Here in this House women and men serve together as equals. There is no discrimination here; therefore, there should be no discrimination anywhere in the state of Vermont."

I sat down, much relieved, and looked up at the gallery, where I caught the attention of a group of women seated in the front row. They smiled down at me, and I smiled back. With a wave, they sent me their gratitude. I caught it like a bouquet. Last year I had been seated up there with them. Today, I was a member of the Vermont House of Representatives in seat 52. In that moment I understood the meaning of public life: my words were not only my own; they also belonged to them, the women in the balcony. That was why I had been elected.

The Equal Rights Amendment was ratified by a vote of 120 to 28. Seeing my happy grin, a legislator stopped me on the way out of the chamber and put his hand on my arm: "Just because you won your first one, don't think you're going to win them all."

But at that moment, nothing could slow me down. Not only had I survived, I had won!

My almost-Victorian words, as I look back at them, did not disguise the intensity of my feeling. The cause of equal justice for women had propelled me out of my seat, and I found the right words because they had always been there: my convictions, held so long in private, had been waiting to be released.

When I first gave speeches, I relied on written texts, each sentence carefully written and rewritten. Later I began to use notes. Not until I became governor and gave five or six speeches a day did I learn to give speeches with no written texts. But by then, I knew what I wanted to say and how to say it, how to read the mood of an audience and relate to it. Eventually I became relaxed enough with audiences to engage in humor, even self-deprecation. Making an audience laugh gave me the greatest satisfaction and delight. Laughter provides instant feedback and is a spontaneous gift of affirmation.

I almost always wrote my own speeches. I once experienced the nightmare of being handed a prepared text that I simply read, and after that I knew better. It was also an occasion that perfectly exemplified the difficulties of my political apprenticeship. It was during my first campaign for governor in 1982, and I was the featured speaker at a Rotary Club luncheon. As the car wound its way up the hill to the Hartness House in Springfield, where the club was to meet at noon, I was anxious not to be late. Rotaries always start on time, my older brother had warned me; he was then a state legislator and club member, and he met me at the door. "You better give a helluva speech. These guys are all Republicans." Springfield was a machine-tool-factory town, and the Rotary Club was a meeting ground for its business leaders.

I scanned the room for a friendly face. There were one or two welcoming smiles, but most people's attention was elsewhere. The men were lining up, pinning their Rotary badges on, exchanging the familiar repartee that brought them together every Monday of the year.

As we filed into the dining room, I realized I was the only woman in the room, except for the waitresses, the pianist, and one newspaper reporter, who gave me a faint smile. Was she sharing my trepidation, or was she, too, putting me to the test, pencil in hand, ready to write the verdict?

The president's clang of the bell interrupted my speculation. I jumped up in time to salute the flag and sing "God Bless America," stalwartly placing my hand over my heart. Was it in the right place? How high above my bosom should it be?

I started to sit down but quickly stood up again, since everyone else remained standing. They had done an about-face to the north and were singing the Canadian national anthem.

When they concluded, I was as careful as a non-Catholic at high mass, seating myself in perfect synchronization with the five other people at the head table. I picked up the *Rotary* songbook next to my plate, as instructed.

"Everyone turn to page nine."

Should a nonmember join in singing the Rotary song or not? "R-O-T-A-R-Y, that spells Rotary," the men sang, trying their best to follow the melody played by the gray-haired pianist, who led them from line to line like a tired but indulgent fifth-grade teacher.

"Everybody turn to page forty-two, 'Row, Row, Row Your Boat.' Come on now, let's hear it." I joined in, hoping someone would notice I was having fun.

I did not touch the square of red Jell-O on its green lettuce bed, or the psychedelic-pink slab of ham. I managed to swallow the mashed potatoes, alternating each spoonful with sips of ice water. The rounded, thick edge of the coffee cup sandpapered my lips. When we got to the vanilla ice cream with maple syrup, I extended my toe to nudge the folder containing my speech, which lay on the floor under the table. Yes, it was there, safe and sound. I reached down for it and scanned the first page. Nothing looked familiar.

My campaign manager had handed me the speech early that morning as I ran out the door. We had decided that this would be a good occasion to unveil my economic-development program: the Rotary Club was the perfect place to prove that I could talk to a male audience about what mattered to them most: business and taxes. I had a rough idea of the contents, but I had not read the final speech until an hour before when I had scanned it in the car. Each point was heavily supported with statistics. I had no doubt that this was the ammunition that would convey my expertise. The only problem was that I would have to pay close attention to the text.

"It is now my pleasure to present to you our lieutenant governor and the Democratic candidate for governor, Madeleine Kunin."

I stood up and moved to the podium, suddenly blinded by the glare of television lights. I could not see anyone, not even my brother. The podium, to my surprise, was unusually high (not a rare discovery for a female speaker) and cut me off sharply at the chin, giving me a child's view of the world. Everything was black. I assumed the men were still there, though I could not have known if, one by one, they had quietly slipped out. For the next thirty-five minutes I looked down at the swimming words of text, wanting to make sure I wouldn't miss any important statistic or point. When I took a furtive glance into the void, I felt droplets of perspiration beading my upper lip. Better look down, I thought; that way they will see only the top of my head.

The last page. Had every man in the room just recrossed his legs, or was that my imagination?

The end.

I escaped the podium and sat down.

Polite applause.

"How do you think it went?" I asked my brother anxiously.

"Too long. And you never looked up."

"I'm sorry."

I had disappointed my older brother, a person I wanted to please, as a daughter would a father. Never again would I do it this way. I would have to learn to use my own words.

I weaned myself from the text gradually, leaving the printed words a few moments at a time, until I found I could do so for stretches of a page or two. For formal occasions, I continued to use written texts, but I composed them myself. Writing speeches became a way to organize my thoughts. I could not imagine giving the task to someone else. For shorter speeches I learned to use handwritten notes, which I would glance at briefly to catch a word that would point me in the right direction. When I stepped into a new area of expertise, where factual information was required, a list of talking points sufficed.

There is a mystery about public speaking that is hard to define. The tension, excitement, and expectation that precede a speech are themselves stimulants to performance. After the first introductory words, I often feel I am functioning on a level that is not entirely within my control, propelled by ideas, emotions, and energy that come from the act of speaking itself. It is like being an athlete, running not only on well-trained muscles but on adrenaline, which the act of speaking pumps out.

As I look back on it, I realize that *all* the work and experience I had after—even in—college helped to prepare me for a life in politics. In my very first career, journalism, I learned how to plunge into new and unknown areas of knowledge; as a reporter you have to know a bare minimum about almost everything. The first meetings of the Winooski Board of Selectmen, which I covered as a twenty-three-year-old reporter for the *Burlington Free Press,* were conducted partly in French by Mayor Armand Rathe; but it was not much easier for me to follow the English-language version of these small-town political skirmishes. Only when I followed the selectmen into the diner across the street for late-night coffee did I begin to discern the battle lines of the debate and get the information I needed to write a story.

In all those school-board and selectmen's meetings, I received the basics of a political education. The question was usually about power and who had the right to exercise it. With pencil and pad in hand and a deadline to meet, I had to sort out the relevant facts and identify the key players, essential skills for a journalist and excellent training for a politician. No field of knowledge was off-limits. Everything had to be described and understood. Curiosity and the urge to satisfy it are the driving forces in both journalism and politics. One of the surprising rewards of political life is the intellectual pleasure one derives from discovering new ideas and information, and from analyzing problems.

I learned not to be intimidated by expertise. I developed an intellectual aggressiveness that stood me in good stead in the unruly smoke-filled rooms of politics, where any subject could come up at any time, unlike one's experience in private life, where one can pick and choose the guests and steer the conversation. That helped me overcome the fear of open-ended agendas, which one might not control.

I cut short my reporting career when I decided to leave the *Burlington Free Press* and become a guide in the American Pavilion at the Brussels World's Fair in 1958. This was the opportunity to go to Europe that I had been looking for. Two years earlier, when I had graduated from college, my mother had urged me *not* to go abroad to study at the London School of Economics (I had received a scholarship for graduate studies that could be used at any institution), and I had heeded my mother's advice to stay closer to home: I went to Columbia University Graduate School of Journalism. But that same year, my brother traveled in Europe, and I had regretted my dutiful choice. Now, in 1958, it would be my turn to return to Europe.

Dressed in my uniform—a gray pleated skirt, gray blazer, gold satin beret—I stood in front of the American Pavilion and proudly displayed the two oblong mother-of-pearl pins on my chest, one lettered "French" and the other "German." These were the languages in which I was supposed to explain America to the world. I was delighted to reverse my childhood journey from Europe to become the bilingual American on this continent. But within days, I found that most of my time was spent telling tired, cranky tourists where the bathrooms were—no simple feat in a circular building.

What a relief, it was, then, when I had an opportunity to work in a special section of the American exhibit called "America's Unfinished Business," located in a tunnel-shaped hut in the rear of the elegant Edward Durell Stone Pavilion. Black-and-white blowup collages of newspaper stories on three subjects—"The American Negro," "The Alliance with Nature," and "The Crowded City"—were pasted on the inside of the tunnel. One section depicted the racial strife in Little Rock, Arkansas, in 1957 in bold headlines: "Integration in South Stirs Student Demonstrations." Photographs showed Governor Orville Faubus warding off twenty-two troopers from the U.S. Army's 101st Airborne (another 350 had surrounded the building) while white parents screamed at nine black teenagers trying to enter the all-white Central High School. The ugly confrontation shattered America's reputation for having achieved racial harmony. The exhibit provoked strong reactions from visitors to the Pavilion from all parts of the world who were shocked by American racism and its accompanying violence. For the first time I had to publicly defend my beliefs as well as my country. I loved the challenge.

Not long after the exhibit opened, a congressional delegation toured the American Pavilion. When they got to "America's Unfinished Business," they became irate. "Why are we airing our dirty linen here at the Brussels World's Fair? The exhibit has to come down immediately," they announced.

"How can they do that?" I asked. "This is the best part of the American exhibition, where we really talk about who we are and what we stand for."

Only a country with strong democratic beliefs could afford to talk openly about its problems, I argued. It would be a great mistake to take it down. So I sent a petition to my senator, asking him to support the exhibit, and gathered signatures from the other guides. I wrote:

> The United States is the only country represented at the Brussels World's Fair which is engaging in this type of self-evaluation. What has sometimes been termed as "hanging our dirty linen" by critics of the exhibit in the United States has, on the contrary, turned out to be a powerful type of inverse propaganda. . . .

When I learned that my statement was placed in the *Congressional Record*, I was thrilled. For me, then, it was the historic equivalent of the Talmud.

The exhibit was taken down, however, and replaced by a display about American health care, sponsored by pharmaceutical companies. I was disappointed and angry. How could the Congress have been so cowardly? But I consoled myself. I had tried. I had exercised my prerogative as a citizen to express my opinion to my congressman.

Today, I see the whole experience somewhat differently. I realize I had enlisted others in my cause and put my concern in writing, exposing it to public view. Instinctively, I had transformed a private grievance into a public debate.

My political tutelage that summer in Brussels was advanced by my roommate at the Brussels World's Fair, Carol Hardin. I met Carol for the first time in the reception lounge of the SS *America*, docked in New York and ready to depart for Le Havre. The president of the fair, Howard Cullman, was making his way through the crowd of guides who had been assembled to meet him before they embarked. Watching his steady progress, shaking hands, greeting each person, I wondered nervously what I would say when he got to me. As he approached, a tall woman with sleek black hair who was seated next to me stood up briskly and bared a dazzling smile as she extended a firm hand to Mr. Cullman. In distinct and certain tones that I had never heard from a young woman, she announced, "My name is Carol Hardin. It's a great pleasure to meet you."

This, I told myself, is how it's done.

Years later, when I would be the one being watched as I worked my way through a crowd from hand to hand, punctuating each handshake with a cheerful greeting, I should have taken other young women aside and whispered, "I wasn't always able to be like this. I learned it from Carol Hardin."

Carol was a niece of Adlai Stevenson, and Stevenson had been my political idol. The night in 1956 when he lost his second race for the presidency, I had been in the Biltmore Hotel on a student assignment from the Columbia School of Journalism. When his marvelous concession speech was broadcast, projected on the larger-than-life-size screen in the lobby, I wept. There was no justice. So when, in Brussels, Carol told me that Uncle Ad was coming to the World's Fair with two of his sons, Borden and John Fell, and asked if I would have time to help show them around, I gasped, "Yes."

Stevenson arrived with a large entourage, and one night the party of about twenty people dined at a restaurant in La Joyeuse Belgique, a part of the fair that replicated old Brussels. I felt I had stepped into a Brueghel painting. Huge platters of food were carried about on long trays; overflowing mugs of beer were balanced on the shoulders of red-cheeked, laughing waitresses in tight bodices and peasant blouses.

"Why don't you sit next to the governor?" a voice suggested to me. Never had I imagined I would get this close to Adlai Stevenson.

"I don't know if this is the time or place to say this, Mr. Stevenson," I ventured. "But I have always admired you very much."

He smiled kindly, patted my knee, and said, "My dear, this is the time and the place."

I don't believe I ate a thing.

The next day Stevenson held a press conference. Standing in the rear of the room and listening to his witty replies, savoring each turn of phrase, I told myself, This is how the English language can be spoken. Walking back through the medieval grandeur of the Grand Place, Stevenson encountered an American GI on the sidewalk. He stopped to shake his hand and said in a hearty voice I had not heard before, "Hi ya, soldier, where ya from?"

I was taking lessons in the art of politics.

SIX MONTHS after I returned from Brussels, at the age of twenty-five, I was married and back living in Vermont. Within the next eight years, my husband and I had four children. For about ten years I was primarily a homemaker engaged in volunteer community activities, except for two years when I was a part-time graduate student—I received a master's in English literature from the University of Vermont in 1967.

During that period of community and family involvement, I was unknowingly preparing for a political life, just as I had done as a guide in Brussels and as a reporter in Burlington. None of the activities I engaged in met the definition of "political," but they taught me political skills.

The difference between community activities and political action is merely one of scale. Similar skills and motivations are required. When I was eventually elected to public office, I discovered that I was far better prepared than I had anticipated. I had underestimated the enormous amount I had learned in the community and was unaware of my ability to transfer my knowledge into public life.

As I lift one layer of experience after another, trying to see how it was that I became a politician, I return to a period in 1961 when I was a newly married young doctor's wife. There was little debate then about the role of doctors' wives: they were expected to dedicate themselves to their husbands' careers. The Vermont Medical Society Auxiliary, for example, existed for that purpose. In the fall of 1961 each state auxiliary was asked to hold neighborhood teas to lobby against the Kerr-Mills bill and the Anderson-King bill, forerunner legislation to Medicaid and Medicare. After serving tea and homemade cookies in the homes of auxiliary members, they would play a record made by Ronald Reagan warning of the evils of socialized medicine. "In your sunset years, you will tell your children and grandchildren how life in America used to be when men were free," Ronald Reagan told us.

I supported the proposed legislation, and I opposed the position taken by the AMA, resenting the assumption that all doctors' wives were expected to adopt it. So I enlisted a group of my friends who were also married to doctors, and we formed an organization; we called ourselves the Study Group for Medical Care for the Aged. Taking my cue from the League of Women Voters, I intended that our group present both sides of the issue. At the time, I was not aware of the Goliath-like proportions of the AMA or my ludicrous audacity in challenging it. I was responding to my outrage and recruiting friends to share it with me.

To my surprise, the rump sessions of our study group caused an uproar within the Vermont organization. How could we oppose the AMA and Ronald Reagan? In an attempt to reconcile our differences, we met jointly with the women in the auxiliary. After the first cup of tea was poured, all common ground was lost. One medical wife, who was even opposed to Social Security, reminisced about the good old days when "we sent Aunt Ida a check every month, and she was very grateful." Tullie Brown, wife of the former dean of the University of Vermont medical school, and a woman of unquestionable status, took up this challenge. She became an ally. Mention of Aunt Ida made her sigh. "My dear, Bill and I couldn't live without our Social Security. It's just marvelous. We look forward to it every month."

The meeting broke up before we could get to Ronald Reagan.

The next thing we did was to arrange a public forum with a representative of the U.S. Department of Health, Education, and Welfare on one side and Dr. Roger Mann, president of the Vermont State Medical Society, on the other. And we gave an interview to the local paper to publicize this forum. This was my first encounter with the press. The next morning I opened the paper with trepidation. What did I look like, and how did I sound? Would I be quoted accurately? Would my husband get into trouble? Who would be offended?

The story was fine but the forum was a disappointment. The representative from HEW was an apologetic, jargon-speaking bureaucrat who seemed most eager to get back to Washington on the next plane. I was incredulous; how could they send such an incompetent defender of the administration? Dr. Mann, by contrast, was a person of enormous presence. He gave an impassioned defense of democracy and equated any legislation regulating medical care with its demise. The panel was so heavily weighted to his side that the motives of the organizers—we medical wives—became suspect. A young first-term legislator from Burlington, filled with righteous indignation, accused us of rigging the event in favor of the AMA. His name was Philip Hoff, and one year later he was elected governor of Vermont.

Dismayed by his accusation, we held a second public meeting. This time, only one side would be presented. The League approach, I had learned, had its limitations.

Burlington's city hall auditorium was packed. The speaker was sharp and well informed. It seemed everyone in the audience had a question. Many had stories. Seventy-five-year-old Helen Kennedy spoke of her fear of growing old: Who would take care of her, who would pay the bills? This was no theoretical debate between two evenly matched sides. For the first time I saw the impact that public policy could have on questions of life and death.

The next day a newspaper editorial carried an attack on our forum. I was taken aback that my actions had unleashed such strong feelings on both sides. The response had outdistanced my intent. I was not yet ready to become a public figure.

But I was saved by circumstance. A few weeks later, we moved to Boston, where my husband became a postdoctoral fellow at Harvard Medical School. While he worked in the laboratory, I returned to my role as wife and mother and anticipated the birth of our second child.

After we had settled in Cambridge, I decided to form a book club similar to the one I had belonged to in Vermont. Every two weeks a group of women, all married with young children, would read a book and discuss it in one of our living rooms. The book club gave us social and intellectual stimulation, which we badly needed, for none of us worked outside the home.

In 1962, Betty Friedan's *Feminine Mystique* was published. For me, the book was an astounding revelation. Friedan confirmed what I had often felt but dared not express: that women had been manipulated to accept their secondary roles. My desire for equality was neither disloyal nor rebellious; it was just. The book club discussion that night in my living room was intense. Some of the women were outraged that *The Feminine Mystique* had placed their choices into question, and others, like myself, felt at last they had been understood.

One of the pitfalls of writing a memoir is the desire to justify the past in terms of the present. Every experience I have had to some degree has been relevant to my political life when seen through the filter of my later work. But when I make an effort to separate fact from sentiment, I acknowledge that there were many difficult times when I had no idea how I could live a meaningful life beyond my role as wife and mother.

I worried that these fragmented child-oriented years would spell nothing, like the magnetized alphabet letters stuck helter-skelter on the refrigerator door. On my thirtieth birthday, a warm September afternoon, my friend Mary Ellen and I sat at a sidewalk café in Cambridge near Harvard Yard. We each had wheeled our one-year-old babies here in their almost-identical elegant navy-blue carriages and had parked them side by side. When one of the babies whimpered, we'd rock the carriage until it fell silent. Then, between sips of espresso, we shared our fears. "What are we ever going to do with our lives?" we asked each other. It was getting late, and we were running out of time.

Today I jest and say that I wish someone had tapped me on the shoulder and whispered in my ear, "Not to worry, someday you will be governor of Vermont." Of course, I would not have believed it.

Still, as I look back, I see that I was acquiring skills that prepared me to be governor. In the familiar cluttered space of my own kitchen, where everything was within arm's length of the telephone, I'd practice, cradle the phone against my ear and talk to the school principal about arranging a children's concert as if I were an executive, while using my other hand to wipe orange juice off the countertop. The person on the other end of the line heard only the voice. They did not see me holding a dishrag. I could pretend to be the person I would become, the woman in a navy-blue suit in her office, behind a polished desk. When a small child threatened to interrupt my reverie by making his or her presence known with a loud whine, I'd hardly miss a beat, deftly reach for the cookie jar, one hand placed over the mouthpiece, while stage-whispering, "Take this and let Mommy talk, please!" Like a ventriloquist, I would take my hand off the mouthpiece and flip back to the voice of the woman sitting behind her desk.

While I may have longed for the peace and quiet of uninterrupted professional life, those split-screen years were important. The interruptions of life matter—they may, in fact, be what is most important. Tidiness is not everything. The ability to layer experience, fold one part over another, smooth out the wrinkles, is a survival skill that is essential in both private and public life. And domestic, motherly skills I learned at home have extraordinary public usefulness. Counting out strawberries one by one to make certain that exactly the same number of strawberries went into each child's dessert dish taught me how much people care about fairness and how to mediate an argument. Cleaning up the third glass of spilled milk in the course of one meal taught me a great deal about the art of self-control. And where better to learn patience than watching a child learn to tie his shoe? Looking back, I see that all of my early community organizational efforts were related to my children.

In 1966, after we returned to Vermont from our two years in Cambridge, I started a volunteer organization to bring professional children's theater to the state. My motivation was simple: I wanted my three children—one, three, and five years old—to have access to live music and theater. To make that possible, I had to enlarge my personal agenda by developing an organization and giving it a name; that is how Lilliput Children's Programs came into being. I had discovered the political imperative: the desire to expand upon personal experience and transform it into a public agenda, to develop an issue of individual importance and merge it into a generally felt community need. I did not need permission to do what I did because I was only a volunteer and therefore no threat to anyone. I could proceed as I wished, unintimidated by rules or experts who might have told me I didn't know what I was doing.

This is why volunteer activities can foster enormous leadership skills. The nonprofessional volunteer world is a laboratory for self-realization. The benign neglect with which such housewifely efforts as mine are often treated can be advantageous. There is no one with the authority to tell you no. There is a tendency to dismiss the value of such work done for no pay, something voluntary, squeezed between routine obligations. And even I would have then described myself as a dabbler with a short attention span, putting my brush down the minute duty called.

But those years, I see now, offered a time of leisurely exploration. I could devote time to different projects without having to decide my life's work. The fluidity of my life allowed me to live in several different worlds at once, and that was a capability I later found useful in public life. I developed Lilliput Children's Programs slowly, asking a folksinging minister, John Nutting, to give the first performance in the basement of the College Street Congregational Church. He agreed. Our costs would have to cover the expenses. I made a list of our friends and sent each one an invitation. We came out even.

Bolstered by this success, I next asked a Vermont couple, folksingers Sandy and Caroline Peyton, to give the second performance. This time we had some change left over. I formed a committee of five friends and turned to them for advice. Do we dare go out of state and engage a professional theater company?

I was learning how to build an organization, a skill that readily could be transferred to politics. When I did not know something, I did not hesitate to ask for help or advice. When one course of action did not work, I tried another until, step by step, I turned an idea into a reality. In a few months, we had organized a series of performances for children in the schools, and two for the public.

The first show took place in an elementary-school gymnasium packed with two hundred wriggling kids. Most rural Vermont children had never before seen live actors onstage. The excitement was electric. I stood in the back, enveloped in a cloud of winter radiator heat and leftover lunch-hour smells. The oohs and aahs made me forget where I was. I experienced the thrilling satisfaction of knowing this performance could not have taken place had I not made it happen.

IT WAS NOT just my eagerness to provide culture for my children, but also my anxieties about their safety that stirred me to political awareness. As a worried mother, not as a politician, I found the courage to act. The ability to build an arc between my maternal role and a public one was an essential part of my political development. Not only did it give me a sense of purpose, but it gave me permission. I was doing this not for myself, to satisfy my ambition, but because I was acting on behalf of others. I did not have to bifurcate my life: private and public person. Each reinforced the other.

I posed a question to myself, and others raised it implicitly: How could I step away from my husband and children to pursue a political career?

My answer was that I did not abandon my mother-wife-woman role; I fulfilled it, with a passion, by dedicating myself to protecting their future through political involvement. This was the paternal role implied by our male political leaders; why could women not have identical political motives? Concern for my children's safety enabled me to span the distance between mother-wife and public person, and that is how my political involvement began and how it would continue. As my children's world expanded, so did mine. My public activities moved out into a wider circle, from my school, to my neighborhood, and to my state. My priorities became more encompassing: education, the environment, and social services.

All political debate is about the effect of policy on the next generation. A standard upbeat ending for a rousing political speech has always been ". . . and we must do this to protect the future of our children and our grandchildren." I was no different from my male colleagues. But the words had a second, personal meaning that exceeded the cliché: my maternal role was activated when I said those words. (Fathers, too, might respond this way.) I envisioned the fate of my own children, as well as others, enabling me to harmonize my maternal and political selves. Often the connection between my political agenda and my children's future was tenuous as I contended with the practical problems of family life, conflicts between my dual roles, and bouts of guilt when I thought I was in the wrong place at the wrong time. And as the issues on my political agenda expanded, there was less connection, perhaps, with my personal circumstances, but I always rooted the validity of my public life in causes larger than myself that mattered to my children's future. That was the only way that such a life made sense.

IN 1966, when we were living on a street in Burlington called Prospect Parkway, I tried to get sidewalks built there. My first visions of impending disaster occurred when I waved my first child, Julia, off to kindergarten. As I watched her skipping down Prospect Parkway in her pretty new dress, swinging a satchel filled with her favorite things, she became smaller and smaller.

A car whizzed by that almost touched her.

"She's walking in the road," I gasped. I chased after her, caught up, and bent down to give her careful instructions. "Always walk on the grass, please, Julia. Promise?" I pleaded.

Eager to leave me behind, she nodded. "I promise, Mommy, don't worry."

As I walked back up the hill, I speculated, What will happen in the wintertime? And can I be certain she won't wander into the road, especially if the other children do?

We had to have sidewalks. I talked it over with a neighbor who also had small children. I soon learned that the neighborhood was divided: those with school-age children would support sidewalks; those whose children were grown were uninterested; some were vehemently opposed.

I turned for help to our alderman, George Little, and he encouraged me to bring the question before the Board of Aldermen. The night the question was on the agenda my husband and I and a handful of neighbors attended a meeting for the first time. We smelled the lingering odors of cigarette smoke and of gray mops sloshing over the marble floor as we squinted in the dim interior lighting. This room in city hall felt like a private club that for many years had kept its doors and windows shut. I saw that another group of neighbors had arrived first, and they were seated in a tight phalanx in the front row. Their backward glances told me they were here to defend their turf. The antisidewalk contingent.

The small team of sidewalk proponents was not prepared for battle. But armed with visions of Julia skipping dangerously down the street, I stood up and presented our case "in defense of sidewalks."

I was not shouted down, but I felt a soft hiss emanating from the glares of my opponents. Arguments were presented on both sides. The aldermen remained silent. One or two began to fiddle with their pencils and leaf through their notebooks. Interest was draining from the room like water through a sieve.

The president of the board had figured it out: this was a no-win neighborhood fight.

"I move the question be tabled," a voice said.

"So voted," the president affirmed.

We straggled out, shaking our heads. The opponents were triumphant. How could they have done this?

But I was not completely demoralized by defeat. I was insulated by my conviction of the rightness of our cause. Not once did I doubt that the demand for sidewalks was just. As we walked down the steps of city hall, I said what I believed, that we were right and they were wrong. (Twenty-four years later, I confess I experienced a special delight, savored only by the vindicated, when I drove down our old street and discovered that someone had achieved what I had not. There they were: sidewalks!)

I learned a vital lesson from the sidewalk fight: it is hard to achieve change with divided forces. Local opposition made it easy for the aldermen to say no. Why risk alienating one group of voters by satisfying another?

The sidewalk skirmish also taught me that I could stand up and speak before an angry crowd, that I could say what I believed, not through self-conscious effort, but by becoming *less* self-conscious. The force of my anger had cleared the barriers that had confined me. Later, I recognized my mistakes. I had assumed, with the arrogance of the righteous, that my concerns would be universally shared. My neighbors seemed to care more about their lawns than about our children—how could they? I dismissed their position because it looked unreasonable, but in time I learned to take other opinions as seriously as my own. Only then could I be well prepared.

So strongly did I feel about the sidewalk question that soon the whole Kunin family moved to Dunder Road, a quiet dead-end street with sidewalks.

But Dunder Road had its own traffic hazards, I soon learned. Our children had to go across an unmarked railroad crossing to get to school. I worried about their safety. After raising the question with my neighbors, I discovered that a number of parents agreed: we decided to ask the city to put up flashing lights. But how would we get this accomplished? Stating the problem seemed easy in comparison with having to solve it. Still, in the laboratory of my neighborhood I learned that defining the problem was the first and most important step. I didn't have to know all the answers in order to begin. There are advantages to being a political newcomer. I found the courage to request the flashing lights at the railroad crossing because I was unfamiliar with the obstacles. Untutored, I refused to take no for an answer. When I was told by one businessman that "Nothing's going to happen with those lights, lady, until somebody gets killed," I reacted like a mother bear in defense of her cubs. I'll show him, I said to myself. And I did.

I figured out what had to be done by asking questions. The first step, I learned, was to testify at a hearing before a quasi-judicial body called the Public Service Board. Until then I had not known such a group existed. I did not think to dwell on my lack of legal knowledge, but in keeping with my League of Women Voters training, I gathered the necessary facts. Next I rounded up a group of neighbors to come with me to the hearing.

The three-person Public Service Board panel listened with interest, ordered a traffic study, and set a date to inspect the site. They concluded that the request for flashing lights to protect children on their way to school made sense, if the evidence supported it. The obstacle was money: it would cost almost three thousand dollars, to be shared by the railroad, the city, and the state. The railroad objected strongly, opposed to setting a precedent that might, after all, marshal mothers at every railroad crossing in Vermont.

I lobbied the Board of Aldermen for their support. Clarence Meunier, my opponent-to-be, suggested I settle for a stop sign, and Bob Blanchard assured me he was pulling all the right strings.

On the day of the site visit, two members of the board and four experts walked, eyes down, along the tracks, inspecting the situation and looking up from time to time to note a car going by. As they were chatting, a small yellow toylike vehicle used for track maintenance headed up the tracks at a rapid clip.

Zoom.

"Whew, that was a close one," exclaimed the chairman of the board as he jumped to safety.

The huddled group nodded in agreement: this was a dangerous crossing.

Two weeks later, I received the official notification: red flashing lights would be installed on Home Avenue forthwith. At least twice a day I drove across the tracks and glanced at the tall, stately lights flanking either side, erect as marshals wearing crossed white bands inscribed with the letters RAILROAD CROSSING.

These two red lights illuminated the rewards that came with risk. The once-distant and impenetrable structure called the political system had responded to my entreaties. For the first time I became aware of my potential political effectiveness. The success at the railroad crossing enlarged my sense of possibility and strengthened my optimism; my efforts had achieved practical results. This is how I began to lay the groundwork for living a political life. The belief that as an individual I could have an effect on an impersonal political system was essential to my growth. It made me believe that I could change the world.

As I look back, my Miranda-like belief in a brave new world could be considered childish. Such daydreams were what sophisticated adults left behind, like the teenage fantasy of becoming a rock star. The political life does, however, require imagination, a refusal to be limited by common sense. I had to envision myself as a heroic figure before I could become one.

Learning political skills on familiar turf, in my own backyard, was safe. It made politics a game, and I was trying out for the team. I could take my time to learn the rules, and I could discover firsthand what women my age had little opportunity to learn: how it feels to win and lose.

Losing, I learned, is seldom final. It depends on how the umpire calls the game, and that judgment, to a large degree, influences what happens next. It is not always devastating to be defeated; the fight itself can give you the boost you need for the next step. And winning, I discovered, sets off a chain reaction; each victory emits a current that sets off the next. Each step is a test, and if you pass it, the feedback bolsters your confidence. That is how I moved beyond the confines of my own backyard into the larger political arena in incremental steps.

At first, when I pursued the issue of flashing railroad lights, I was on familiar ground, speaking out as a private citizen. But as I became more deeply involved in the process, gathering signatures and testifying before the Public Service Board, I stepped over the line from private citizen to public advocate. I was pulled into politics by the sequence of events. By the time I recognized that I was standing on political ground, it seemed right to be there because that is where the decision would be made. I was following the issue to its logical conclusion: the power center where the votes were cast. When I pursued a similar course with the Equal Rights Amendment, that is how I discovered I wanted to be in the Vermont state legislature, sitting in my seat and voting.

When I went out campaigning, I distributed a flyer with my hand-drawn pen-and-ink drawing of railroad crossing lights. "Madeleine M. Kunin helped YOU get these flashing lights at the Home Avenue railroad crossing. YOU can help Madeleine M. Kunin by voting for her for district Representative to Montpelier—where she can accomplish even more."

Today, the flyer is embarrassing to me. Then, it may have helped me win.

When I became a state representative, the kitchen that I had once been eager to exit was now sometimes comforting to reenter. On a Monday morning, Esther Sorrell and I would confess to each other that we had spent the weekend baking bread. Kneading, slapping, punching, throwing the dough from side to side felt wonderful—a suitable outlet for our frustrations. When I opened the oven, I had produced something edible that would nurture my family: a beautiful, golden loaf of bread. This was the reality I craved.

One Friday afternoon during the last week of my first term in the legislature I stopped at the shopping center to pick up groceries for dinner. It had been a frantic week, as legislators had scrambled to get key bills passed before adjournment. For the first few minutes, pushing my metal cart through the aisles, my mind was still in the capitol, under the golden dome, but then I had to decide: margarine versus butter, brown eggs or white. Everyone in the store was equally engrossed in trying to figure out "the better buy."

The world I had just left behind in Montpelier came to seem like that of an exotic tribe absorbed with its own customs, speech, and garb, unrelated to what happened here in the supermarket. What did it matter to my fellow shoppers if a bill was passed or not, an amendment rejected or accepted? The momentous significance I had attached to the progress of legislation just an hour ago was now melodramatic. How could I have taken myself that seriously?

I continued pushing my cart, joining the rhythm of the parade going up one aisle and down the other. Dairy products, aisle 2; soups and cereals, aisle 3. Everything in its place.

"How's everything in Montpelier?" a voice interrupted.

Before I could think of an appropriate reply, I heard, "I want to tell you, you're doing a great job."

"Thanks, thanks. Nice to hear that." I smiled.

With hindsight, I realize that there was a political benefit derived from the years when I had been pushing my shopping cart full time, as it were: I was more connected to what politicians considered less important, to the small occurrences of daily life. The fact that women have been largely responsible for coping with such family problems made me privy to information that seldom reached the committee rooms where official decisions were made. Concerns about child care, pollution, health care, and crime—all these emerged during those years in the stories we women shared with one another. Worry about a child's teacher, concern about a recent robbery, anxiety over not being able to afford to send a son or daughter to college, a grandmother moved reluctantly to a nursing home, dismay at polluted air and contaminated water—these were daily realities that shaped my values and defined my political agenda. I did not have to glean such trends and statistics from reports; I could verify them with personal accounts.

IN 1970 my husband had an opportunity to take a sabbatical from the University of Vermont. We could go to Bern, Switzerland. Enticing as this offer was, I had some misgivings. I had just started a new career, teaching English literature at Trinity College. If I left after only a year, could I ever get this job back, or any job? But I was also exhausted with the dual demands of teaching and a new baby. Last year, our fourth child, Daniel, had been born, and my mother had died three months after his birth. A return to Switzerland would bring me close to Aunt Berthe, my mother's oldest sister, who loved me like a daughter.

That sabbatical year—1970–71—was the most family-focused year of my life, and it also had a profound impact on my political growth. As an immigrant to the United States, I had grown up with a dual identity, European and American. Now, thirty years later, when I returned to Switzerland, I saw Europe with new American eyes. Switzerland, for all its comfortable childhood familiarity, to me seemed *kleinlich*, as my mother used to say, "small-minded." And the role of women was strictly delineated.

My daily life was happily centered in domesticity. I wanted to treasure this period of togetherness when we, as a family, were dependent upon one another in the unusually close way experienced by Americans abroad. But as I shopped and cooked and pushed Daniel's stroller down the street in Bern, I was already moving on to the next stage of my life, for I was gaining an understanding of what I did not want.

My kind next-door neighbor on Steinhübeliweg, Frau Albert Ruedi, taught me how to knit. I liked to feel the wool slide through my fingers and hear the needles click. Amazed, I held out at arm's length a completed sweater for my husband. During our afternoon talks, Frau Ruedi told me about her life. She spent much of her day preparing for her husband's return from work. He was an engineer, good with his hands, but lacking in words. Her only son, Albert, was the apple of her eye. Over tea, she told me that whenever they visited her husband's family, the men would eat at the table while the women hurried back and forth from the kitchen carrying large platters of food. Never did husbands and wives sit down together.

When she instructed me in the intricacies of adding and subtracting the correct number of stitches, I thought I detected regret in her voice, or perhaps I was imposing my values on her. I asked myself, How could she be satisfied with such an ancillary life?

Frau Ruedi's gentle revelation of herself as someone who knew the world was filled with possibilities, but not for her, served as a poignant warning. Much as I would like to transform myself into some ideal of the devoted wife and mother, Frau Ruedi confirmed for me what I had always known, that adhering to that ideal requires more sacrifice than women should be asked to make. I knew myself incapable of it. The very thought would turn devotion into anger.

Switzerland provided an incubation period, allowing me time to read, think, and redefine myself. By the end of the Swiss sabbatical year, a more independent self had begun to take shape. Also in that year, Swiss women achieved the right to vote for the first time. When I turned on the television to watch women and men debate the pros and cons of this issue, I felt I was watching a rerun of a historical documentary, translated into German, of the American suffrage movement. My curiosity was such that I attended several meetings of the women's suffrage group in Bern. Although women could not vote in federal elections, a number of Swiss women held public office at the cantonal level of government (equivalent to our states). I met the female mayor of Geneva and several women who served on Zurich's city council. I was asked, as an American visitor, What is the political status of women in America? I was embarrassed to acknowledge that although women had had the right to vote since the passage of the Nineteenth Amendment to the Constitution in 1920, few women held elective office. Only thirteen women served in the U.S. House of Representatives, and no woman had been elected governor in her own right.

Thus it was that in Switzerland, the year that Swiss women won the right to vote in federal elections, I began to think about running for office when I returned to the United States. The example of the Swiss women's participation in public life, despite the obstacles of living in a decidedly patriarchal society, made me think it might be possible for me to get politically involved when I got home. If women could become political activists in Switzerland, think of what could be accomplished in America.

A year later, I ran for public office.

4

"What if I run, get elected to the legislature, and find out that I'm no good at it?" I posed the question that was bothering me most to an elfin-faced college math teacher sitting behind a gray desk in his cinder-block office. I waited for his assessment as I would a final grade. Math had been my worst subject. Vincent Naramore ("Vinnie" to close friends) was a political guru. In the days when polling did not pretend to be a science, he was much in demand, holding morsels of political percentages high in the air and waiting for the Pavlovian press to jump. Usually, they did.

Each year, up until the early 1970s, the week before Election Day he polled the 823 citizens of Salisbury, Vermont, and his results were considered dependably prophetic. As went Salisbury, so went Vermont. (This went on until Charles Ross, a candidate for Congress, found out where Salisbury was located on the map, hopped in his car, and saturated the town, going so far as to give a pine tree to each likely voter. He got 90 percent of the vote in Salisbury, but lost the state.)

On that spring day in 1972, my question hung in the air too long for comfort, like a loud cough at a concert. I crossed and uncrossed my legs, hoping the silence would be struck down by a strong affirmative answer like "Don't be silly, you'll be great," for example.

Professor Naramore looked at me with a kind smile and said, "Well," and paused for a suck on his pipe that revealed more lung capacity than one would expect from such a slight man, "if you find you're no good at it . . . you won't stand out."

I burst into laughter. What a wise man. Vincent, everything they say about you is true.

That night, I wrote my press release for the *Burlington Free Press*.

> BURLINGTON—(Special)—Mrs. Madeleine M. Kunin of Burlington announced Tuesday she will be a Democratic candidate for the [Vermont] House of Representatives from district 1-8. She declared she is

seeking the House seat because "the 1973 legislature is going to make some vital decisions which will affect all of us, especially in the areas of environmental controls and the property tax. If we do not act now to remove the oil tanks from the Burlington waterfront, to control sewage going into Lake Champlain and to stop air pollution, our children will ask us why we sat by with our hands folded."

Mrs. Kunin, 38, stated more women should participate in government "not just because they're women, but because they have something to contribute.

"We must work together to try to find fresh solutions to old and complex problems, such as creating an equitable tax system and to pay for public schools," said the candidate.

Mrs. Kunin ran against Alderman Clarence Meunier in the Ward 5 Democratic caucus in Burlington and was narrowly defeated.

A former English instructor at Trinity College, she was a *Burlington Free Press* reporter, a member of the Governor's Commission on the Status of Women, and founder of Lilliput Children's Programs. She is a member of the League of Women Voters and a coordinator of the Women's Political Caucus.

Mrs. Kunin graduated from the University of Massachusetts, Columbia University School of Journalism, and received an M.A. degree from the University of Vermont. She and her husband, Dr. Arthur S. Kunin, have four children.

My life story, in six column inches. Squeezed together in tidy type, it looked presentable, even logical, making it seem inevitable that I would run for the legislature. The other time my life had been neatly delineated was when I had become engaged, and the announcement made me look like the person I wanted to be—the woman about to be married. Now I concentrated on my picture with the worry of someone who looks in the mirror to see if the light will be cruel or kind. I seemed to have carried it off, keeping the loose strands of doubt tucked neatly behind my ears.

But could I live my life as I had written it down? "She and her husband, Dr. Arthur S. Kunin, have four children." I wrote the release as if I were a man, as if it made no difference, as if the children were Arthur's as much as they were mine. I knew better. My children were young. How could I be a good mother to them, and a good politician? How much could I ask my husband to help? Could I find reliable and loving baby-sitters? Would

I come home at the end of the day, with guilt seeping from my heart, like calcium from my bones, making me vulnerable for a fall? And what would the voters think when they read "four children"? They could read between the lines. When they matched that sentence with my face, would they shake their heads and ask, "But who's taking care of the children?"

I knew that my political success would be judged not only by how well I represented my constituents in Montpelier, but also by how ably I fulfilled my motherly duties at home. Isn't that how I myself had passed judgment on other women in public life when I had felt stuck at home? Why should I expect greater tolerance from others than I had been capable of expressing myself? I was familiar with my ambivalence over other women's success; deep down, I thought they would pay a price. What would mine be? The bad-mother nightmare: a child run over in the street? Or something less dramatic but equally condemning: a bad report card, truancy, a temper tantrum in the Grand Union supermarket? "What can you expect, she's away so much, politicking in Montpelier," the voice would say from the next aisle over.

I sought out other voices and turned to the women legislators I knew. I was fortunate to live in a city with four female role models. Esther Cohen was one of three women from Burlington serving in the Vermont Legislature (out of a total of seventeen). She was a widow, and her children were grown; I was cheered by her encouragement. Evelyn Jarrett, also a widow, was of the same generation; politics filled these women's lonely days and nights. I barely knew Lorraine Graham but found we had something in common; she had a child the same age as Daniel, who was two and a half. And Esther Sorrell, who was running for the Senate, had a daughter Michaela, the youngest of five children, age ten, my daughter Julia's age.

Seven years before, the Supreme Court had required Vermont to re-align its legislative districts in proportion to population. The result was a political upheaval that shifted power from Vermont's 250 rural towns to cities like Burlington, where Democrats were now being elected. (Prior to reapportionment, each town had had one representative, regardless of population; the town of Victory, population forty-two, and Burlington, population thirty-eight thousand, each had one representative.) After the "one man, one vote" decision in 1965, Burlington gained twelve and one-half new representatives. (The half district spanned Burlington and neighboring Winooski.) In the scramble to find new candidates to fill the Democratic slate, women were recruited.

The women who got elected represented the first wave of progressive women, supporting programs for children, education, and the poor. They seemed to exist in a world apart from politics, exerting their influence with a no-nonsense grandmother's hand, reminding the boys "to do what was right." Holding their square purses in their hands, these women had stepped into the great hall of the mostly male House of Representatives. They feminized this vast male space, enabling my shoulder-bag generation to walk in as if we had a right to be there, swinging our bags at our sides.

I had one more call to make. I had to speak to my brother, Edgar. He had always been positioned at the bench marks of my life: which college to attend, where to accept my first job. It was he who had urged me to come to Vermont, as he had done, to work for a small-town newspaper and get experience before trying to break into the big league in Washington or New York. And when I got the offer from the *Burlington Free Press*, he was the one who had said, "Take it."

Now he was the political pragmatist. This would not be a good year for a Democrat to run, he told me. He was working in Washington, where the word was that Nixon would win in a landslide, McGovern would get clobbered, and every Democrat would be dragged down with him. "Don't do it," he advised. "Wait."

Something in me rebelled. I did not want to be the careful and obedient younger sister, accepting sound advice. I searched for a counterweight.

I went to see Vic Maerki, a *Burlington Free Press* reporter who had been a tough and sometimes terrifying mentor. His beat had been the legislature. I had listened to him describing the power plays and personalities as he strode around the newsroom, cornering anyone in his way.

Now I asked him, "What do you think I should do?" I expected a stern answer. His weekly column, "The Way I See It," was harsh on politicians.

"Go ahead," he said.

"Vic, you mean it?"

"Why not? Give it a try."

I said thank you—more than once, for he had given me what I needed: male approval.

Filled with resolve, I lost it on the way home. What to make for supper, spaghetti or meat loaf? Time to pick up Daniel from nursery school. Today was my turn for the Hebrew-school car pool. How could I fit anything else into my life?

It was too soon. I wasn't ready. I didn't know enough about the issues. I would be giving up the pleasure of being with my children, and what would I get in return? Would it be worth it? In my daydreams, I had calmly walked out the door and waved good-bye, briefcase in hand; the children were miraculously older, and I was wiser than I was now. Everybody in the picture was smiling. Take your time; do it right. Wait.

I'll make spaghetti. That will be faster if I use canned sauce and throw in a fresh tomato and some basil. The family won't mind.

As that decision fell into place, I decided, I can't wait. I've got to run. Somehow, I will manage. I can bake brownies at night. The time is now, crazy as it sounds. I have to jump, ready or not.

The saying "Timing is everything in politics" applied to me. Strategically, it was a good time to run. I would be running for an open seat, pulling into the parking lot just as George Little, now the legislator from my district, was pulling out. A moment's hesitation, and someone else would take the spot. I knew the value of an open seat, having done battle with an incumbent alderman in the Democratic caucus.

When I had gone to see George to ask his advice, he had urged me to run. "The hardest part is making decisions," he said as he reminisced about his time on the Appropriations Committee. "I would sit there trying to make up my mind which way to go and stare out the window at these two squirrels, running up and down the side of the tree. I can still see those squirrels."

He stopped his reverie, bent down, and opened the doors of two white cabinets behind his desk to take out a stack of legislative reports. "Here, I'm happy to give them to you. They've just been gathering dust. Maybe they'll give you a head start. Best of luck." He never once mentioned that he was a Republican and that I was a Democrat.

I filled my arms and staggered out. I had to run for office, or else I would have to return the reports to George.

It is difficult to describe one's mental readiness for a race, but athletes know when they are primed to go, and so do many politicians. These decisions are complex, not easy to parse, because they contain the experiences of a lifetime as well as the perception of the moment. The issue of the moment for me was the women's movement; it was that timer, set years ago, which had gone off, telling me it was time to run. Without it, I might have waited until my children were grown, acceding to the expectations for my generation of women. Instead I was inspired to defy them. The bold new vision of women's lives that was emerging in the words of Kate Millett, Germaine Greer, Gloria Steinem, and Betty Friedan told me that I did not have to plot out my life patiently and sequentially—first raise children, and then, when they left home, plan a career to fill the empty nest. Instead, things could happen in rapid succession, confusion, or even simultaneity. I could run for office while my children were young and I was energetic. I did not have to incubate my ambition or my vision for a gestation period of ten or twenty years. I could give birth to it now.

The women's movement had a second effect: it made me feel normal. I cheered the feminists as they marched by because their shouts—angry, sad, and outraged—voiced my muted rebellion against traditional expectations, validated my quest for equality, and told me it was worthy. When I had asked the question, How might I lead a meaningful life? I had been on the right track. I was not maladjusted. It was society that was wrong and had to be changed. The women's movement, therefore, not only enlarged my sense of personal possibility but gave me a public mission and a purpose: to further equal opportunities for women.

The political focal point of the women's movement then was the Equal Rights Amendment. The controversy over its ratification expanded what had been a limited feminist discussion, staged in friends' living rooms and university lecture halls, into a public policy debate argued in the Congress and in statehouses. I had a premonition that this was how it would be. It was as if I had been poised on the sidewalk, waiting for the parade for women's rights to come by, tapping my foot to a distant familiar music, imagining the colors of the uniforms and the sound of the drums, long before the band appeared. At first, I thought I would stay at the sidelines, watch the marchers, and greet them with a wave. Instead, I joined their ranks.

It did not take much effort to draw me in. When the debate began in the United States on the ERA, my family and I had been in Europe, and I had determined that when we returned to America that fall, I would become involved in politics. When I was asked by Caryl Stewart to lobby for the Equal Rights Amendment and help form the Vermont Women's Political Caucus, I recognized the call I had been waiting for.

The outspoken feminists of the 1970s paved the way for women like me. They had staked out new territory and, in the process, created space for us to position ourselves at a safe distance apart from them. I could not have entered the political arena without their vanguard attack. Their aggressive feminism broke the old icons, enabling the women who followed them to pick through the rubble and reshape their lives.

The nexus between my personal feminism and my political agenda had both positive and negative consequences. The danger was that I might take political defeat on an issue like the Equal Rights Amendment as a personal rejection. I also might be thought to be driven by a single cause.

The advantage was that women's issues allowed me to achieve perfect symmetry between my words and my beliefs, the highest personal reward of political life. In time, living a political life became, in itself, a never-ending exercise in personal liberation, initiating me into once exclusively male rites of power. But feminism sometimes fell short when it came to practical realities. It couldn't tell me how to integrate the two parts of my life: mother-wife and politician. That was a cloth I was to weave and unweave and weave again, like Penelope, alone. Neither did feminism determine my long-term agenda, which perforce became all inclusive.

Feminism did, however, make me angry enough to act. When I lobbied on behalf of the Equal Rights Amendment in 1972 before an all-male legislative panel, I rebelled against my powerlessness. This decision could not be left to men acting on our behalf. We, as women, had to be there, casting our votes. The vision of me and the others, women seated among men, armed with equal power, poised to speak and to vote, was wildly exhilarating.

The debate over the Equal Rights Amendment in the Vermont legislature in 1973 was far less volatile than the Clarence Thomas hearings in 1991. The power imbalance, however, was the same. We, the women, were the pleaders, seated on one side of the table, and they, the men, were on the other, with the power to decide. The humiliation of having to *ask* for equal treatment under the law, of their treating ratification of the Equal Rights Amendment like a political favor, provoked an inarticulate internal fury, which we learned, in time, to express through polite dissent. It was a sensation I was to experience again, eighteen years later, when, as former governor, I testified with a panel of pro-choice women before the all-male Senate Judiciary Committee on Judge Clarence Thomas's nomination to the Supreme Court. Our powerlessness provoked rage. Watching Anita Hill testify before this panel became a defining moment for a new generation of women, who, like me, recoiled at the unchallenged display of male power and female vulnerability.

There was another reason to be in the legislature. Newly enacted environmental laws needed support. Advocates for ecological initiatives were vocal on the outside but silent within governmental ranks. The environmental movement had officially emerged on Earth Day, 1970. In Vermont it focused on Act 250, a comprehensive law that regulated development, opposed by developers and landowners in the Northeast Kingdom, as Senator George Aiken called that part of the state. Act 250 had been initiated by former governor Deane C. Davis, who had been outraged by the sight of raw sewage sliding down a hillside during a tour of ski-resort developments, but a year later, environmentalists and developers remained bitterly divided over it, and a call for its repeal had been issued. I wanted to be in the legislature to argue for the defense.

I have sometimes wondered if I would have run for public office in any state other than Vermont. More than elsewhere, it is a state in which public life is equated with public service. Its small population is conducive to personal campaigning. Even statewide races are less negative and more issue oriented than in many other states. Running for public office seemed more manageable than it might have elsewhere. But the decision to step over the line from private person to public figure is, in the end, the same in every state of the Union. And the political process is highly competitive, regardless of location. To enter, I had to be willing to fight.

There is no doubt that I would have had great difficulty in getting elected in Vermont in 1972 if I had come from anywhere but Burlington, the largest city in the state and a Democratic stronghold. Many rural towns prided themselves on never having sent a Democrat to Montpelier, and the rural-urban schism was wide. (After I was elected, a legislator confided to me that I had a big hurdle to overcome. "What is it," I asked, "that I'm a woman or that I'm a Democrat?" "Neither," he replied. "You're from Burlington.")

In my Burlington legislative district four people were on the ballot for the two seats. Evelyn Jarrett, a six-year incumbent, was a Democrat. As for Robert G. Morgan, the Republican candidate, I read his literature with trepidation. "Born in Burlington and educated in the public-school system . . . and the University of Vermont. . . . He is the owner of One Hour Martinizing on North Avenue and a partner in the antique business with Arthur P. Rainville." That was worrying—a native Vermonter and local businessman. What I did not know was that he would make no effort to campaign.

David Mahan was a last-minute third-party entry into the race. On October 27 this twenty-one-year-old student at the University of Vermont became a candidate of the newly formed Liberty Union party. He told the press he "could pick up many votes in the student-oriented district." With his announcement the *Burlington Free Press* report concluded this would be "a hotly contested race." The incumbent, Evelyn Jarrett, "running in both Democratic and Republican slots . . . appears to be a certainty for re-election while Mahan, Democrat Madeleine Kunin and Republican Robert G. Morgan battle for the remaining seat. Mahan said he decided to run because 'I feel the Democratic and Republican parties are basically both the same, because they only have the interests of the large corporations in mind rather than the people of Vermont.'" (Years later, in my second gubernatorial reelection campaign, I heard the same views expressed by challenger Bernard Sanders, then mayor of Burlington, an independent challenger for my position.)

In 1972, few people were paying attention to third-party rhetoric. But as a nervous new candidate, I did. When Evelyn Jarrett agreed to campaign as a team with me, I was grateful. We posed for a joint poster—two women seated on a love seat chatting. We sent out postcards with the same picture. On the back was written: "Working together for better government in Vermont: Evelyn Jarrett and Madeleine Kunin, elect both Democrats in District 1-8."

Evelyn was unusually generous, an older woman taking a younger woman by the hand. When we campaigned door to door together, she defied exhaustion. "Come on, Madeleine," she'd call, as she sprinted up another steep driveway and I followed behind. Knocking on *every* door became a personal obsession. We were good for one another, cheering each other on. I dared not give up with Evelyn marching in front of me. She lived in a part of the ward called the hill section, decidedly more Republican and affluent than where I lived in the South End, which was more working class and Democratic. Our two-member district included some six thousand people. We spent $581.17 on the race, raised in five-, ten-, and twenty-five-dollar contributions. Raising money for my first political campaign hadn't been easy, but I felt comfortable asking my friends to contribute in small amounts. They organized one joint fundraiser: a beer-and-cheese party for six dollars per couple, a huge success. (It seems we predated Brie and Chablis.) My two largest contributions were each twenty-five dollars, a conspicuously generous sum. I sent Evelyn, who had become ill in the final weeks of the campaign, a financial report after the election:

> Enclosed is our expense and contribution account for the campaign. It may seem like a lot of money, but I think we have to bear in mind that it was a campaign for both of us, making the cost for each one not too high. Since most of the push was for my benefit, I will leave it up to you what you would like to contribute.
>
> I trust that you are getting your strength back and by the first of January will be raring to go. I'd be happy to get together with you before then, and perhaps Lorraine and the two Esthers as well, for the experts to initiate the novices. Any advice will be gratefully received.

Accustomed as I have become to the thick computer printouts of later campaign finance reports, I feel nostalgic when I look at my list of hand-written contributions and expenditures, tucked into a yellowed file—I drew a line down the center of a single, lined white sheet of paper to delineate the two columns. The largest expenditure was for printing: $209.09. The smallest was for mimeographing: $4.00.

IN 1972, Evelyn Jarrett and I faced a major decision: Should we buy time for a radio commercial? I remember thinking that crossing that threshold would change me from being a neighborly, face-to-face campaigner into a professional politician. My words would be released into the airwave void where anyone, anywhere, could hear them—driving to work in the car, doing dishes in the kitchen, milking cows in the barn. I wouldn't know who the listeners were; they wouldn't know me. My voice would become a detached stream of words, poured into a thirty-second container of sound. My campaign would no longer be a neighborhood solicitation, like collecting for the Heart Fund. Paid advertising would make me a commodity, bought and sold, for the right price. (In my first gubernatorial campaign, the young partner of the fledgling advertising firm that did our media told a newspaper reporter that selling the candidate was "just like selling a can of beans." I never forgave him.)

The message, separated from the messenger, is the essence of campaign advertising. Your hand, your voice, your eye contact, cannot be everywhere, so you have to allow yourself to be replicated, either in whole or in part. My first reaction was schizophrenic: This is not who I am. I am someone else: me. I cannot recognize myself, disembodied. I wanted to maintain control over myself, remain the person who appeared on a constituent's doorstep, said hello, smiled, shook hands, and had a conversation. It was hard to let go.

Consciously, I did not admit to media anxiety; instead, we talked about the cost. Think of the waste, Evelyn and I agreed. One hundred and seventy-five thousand people lived in the listening area. They would be bombarded by a message intended for a few thousand voters.

Then why did I do it? Because I wanted to win. After much discussion, Evelyn and I agreed on two ads, one with me leading off, and the other with her featured first.

This is Madeleine Kunin.
This is Evelyn Jarrett.

We are the Democratic candidates for the Vermont House, district 1-8 in Burlington. If you believe, as we do, that our children
and our grandchildren should inherit a beautiful Vermont, then
vote for us—Madeleine Kunin and Evelyn Jarrett—on Tuesday,
November 7.

I formed a campaign committee of neighbors and friends who contributed their time, as they would if they had been invited to a potluck supper
and asked to bring a casserole. The campaign itself was run out of my
kitchen, and my campaign manager was my best friend, Nicky Roth.

This was a cozy, homespun affair. In later statewide campaigns I moved
the operation out of my house and onto the factory floor, but the dynam-
ics of every campaign remained similar: I would have to ask for money.
With each race, the target rose higher, and the task became tougher.

"It must be so hard to ask for money for yourself," a friend observed.
She was right. I didn't mind raising money for others or for a cause, but
asking for myself made me pause, hesitate, and apologize. Please, don't
write too large a check, I'd say under my breath, right after I had asked
for a contribution. I was afraid money would cheapen me. The fear of
political prostitution is a vivid metaphor for women. Love, if genuine,
should be free.

Until recently, lack of an independent income has kept many women
from establishing a businesslike connection between power and money.
What for many men is a normal bartering system is a new experience for
most women. The women who have sufficient wealth to become large
contributors to political campaigns and who are comfortable in that
power exchange are the exception. To link money with worth is an alien
concept; it runs contrary to women's upbringing and instinct.

Fund-raising without blushing became easier for me when I could separate my campaign from myself, when I could assure myself that financial
contributions provided a conduit for a contributor to give to a cause, or
political party, or just be part of an inner circle. It had little to do with me
personally, I told myself when I opened the envelope and saw checks
made out to the Madeleine M. Kunin Campaign Committee.

One of the ironies of politics is that asking for money requires a sturdy
ego, but asking for increasingly large amounts of money requires a sub-
mersion of ego. I learned to ask for campaign funds by detaching myself
from the request and connecting myself only to the abstract idea of the
campaign. There were two poles: one, Madeleine M. Kunin, a person
whose signature appeared on fund-raising letters and whose voice solic-
ited on the telephone, and the other, the Kunin campaign, this thing that

made demands. If a check was made out accidentally to me, Madeleine Kunin, I got it out of my hands as quickly as possible. The worst thing someone said to me, when handing me cash, was "Go get something nice for yourself."

"Oh, no, please, I can't accept that," I stammered as I pushed the crumpled bills back into the palm of his hand.

"How do I make out the check?" a contributor whom I had long been wooing asked with a smile, pen poised above his checkbook.

"Please make it out to the Madeleine M. Kunin Campaign Committee," I recited, absolved of venial sin. Not only did that complete the transaction, it removed it from me.

I pictured the contributor list, neatly typed, in straight columns, as gray as the stock market report. During my first campaign for governor, we posted each day's contributions on the office wall, and the growing list of names and dollar amounts both cheered and shocked me. Hanging up the names in a public space, like so much laundry, washed out the taint of money. Disclosure was the cleanser. And yet it was difficult, at times, for me to look at the list. Names represented commitments and expectations of people who were betting on a winner. What if I lost? Did they know the extent of their gamble? Should I have been more forthright in explaining the odds?

Anxious as I was about the list, I loved to see it grow, and I added names myself, after going through the morning mail, standing like a schoolteacher with chalk in hand at the blackboard. The political war chest is aptly named; it allows the candidate to go into battle. Each contribution not only enables one to pay staff and buy precious television time but success in fund-raising is in itself taken as a demonstration of political power. A candidate without money is not serious. A candidate who either is independently wealthy or raises large amounts of money automatically has to be reckoned with. Often a war chest itself will fend off opponents, like a nuclear deterrent.

A good fund-raiser looks like a winner. (A winner, of course, is also a good fund-raiser.) The most arduous fund-raising takes place immediately after a disappointing poll, when money simply dries up, like a puddle in the sun. Conversely, the most effortless fund-raising occurs in the final days of a close race, when dollars pour in with no effort. Interest is high, and money, the donors know, will make a difference. The worst part about fund-raising is when it becomes an end in itself, an obsession making the actual campaign seem secondary.

Over the course of six statewide races, I never resolved my ambivalence about raising money. In my first campaign I felt a sense of triumph, as if I had gotten over a special female weakness; I had demonstrated political mettle by being able to raise money like a man; I had shed my squeamishness and accepted the task as a necessary chore. It was a means to an end that everyone seemed to understand. When I raised less money than my opponents, my underdog status permitted me to lay claim to a kind of virtue, but as an incumbent, when my position changed and I succeeded in raising as much as and sometimes more than my opponents, I was pleased to achieve such parity but became increasingly ambivalent about the process.

We counted checks during the campaign just as I had counted my tips when I worked as a waitress at Chef Karl's in Lenox, Massachusetts, to earn money for college. Then I would make neat piles of the dollar bills and stack the quarters, dimes, and nickels in columns, recording each day's stash in my notebook. This is how I would escape my servitude: it was not money I coveted, it was an education. The next evening, when I smiled at my customers, sizing each one up while pouring ice water into the glasses, I hoped they could not see me already counting the tips that I envisioned placed on the pretty silver-plated tray. But at night, in the cavern of my bedroom, I glowed like a fairy-tale miser who had opened the treasure-chest lid. Now, after a fund-raiser, I would ask my staff about the totals as crudely as I had counted the quarters then. Yes, it was vulgar, but it was a means to an end, was it not?

So I would stand in the front of a living room fireplace, wearing my navy-blue suit, accepting applause from a friendly crowd at a wine-and-cheese fund-raiser. I'd give a good talk. Then someone else would make the pitch.

"If we want Madeleine to win, we've got to help her stay on TV. You know how terribly expensive those ads are. Just make it out to the Kunin campaign."

Perfect.

I never completely overcame white-gloved disgust about touching political money; at the same time, I would be amazed by my eagerness for it. Then I would ask myself who, in fact, I was becoming. Was this the person I wanted to be?

With each subsequent election, the problem worsened, and drawing the line between good and bad contributors became harder. Never was there a quid pro quo, but as each gubernatorial campaign became more expensive, the pressure to raise more money intensified, and I would have to go off to California, Chicago, New York, and Boston for fund-raising events. On a plane, flying across the country, I would feel captive of the process, wishing I could be home in Vermont.

One afternoon in Los Angeles, I and Debbie Landau, my campaign manager, met with a well-known Hollywood fund-raiser. I was the incumbent governor of Vermont, running for a third term. The man beckoned us into his office, seated us in front of his desk, and promptly picked up the ringing telephone. Clearly his secretary had not been told to hold calls. While he carried on a long conversation with a very important person (whose name I shall never know), I looked at Debbie and she looked at me; we shrugged our shoulders in dismay and resignation. This so-called kingmaker felt compelled to display his power in front of me. It must have given him special pleasure to put down a governor. When he finally turned to us, I could barely speak, afraid my disgust would show. Any illusion I might have had that wealthy out-of-state political donors might be interested in who I was or what I stood for was wiped away. Raw, ugly power had been thrust like a fist into my face.

After I left public office, I received a phone call from a woman running for the United States Senate. I heard the nervous anxiety in her voice—I wondered how far down on her calling list she was that day as she recounted how much money she had already raised and immediately dwarfed it by describing her opponent's commanding war chest. She needed to raise at least that much. No mention was made of anything else; no issues, no ideas, no people. As I listened, I wondered if that tired, driven woman ever had been me.

For a long time, I accepted the practical reality that for any politician under our current system fund-raising was a necessity, a means to an end. But the relationship of fund-raising activities to campaigns themselves has changed. I heard a U.S. Senate candidate in 1992 proudly tell a roomful of contributors that she had taken a pledge not to spend more than half of her time fund-raising; most candidates, she said, spent 90 percent.

I never calculated the percentage of my schedule devoted to raising money, but it became obvious that increasingly it took me away from my job as governor. What once had been one chore among many threatened to be a greedy taskmaster.

The prognosis for meaningful campaign-finance reform in this country is not good. As a state legislator, I sponsored bills to limit spending for state candidates and to promote public financing by means of an income-tax check-off that allowed for matching funds. No action was taken. Reform at the federal level looks equally unpromising.

Individual candidates can try to change the system by setting parameters: small contributions from many people are less problematic than large contributions from a few donors. I know I took comfort from having a longer list of contributors than my opponents, more women donors, and many more small contributions. But while I never, in any of my campaigns, found a fund-raising angel, a person who could spend a few hours on the phone and turn up ten, twenty, or even fifty thousand dollars, I confess to being envious of those who did. I did, however, have extraordinarily hardworking supporters, both men and women, who helped me raise money and never dreamed of asking for anything in return. These people made it possible for me to get elected without feeling compromised. But in return for a contribution, people often hope for access to the candidate, possession of the politician's time and attention. Increasingly, that, too, disturbed me as I found myself smiling at dinner partners whose contribution had seated them by my side.

The negative side of fund-raising had one positive consequence: it forced me to try to depersonalize the campaign process. Some distancing is essential to political survival. If every word of public praise was accepted as a measure of self-worth and every criticism taken as a personal loss, no politician could maintain emotional equilibrium. Praise, I confess, is the more difficult to renounce; its rarity alone makes it hard to reject.

Political life buffets its charges between emotional extremes of love and hate. Uncertainty about where one is anchored at any given time moves under a calm surface like dreams, vaguely remembered from the night before, which cannot be acknowledged in the light of day. How did I deal with these wild mood swings without causing irreparable damage to my psyche? One way was denial. Another was modified schizophrenia.

Some mornings, when I looked into the mirror to brush my teeth and comb my hair, I would stare at the reflection and say, This is the real Madeleine Kunin. The person on television last night was someone else.

The distance between me and my political other seemed especially great after I recorded my first solo half-hour interview on Vermont public television with Jack Barry in 1975. When I got home, I set the kitchen timer for eight o'clock, the hour the show would be aired, and then went about the business of preparing supper.

At the appointed hour, I gathered the children around the television set to watch Mommy. But they wanted to watch something else.

"No," I said, "keep still. I want to watch my interview."

"Please, please, we want to watch—"

"Shut up."

"Oh, gee, come on, Mom."

"Keep quiet."

I was entranced. There, on the screen, an intelligent and attractive woman was holding forth on the issues of the day. She was articulate, calm, and self-possessed.

"Boring, it's so boring."

My voice rose. "Keep still, please. I mean it, I really, really mean it." I underlined each word menacingly.

My television voice continued uninterrupted. On camera I smiled, nodded, and smiled again.

Who is this woman, I asked myself admiringly, talking so skillfully, so unperturbed?

"Now can we switch the channel?"

"He hit me."

"She started it."

"I did not."

"Stop it, both of you!" I yelled above the din. "I want to listen to myself. I can't hear a thing with all your fighting!"

"Aw, Mom, we've watched enough."

What if the listening audience could see me now, I thought with amused horror, here in my living room yelling at my kids?

With time, I learned that a degree of detachment is a practical necessity for living a public life. That is how I could allow myself to be sliced, edited, and excerpted, by Xerox, fax, and film. Distortion was inevitable. I believed that without it, I, Madeleine Kunin, the candidate, could not have reached the voters.

And yet, I could not remain detached. My ego was out front, like the carved figureheads of women attached to the prows of sailing ships. There was both danger and excitement in being positioned at the prow, the first to dip and rise. Coming up, after having been down, the waves washing over my head and shoulders, was exhilarating.

A political person, like an artist, musician, or writer, draws colors, shapes, and sounds from the depths of her being, not knowing what is buried there until it surfaces. Sometimes I felt like a surprised diver, holding a cluster of salt-encrusted pearls in my hand. Ideas, passions, and beliefs lay buried until they were brought to the surface and transformed into something else, called politics. Then I knew precisely who I was and what I believed. I survived emotional whiplash by learning to go forward and then retreat, back and forth, to take risks, and then to seek safety; to expose my ego, and then protect it; to blame or praise myself, and then to blame or praise others.

The equilibrium was not always perfect. There were times when I experienced great anxiety that I had made myself too vulnerable, that I could not cope with the exposure and all that flowed from it. Sometimes my ego felt as thin as silk; one more pull and the threads would tear. But quietly, I knew I had to build my inner reserve and sustain my outer supports of family and friends. That would be the bedrock of my private reality.

Throughout my political career, I met from time to time with a small group of women friends who were not involved in politics. We had known one another for many years. When we got together for lunch or an afternoon at the lake, we gossiped, laughed, and excerpted the commonalties of our lives. Their unquestioning understanding and affection gave me strength, and more and more I came to value the experience of retaining these friendships.

As I continued to construct my public life, I became more adept at revealing my feelings, thoughts, and ideas. Public life, at its best, magnifies private dreams, projects inner images onto a large screen. At such rare moments, the private and public self are merged into one voice, one image, and the split between the private and public self is eliminated.

IN MY FIRST legislative race, in 1972, my fear of public failure enabled me to tap a new reservoir of energy. I was so driven that I was afraid to stop campaigning. After swallowing my last bite of supper, I would get up from the table, kiss the children, tell my husband I'd do the dishes later, get in my car, pick up a friend to join me, and walk from door to door, almost every night. At each house, I would introduce myself with the words, "Hi, I'm Madeleine Kunin, and I'm running for the legislature from this district. Just wanted to say hello." I would take a brochure from the pile and hold it out.

Usually the person at the door would say something pleasant, such as "Come on in." If there was a long pause, my eyes would search for a picture, a knickknack, a baby, a dog, a picture of the pope—anything that I could talk about. My goal was to connect with these strangers on the other side of the threshold as they eyed me and I eyed them. I could be neither too aggressive nor too shy, a pleasant neighbor returning a cup of sugar borrowed yesterday. Could I make the proper impression, so that when that person stepped into the voting booth and saw "Kunin" on the ballot, something inside her head would click, "yes"?

When the first awkward words turned into banter, I would be thrilled. I discovered how to say unimportant things easily. To my surprise, issues were seldom raised. This was just a friendly call. At the very end, I would remember what I had to say. "I'd appreciate your support in November."

"You've got to be more direct," I was told. "Ask them for their vote."

I found it hard to do. "I need your vote," I rehearsed. It sounded crude. I compromised: "I would appreciate your vote."

In some houses I was greeted warmly as a welcome stranger, the front doorbell not having rung in a long time. In one house, a fluted crocheted doily sat on top of a large television set beneath a faded plastic plant. The easy chair sagged with the indentation of the constant viewer. The side table held a water glass, a Kleenex, and assorted bottles of pills. A small, white-haired woman was at the door.

"Come on in, dear, have a cup of coffee, sit down," she said, hurrying into the kitchen to take the plastic cover off a plate of cookies. "Please stay."

"These are delicious," I murmured, as I explained that I was campaigning.

She told me about her husband, what a good man he had been, how they had done everything together, always.

I nodded, listened, and thought of my mother.

How will I get out of this living room? I wondered. I looked at my watch and reached to the floor for my purse. "I wish we could stay longer, but we've got to move on, we've got the whole street to cover tonight," I said, as I groped for my things. As I pulled myself away, I vowed that I would remember this woman and her sad eyes, this room, this house, this street.

I climbed the stairs to a third-floor apartment where I was greeted by a thin, stringy-haired woman with a child pulling at her skirt. "I can't vote," she said. "I'm on welfare. I don't pay taxes."

"Oh no, you don't understand," I said, trying to expunge the look of terrible humility from her face. She looked as if she wanted to dissolve. I wanted to shake her, but she would have broken. I told her she had the same right to vote as every other citizen, but she was skeptical. After five more minutes, she agreed to register to vote, and as she signed her name at the bottom of the form, I knew I wasn't giving her anything she thought she needed; I was just making myself feel better.

At a top-floor apartment on Battery Street, in the part of town that I had only driven through before, I was hit by the smell of cats when the door opened. An elderly man stood blinking at me, in undershirt and suspenders hitched to a spotted, drooping pair of black trousers. Behind him, dirty dishes in the sink, dried-up bits of food on the table, cat food scattered in tins on the floor. A skinny gray creature rubbed against my leg; two more chased each other across the linoleum.

Is this how he lives? I asked myself in disbelief.

"Sorry for the mess," he said. "Haven't been too well lately, couldn't get out."

As gently as I could, I asked if he needed any help.

"Should be getting the check any day now," he said, running his fingers through his strands of hair.

I took his name and address. The next day, I made some calls. No one, I thought, should have to live like this.

Some nights, Arthur came with me to campaign. He was very direct, talking to constituents straightforwardly as he would to his patients. Sometimes when people didn't know what to say to me, they would talk to him. And I liked sharing this part of my world with him.

At each doorway, I felt I was opening the curtain to a play, getting a glimpse of people's daily lives. The willingness of strangers to open up their doors to me was surprising: rarely was anyone rude. Only dogs were unpredictable. Occasionally, I detoured around a bark, not wanting to test its bite. Only once did I feel menaced—by a beer-bellied man who let me know how much he hated politicians.

After a few weeks of this, I prided myself on having overcome my shyness. I am finally getting it right, I thought. At one house, after I introduced myself, I spotted a bright, framed embroidery on the wall, a hand-stitched Vermont scene with green fields, a brown cow, and a red barn.

"That's a lovely picture," I said after I handed the lady of the house my brochure. "Did you make it yourself?"

"Yes, come and see what else I've done," she said as she led me into the bedroom with flowered wallpaper and opened up the cedar chest. One by one she took out her pieces of embroidery: a chair cover, a pillow, and more and more pictures, and I gushed appropriately. I was running out of adjectives, but I felt certain this woman would remember me, possibly forever. This was not mere chatter; this was an investment.

Finally, I said, "I'm so sorry, I would love to see more of your work, but we have to move on." As my friend and I got to the front door, the woman turned to her husband, who the whole time had remained in his Barkalounger watching TV, beer in hand. "Did you give them something for the Red Cross?" she asked.

"Oh, no," I groaned. "I'm here because I'm running for the legislature."

"Sorry, can't hear you."

"I would appreciate your vote," I said as slowly and clearly as I could.

"Sure, sure, dear, we'll be there," she said cheerfully as she closed the door behind me.

A few weeks before the election, Elaine Little, the wife of the Republican legislator George Little, agreed to ask her close friend (and good Republican) Emmy Lapham to hold a neighborhood tea for me. I was not to tell a soul that Elaine had been the instigator. At this tea I would have an opportunity to infiltrate the Republican section of the district. A hint of conspiracy hovered in the air of Emmy Lapham's deep-carpeted comfortable living room as the women sipped their tea and balanced Emmy's good china on their laps: these Republican women were meeting with a Democrat! Most were older than I was and had led more traditional 1950s lives. I was sensitive to the difference between us, but I need not have been. In that sunlit room that afternoon I heard words that I would hear repeated in many other rooms: "It is time," the women agreed, "for more women." They were decidedly *not* feminists, but they *did* want to help a woman get elected. Gender, I would discover, was a far more cohesive force than either age or political party. The unspoken recognition of mutual experiences in those years transcended our differences.

On Election Day, I was introduced to the realities of ward politics. The declared objective of Democratic party workers was to get "our" voters to the polls, a process more impressive in theory than practice. In Vermont there is no party registration—Democrats, until recently, were a minority that survived by being discreet, and Republicans opposed party registration because they considered party affiliation nobody's business, certainly not the government's.

In some Vermont rural towns little has changed since the early days. Once when I was campaigning on Memorial Day for lieutenant governor, I talked to a family enjoying a picnic in the village green. They were from Middletown Springs.

"What party are ya?" the father asked with genuine curiosity as he stood up to shake my hand. The parade had finished, and I was moving through the lingering crowd. Anyone sitting down was fair game.

"Democrat," I said.

Silence. He scratched his head and looked at me with interest. "Yup, we had a Democrat once," he recalled, "but he died."

Burlington was different. Weeks before the election, the checklists would be studied, discussed, marked, and treasured: *D*'s and *R*'s and *I*'s, marked in different-colored inks next to each name, followed by a phone number. The lists had been passed down from generation to generation as political heirlooms.

On Election Day in 1972 each party had a side checker seated at the polls who would cross off the names of those who voted. The list would be rushed back to headquarters where it would be checked against a master list. Democratic headquarters was in the Montys' kitchen, steaming with coffee and sticky with doughnuts. By three o'clock, volunteers began to work the phones. I got there in time to hear Alderman Bob Blanchard go to work.

"Hello, Père?"

"Ça va? I'd really like you and the family to come down here and vote. Just vote the straight ticket like you always do. That's what I did. It's much easier that way.

"How are the kids? I see Annette's old enough to be on the checklist. Does she need a ride from work? Happy to do it. We'll have somebody there at five o'clock sharp."

Only a short time before, Bob worked against me, when I ran against Clarence Meunier. This time, he was on my side. My memory was short. What a pro, I said to myself.

WHEN I STOOD at the polls for the first time in my campaign for the legislature, I watched voters coming in, one by one and in pairs. This was the moment of reckoning. What were they thinking? Had they been influenced by the brochures that we had distributed door to door? What about those handshakes, smiles, and conversations? Had they read an article about me in the paper, or seen me on TV, or listened to one of my radio spots? It seemed as if I were existing in two unconnected worlds: the campaign, which had gone on for months, and the election, which would be decided within hours. I scrutinized the faces of the voters. They told me little.

I learned to stand at the polls and bear it by performing a mental Houdini act. I could become invisible at a moment's notice. When the body language of the voter told me he or she was happy to see me, I could make myself appear and say hello. If the voter kept his eyes on the ground, I too looked down, scouring the sidewalk as if for a lost contact lens. And for those who took pains to make a wide detour around the candidates, I simply disappeared. I shouldn't be here, I'm making people uncomfortable; it's crude to put yourself on display like this, I lectured to myself.

Just then another person would walk by and smile. On the other hand, if they see I care enough to stand here, shivering in the cold, I might get their sympathy, I reconsidered.

A woman, pulling her toddler behind her, gave me a quizzical look. Of course, they may also think I'm a fool, I admitted.

To pass the time, the small huddle of candidates and volunteers shifted from foot to foot and talked about the weather. Never had I heard weather analyzed in such exquisite detail. Nothing equals the level of sophistication that politicians rise to in a discussion of climatic conditions on Election Day. Was rain good or bad for Democrats?

"Two years ago it was sunny, and we lost."

"But remember the time it was cold in the morning, and then it warmed up by noon?"

"What we need is a good snowstorm. Keeps Republicans away."

"Democrats come out no matter what."

"And they don't mind waiting in line, either."

"For sure."

"Sure?" I asked with hope.

Just then a car pulled up to the curb. A group of remarkably sturdy elderly women were lifted out, one by one, and stumped into the polling place, supported by their canes. The volunteer driver, sporting a Republican button on her chest, smiled. My heart sank. I recognized one of her charges. When I had knocked at her door and told her who I was, she had cut me short. "My dear, I have never voted for a Democrat. If there was a cedar post in the backyard, and it was marked Republican, I would vote for it."

We turned to the other subject we knew best: voter turnout.

"How many, so far?" I asked.

"Twelve hundred by noon. Last year, we only had nine hundred fifty. But, of course, it wasn't a presidential year."

"Guess that's a good sign."

"It slowed down in Ward Three this morning; one of the machines was down."

"Oh, that's terrible. Did people wait?" I asked.

"Some did. But a lot of people left, had to get to work."

I mourned the votes lost.

"Hear they're arriving in droves in Ward Six. Hasn't let up since seven o'clock this morning."

"Wow, that's great."

I would delight in the numbers. Sheer quantity seemed good. Like a good member of the League of Women Voters, I applauded good citizenship, not thinking that I might not be the beneficiary.

I learned that political campaign rituals demand intrusion on someone else's space with a handshake and a word, and each time I approached someone I realized that the person so accosted might turn away, be curt or angry. As I went from door to door and stood for hours at the polls, I learned I could recover quickly from verbal affronts. I developed a short memory for pain and a strong recollection for praise. My anguish would be erased by the next kind word. "Rolling with the punches" is the vernacular. On the campaign trail, I began to know what it meant.

"Pressing the flesh" was another expression I defined for myself. I hated the sound of the phrase, but nevertheless, I shook every hand I could reach, and I came to understand why politicians attribute magical powers to the handshake, harkening back, perhaps, to the time when a handshake sealed a bond. Some politicians place great faith in the gesture, using both hands to close on a stranger's, like a sandwich. Others clasp an arm or squeeze a shoulder, so eager are they to embrace the voter. I understand why. With a satisfying, firm handshake each person feels the current pass from one to the other. In those seconds, one feels completely understood. The handshake, more than a word, creates connection. When I campaigned in factories, hearing my heels click on the cement floor as my entourage and I wove a careful path around machinery, grime, and noise, my extended hand was a gesture of equality. It said what we knew: I don't care that your hand is rough and dirty and mine is soft and clean; you don't either. I am not too proud to touch you, and you are not embarrassed; we're on common ground. Some workers would wipe their hands off on a rag before they met my hand, halfway. Others would stay by their machines, hoping to avoid me, feeling the distance between us should be maintained. I learned to respect that, too.

For a few voters a handshake is a test of the candidate's pain threshold. Occasionally a sadist would laugh with satisfaction when I yelled "Ouch!" For my part, a handshake gave me some control; it allowed me to define proximity. I would reach for his hand, but no more. Using my arm like a pole, I could keep a stranger at a safe distance.

I discovered that rings hurt, and that it is bad form to wear gloves. The grasp, to be meaningful, must be flesh to flesh. I marvel now to think how much meaning I placed on each handshake, believing that something like a blood transfusion occurred. I felt I was extending life to old people, adult approval to children, and during a few grandiose moments I thought my hand was a gift. Still there were awkward moments when I extended my hand, and no one took it. Had anyone seen my arm jut straight out, cut down by rejection, like a fallen limb?

I learned from hands. A limp hand, like a dead fish, was unpleasant. Especially when a woman didn't grasp back, I wanted to tell her to stand up for herself and squeeze.

The calloused hand, the firm grasp, the blue veins, all held messages I absorbed through my skin. I gathered visceral knowledge. That brief touch linked me, as in a square-dance do-si-do, with a circle of people I would have never encountered had I stayed at home, looking at my manicured hands.

ON ELECTION DAY, November 1972, voting was heavy; at least an hour's wait. Were people taking their time to split their tickets to vote for Nixon for president, Tom Salmon for governor, and me? A good sign. Or, if it took so long, was something wrong with the machines? Would they get discouraged and leave?

I received early results from Ward 6, the Republican part of the district, where it looked good, but I was afraid to celebrate until I heard from Ward 5. Around ten-thirty, the telephone in our kitchen rang. It was Mary Evelti, who had just finished counting votes at St. Anthony's. "Congratulations," she said, in her warm, kind voice.

I jumped up and down like a child, hugged my husband and everyone within reach. It felt so great to win because I was deliriously happy not to lose. When I had declared my candidacy, I thought I had overcome the fear of failure. I joked and said that if I lost the election, it would be different from having a soufflé fall in the privacy of my own oven. But not until that moment in the kitchen did I know how dreadful losing would have been. When my brother called, I was thrilled to give him the good news. I would not have liked to tell him bad news. That I had succeeded against his better advice was both a triumph and a relief.

The next morning, I had difficulty connecting the new person I had become—a member of the Vermont House of Representatives—with myself, Madeleine Kunin, wife of Dr. Arthur Kunin, mother of four children. Could I still wear jeans to the supermarket? Would my children have to get all A's in school? What if our lawn wasn't mowed and our garden not weeded? How public would my public life become? I had donned a uniform with epaulets and brass buttons, and everybody would know who I was.

Privately, I felt shy. Publicly, I was poised. I act like a politician, therefore I am a politician. I have not changed, only allowed my other side to show, I said to myself.

What would life be like in Montpelier? I might actually influence how people lived their lives! Could I achieve something worthwhile? Would I know when to be aggressive and when to be quiet? Could I earn other people's respect? A great part of success or failure in politics is based on trust and friendship. How long would it take to build these bonds?

My official life as a legislator began on November 20, 1972, when I received a telephone call from Joyce Wasson, secretary to Democratic governor-elect Thomas P. Salmon. I picked up the phone in my kitchen with one hand, emptying the dishwasher with the other.

"Representative Kunin?" the voice asked.

"Er, yes," I said. That was me. I put down my bouquet of knives and forks.

"The governor would like you to come to a meeting tonight with all the Democratic legislators at seven-thirty at the Brown Derby in Montpelier. We hope you will be there."

"Yes, yes, of course, I'll be there. Thank you."

What had I just said? I had answered instinctively. My political life had begun. I was an elected official responding to the call of the governor. Now, to get there, I had to rearrange my life. How on earth would I do this? Only one thing made me feel better. That morning I had made red Jell-O. I opened the refrigerator and looked at it lovingly; it was almost firm.

Now, two things had to be done: find a baby-sitter and figure out transportation. I spent much of the day looking out the window (it was snowing) and listening to weather reports. This is how it would be for the rest of the winter; regardless of snow and ice, only a major storm would keep me home now. I would have to accept that reality and cope with it, gritting my teeth in anticipation of the icy road.

First, to arrange the schedule. I had to leave the house by 5:45 p.m. to get to Montpelier on time. Fortunately, there was a car pool I could go with: I would meet Esther Sorrell, Esther Cohen, and Lorraine Graham at Esther's house.

Next, find a baby-sitter. Adam and Julia were sick with 102.5-degree fevers. I couldn't leave them in a stranger's hands. Leaving just before supper was bad enough. After several phone calls, I reached Mrs. Mabel Fisher; she was now retired but had been the children's favorite baby-sitter; could she come again, just this once?

"Yes, I'll be glad to help you out."

"Oh, wonderful, thank you, thank you," I said, relieving myself of guilt. As if it were a suitcase, I put it down, and she so kindly picked it up. What would I have done without Mrs. Fisher? This self-effacing, overly generous grandmother gave my children love and gave me the chance to begin my political life. Without her, my choices would have been much more narrowly circumscribed. At the very least, my political life would have had to wait until my children were older. That same week I employed Phyllis Sweeney to come and clean the house one day a week. (When I was elected governor, we extended it to two days.) One of the ironies of the women's movement is that women like me obtained our liberty because of other women who agreed to help us as our housekeepers, baby-sitters, and cleaning women.

As I prepared to leave, Daniel, the baby, screamed and clung to my skirt. "Don't go, Mommy, don't go." Julia felt sorry for him and tried to tell me what to do. I felt rotten. How could I do this? I literally tore myself away, pulled clinging hands off me like burrs, ran out the door, jumped in the car, and rushed to arrive at Esther's house in time for the car pool.

When I pulled up to her house, I glanced in the backseat. There was Daniel's baby blanket. He had never gone to sleep without it. His "blankie" was his life. Once, it had been left in a taxicab, and that had been a disaster. With a note of panic in my voice, I asked my women colleagues, waiting and ready to go, "What should I do?

"I hate to make you late. I'm really sorry." Suddenly I felt exhausted. Montpelier was far away.

"Go back," Esther advised.

"We'll meet you at the parking lot at Sears," Lorraine said kindly. I loved them for their understanding. But was this how it was going to be from now on? Was this ratty, gray, many-times-mended baby blanket a sacred omen?

Daniel, what are you telling me? I almost sobbed to myself as I hurried home.

In fact, no subsequent departure would equal this one, but I would hear the sound of tearing fabric pulling me in opposite directions often enough. At the end of each legislative day in Montpelier, I would feel the gravitational Mommy pull, demanding that I get home in time to read a story and kiss the children good-night. But in between, I concentrated on my new life.

Once we left the Sears parking lot that night, my world changed; I became a member of the car-pool club. The drive was treacherous, but Lorraine steered her eight-cylinder red-and-white Mercury Marquis like a battleship through enemy waters. We arrived exactly on time. As we talked in the car, the women whom I had admired from afar—Esther Cohen, Esther Sorrell, and Lorraine Graham—treated me as an equal. Amazing how quickly the transformation in status took place, simply by garnering votes.

The Brown Derby restaurant was attached to a motel, a roadside stop that had become a favorite watering hole for legislators. The decor was early fifties: red Naugahyde booths quilted with brass buttons. Dim lighting was as kind as a mottled mirror. The air held a week of smoke, one layer resting lazily on top of another; in those days, I lit up, too, to look as if I knew what I was doing. The room was filled with men, backslapping, handshaking, laughing grown men; the scene looked like a twenty-fifth college reunion. This is it, I said, as we went through the door; I was a participant, not an observer.

An older, refined-looking representative named George Sloane asked me, "What do you do?"

I was grateful for his approach but not prepared for the question. "I used to teach at Trinity College," I said, hoping that would be satisfactory. I wasn't used to sticking handy labels on myself.

Danny DeBonis, bouncy as a puppy, grabbed my arm. He was from Poultney. "Know where that is?"

"Sure, didn't Horace Greeley come from there?"

"Didn't think you people from Burlington knew anything," he laughed. He told me he went ice-skating every night during the session. Relieves the tension, he explained.

"What do you do?" I asked.

"I'm a poor farmer." He laughed again, encouraging my skepticism. Later I learned he subdivided farms and did very well selling off the pieces to a group of lawyers from New York.

I observed another new legislator, Jordon Cole, a minister from Putney, taking careful notes; should I? Would this be like school?

Sam Lloyd introduced himself, a freshman legislator from Weston, who owned a bowl mill and acted in summer-stock theater. They had never sent a Democrat to Montpelier from his district before; he represented four small towns and reeled them off as if reading a bus schedule:

Weston, Mount Holly, Ludlow, and Londonderry. I will always remember Sam, we were both from the class of 1972.

Time to take a seat and go around the room and have each new legislator introduce himself, we were told. Sam's voice boomed out first; I envied his elocution. On the floor of the House he would never have to use a microphone. Next, David Shaffe, from Bennington, stood up. Before this gangly, bald-headed young man could say his name, applause broke out. Everybody knew he had defeated powerful Marshall Witten, the Republican chairman of the House Appropriations Committee, who was known for his tough interrogations. He had had a way of sniffing out Democrats and then pouncing on them, George Sloane explained in my ear. David the dragon slayer was a hero before saying a word.

My turn. I felt very conspicuous, young, and female in this crowd of mostly men. I stood up, said my name and district, "Chittenden, one-eight," and sat down. Polite applause. I had survived, for now. This was a club like no other. How you sit, how you stand, how you talk, and how you smile were scored and notched with a penknife into the doorpost.

I was introduced to Mavis Doyle, a middle-aged reporter from the *Rutland Herald*, the last of her kind to have a sense of history. She scrounged the statehouse for news like a bag lady picking through trash cans. Her motto was old-fashioned; she lived by it without embarrassment: "Comfort the afflicted, and afflict the comfortable." (Several months later, when my committee chairman, Orrin Beattie, was bottling up a bill that the governor desperately wanted, she commented to me, "That little guy has brass balls." Her dislikes were equally clear. In almost every story she wrote about Republican legislator Richard Snelling, she would start with: "The portly Shelburne industrialist...," which drove him crazy.)

I felt only somewhat more secure being a Democrat. In those days, being in the minority meant the press might be on your side. She would do a terrific story on the new women, Mavis assured me that night. I was not eager.

"You'll do great things," she said, with a wide, expectant smile. I covered my apprehension with a gaudy grin, hoping she could not see my thin soul.

We listened to the newly elected governor give a speech to rouse the troops. He had been elected on a platform promising property-tax relief, and we were to be his foot soliders in the battle ahead. Everyone seemed ready. Some legislators asked questions. I wondered when I would have the courage to stand up and ask a question of the governor.

Following his speech, an after-the-game locker-room mood of celebration made the room seem sweaty; our team, the Democratic underdogs,
had won. How good it felt. This is what being a Democrat means: part of
a huddle. Only I wasn't a political sociologist studying the species; I was
one of them.

Joe Jamele, whose desk had been next to mine in the newsroom when
we were both reporters at the *Burlington Free Press*, grabbed a beer and
came over to chat. He had been Salmon's campaign manager, credited
with pulling off a major upset. He had not recovered; the greatest time of
his life was the campaign, and especially election night. It was unbeliev-
able, he said. Would I ever experience such euphoria, and envelop others
in my nostalgia?

As I dutifully followed my car-pool companions back to the parking lot
of the Brown Derby at nine o'clock, I wondered whether we were missing
anything by leaving early while the guys stayed to drink. Would this be
the pattern? The girls go home, and the boys stay to smoke cigarettes in
the tree house? That night I enjoyed the virtuous feeling of being a good
girl, a necessary antidote to my wrenching afternoon departure from my
children. But how would I figure out how to be one of the boys without
abandoning the two Esthers, Lorraine, and Evelyn? And would that be
dangerous, or could I find a safe seat at the bar?

On the way out of the Brown Derby, I saw two legislative wives waiting patiently in the lounge, side by side in their easy chairs, near the
yawning receptionist. They had been waiting all this time? I smiled and
said hello. I could have been one of them, a backstage political wife,
waiting on the other side of the door. At one time, I would have envied
them for being seated this close to power, but now I felt sorry for them.
The script had been updated, but these women were continuing to play
the roles they had been first assigned and memorized. I wondered, fleetingly, what they thought of this new walk-on part played by someone like
me.

There would be other nights when the decision whether to go home or
stay was harder to make. At times I agonized whether I should stay for a
public hearing, a dinner, or simply to have fun. I would feel the need to
unwind, laugh, tell jokes, and share stories with those who had experienced the same skirmishes on the floor of the House.

And we women legislators, when we did join forces, enjoyed a special
camaraderie. One afternoon, during my first legislative term, four of us
recorded an educational television program together—two Democrats,
two Republicans. This was my public-television debut. Usually, only the

male leaders had been interviewed. I didn't want to watch the program when it was televised that evening (I was too embarrassed by my performance), but I did want to stay in Montpelier for a public hearing and have dinner with the women. Should I go home and be a good mother and wife, or stay and have a good time? I called home.

My husband encouraged me to stay and join the party. He would take care of dinner for the kids. Great! So the four of us women had dinner together at the Holiday Inn and then retreated to a guest room to watch our program. I was surprised that we sounded so confident and informed, discussing not only women's issues but also drug laws, highway funds, facilities for juvenile offenders. For a wrap-up, Jack Barry, the host, concluded, "Well, you can see that brains and beauty do mix; they're legislators, they're ladies, and they're lovely."

Louise Swainbank, a seemingly prissy retired Republican schoolteacher from St. Johnsbury, burst out with "Oh shit!"

We fell on the bed and roared.

"Louise! Did Louise say that?"

"Jeezum Crow, I never thought I'd hear you say that," Esther guffawed, slapping her knee.

It felt so good.

My next command performance was Orientation Day for new legislators, December 5. It was snowing at eight-thirty that morning. I scraped the slush and freezing rain off the car windshield, telling myself I was like a postman, I had to deliver myself to Montpelier. I gripped the wheel, preparing for thirty-eight miles of hell frozen over. Even now, when I see the sign on the interstate that marks MONTPELIER, 5 MILES, I recall that morning. I would make it. Only five to go.

When I spotted the golden dome of the statehouse, I smiled and became proprietary; this beautiful sparkling jewel was mine.

As I hung my coat in the coatroom, spied my mailbox with my name on it, I began to feel I belonged. I was one of them. It was a world of topcoats, mufflers, and galoshes, not high heels. I told myself the women were not outcasts, only small in number. I will try not to huddle with the women, I told myself as I found a seat in room 11, in front of a row of other women, but within talking distance of them. I turned around and smiled.

The chairman of the legislative council, Donald Smith, described how bills were prepared. His voice was as monotonous as the process he described. He was followed at the podium by the lieutenant governor, "Jack" Burgess, who gave us a high-school civics lesson, flapping his arms like chicken wings for emphasis. I paid close attention. We were assured that every member is equal, that there is majority rule and protection for the minority, but I had the uneasy feeling that things wouldn't work that way. The Speaker, Walter ("Peanut") Kennedy, hinted at how it really worked: occasionally, he explained—and then he smiled like the used-car salesman he was—he chose not to recognize someone who had risen to be recognized and speak.

Governor-elect Salmon entered. Everyone rose and applauded. When he finished speaking, they rose again. This was protocol.

It was almost over. "Any questions?" Bob Picher, clerk of the House, asked.

The real question I had I could not ask. What kind of legislation should I propose, if any? How does one go about the actual process of writing laws? It seemed as overwhelming as if someone had asked me to carry the tablets down Mount Sinai.

The last speaker was Bill Morrisey, a reporter who oriented us to the ways of the press. "Now," he smiled, "you are all fair game."

My first political lesson took place that afternoon. I had hoped to meet with Speaker Kennedy, from Chelsea, to discuss my committee assignment. I knew the rules: I could state my first, second, and third choices, and he would decide.

"You're just the woman I want to see," he said when he spotted me hanging up my coat after lunch. I followed him through the labyrinth of stairs and offices behind the House chamber and into his tiny domain for my audience. There was barely room for two desks, one for him, and one for his secretary, Sylvia. The walls, lined with signed photographs of former Speakers, extended this cramped space into history. Squeezing so much into one small room made the air thick.

I had hoped to have a give-and-take conversation. I thought I'd like to be on the Health and Welfare Committee, I told him. In truth, that was the only subject I thought I might know something about—at least I understood the meaning of the words "health" and "welfare."

"How about Government Operations?"

I had no idea what the committee did.

"Well, I wonder if it will be my cup of tea," I replied tentatively, wishing I had something, anything, to take a sip from.

"Well, Madeleine, it's going to be a very important committee this year. We'll be doing reapportionment, and I need a good Democrat from Burlington to serve on the committee."

I nodded. At lunch, Mavis Doyle had warned me not to accept Government Operations. For some reason, she had already known the game plan. "You don't want to be there with a bunch of Neanderthals. It's been a graveyard for Democratic bills."

"I need someone who can count, someone with brains," said Kennedy. I was flattered, but I remembered Mavis. What could I do?

Suddenly I became aware of other people in the room. I turned around, and there were four more legislators, seated silently against the wall, waiting their turn.

I turned to Peanut and said, "Well, I'm not violently opposed to it [that is, 'I won't make trouble'], and I might even become enthusiastic."

The next day when committee assignments were announced, I was one of two Democrats on the eleven-member Government Operations Committee, chaired by Orrin Beattie, the Speaker's right-hand man. I would have heavy reapportionment water to carry. My cohort, Pat Candon, a retired postmaster from the town of Pittsford, whose smile became more ruddy and bright as he became more nervous, always let me lead the Democratic charge. "I'm right behind you, Madeleine," he would chuckle. And sure enough, he was.

That afternoon, I transformed myself from briefcase-carrying legislator to car-pool mother and wife. I rushed back to Burlington to pick up Daniel from nursery school, stop at a phone booth to make a call about jury duty, and cancel a dental appointment. Next stop: find a glass of water to take two aspirin for a splitting headache. Next, buy pastry at the Pâtisserie, pick up chicken for dinner, and get Hanukkah candles.

After the first week, I decided that the Vermont statehouse was a good environment to be in. For the first time, I was Madeleine Kunin—not just my husband's wife, my children's mother, or my brother's sister. "I have my own sense of identity," I wrote in my journal with pride.

Well into that session, Orrin Beattie reported that he had been asked how he liked having two women on his committee—Judy Rosenstreich, a Republican, and me. "Oh, they're bastards like everyone else" is what he said.

I laughed with the others. A bastard was fine, I knew. As long as I wasn't called a bitch.

The challenge, I realized, was to remain on good terms with people I disagreed with. It's very stimulating, but when I discuss the ERA, it's impossible, I concluded.

"Do you want to be a man or a woman?" Melvin Mandigo, a member of my committee whose profession was artificial inseminator, once asked me during a discussion of equal rights.

"I want to be a human being," I replied.

"I like being a woman," Representative Lucille Molinaroli piped up.

"So do I," I retorted, giving up.

Vince Naramore was wrong. Whether I was good at it or not, I *did* stand out.

5

"The chair appoints the following members to escort the governor into the well of the House to give his adjournment address: the member from Montpelier, Mr. Giuliani; the member from Stowe, Mr. Dewey; the member from Rutland, Mr. Candon; and the member from Burlington, Mrs. Kunin."

"Did he say Mrs. Kunin?" I swiveled my chair around to my seatmate.

"Think so."

"Will the committee please assemble."

It was past midnight; the clock under the balcony had been stopped more than an hour ago.

"They always stop the clock the last night of the session. No one wants to be caught charging legislative overtime," my colleague explained.

The legislature could do anything on the final day of the session. Rules scrupulously honored for months were now suspended at a dizzying rate, seemingly by fiat. The bills the Speaker wanted passed were called up in rapid succession and approved with minimum debate. Others were relegated to death row. A disappointed legislator would register a weak protest when he discovered his pet bill had died. Sympathetic murmurs would be heard, but they were quickly silenced by the bang of the gavel. The rapid, staccato rhythm was maintained. The Republican leader, Giles Dewey, a retired farmer, would wait on the Speaker like a faithful butler, rising to make a motion each time he received a nod. The arrangement worked beautifully.

"Mr. Speaker, I move that the rules be suspended to take up H. 246 for immediate consideration," Dewey recited.

"The member from Stowe, Mr. Dewey, moves that the rules be suspended to take up H. 246 for immediate consideration," the Speaker echoed. "All those in favor?"

A tired choir of "ayes" was heard.

"Those opposed?"

Not a sound.

The ritual was as scripted as a mass. Most members were expected merely to say "Amen."

I had begun to lose interest and retreated to my mental balcony, observing the performance through mother-of-pearl opera glasses. My eyes now focused on the baroque House chandelier, and I had been studying its ornate twists and curves when the sound of my name brought my attention back to the House floor. I had gotten only halfway around the chandelier, counting twelve light bulbs.

"Looks like you're part of the inner sanctum, young lady," my seatmate said.

I stood up.

"Excuse me," I said, as I slid past him and joined the dark-suited men assembled in a cluster, rubbing shoulders in the center aisle. I wished I had combed my hair. I ran my fingers through it as casually as I could. I looked down at my new black high-heeled shoes. I was wearing a bright-red dress. Suddenly I was happy.

Like a fife-and-drum corps, our little group marched out and then marched back in again with Governor Salmon in tow, stopping briefly at the doorway to wait for the signal to step into the House chamber.

The Speaker struck the gavel hard. "Please rise to welcome the governor of the state of Vermont for the purpose of making his adjournment address."

Our phalanx moved forward. Delicately I placed my hand on the crook of Governor Salmon's pin-striped elbow and walked with him lightly to keep pace with the others, almost skipping down the aisle. I wanted to look calm and official; later I was told I had been glowing like a valedictorian.

Why had I been asked to join the Democratic and Republican leadership in this procession?

Did this mean I was not the outsider I saw myself to be? Or was I an accidental choice, the first name on a list, when the Speaker said, in the nick of time, "Hey, fellas, we've gotta add a woman"?

Never mind. How easy it was to march in step. How quickly I felt I belonged there. Peace settled on this great hall in its waning hour; everyone was exhausted. Rancorous emotions that an hour ago had puffed furiously through the chamber, making the air unstable, had dissipated, like a man's breath on a cold day.

The play was over. The actors were taking their final bows, victor and vanquished, hero and villain, in unison, before the applauding crowd. And I was one of them.

This small tight band of politicians controlled the House. I had seen them in action these past months: five or ten mandarins—committee chairmen, party leaders, and the Speaker—writing notes, giving nods, shaking hands, speaking in a code that all but an unwitting and rebellious few understood. Seated among the members without insignia, they seemed equals with the rest, but when I looked carefully I thought I caught the occasional glint of a hidden scepter.

Election to the Vermont Legislature had brought me into the first circle of power, one voice in a chorus of 180 members. Real power was concentrated with these high priests who orchestrated the mass.

I could not yet bring myself to acknowledge that I wanted power; it was not a desire I could articulate even to myself. I framed my ambition in more comfortable language: that I wanted to have an impact, to get something done, to carry out my new responsibilities as effectively as possible.

Simultaneously, I was worried about the price of political success. One day during the term, I noted in my journal:

> *The most difficult strategy is how to work within the power structure in order to get what I want and, at the same time, to have the guts to oppose the structure when I disagree with it. Nothing can be accomplished by speaking with a single voice; it is quickly drowned out in a chorus of no's. The key to success is to form allegiances with the sources of power without compromising personal values. One has to be informed, know all the angles, both factual and political, and do a tremendous amount of lobbying. I have to learn whom to trust; this means that I can't be either overly suspicious or naïve. It is a delicate balance.*

I had already experienced the embarrassment of feeling ostracized, both in the committee I had been assigned to—Government Operations—and on the floor. The first amendment I had offered had been shouted down—a proposal to cut several thousand dollars from the multimillion-dollar Highway Fund and transfer it to the General Fund for day care. A few nights before, I had attended a public hearing in Montpelier on the subject of day care, and the memory of it still resonated in my head as I stood up to propose my amendment. The hearing had been packed on that cold winter night. The smell of wet snow melting on wool hats and mittens permeated the overheated hall. Mothers who were anxious to keep their jobs and care for their children had driven from all over Vermont to ask for help in the capitol.

This was my first public hearing. The red velvet curtain of the formal legislative process was pulled open, revealing a jumbled scene of real-life parents, children, day-care workers, all telling their stories, exposing their needs. The sour smell of life, the sounds of coughing, the sight of runny noses, made it impossible to keep my distance. I had to act. But how? I wanted to transform these stories into language that could be understood by my legislative colleagues. I took it upon myself to become an interpreter, to find a common language between these two worlds. Dollars, it appeared, are what both sides understood. The withdrawal of federal funds for day care had created the problem; finding state funds might fix it. At the very least, an appropriation for day care could forestall the projected closure of many needed centers.

When I examined the Highway Fund, I assumed that a few thousand dollars less would not matter much. I did not yet know that the Highway Fund and the General Fund had been engaged in a fifteen-year cold war, each equipped with troops guarding their borders. But the moment my amendment reached the floor, the chairman of the Appropriations Committee reached down for a round of ammunition. Then he looked at me, and fired.

"When you touch that Highway Fund, you're taking away maintenance money," Emory Hebard warned.

Knowing the legislators' taste for pork, he held a piece in front of each member's nose: "There isn't a town in the state of Vermont that hasn't been counting on that money. It's already printed in their budgets for Town Meeting Day. If they don't get what they've been promised, I guarantee you'll hear about it."

Heads nodded; eyebrows rose; an ominous murmur filled the room.

"If you cut back on maintenance now, it'll definitely cost you more later."

I was ready to give up. But not Emory.

"Just like the front steps of my store, I can skip a paint job one year and maybe even the next, but the third year, that paint will chip, the wood will rot, and in no time, the steps will sag, and before you know it, the whole damn thing will fall down. The next year, I'll have to buy new lumber, nails, and paint, and build a new set of steps. Better to save the money and paint the steps this year. I urge the members of the House to defeat this costly amendment proposed by the member from Burlington."

"All those in favor, signify by saying aye," the Speaker said in his catechism drone.

"Aye," I whispered, as bravely as I could.

"All those opposed?"

"No!" The baritone legislative chorus had taken a deep breath, filled its chest with air, and with one colossal exhalation knocked me down.

Now I knew where the power was: in the Appropriations Committee. The best place to amend the bill would have been in the committee room, not on the floor. I also learned something about the art of public persuasion. Every speech Emory Hebard gave started with a cracker-barrel story; this Northeast Kingdom conservative never once mentioned that he had graduated from Middlebury College with a Phi Beta Kappa key, but he did mention that he had been a storekeeper and a lister (property appraiser).

I decided to ask Emory Hebard for advice on getting money into the day-care budget.

Day care was controversial. Most legislators thought the state should not get involved in paying for it; mothers should stay home and take care of their own children or else find a relative or friend to help out. That's the way it had always been done. "If the state subsidizes day care, these women will just go out and buy Cadillacs," I had heard one legislator comment.

"It's day care that leads to the breakdown of families by taking responsibility away from the mother," another chimed in.

"Pretty soon, before you know it, they'll make it mandatory. Socialism, that's what we're coming to," his friend agreed.

Emory, to my surprise, was pleased to be consulted. "Why don't you put together a resolution to create a study committee on day care? I might even sponsor it with you, if that would help."

And he did. When the resolution came up on the floor of the House, cosponsored by the conservative Republican member from Glover, Mr. Hebard, and the liberal Democratic member from Burlington, Mrs. Kunin, heads turned. The vote was unanimous. That day-care-study committee was my first legislative victory.

Meanwhile, on the Committee on Government Operations, I was usually outvoted, on party lines, 9 to 2. Soon, however, I began to envision new alliances. To my surprise, I had begun to warm up to some of the Republicans on the committee. Melvin Mandigo, whom I had considered an ultraconservative among conservatives, intrigued me. I admired the passion and directness of his views. He was precisely the person he proclaimed himself to be, a trait I appreciated. He was friendly, always framing his argument on principle, never holding a personal grudge. He made me laugh; he could even laugh at himself when he recognized the hopelessness of his position. I was thrilled to discover I could like people whom I vehemently disagreed with, and that they, in turn, could like me.

Then there was Cola Hudson, who sat to my left. He jokingly threatened to form a committee for equal rights for men. I cannot recall that we ever voted the same way on anything. But we became friends, recognizing in each other a driving credo. That summer I visited Cola in Lyndonville, where he worked as a custodian in the elementary school. I invited along my student intern and a young woman from Switzerland. We met at the steps of the Lyndonville Library. Cola was nervous: three women talking to him, all Democrats. He was a bachelor, and a Republican, by religion.

"Hi, Cola." Someone passing by waved.

He replied without introducing us. We politely kept our distance.

Cola took us to the East Haven Field Day celebration, a local fair. We understood the protocol. Stand back. At last Cola found what he was looking for. "Oh, there's a couple of Democrats," he shouted. "Come on over." He waved to a man and his wife coming toward us from the cotton-candy booth. "I'd like you to meet some Democratic friends of mine."

I teased Cola. "Guess they're the only ones in town, right, Cola?"

He grinned.

He was a shy man, more given to a Vermont "yup" or "nope" than whole sentences. Just the same, he had strong opinions and reassuring laughter. His life, so narrowly circumscribed by this rural Vermont town, encompassed wisdom.

Later that summer, my family and I visited Cola. This time he met us in front of the IGA, and we followed his light-green 1957 pickup truck out of town. We turned off the paved street, went through a covered bridge, and got on to dirt roads; after three turns, I knew we would never find our way again without him. Cola slowed down. There, at the end of the road, was a gray farmhouse weathered down to bony wood, with a tin roof and a gentle sag that allowed it to lie comfortably in the curve of the landscape, like a cat in an armchair.

We got out. From the house a sloping plateau of green fields spread out in front of us like a blanket, rimmed by a one-hundred-and-eighty-degree arc of mountains. Such grandiose generosity: Burke Mountain, Kirby Mountain, Stannard Mountain, East Haven Mountain, and a stretch of the White Mountains regaled the horizon.

"The place used to belong to my grandparents," Cola explained. "They came around 1905. Now, it's just me and Archie and George living here.

I've had lots of offers to sell it, but it's not for sale." He said it as if I had just made an offer. How could I? There was something sacred here.

"Even when you tell 'em that, they sometimes come back, just to look," he said. He knew what he had.

Cola warned us about his brother Archie. "He's kinda moody. When he's in a good mood he's just as nice as can be."

Archie came to the door, a lumbering overweight man, with thinning blond hair, green work pants, a plaid shirt that gaped open at the belly, and a leather lanyard with a pretty clasp hanging from his neck.

"That's very interesting," I said, pointing to the clasp, the first object to hit my line of vision.

"I've got a whole collection of them." He smiled happily, and led us inside the door to show us his box of lanyards. Just behind him was George, a neat, chunky little person, as self-contained as his brother was overflowing.

Stepping inside the house, I felt like Snow White visiting the Seven Dwarfs. It looked as if nothing had changed in a hundred years, except that the floors had been scrubbed by a succession of mops that had nibbled away at the linoleum around the edges and painted it gray. I inventoried a few worn hooked rugs, one rocking chair, a fine brass kerosene lamp "that had always hung there," and two small, antique school desks. The best piece of furniture was a glass bookcase; like an altar, it held Cola's green-bound collection of *Vermont Statutes Annotated*.

I stepped back outside, wanting to give Cola and his brothers, and me, a chance to recover. Cola started an outdoor fire.

"Can't bring myself to buy charcoal, so I use wood," he said, as he lit a match. Was it that they could not afford charcoal, or was this the old-fashioned way? I nodded approvingly.

The brothers presented us with a feast: homemade potato salad, tossed green salad, hot dogs, hamburgers, pickles, cottage cheese, iced tea, Kool-Aid, and ice cream and strawberries. We stuffed ourselves. After lunch, Archie and Cola took us for a walk through a field of wildflowers to the top of the hill behind the house "where we used to see bears and once saw a moose," he explained. "Not everyone is as fortunate as I am," he said, as he scanned the view.

His salary was small, his taxes a burden: "Lister told me the other day that property taxes are going up one hundred dollars, don't know where it's going to come from."

What Cola also did not know was that on that day he was adding fresh zeal to my environmental fervor. That farm could not be lost to a developer. Years later, I promoted a land-use tax, and as governor created the Vermont Housing and Land Conservation Fund to help keep such vistas open. When I signed the legislation, I thought of Cola and his brothers. For his part, Cola, as expected, voted against it.

When our committee met for the last time at the end of the session, Cola took a package out of his briefcase; it was a copy of Ralph Waldo Emerson's essay "Friendship." On the inside cover, he had written: "To Madeleine. A true and valued friend. A *Vermonter* in the finest sense of the word."

OUR COMMITTEE's first assignment was to review four contested legislative elections and decide who were the rightful winners. Had there been sufficient infraction of election laws to invalidate the initial conclusion in each case?

The Goshen town clerk testified that after the election, she had stored the ballots in shoeboxes overnight in her pantry for safekeeping; the next day she called the Republican chairman in to help her with the recount.

Shocked to find that the Democratic candidate had won by two votes, she blurted out, "Never had elected a Democrat, and didn't expect to. Must have been something wrong."

She was right. After the recount, the Republican candidate won by two votes.

"Perhaps we should seal the ballot boxes?" I ventured.

The committee tended to agree.

I agonized over each case, moving my fingertips down the pages of the election laws, line by line, certain I would find truth embossed in print. Fresh from my own political victory, I knew the world of difference that existed between losing and winning.

Arie Rothenberg, the Democratic chairman, stopped me one afternoon in the midst of our deliberations as I was walking down the statehouse corridor. "I've got it straight from the horse's mouth. They'll seat two Democrats and two Republicans." He smiled, telling me not to worry.

"No," I protested indignantly, "you don't understand! It's not going to be that kind of political decision!"

But it was. I consoled myself that we had reached that conclusion only after much deliberation and discussion.

The committee next set out to revise the election laws. The question was: Who has a right to vote and who does not? The Supreme Court had recently ruled against lengthy residency requirements for voting, making Vermont's law unconstitutional.

The committee was upset. Shorten the residency requirement, and anybody might be able to get on the voter checklist. "Voting is a privilege, not a right," they chorused to one another.

I was surprised to find myself in the minority. Wasn't it the other way around: a right and not a privilege?

Round and round we went. The mentally ill, the poor, hippies from the communes, and college students were not fit to vote, at least not unless they registered thirty days or more before the election, my colleagues kept saying. At last, I figured it out. These tardy voters who had moved into town the night before the election would very likely on the next day vote "Democrat."

Even prisoners might vote, announced Edward Conlin, the representative from Windsor, site of Vermont's maximum-security prison. He was incensed that inmates had gotten on the Windsor voter checklist. "Gotta stop 'em. Right now," he fumed. "They could take over the town."

Some enterprising Democratic party workers had registered six inmates to vote. The only residency requirement was a form they were asked to sign that stated that they would "remain in Windsor indefinitely."

When asked why they signed it, the prisoners dutifully replied that if they had refused, they would have been accused of trying to escape.

Conlin's proposal was to require them to vote absentee from their hometown. "Only one of those fellows is from Windsor, I can tell you. The rest are all from Chittenden County," he said, looking pointedly at me.

I voted for the bill.

On dull days in the House, I felt fortunate to sit in front of Al Foley, a retired Dartmouth professor known for his Vermont humor.

During a long and often tedious debate on the lengthy general-appropriations bill, our wandering attention had been revived by a small (ten-thousand-dollar) line item to restore the Bedell covered bridge spanning the Connecticut River. (I later suspected Emory Hebard had stuck it in as a decoy: give them something to chew on while the multimillion-dollar items slip by without debate.)

Everyone in the chamber had something to say about the Bedell covered bridge. First of all, did it belong to Vermont or New Hampshire? The boundary between the two states was closer to the Vermont shoreline, but the bridge, it was agreed, belonged to New Hampshire. So why should we pay one red cent to repair it? Back and forth, they argued.

"It ain't worth it."

"But it's a historic covered bridge."

"Let 'em pay for it."

Then Al Foley stood up, pulled his microphone out of its desk socket, and commanded silence. "Mind you, Mr. Speaker, I have no great love for New Hampshire. As long as Meldrim Thomson's governor, with my opinions, he wouldn't let me step into the state of New Hampshire. But I say, let's give them the ten thousand dollars, and shame the bastards!"

The bill passed.

Back in the committee we took up a parole bill—a simple enough bill to all appearances, but like every other piece of legislation, I discovered, complex.

The first person to testify was the bill's sponsor, Russell Sholes, a member of the Institutions Committee, who asked that the parole board be expanded from three to six persons, and that each member have law-enforcement experience.

Then we heard from Rudolph Morse, the executive secretary of the parole board. He would have to make the decision in cases where there was a tie. He thought having five members would be better.

Morse was an intriguing witness. A Vermonter whose family lived here for many generations, he first made it clear that he was against change. "Don't like that new corrections commissioner they brought in, with his Washington ideas about computers; he just wants to spend lots of money and even expects me to help him get it from the legislature!"

The committee was won over.

But he had no illusions about prison. "It's purely punitive, seldom is there any rehabilitation. We're just keeping a man away from his family and making them dependent on welfare, taking something out of the economy.

"No reason to keep people in jail unless they are a threat to society. It's very hard to evaluate people because when you're face-to-face with a man you tend to sympathize with him, no matter what the record shows.

"The board shouldn't be made up of experts but of ordinary citizens. It should be like a jury, where a man can be judged by his peers. Lot of them are there because they're poor, you know. But we should pay the board better, so they'll come regularly."

Because of his unquestionable credibility and experience, Morse could move the parole discussion in a new direction, bringing the committee along with him. We gave him what he wanted, including an increase in the per diem to parole-board members.

I enjoyed the happiness that comes in casting a unanimous vote, a particularly pleasant sensation after having voted so often in the minority. I was one of them. But the intellectual satisfaction achieved in arriving at a shared conclusion was also important; it made me believe that if the facts were fairly presented, good policy decisions would be inevitable.

Compassion in the political process came from surprising sources. When the supplemental-appropriations bill was up for action, it contained a large increase for welfare; the recession of the early 1970s had hit Vermont, and part of the increase was to pay for high fuel costs.

The floor of the House divided into two camps: conservatives and liberals. There was no doubt where I belonged, but I was worried. How many of us were there? The anger unleashed by the debate was unsettling.

"I say, let's not give 'em another nickel. Long-haired hippies, coming in from out of state, that's what they are."

Heads nodded.

"They're just a bunch of bums who don't want to do a decent day's work. The worst thing we ever did was have the state take over welfare. When the towns were in charge, we knew who deserved it and who didn't. Cost a lot less money, too."

In those days the names of welfare recipients were published in the annual town report. Some towns were so prosperous that they had none.

The welfare increase was going to go down to a resounding defeat. How could it be saved?

Up stood Red Hooper, from Johnson. If an out-of-stater were to photograph a typical, old-time Vermonter, Red Hooper would be his subject.

The first thing I had noticed about Red was his enormous hands. Their colossal strength continued in his arms and shoulders; at seventy-two he was a powerful man. And in defiance of his years, but in keeping with his name, his hair was an unruly and abundant red. When he spoke, members cocked their ears, papers stopped shuffling. He was hard to understand because he spoke softly, and his Vermont accent was as thick as maple syrup oozing down a pile of pancakes. Red Hooper had been elected years ago, then quit the legislature to work for the state as a game warden and now was retired. Some said he had been a first-rate game warden because he knew all there was to know about poaching. He could walk through the woods tracking an off-season hunter for ten or twelve hours. Then he would sneak up on him, real quietlike, and catch him red-handed with his doe. Years later, at Red Hooper's funeral, every game warden in Vermont showed up, in uniform, standing ramrod straight in two columns on either side of the walk leading from the church door. An honor guard fit for a king.

The first spring I served in the legislature, Red invited my family to visit his maple-sugar operation when they were boiling sap in the sugarhouse. He had built it himself, once took a tumble off the roof, "but didn't get hurt a bit," he said. "Just landed on my head, got up, and walked off."

The children and I joined him for a walk in his maple grove to check the tubing. I looked and listened, transfixed, as he described what he saw in the woods. It was as if he were following an annotated text, for every track, rivulet, and fallen leaf had meaning.

The few times Red spoke on the floor of the House, it was on fish-and-game bills. He always had the last word. What was he doing now, the turning heads asked during the debate on the welfare bill, getting up on this one?

"Mr. Speaker," Red began slowly, "I don't know if I'm speaking out of place or not, but I would like to say a word or two about this bill."

"Go right ahead, member from Johnson," the Speaker said amiably.

Red explained that one of his many odd jobs was to serve as town overseer of the poor, to fill in on weekends in case of an emergency when the welfare office was closed.

"You may recall, it was pretty darn cold this weekend. Lots of pipes froze. Had trouble starting my car. May have happened to some of you folks, too. Well, about three o'clock in the afternoon, I got a call from some woman living in a trailer. Needed help. I got in my pickup and set off."

The hall was quiet. What was Red up to?

"I got to the trailer. Hard time finding it on a day like that. Couldn't see much. The roads were real bad. When I opened the trailer door and got inside, I took my gloves off. Then I put them right back on again. It was just about as cold inside as it was outside.

"Five little ones were huddled together on the sofa wearing all of their clothes, jackets, mittens, boots, everything. Covered with quilts.

"I went over and checked the stove. Empty. I got back out to my truck for some kerosene. Took it with me, just in case. Took a little while for the stove to start up. You know how it sputters at first, after it's been empty awhile?

"One of the little ones got off the sofa, put her hands over the grate, and began to cry.

"I don't know much about this welfare budget that you've all been discussing here. All I know is that those little ones were cold."

He sat down. Not another word was said. The vote was taken. The budget passed.

My own emotions sometimes surprised me, how quickly they swam to the surface. One Friday in April, I spoke in support of a bill to strengthen Vermont's laws against child abuse. I did not expect opposition.

Up stood Stub Earle, the member from Eden, the last member of the House to keep a spittoon by his seat, which he used with impressive accuracy. Whenever he spoke, his cheek bulged with chewing tobacco. He liked to defend what he considered an endangered species: "Vermont woodchucks." Usually he brought down the house.

"If I vote for this bill," he asked, pulling the cord of the microphone out of his desk in big swirls, as if it were a lasso, "what happens to my right to discipline my kids? Kinda old-fashioned, I guess, but I believe spare the rod and spoil the child."

I imagined a transformed Stub Earle: a child abuser beating up his kids. Anger erupted in my stomach and threatened to rise in my voice. How could he say this? I said to myself, fearful that I would scream at him or burst into tears.

"Representative from Eden," I replied, "there is a big difference between discipline and abuse. You as a father would still have the right to discipline your children." As I spoke, the photographs of abused children I had seen that afternoon in a national report came into view. I saw the burn marks, the broken bones, the emaciated bodies, and the scared, sad eyes. But as I looked around the chamber, I also saw that others were grateful that Stub had spoken. A man's home was, after all, his castle, and no one wanted the government to butt in. "The largest number of abuse cases occur with children under two years of age who cannot defend themselves. These are the children the law must protect," I went on.

Stub moved his tobacco wad around to the other cheek. "Well, just wanna be damn sure that no sheriff is going to knock on my door for no reason," he said and sat down.

How thin the membrane of legislative formality was, permeable at any moment by a surge of emotion. Stub Earle had touched a delicate nerve: the female fear of male violence, and all the more ominous because he believed that "discipline" was his parental prerogative. I could not say to him what I thought: You have no right to hit your kid and call it discipline. The fact that you're a father does not allow you to use brutality.

As I spoke, I imagined I saw his muscles flex, ready to strike. I had to choose my words carefully, or I would provoke verbal violence against me here on the floor of the House. He had the power to kill the bill. I did not want to incite him. My rage may have stemmed from my suddenly seeing him not as a funny backwoods character, but possibly as a dangerous man. And like an abused wife, I had to placate him in order to protect myself.

With relief, I watched the bill pass.

The legislature, I learned, could assume many guises: cuddly as a teddy bear one moment, prickly as a porcupine the next. Happy as one big, boisterous family around the Thanksgiving table on a Thursday, divided like a couple in divorce court on Friday. What amazed me was that the angry combatants could meet on the street the following day, embrace each other, share a beer, and plot against a new and unsuspecting foe.

I began to understand that this band of legislative players always needed one another; they could not be typecast in single roles. Rarely was any one person a villain for long. A few weeks later, Stub Earle and I worked side by side to win passage of a bill that required nickel deposits on bottles and cans. Farmers and environmentalists had joined forces against the bottle lobby, each for separate reasons; farmers didn't want their cows choking on glass tossed into the fields, and environmentalists wanted to recycle trash and clean up the roadways.

New coalitions would form continuously, and old grudges would be discarded as lightly as cellophane off a cigarette pack. The political adage "Don't get mad, get even" was stated with bravado but seldom followed. Events moved quickly and memories were short. But the cliché "Politics makes strange bedfellows" was exemplified daily. As was horse-trading.

A bill requiring mandatory sentences for an assault on a policeman, jovially referred to as the bop-the-cop bill, came up. I opposed mandatory sentences because I believed it would set bad precedents and limit judicial discretion.

The problem was the bill's sponsor, Democratic senator John ("Jack") O'Brien from Winooski. He had the temperament and looks of an agitated red rooster, and this was his pet bill. Any House member who dared to vote against Jack's bop-the-cop bill would be crucified in the Senate.

When Jack's bill came up on the calendar, he seated himself in the visitors' gallery and took out a roll-call sheet and a pencil. Every House member knew he was there.

Seated on the aisle in the back row was Bob Graf, a Republican elder statesman known for his shrewd political wisdom.

"What should I do?" I whispered to him.

"It's a terrible bill," he replied.

Relieved to think I wouldn't be alone in voting no, I vowed to stick to my principles, and when my name came up, I voted no.

Graf missed the roll call the first time around because he was not in his seat. The second time his name was called, he voted yes.

I was dumbfounded.

"How could you?" I mouthed as I turned my seat in his direction. You wanted to see which way the wind was blowing, didn't you? my look implied.

He shrugged. Later he explained with a smile, "When I'm in a bind, I represent one-half of my constituents by voting one way in the committee, and I represent the other half by voting the other way on the floor."

Only a handful of us had voted against Senator Jack O'Brien. We huddled together in the hallway, wondering when our sentence would be handed down.

Mine came a week later when my transporation bill, creating a new agency of transportation, came up in the Senate. I had worked on it all session and was proud of the achievement. In less than a minute, it was defeated by one vote, cast by Jack O'Brien. He told his seatmate he didn't like the bill's sponsor, Mrs. Kunin from Burlington.

"Should have voted with Jack, Madeleine," I was told by a fatherly senator. "Then your bill would have gone through."

The bill was an administration priority, though, so I recruited John Gray, the highway commissioner, to help me lobby for reconsideration. The next day, the bill passed. I cheered for the bill's passage, but I was really ecstatic because I had been able to escape Jack's revenge.

I had asserted my independence, but I was not a free spirit. The legislative process by nature is collegial. The fact that I had an equal vote meant that I could further my issues with the same power that other legislators promoted theirs. Just as I did not know whom I would need next, they did not know when they would need me. Mutual dependence created a surprising egalitarianism; never could any of us be permanently marginalized.

Legislative bargaining power gave me leverage for my priorities. As long as I could clearly distinguish between striking a mutually agreeable bargain and compromising my beliefs, I would be safe. As I monitored that dividing line, parceling out my bargaining chips sparingly, I worried whether that distinction would ever blur. It was not always the bargains made that conferred power; it was the implied promise or threat of future votes that I and every legislator carried that gave me legitimacy.

The nature of the legislative process forces an uneasy but momentarily genuine intimacy among the members. Each person has to be sufficiently accommodating to preserve a spirit of civil interaction. We were trapped here together under the golden dome, like sailors at sea, and there was no way to jump ship. Neither were there many places on deck where I could detour to avoid ideas or people I didn't like.

In private life, I could pick my friends, select my issues, walk along a cordoned-off path among people who thought and behaved like me. The legislature was different. I never knew whom I would bump into coming around the corner. No matter; I had to be polite. Be nice, you're in a very tight space. I was heartened to remember that they had to be nice, too.

Learning to be tolerant of people I vehemently disagreed with was trying but also stimulating. Not only was I intrigued and sometimes entertained by an astonishing spectrum of political opinions, but I had to respond with a vigorous defense of my assumptions. I had not understood the intensity and fragility of my own beliefs until forced to defend and articulate them under fire.

Sometimes, to mutual astonishment, dueling partners from the right and left would meet midway. Melvin Mandigo, my conservative nemesis, and I roared with laughter one afternoon when we defended, with equal vigor, the importance of individual liberty. We accidentally banged our heads together, having simultaneously jumped to a point of common agreement from two different directions. When we recovered we were equally shocked by this sudden display of unanimity.

The first time I had a ringside seat at a fight when the gloves came off between Democrats and Republicans on the floor of the House, I was as wide-eyed as Orphan Annie. Like an unexpected change in New England weather, the mood in the House turned ugly in the midst of a lengthy debate on property-tax reform, the centerpiece of the Democratic agenda. The issue seemed minor: the question was whether the governor was listening to House debate from a loudspeaker in his executive office, taking notes, and preparing rebuttals for his legislative lieutenants. The Republican Speaker, finding this outrageous, had had the PA system turned off. "Never have I seen the executive misuse his powers like this," the Speaker said with forced fury, his spiky crew cut puncturing the air above his head. He had made the unusual move of stepping down from the podium in order to speak from the floor.

Tapped by the Speaker's baton, Orrin Beattie, chairman of my committee, rose. "We must defend the separation of powers," he said, his face turning red with patriotic indignation as if the Constitution itself were about to be ripped to shreds.

Democrats responded with equal vigor: turning off the legislative loudspeaker in the governor's office was an outrageous insult to the executive; every governor had been given the courtesy to listen to legislative deliberations. Not only that, it was an infringement of the constitutional right to freedom of speech.

"This is an all-time low level of debate," Henry Carse, a moderate Republican, admonished. A recess was called, huddles formed, and ten minutes later, the loudspeaker piped into the governor's office was turned back on.

In the heat of battle, I found myself feeling warmly about all Democrats. These were my people, regardless of what I had thought of them moments before. We were soldered together like little tin soldiers, all pointed in the same direction. One by one, our names were called, and we snapped back smart yeses as if this were a military drill. The purity of the process left no room to hide; everyone knew who was with us, who against us. The distinction between good and evil, friend and foe, was obvious; it could be seen in typeface set in two columns of ayes and nays printed in the next day's House *Journal*. When I voted in the minority, I could feel one of two ways: bravely heroic or embarrassingly ostracized. Either way, the minority became a tight band. When I voted with the majority, I enjoyed the double reward of being right and of winning. It was fun to be jostled by the good-natured camaraderie of the other names on the list, filling up the room, crowding out the others.

No matter which way I voted, the formality of the process, the necessity to make a decision, made one safe. Everyone had to choose sides; everyone had to be counted. Even when one had second thoughts, there was little time for them, or for recrimination, because the next day there would be a new list of winners and losers. The speed and certainty of the process shielded me from prolonged self-doubt. Here, everything was condensed to its essence, making it seem both more and less real than life. Every vote dealt with real people and problems, abstracted into the formality of legislative language and the predictability of the legislative process. It was impossible to dwell on a question or to let the echo of an earlier debate linger. The merciless calendar moved on, forcing one question offstage to make room for the next. Engaged in this marathon of having to debate and decide, debate and decide, in rapid succession, gave me a new athletic agility to deal with conflict.

Most of my life, I had detoured around conflict, even when it meant taking the long way home. As daughter, sister, mother, and wife, that had been both instinct and expectation; my role was to keep the peace. When fighting broke out at the dinner table, on the playground, it meant that I had failed; I had not found the right words, tone, or touch. Here I discovered that fighting was not disastrous. It was an integral part of the rhythm of legislative life. Even as I honed my new skills, I still hesitated to use them.

"I hate the end of the session," I told the Republican president pro tem, when I felt tension building between the Senate and the House prior to a blowup. He turned to me in surprise, rubbed his hands together, grinned, and replied, "Why, that's the best part. I love to fight."

And he did.

I didn't. But I learned to fight for what I wanted.

In the House, the big battle that first term was over reapportionment. After some twenty-five informational hearings, our committee began the brutal task of voting on a reapportionment bill. Politics was suddenly stripped of its finery, exposing raw, naked power. The fight was for survival. For months, the discussion had been at a high plane; we were to design legislative districts that were fair, equal, and respectful of tradition. Everyone agreed on the standard. No one had pointed to the truth: we were deciding who would come back here and who wouldn't. In the final days, the thin veneer of civility wore off, like makeup at the end of the day. Bargains were openly offered: you vote for my plan, and I'll vote for yours. I reminded myself, as I looked out the window, searching in vain for George Little's squirrels to distract me, that we were making decisions that would affect people who would never enter this room and would remain ignorant of the bargains struck here. As we cast our votes on each legislative district, delineating Vermont's land like cartographers on a binge, I, too, enjoyed the power to say who would vote with whom.

I had concentrated my efforts on Burlington, on new legislative districts that would coincide with the aldermanic districts there so that, at long last, the confusion between overlapping and conflicting districts, causing disarray and complaints, would be overcome. It made perfect sense, I thought. But when the Burlington plan came to a straw vote, the committee voted no 7 to 4.

"What?" I exclaimed in disbelief, staring at the hands raised in opposition to my plan, fearing they might strike.

Earlier discussions of my proposal had prompted little comment, and I had assumed, therefore, that I had committee support. Now I saw that the chairman and Judy Rosenstreich had voted against me. Did Orrin want to teach me a lesson? Was Judy jealous? Did she want to demonstrate her independence from the other woman on the committee? Or was it my fault, had I been too aggressive, too impudent? Should I curb my repartee? What I did not know was that the Democratic representative from Winooski, a neighboring town, which would lose half a seat under my proposal, had lobbied the committee against my Burlington proposal. A victory for me would be a loss for him.

After the straw vote, I dug my heels in. I told the committee I was serious, smiling like a mannequin whose arm had been unscrewed. I paused after each word as if I were reprimanding my children. I was deadly serious, I repeated.

In winning the next round, I learned that victory also had a price. I had made an enemy. Arnold Tibbetts, the representative from Marshfield, had voted with me, certain that in return I would vote for his proposal to separate Marshfield from Plainfield; he lived in fear that the radical Goddard College students in Plainfield would vote him out of office. Despite Arnold's apprehensions, it made good sense to keep Marshfield and Plainfield together; they always had been part of the same district.

When I voted against Arnold, his anger exploded. I steadied my chair and looked over at Cola. He whispered to me, "Hang in there, Madeleine." What a superior human being. I felt I could hand him my soul for safekeeping.

I vowed to stay quiet in the discussions from now on, at least for a day or two. The rifts in the committee made me fear my own hostility. The chairman told me, "I don't want you to get too tough." I feared I knew what he meant.

But I asked myself, How else can I survive in this place? Humble acceptance of defeat is demeaning, even masochistic. I had to fight back for my Burlington reapportionment plan. I wanted it to win. I couldn't mask that ambition behind a sweet facade. The intensity of emotion unleashed by this debate was disturbing to me—love and hate, generosity and greed, trust and suspicion, silhouetted in black and white on a giant screen in the committee room. In real life, these same people would have been sketched in charcoal grays; it would have taken years to see their characters so clearly defined, if ever. I was astonished not only by what I saw in them, but by what I discovered in myself. I had a fierce drive. I wanted to succeed. I wondered, Have I always had that capacity for combat, and is it only now exposed? What happened to the feminine side of me, the lady who smiled pleasantly and was nice?

Orrin Beattie, the chairman, was my teacher and demonstrated a wily toughness that was disturbing to me even as I admired how brilliantly it worked.

One Friday afternoon toward the end of the session, Speaker Peanut Kennedy came to our committee to tell us which bills should have high priority and be reported to the floor. We got into a discussion of rape, a subject that came up around a bill that would have given game wardens law-enforcement powers.

The Speaker described a hypothetical rape scene in the woods. If a game warden—lacking the power to make an arrest—came upon the scene, would he have to stand and watch while waiting for a deputy sheriff to arrive and make the arrest?

Someone said, "They'd all stand in line."

Laughter.

"And enjoy it."

More laughter.

The sound of my own laughter came from a sound track. It seemed to echo through the room like a shriek. Surely, I had not made it. My hand sprang up and covered my mouth.

The smiling faces around the table were enjoying the imaginary scene, as if they were watching a home video. I turned away, feeling violated.

Judy Rosenstreich proved she could take it. She pointed mischievously at Arnold Tibbetts. "Arnold, you're blushing."

I was warmed by his color. I pressed my knees together tightly and smiled weakly. Is this how they will try to keep us under control, flaunting their ultimate power? Never, I vowed from my pillow that night, would I let such humor pass again.

On the floor of the House I found new courage. I was determined to win passage of H. 492, a bill I had introduced that would require lobbyists to disclose their expenditures. In the aftermath of Watergate there was a mandate for political reform, and I agreed with a newly formed national organization called Common Cause, which advocated lobbyist-disclosure legislation. The Speaker sent my bill to the Committee on General and Military Affairs, chaired by Representative Henry Hicks, an irascible labor leader from Weathersfield. He made it clear he would not let the bill get to the floor.

One by one, I approached his committee members.

"What should I do? Can you help me get the bill out?"

"Well, Madeleine, sure would like to help you out. See what I can do."

The shifting from foot to foot and sidelong glances told me they would stick with their chairman.

I went directly to Henry. "Will you allow the bill to get out so it can be debated by the House?" I asked, straight to his face.

He scowled. That was the only expression available to him. I was an annoyance, something he would like to shoo away, a buzzing mosquito.

"The bill? Will you vote it out?" I persisted, bracing myself for a swat.

"Nope. Try again next year, when I'm not around," and he took off. His voice had sounded like a snowplow scraping pavement.

The next morning I pulled out my last card. I went to see the Speaker, having obliterated his sexist humor from my mind.

"Do you have any advice, Peanut? I've tried everything. I talked to all the committee members. They're going to stick with Henry. Then I asked Henry straight to his face. All he said was 'Try again next year.' I refuse to give up. It's an important bill," I said, having a sense of its popular support.

"Well," the Speaker said, as he crossed one leg over the other, smiling a Machiavellian smile, "this place needs a little shaking up."

He leaned forward. "There is something in the rules. But you can't tell anyone that I told you this."

His chair edged closer. "Let me tell you what you can do. It hasn't been done very often, but it just might work. First thing in the morning, before the orders of the day"—he meant the beginning of the day's calendar—"you can stand up and move that the Committee on General and Military Affairs be relieved of the bill. That way, it's out on the floor. The rest is up to you."

I waltzed out of his office.

By 9:15, morning prayers were over, and the members of the House were busy threading the laces of their bill books into the punched holes on that morning's new bills, tying them in neat bows.

I stood up at my seat.

The Speaker, barely looking up from his perusal of the calendar, said, "Member from Burlington, Mrs. Kunin."

"Mr. Speaker," I said, trying to sound as casual as I could, "I request that the Committee on General and Military Affairs be relieved of H. 492."

"All those in favor?" the Speaker responded.

A few muttered ayes. Most members did not bother to look up.

"Opposed?" the Speaker innocently asked.

A second later, the gavel fell. "The motion passes. The Committee on General and Military Affairs is relieved of H. 492."

Midsentence, Henry Hicks woke up.

"Nooooo," he bellowed like a wounded moose.

Too late. The bill was out of committee and on the floor. There was a buzz of conversation: something had been set in motion, and right under Henry's nose. The press picked up the story with delight. I pointed out to reporters how heavy the lobbying had been by the beverage industry against the bill proposing a deposit on bottles, by the utilities against a "lifeline"* proposal for reforming electric rates, and by bankers to raise interest rates on home mortgages.

"House Pulls Lobbyist Disclosure from Hicks," the headline in the *Rutland Herald* said. "A bill requiring lobbyists in the legislature to disclose contributions and expenditures goes to the House floor Tuesday because of quick work Friday by its sponsor."

The *Burlington Free Press* reported:

> The committee chairman, Rep. Henry Hicks, R-Weathersfield, had pledged that the bill would die for lack of action in his committee.
>
> However, in an unusual move Friday, Rep. Kunin made a motion on the floor to relieve the committee of the bill. The result was a blitz; opponents of the bill were caught off guard, and the motion passed without debate.
>
> As a result, the bill will be on the House floor for action Tuesday.
>
> There are now more than 120 lobbyists in Montpelier, and the only official, publicly available information about them is a list of their names filed at the secretary of state's office.

My outsider status gave me, I thought, an uncluttered view of right and wrong. As a woman among men and as a newcomer among old-timers, I had not formed fond attachments to the permanent appendages of the legislature—the lobbyists. Those I had begun to ally myself with were public interest groups such as the Low Income Advocacy Council and the Vermont Public Interest Research Group, started by Ralph Nader, which I viewed more kindly, because they were outside the system, like me.

Only as an unindoctrinated plebe could I seize the unwritten rules of the club and tear them up. In retrospect, I am awed by my innocent

---

* Legislation would have set a baseline low rate for poor and elderly customers.

indignation. Peanut Kennedy was right: the system needed shaking up. As a seasoned politician, he knew that a freshman legislator could wield an earnest scrub brush for good government, and slosh the issue around the House floor, not caring whose boots got splashed.

My allies were vocal. The bill was widely praised in newspaper editorials calling for more open government.

From the inside the view was different. I was a problem and possibly a menace. Henry Hicks was not an isolated curmudgeon; he was the lion at the gate, attending to his assigned post to defend the legislative realm.

Now that the bill was on the floor, it was mine to defend. My task seemed straightforward: to convey to the members of the House how strongly the public felt about political reform; to show them that the lobbyist-disclosure bill could purify the process and restore public confidence. My argument was beautifully clear.

But I was nervous. That weekend, I prepared my remarks carefully, leaving little to chance. The facts would be persuasive.

But like a wild-eyed missionary intent on salvation of the natives, I was blind to the consequences of breaking cultural taboos. I had wrested a bill from the chairman, and thereby broken the club rules. Worse yet, I was threatening to disrupt the chummy, long-standing relationship between legislators and lobbyists. My punishment was isolation. I was to be left to wage my fight alone. The normal backup of a committee would be lacking.

Immediately, the tribal elders, the committee chairmen, moved into formation. If one chairman's power to hold a bill captive could be challenged, they might be next. First on his feet that Tuesday afternoon was Timothy O'Connor, chairman of the House Judiciary Committee, a good Democrat and frequent spokesman for Governor Salmon. "The wrong people are on trial," Tim lamented. "The lobbyists are on trial when we should be on trial. It's up to us to do what's right."

"Legislators," the next person objected, "are not duped by lobbyists. That is an insult to this body."

O'Connor made a motion to send the lobbyist-disclosure bill to the Judiciary Committee, where it could be carefully examined.

I objected. I knew that the Judiciary Committee would kill it. O'Connor's motion was shouted down.

Saved.

Jack Morgan, a Republican from Woodstock, stood up. "I move that we send the bill back to the Committee on General and Military Affairs, where it belongs."

Again, I protested. They would never let it out again.

I survived, 106–34.

I was growing confident. The votes were there.

Emerson Peake of Rutland Town stood up. He was resentful of the way the press had reported the controversy over the bottle-deposit bill and felt the lobbyists had been maligned. "I feel that the press—as far as the bottle bill is concerned—is by far the biggest lobbyist in the state," he protested. There was general agreement, judging by the silent nods I saw. The notebook scribblers at the press table smiled knowingly at one another.

That night, they quoted Peake accurately and added, "Peake accepted a junket to a hockey game in Montreal that was financed by a lobbyist for the Vermont Wholesale Beverage Distributors Association and by the Molson Brewing Co. of Canada, both opponents of the law."

Timothy Payne spoke against the bill. But again, the press reports made the observation that Payne had recently had his picture taken lugging several cases of beer into the bus bringing legislators to the lobbyist-financed junket to Montreal.

One amendment, proposed by Emory Hebard, was adopted, requiring all lobbyists, even those spending less than one hundred dollars, to register. Hebard called these few the "semipros." I did not object.

At 4:50 that afternoon, after three hours of debate, I allowed myself to savor victory, licking it off the tip of my finger like icing. But then I had to push the bowl away: as the Speaker was about to start the roll call, Amos Colby got up and thoroughly denounced the bill. I was patient. Colby was not a heavyweight. Then, to my amazement, Oreste Valsangiacomo, Democratic whip, rose.

What's happening? I asked myself.

Val started out benignly. "Mr. Speaker, we've had a lengthy debate on this bill. Some of the members have gotten confused with all these amendments. I see that there are more amendments waiting to be discussed. Tomorrow we have a light calendar [Not true, I muttered to myself.] which would give us lots of time to debate this bill. I move, Mr. Speaker, that we adjourn."

Oh no. Just when victory was about to be enjoyed, I felt it pulled from my hand.

I rifled through the rule book. A motion to adjourn was nondebatable. Later I discovered I could have asked for a rules suspension to make the adjournment motion debatable. Now, helpless, I stayed in my seat, hoping for a miracle.

The motion to adjourn carried on a voice vote. The wall of positive support that had withstood prior amendments had crumbled. The high optimism of only a moment ago was suctioned from the room, leaving the air thick and stale with tired words.

I sent the Speaker a note. "Do you think I should stop knocking my head against the wall?"

He replied, "Not until the calluses give you a problem with hats."

I laughed, but then asked myself, How could Val have done that? Val knew the rules; he had the strategic repertoire of a chess master at his command, and nothing he did was without design; now he was poised for checkmate. In the interim between adjournment and the next day's reconsideration, the lobbyists would have time to rally their troops and sow doubt among the bill's supporters.

The truth was harsh. It was the Democrats who were scuttling the bill. I went straight to Governor Salmon's office after adjournment and asked Norm James, his press secretary, for help. Could he work on those Democrats? Instead, James grilled *me* about the bill.

Early the next morning I appeared before the Democratic Steering Committee to make a last-minute pitch for party support. I told them this should be a Democratic issue; we should be the party to stand for openness in government. Their silence was transparent. My plea was politely tolerated.

The bill came up again the next day. A flurry of amendments showered down; it was difficult to distinguish friend from foe. Which amendments should I accept or reject? Each person who rose to speak against the bill had left some bruises on the legislative body; at the end of an hour, I sensed imminent collapse. Doubt had begun to infect the chamber like a disease, causing the members to squirm, whisper, and cough. The final blow was wielded by Frank Esposito. Earlier in the session he had gotten furious at a League of Women Voters lobbyist who, with unusual candor, had suggested that if he could not support a bill that required bottles to be recycled, it was time to recycle him. He had not been amused.

Now he rose from his seat like a provoked bull, his hand pawing his desk for a copy of the bill, which he then held at arm's length. He informed the body that this was a very poorly written bill. Sloppy drafting. "I've never seen such a bad bill," he puffed, as he turned the pages with mock amazement. "First of all, it contradicts the federal law, the definitions are vague, and it will be impossible to enforce." For fifteen minutes, point by point, Esposito went on, snorting, kicking up dust, getting ready for the charge.

Finally I rose and asked, "Member from Rutland, what exactly is your point?" Like a dutiful schoolgirl, I had thought that if I could answer every question, I could placate him. My last hope was to win the sympathy of the House by exposing him as a bully who was picking on me. It was an uncertain strategy. I didn't know how to break the chain of his interrogation with a reply that would allow me to regain control.

Later, I chastised myself for having been too polite. I replayed the scene as it should have been: I jump up from my seat and yell, "Esposito, lay off! Stop trying to kill this bill." The crowd cheers.

But Esposito had done his job well. Royal Cutts, whose new, extremely large white teeth fascinated me, rose from his seat. His black pin-striped woolen jacket was bejeweled with insignia from the Grange; he had been its state master. I was impressed. Cutts reminded the House that he chaired the Natural Resources Committee, where fierce lobbying had occurred against Vermont's new environmental law, Act 250. Until now, I had thought him an ally who stood up under pressure.

"This bill is too far-reaching, it is unnecessary, and I certainly hope to see it killed. Why, everyone who has testified in my committee this year would have to register," he bemoaned.

"A good thing, too," I muttered.

Cutts had caved in.

The last speaker was Peter Giuliani, a Republican committee chairman, who felt duty-bound to defend the honor of the legislature. The only purpose of the bill, he said, would be to protect the legislature from corrupting influences. "Who needs it?" he asked rhetorically.

I had a split-second internal debate about whether to answer Giuliani's question and sum up the argument. I convinced myself it wasn't necessary. Besides, if I spoke again, I risked another motion to adjourn, and then all would be lost.

During the roll call I felt as if it were my life that was being voted up or down: "Yes . . ." "No . . ." "No . . ." "No . . ."

"My God, three in a row." I panicked as I drew a line across four hastily penciled vertical strokes to keep score.

"Yes . . ." "Yes . . ."

Ah, two together. Would that make up for the others?

"Listen to the results of your vote," the Speaker announced, giving me a knowing look.

"Those in favor, sixty-four; those opposed, seventy-one."

I was devastated. My face flushed bright red with anger and humiliation. I was about to cry. Clare Parker, who had made his living selling ice,

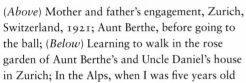

(*Above*) Mother and father's engagement, Zurich, Switzerland, 1921; Aunt Berthe, before going to the ball; (*Below*) Learning to walk in the rose garden of Aunt Berthe's and Uncle Daniel's house in Zurich; In the Alps, when I was five years old

Photos from author's personal collection

(*Above*) With
brother Edgar and
dog Brownie on
North Carson Road,
in Los Angeles in
1941; (*Above, right*)
Wearing favorite
headband, at P.S.
101, Forest Hills,
New York; Class
of 1956, University
of Massachusetts;
(*Right*) Freshman
legislator, at the
statehouse mailbox

Photos from author's personal collection

Sanders Milens

Family portrait, 1972: (*l to r*)
Adam holding Kitty, Madeleine,
Peter, Arthur, Julia, and Daniel
in the center

Personal collection

(*Above*) First committee
assignment, Government
Operations, with Representative Patrick Candon (*left*)
and Representative Cola
Hudson (*right*), 1973;
(*Right*) House Appropriations Chair, 1977; Floor
huddle, as Vermont House
debated $2.7 million supple-
mental budget, 1978

Donna Light: AP

Donna Light: AP

Michael Sinclair: AP

(*Left*) Announcing bid for lieutenant governor, 1977; (*Below*) Dropping the gavel to call the Senate to order after oath of office as lieutenant governor; (*Below, left*) "The Chair votes NO." Casting the tie-breaking vote against an antiabortion amendment attached to the state budget, 1979

Donna Light: AP

Donna Light: AP

(*Right*) Announcing campaign for a second term as lieutenant governor, 1980; (*Below*) With Republican Governor Richard Snelling at Island Pond, Vermont; Annual milking contest between Vermont's lawmakers

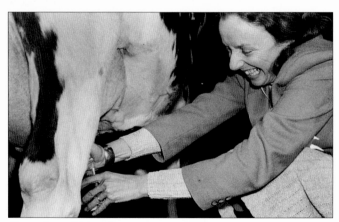

Photos: Donna Light: AP

(*Right*) Gubernatorial campaign kickoff, 1982; (*Below*) Conceding the governor's race to Richard Snelling, 1982; (*Bottom, right*) A thumbs-up gubernatorial campaign, 1984. The sign in French says, "This time, Madeleine"; (*Bottom, left*) Explaining proposal to increase state aid to education, 1984

Donna Light: AP

Toby Talbot: AP

Toby Talbot: AP

Toby Talbot: AP

Vyto Starinskas: Rutland Herald

With Geraldine Ferraro in
Burlington, Vermont, 1984;
Reelection campaign, 1986

Toby Talbot: AP

was seated to my right. Now he handed me a note: "The whole damn House is not worth the salt in one teardrop."

The Speaker sent me down a note:

> Madeleine. It was a whale of a try, and with all the odds stacked against you, you fought an excellent and brave battle. You also gave many people cause to think. The news media will be kind to you, rough on the opponents. There will be another day and you will try again. Cheers! I have been beaten by experts myself.
> Sincerely, Pean.

I held it tight, as I sought self-control. I did not want to give anyone the satisfaction of seeing me cry. Where were my friends? No one had risen to speak in my defense, including those who, the day before, had offered me their praise.

Disappointment turned acidic. I would never forget and forgive. I suspected people had gloried in my defeat. I remembered a remark made to me after Vermont's passage of the Equal Rights Amendment: "Just because you won your first one, don't think you're going to win them all." Breaking the rules deserved punishment. If I had pulled this off, no one would have been able to control me.

I retreated to the ladies' room, where I could pat powder on my nose.

"I wonder," a soft voice said, out of the blue, "if the outcome would have been different if you were a man." Drying her hands at the sink next to mine was Mrs. Patrick Harte, a woman in her late sixties, the wife of a South Burlington legislator.

Just what I had not dared to express, but darkly suspected. "Maybe, but who knows?" I answered, grateful for the question I dared not explore further. I knew that was too easy an answer, and I did not want to give in to the comfort of paranoia. Nevertheless, her words were as soothing as a mother's; she had understood.

I was surprised the next day when legislators appeared to ask for my forgiveness. That I was genuinely angry was disturbing to them. For several days I clutched my anger to my chest like a huge notebook protecting me on my way to school.

Looking back, I see that I came close to losing faith in the system, not only because of my personal defeat but also because the system had raised its fist in my face. I was unprepared for the blow, because, at first, the outside world had stroked my hair, telling me I was being a brave good girl. The press and public had cheered when I unfurled my banner of truth and held it high, like a Joan of Arc, certain that I would be followed with righteous fervor. Political schizophrenia seized me; which world was reality, this stuffy chamber of recirculated air, or the green world beyond, framed by these high arched windows?

To lead an effective political life, I knew what I had to do: live my life in two dimensions, never straying too far from either politics or life. This chamber had a limited perspective, but I had to go through it to reach a wider vista.

When I recovered, I discovered that I had, in fact, been more successful than I thought. The press blatantly took my side—of course it was in their interest to do so. The *Burlington Free Press* wrote: "A major bill designed to end secret lobbying campaigns in Montpelier was killed in the House Wednesday by a seven-vote margin. The legislation was strongly opposed by most of the state's 120 registered lobbyists." An editorial called the legislature "special interest pawns" and applauded my efforts.

Mavis Doyle wrote for the *Rutland Herald*:

> Opponents of the bill were jubilant at killing it. One of the first opponents to leave the chamber after the vote was Rep. John Mulligan, D-47, of Castleton, who emerged with a big grin on his face.
>
> Mulligan was immediately congratulated by Bernard Freeman, the lobbyist for the Vermont Association of Realtors.
>
> All but three legislators who took a junket financed by several lobbyists to a Montreal hockey game last month voted against the bill.

Mavis had no mercy.

By the end of the week, I sensed that I was being treated with new respect. The fact that I had come close to winning was an indicator of potential influence. I took comfort knowing who my opponents were and who my friends were. For the moment.

ON NOVEMBER 13, 1974, I sent out letters to my fellow Democrats, announcing I would run for minority whip. The position was second in command to the Democratic leader. Mary Chambers, a New Hampshire legislator who had been a member of our women's book club, gave me the idea when she told me she was now minority whip in New Hampshire. (Only years later did I learn that she had been appointed, while I had to be elected.)

I went back and forth on the decision. Finally I made a list, telling myself this was the intelligent way to evaluate it.

Cons

1. It would lock me into a party position, and I would have to support the party and the governor when I might not want to.

2. The responsibility: Can I handle it, do I want to stick my neck out, can I get a following, votes?

3. John Murphy, also running for the post, is a nice guy. Why oppose him?

4. Fear of losing face, fear of criticism, of being accused of being too ambitious—who does she think she is?—increasing divisiveness in the party when this is the year we should all stick together.

5. Basic lack of confidence, that lonely feeling of being out there by yourself and not being certain you are right.

6. The time and energy it would take would be diverted from enacting bills.

Pros

1. A woman seeking a party position for the first time might set a precedent, encourage others, even if I fail.

2. It would present another liberal dimension of the party in an official capacity, build a respectable coalition to affect party policy decisions.

3. The challenge and the desire to meet it, to prove something to myself and others that I can do it.

4. Security—having a label is nice, makes position more official.

5. Belief that I can do the job well, that I can speak on the floor, that I could unite the liberal wing of the Democratic party.

6. Exciting time for Democrats to influence the legislature, not be given second-class-citizen status.

7. Good to be part of the action.

8. Mary Chambers did it in New Hampshire.

9. I have some support from Burlington and surroundings. When I optimistically add up the votes, it looks good; at least I would get a reasonable number even if I lost.

10. Losing would not be too bad if I don't lose disastrously. It would still make a point. I'd be considered someone to be reckoned with, and it would force consideration of more liberal viewpoint.

Ten reasons in favor, six against. After I mailed the announcement letters, I said to myself, I hope I'm doing the right thing. And part of me still yearned to withdraw, I confessed, but in the next sentence I wrote in my journal,

*I only grow if I go forward. What drives me? I could be satisfied
with what I am, doing an adequate job.*
    *Well, it's done, curious about the outcome. I plan to be a grateful
loser, hopefully. No grudges.*

A month later at the Democratic caucus in Montpelier at the Brown
Derby restaurant, I was elected assistant minority leader by a vote of 40
to 26. Minutes before the vote, Tom Candon, the minority leader, came
up to me and asked, "Are you still running?"

"Of course," I said, astonished by the question.

"I heard you were going to withdraw," Larry Powers, a freshman legislator, told me.

"Hell no." I laughed. That's what the boys had hoped I would do. They
did not know that I was prepared. Lorraine Graham, my car-pool buddy,
lined up the Burlington vote, approaching Sadie White, Alfred Couture,
and Clarence LeClair. They could not say no to Lorraine. I asked Maedean Bartlett, a widow from Richford, to nominate me. She was surprisingly encouraging and brought most of the Franklin County delegation
with her. She had voted against the Equal Rights Amendment but seemed
tickled by the idea of nominating a woman for minority whip. She was
nervous but sincere when she addressed the Democratic legislators, stressing that I would pay attention to all the members of the House. A conservative woman, I was certain, would sound a reassuring note.

The liberal perspective was provided by a young legislator I had asked
to speak on my behalf—Steve McLeod, from Barre, who pointed out that
I did not always agree with the party leadership, that I got along well with
Republicans, and that I would bring a necessary new element into the
party. I was glad I had asked him to talk when I noted that my opponent
had asked twenty-three-year-old Mike Obuchowski: we had each
thought of the youth vote.

John Murphy was my opponent, a machinist at the GE plant in Ludlow
who spoke up for the "little guy." Later, I was to appreciate his first-rate
political instincts; then, I saw him as a likable caricature of an Irish good
old boy. If I had known him better, I suspect I would not have wanted to
run against him.

The Murphy supporters had green shamrocks with the letter *M* pinned
to their chests, and for a moment I wished I had thought of something for
my team. John Mulligan, Murphy's nominator, was funny: "He's a man
of small stature when you measure him from the ground up, but not if
you measure him around." I longed to have a touch of Irish humor.

The vote was by secret ballot. Steve McLeod and Mike Obuchowski were the ballot clerks, and midway through the count, I noticed that Steve's pile was thicker, and he looked fairly cheerful, I decided, after scanning his face as if it were a weather map. I took heart.

When the winner was announced, Murphy immediately got up to announce his support for me, and I reached out for his hand—an instantaneous response. I kissed Lorraine Graham and hugged Maedean Bartlett. Tom Candon was too shocked to shake my hand. I knew, by his look of rude surprise, that he was not pleased. He had deliberately underestimated me and had hopes my candidacy would disappear; if I won, he knew I would be trouble. And he was right. I confess to feeling a zing of gleeful triumph shoot through me when I realized that, over the sputtering objections of my own leader, I had become the first woman elected to a legislative leadership position.

He did not know what to say. He could not congratulate me, but neither could he castigate me; under the circumstances, he needed time to figure out how to manage me.

In deference to Murphy and to the bruised spirit of party unity, the vote totals were not announced until later. It was not necessary; everyone knew what victory meant. That afternoon, Timothy O'Connor asked if I would second his nomination for Speaker, to which I immediately agreed.

Who would have believed it? I asked myself in wonder. A year ago I would not have dreamed of being asked for my political hand to help get Tim O'Connor elected. Neither did I think I would give it. Tim had regarded me as a troublesome feminist, and I had seen him as an obstinate Irishman. We jousted back and forth over the Equal Rights Amendment, pretending it was a game, when deep down I bristled at his teasing.

I pondered the significance of my need to prove something to myself, calling my running for Democratic party whip at once a "terrible drive" and "rewarding." What pleased me was the discovery that I could be outspoken, disagree with people, and still win their respect. This is precisely what I had wanted to achieve in my freshman term: be true to myself and yet effective within the political system. This election assured me that I could win the support of my peers, a critical internal constituency, essential for my long-term success with my external constituency. Without their help, I could not keep the promises I had made to the electorate and to myself.

I had cracked the power molds, like a series of Russian matrioshka dolls, one inside another. Now I had gotten to what I believed was the core. My appeal to the membership to support me as whip was based on what I feared most but what was, in fact, my advantage: being an outsider, not an insider. I promised to carry their views into the inner sanctum and make them heard there; therefore, I was trusted. What I would not know until months later was that the moment I became an insider, I gave up my heroic outsider status and soon became suspect as a member of a powerful coterie.

Geography had been most important to my victory; I had the complete support of the Burlington delegation. Gender was tangential, but it added excitement and underscored my outsider status, making my incursion into the male power center visible. And the election permitted me to cross a line that had separated women from men; I was making a public declaration both to myself and to the legislature that I wanted power.

My assessment was quickly affirmed; leadership meant influence. Tim O'Connor announced at the caucus that if he were elected Speaker, he would not make any committee assignments without consulting first with the leaders and whips of both parties. I would be there in the room when power was to be allocated. I would not be punished by exposing my ambitions; I would, to my surprise and relief, be rewarded.

6

I DREAMED WE LIVED ON TOP OF A MOUNTAIN AND I WAS DRIVING down an icy, winding road. As I maneuvered the hairpin turns, I asked myself, Why do I live up here, where it is so high and dangerous? I dared not look over the edge. I drove carefully. And to my surprise, I made the descent.

In another dream, I was a trapeze artist, standing on a platform circling a tall pole. How did I get up here? How would I get down? I felt the pole sway. I would have to jump. Then I woke up. I was enormously relieved. It had only been a dream.

Had I reached these dangerous heights only to fear a fall? Were these dreams warnings or a natural expression of anxiety? Being minority whip made me both more confident and more apprehensive. This is where I wanted to be—in the inner circle, where I could be an advocate for a progressive agenda and the legislators who would help promote it. But the risks that came with power were many. My one vote could be negated by the others; those who looked to me to intervene on their behalf might be disappointed if I could not achieve what they wanted, and power would make me both liked and disliked. I feared my friends might ask, "Why couldn't you have done more?"

As I was about to formulate an answer, the page handed me a note while I was seated in the House chamber the first day of the new 1975 legislative session. "Leadership meeting at 10 a.m. in room . . ." I retreated to a whitewashed brick basement room below the statehouse where the leadership group had assembled behind closed doors. Our task was straightforward: to decide which legislators would serve on each committee. I took my seat and listened to the staccato judgment calls. The privilege of seclusion had stripped the exchanges of gentle modifiers. Firing from the hip, the men shot down their peers with sharp one-liners. A person's fate was decided in an instant.

"No brains and stubborn as hell, he'd be a disaster."

"Fish and Game, that's where he belongs."

"She never voted with us, forget it."

"Remember how he screwed up reporting that bill? Not chairman material."

"Wrong county. We need someone from down south."

"Can't be trusted, give him his third choice."

How crude it was! Once a person's imprint had hardened in the clay of perception, there was little opportunity for redemption. Nothing was forgotten. Did men and women have to be flattened into cartoon characters for others to see them clearly? There was no time for lengthy biographies, for ambiguity and complexity; people were either smart or dumb, loyal or disloyal, strong or weak. Carving up the legislative kingdom into 150 slots while balancing party, geography, and bias was difficult enough without extraneous details.

When would it be my turn to be labeled and slotted? The first day of the session, Mavis Doyle pulled me aside. "You're in line for a chairmanship. They'll have to give it to you."

"I don't think I'm ready," I protested, just now absorbing the full significance of my leadership position. I'd better think about this and ask for what I want, I thought to myself, but I may be too late. Maybe my fate has already been decided, in another room, smaller than this one. During one early morning meeting, the Republican leader, Richard Snelling, made a novel suggestion: Why not give both the Republican and Democratic whips a seat on the Appropriations Committee? He liked the balance.

Jim Douglas and I looked at each other. We had served together on Government Operations. Would we take the next step in tandem?

I made a weak effort to suppress my delight; this was a plum appointment. In my first term, I had traced the root of power straight to this committee. Mavis never mentioned the Appropriations Committee without the prefix "powerful." These were the high priests of the legislature, the keepers of the purse who humbled all others. As a member of that committee, I could listen, ask questions, learn, and have a significant impact. But why was it being offered to me? Possibly this was a preemptive strike by Snelling and Candon: give her the Appropriations Committee, treat Jim the same way, and she'll have nothing to complain about.

They were right. I was happy. What neither Snelling nor I could have known was that this seat would give me the credentials, eight years later, to run against him for governor.

At two o'clock that afternoon, flushed with adrenaline, I left the back room, went up the stairs, and stepped into the House chamber to attend the opening joint session of the House and Senate. This would be the last time that Lieutenant Governor Jack Burgess presided. He had been defeated in the 1974 election by a feisty Democratic legislator from Burlington, Brian Burns.

As I waited for Burgess to speak, I was surprised to find myself admiring the man who was making the introduction: Jack O'Brien, the senior senator from Chittenden County, whom I remembered for holding my highway bill hostage. Now Jack sounded like a statesman. "We thank you for your fair leadership and we will miss you." Just the right words.

Burgess was genuinely moved by the long applause that followed. His grateful smile made me feel sorry for him: a defeated public servant with no place to go. A shadow fell on the podium. I caught it, but only fleetingly, not allowing myself to dwell on the fate of this bygone politician who was stepping down just as I was stepping up.

The senator from Caledonia, Graham Newell, rose to present the report of the Canvassing Committee, a vote-counting formality that confirmed the number of popular votes cast for the constitutional officers.

I took pleasure in Newell's precise language. A Lyndon State College professor in a worn tweed jacket, he took his responsibility seriously, exuding a pedantic but welcome decorum. This was an orderly process, where reason and fairness prevailed, his manner implied. On command, the pages began to distribute different-colored paper ballots for each office to the legislators. They assembled near the podium and minutes later dispersed once more to collect them. The Canvassing Committee carefully counted the ballots. The election of each constitutional office was confirmed, as expected.

Two years later, I would see that honored tradition violated. In 1977, the legislature snatched victory away from John Alden, who had won by twelve hundred votes, and handed the election to T. Garry Buckley. Because Alden did not have more than 50 percent of the total, the legislature had the power to decide. Alden had made enemies, switching party allegiance from Republican to Democrat. "But he won fair and square," I told the Speaker, right after the vote was announced. How could the legislators be so devious, so bent on revenge, and not understand that they had committed a cardinal sin by overruling the popular vote? The press raved; the legislators were unrepentant, and Alden lost the election. A year later he left the state. The dark side of this bright chamber had been exposed like a bad tooth made visible only by a wide grin. Once having glimpsed it, I never forgot it was there. When it was my turn to have my gubernatorial election confirmed by the legislature in 1987, I remembered John Alden. Almost no one else did.

Newly anointed in my leadership position, however, I was as trusting as a convert to a new religion. One by one, the vote totals were announced for governor, lieutenant governor, secretary of state, and treasurer. Each time I joined the chorus of applause, savoring the ritual rhythms. Sitting in the visitors' gallery, Linda Burns, wife of the newly elected lieutenant governor, beamed when the vote for her husband was announced. I smiled at her, hoping to connect with her happiness.

Two years later, when Brian Burns would lose the Democratic primary contest for governor to Stella Hackel, I was at what was supposed to be the victory party at the Redwood Motel, where Brian's friends filled two adjoining wood-paneled motel rooms. But everyone knew he would lose, and when the time came, it was as if a man with a severe illness had suddenly expired. Grief arrived on schedule but with unexpected force. I sat on the edge of the double bed, concentrating on fragments of potato chips sinking into the crusted-over onion dip, trying to listen to the early returns. Campaign workers spoke in hushed tones; this was going to be a wake. By ten o'clock, it was over. Brian gave a fine speech. The dreadful part was when Linda broke down and cried, and the two went arm in arm into the other room.

ON NOVEMBER 3, 1976, the day after the election, I left home early to attend the funeral of Robert Branon, a former state senator, Democratic party chairman, agriculture commissioner, father of nine, and prosperous farmer from Fairfield, in Franklin County, one of the few Democratic strongholds of Vermont, populated largely by hardworking French-Canadian dairy farmers who shared political power with the Irish. There were two political fiefdoms, the Howrigans and the Branons; one or the other had always gone to Montpelier. With Robert Branon gone, it would be Francis Howrigan's turn.

The church was packed. Both the winners and losers of yesterday's election were escorted in groups of twos and threes to the VIP section up front. United States senator Patrick Leahy and his wife, Marcelle, arrived with the O'Brien family—Leo and Stella, Danny and Sandy. The newly elected governor, Richard Snelling, was escorted to the front row with his wife, Barbara. Was it the trooper at his side or his new stature that created the energy field around him? A ripple of recognition traveled through the pews as heads turned and necks craned to catch sight of him. Most people in this church had voted for his opponent yesterday; today they wished to be forgiven. "Isn't it an honor for Robert that the governor is here?" the woman behind me said to her husband.

A few feet behind him, the ushers escorted Governor Tom Salmon, last night's loser for the U.S. Senate seat against Robert Stafford. He looked like a boxer just out of the ring, his jacket, a terry towel. He walked slowly and genuflected deeply before stepping sideways into the pew, where he sank down next to his wife, Madge. How quickly power had washed off his body, leaving it heavy where it once had been light. This had been an ugly race; the scars of it were visible on his bent back. Was he lowering his head into his hands in prayer, or was he mourning his loss?

In walked Stella Hackel, who had received the news of her defeat to Richard Snelling only a few hours ago. Hands reached out to her. She smiled and draped her coat over her shoulders. These were the people who had liked her best; she had done well in Franklin County. She seemed happy that it was over. I felt guilty that I had not helped her more. I had been put off by her conservative politics. Only much later, when I ran for governor myself, would I appreciate all the obstacles she had faced.

Two somber rows of legislators filed in and took their seats. Everyone was here. Judge O'Brien, Judge Costello, Dr. O'Brien, the Cains, county Democratic chairmen from every corner of the state. This was the political family, victors and vanquished, now exhausted, sitting down together.

The church was plain: red brick on the outside, whitewashed walls on the inside. The only luxury was the brilliant blue-and-red stained-glass windows, looking startlingly hedonistic here. The donors' names were etched at the bottom: Mr. E. LaChance and Mrs. E. LaChance. In between pauses in the liturgy, I speculated on their first names. Was it lack of space or modesty that had prevented spelling them out?

Two rows of young men stood against the side walls. They stretched their ruddy necks now and again to find comfortable positions within the white circle of their starched collars. I heard a baby gurgle and felt a child's foot banging the back of my pew. I turned around and smiled at the mother, struggling to keep her infant quiet and her little boy still. The whole town had turned out to honor the patriarch. The organ boomed out a few deep chords, and a woman's voice sang out with astonishing power to lead the congregation in "Onward, Christian Soldiers." I was swept up in the surge of sound, claiming the music but not the words. I stared at the flickering candles, breathed the incense, and thought of Madame Bovary.

The organist slowed. The Branon family had begun to come down the aisle: four sons and four daughters, husbands and wives, babies in arms, and grandchildren held by the hand, all in their dark Sunday finery. Mrs. Branon, holding a son's arm, walked proudly, carrying her small, round body ramrod straight. I recalled a discussion we had had not long ago in the ladies' room of the Elks Club in Barre during a legislative dinner. She was in one stall and I in another, and two of Bob Branon's daughters were combing their hair at the sink. She agreed with her husband about the ERA. No need for it. Her daughters disagreed. We had a spirited debate, looked at one another in the mirror, and burst out laughing. "What a place to have this discussion!" we exclaimed all at once.

How, as a widow, would she manage? She was of the generation of women who had never learned how to drive. But I suspected a core of strength supported that plump exterior.

I counted four priests at the altar. The altar boys brought out two golden chalices, a small pitcher, and a covered bowl of wafers. Each move was executed with the precision of the newly tutored who know they are being observed. The priest invited those who wished to do so to take Communion. Two rows formed silently at the head of either aisle. Who was Catholic and who was not? The separation was uncomfortably public. I was grateful that we few Jews could remain seated with the Protestants.

There was no eulogy. The priest's words were spare: "On behalf of the Branon family I would like to thank all the people who came. Robert lived a good Christian life. And now, thank the Lord, the long agony of his suffering is over."

He had died of cancer. I wished I could look at death as a blessing, a return to the Lord.

He remembered to add, "There will be food back at the house. Everybody is welcome."

I stepped out of the church into the cold November air and caught a whiff of manure in the icy breeze. Adjusting to the light, I was startled to face a large red barn situated directly across the road. There was no transition between the church and the land, not even a fence. It seemed as if the church grew out of the earth, like the barn.

We walked to our cars on the blacktop road. I joined the funeral cortege, passing by a mailbox that said MOO ACRES. I stepped carefully, looking for an island of hard snow in the sloppy field of mud surrounding the white burial tent at the gravesite. It was good, I thought, that Robert Branon had died now, before the ground was frozen, so that he could be buried in the land he loved. Here the cemetery blended into the landscape, a quarter of a mile from the church and a quarter of a mile from the farm. And politics was not far removed from either, as rooted in the soil as the stubby yellow cornstalks left in the surrounding brown fields. Branon had taken care of his people, making sure Franklin County received a good share of the state dollar: a new paved road, money for flood relief, more funding for a new vocational school.

Back at the house we feasted on homemade biscuits and chicken fricassee, salad, cupcakes, brownies, and hot coffee. The steamy kitchen exuded warmth and clattered with life. The hand that had given and had taken away had been stayed; here was the power and the glory. There at the gravesite, with his mournful blessing, Father Robert Giroux had washed away all of our sins.

THE RITUAL of the first day of the legislative session was now comfortably familiar. I was a seasoned, second-term legislator. I watched from my seat, number 126, on the upper-left side of the House, as my brother, Representative Edgar May, got up from his seat on the lower right and walked to the well of the House. He had been named to the Canvassing Committee, his first official act. He had been elected to the legislature last November from the town of Springfield, in southern Vermont, where he and his wife had settled after they returned from Paris. He was the first Democrat in memory to be elected from Springfield.

A page dropped a note on my desk. It was from a photographer from the afternoon newspaper the *Barre-Montpelier Times-Argus*. Could he take a picture of the two of us, right after the session, in the House chamber?

"Yes," I wrote back.

We posed in the doorway of the House chamber, brother and sister, side by side. That afternoon, the photograph was printed three columns wide, on the front page. I was startled that they had played it so big. I took the picture home to the family, for the children, who would be excited to see their uncle and mother together on the front page. The two of us looked as thrilled as if we had won the lottery. I looked proud of him, and he looked proud of me. Our grins were surprisingly similar.

As Edgar distributed and collected ballots for the Canvassing Committee, he received warm greetings in return.

"Congratulations, welcome to the club."

"First time we had a Democrat from down there."

"Here to check up on your sister?"

Judy Rosenstreich said to me, after shaking his hand and giving my brother an approving look, "I bet your brother will be Speaker one day."

I did not disagree.

I watched Edgar with admiration from a distance. Up close, I knew he riveted people with his bright-blue eyes and intelligent smile directed right at the person in front of him, exuding uncommon charm.

"I'm happy to be here, thank you, thank you." He smiled. He moved from one seat to the next, collecting ballots and compliments in equal measure, leaving a wake of chatter behind him.

I wondered whether my newly gained power would be eclipsed by my older brother. The thought of becoming, once again, Edgar May's sister was, I confess, upsetting. I was saved from exploring this dire thought when I heard my name called. I was being requested by the Speaker to join the committee to inform the governor that the House was organized and ready for action. Four of us assembled: Tom Candon, Richard Snelling, Jim Douglas, and me. It was hard to keep a serious mien; everyone, even the governor, joked and laughed on the first day of school, and I joined in, giddy with the delight of being a class officer.

Back at my seat, I reassured myself. There would be room for both Edgar and me. I had my own identity here. I had worked for it. My political life was my creation; it had not been bequeathed to me as a sister, mother, or wife. I treasured my title, "Madeleine Kunin, State Representative." (I could not foresee that in time my brother would find it equally disturbing to be "Madeleine Kunin's brother.")

I was Edgar's younger sister by four years, and I had looked up to him for most of my life. We both had come to America as children from Switzerland with our mother in 1940. Because of my father's early death, when Edgar was seven and I was almost three, he played a dual brother-father role, giving his judgment unusual weight. As a child I was not cognizant of the burden this placed on him. I only wanted his approval while simultaneously wanting to free myself from it. I envied him for his ability to rebel against my mother without suffering retribution. I had felt bound by the tender ties of being the good daughter, and then the mother and wife. But here, in the legislature, for the first time I had attained a new if tenuous equilibrium; by day, I was a political person, and at night, a wife and mother. Could he understand the journey I had undertaken to arrive here? How new and fragile my dual life was, and how different, inevitably, it would be from his? Nothing in my life had foretold that I would sit here, in seat 126 in the Vermont House of Representatives, but almost everything had predicted that he would. I wanted to hold on to my place and not give it back, as if we were children fighting over a ball in the playground.

THE PRECISE MOMENT when my brother's life and mine diverged was Mother's Day, 1961. We had arranged to meet for a family celebration at a convenient midway point between the two of us. We decided on Tuttle's bookstore, on Route 7, in the center of Rutland. On that first warm spring Sunday, my brother picked my mother up from her home in Pitts-field, Massachusetts, and my husband and I drove down from our home in Burlington. We met in the store's black-asphalt parking lot.

I stepped out of our car, cradling my perfect, pink-bonneted five-month-old daughter, Julia, in my arms as she squinted in the spring sun. I extended her to my mother and brother like an offering. And my brother held his Pulitzer Prize in his hands. I took the prize and gave him the baby. My mother exclaimed over both. We took pictures, admiring the baby, admiring the prize.

Edgar had received the prize a few days before for a series of articles he had written on the welfare system for the "Buffalo Evening News." He had posed as a welfare recipient to get the inside story. (Later he developed the series into a well-received book, *The Wasted Americans*, which would call him to the attention of President Johnson, who then asked him to serve as inspector general in the War on Poverty.)

Julia had to be nursed. I asked the woman behind the bookstore cash register if I could use a back room to nurse my baby. She obligingly led me to a book-lined storage room that assured me privacy. "It will be nice and quiet here." She smiled. I would not have dreamed, then, of nursing a baby in public.

I loved the smell of books. As Julia made soft, satisfied noises at my breast, I scanned the shelves, drinking in the titles with a thirst of my own. I thought how much my life now differed from my brother's. We had started out on similar tracks. On his advice I had decided to enroll in the Columbia School of Journalism. John Hohenberg had been his journal-ism professor at Columbia; he would become my professor, too. I had agreed. On Hohenberg's advice, Edgar left school and headed for Ver-mont to seek a reporting job. He landed one at a weekly newspaper, the *Bellows Falls Times*. After I graduated from Columbia, Edgar urged me to follow his footsteps. The job market for women reporters in 1957 was limited; almost every opening was on the women's page. I was determined to avoid the narrow niche of society-page reporting that would have kept me entangled in bridal veils and wedding gowns. So when I learned there was an opening for a newspaper reporter at the *Providence Journal* in Rhode Island, I applied. During an interview, the shirtsleeved editor seated behind the maple desk paused, took a drag on his cigarette, leaned forward to look out the window at the asphalt below, turned to me with a worried look, and said, "The last woman we hired got raped in the parking lot."

I blushed as if the fault had been my own. How could I have even thought of working here?

"Oh, that's terrible," I muttered, and clutched my purse.

I applied at the *Washington Post* and the *Washington Star*. The interviews went well. Two weeks before graduation I got a call at ten o'clock in the morning from the *Post*'s editor, Alfred Friendly, Sr. "We're considering three people to fill a reporting job. We've looked over your resume and you're very high on our list. Just wanted to make sure you are still available," he said.

"Yes, yes," I replied, trying to keep my breathlessness a safe distance from the perforated receiver.

"We'll call you back this afternoon."

"Fine, I'll wait for your call. Thank you so much, so much. . . ."

That afternoon I received the call, as promised.

"Miss May?"

"Yes?" I exhaled.

"This is the *Post*. Just wanted to let you know, we decided to give the job to a man."

"Oh, I see. Thank you very much." I hung up without objection. Without rage. None could be expressed because that is how things were expected to be. Instead I turned on myself, certain that my rejection had been my fault, that had I been smarter, I would have gotten the job.

Neither the law nor the language for gender bias had yet been invented. But my experience of it was already quite extensive. While at Columbia, I had applied for a part-time job at the *New York Times*, hoping for a copy-girl job in the newsroom. The personnel director noted on my resume that I had waitressed in the summers while in college and said sweetly, "We don't have anything in the newsroom for you, but I could see if we could get you a waitressing job in the *Times* cafeteria."

I envisioned myself in uniform bringing coffee to my byline heroes—

Clifton Daniel, James Reston, and Meyer Berger. I felt nauseated. "No, thank you," I said, got up, and walked out.

Years later, when I was governor, I caught a glimpse of that dining room when I was on my way to the publisher's dining room, where I was hosted by Arthur Sulzberger at an editorial board luncheon. I could not yet tell the editors and writers assembled around the table that story, but I was able to share a more recent one. Only a few minutes earlier, I and Liz Bankowski, my chief of staff, and the state trooper who accompanied me, wearing civilian clothes, were waiting at the designated door on West Forty-third Street to be escorted into the *New York Times* building. Without a moment's hesitation, the gray-uniformed guard reached for my trooper's hand and said, "Pleasure to meet you, Governor." Young Jim Dimmick smiled with embarrassment and pointed to me.

At Columbia School of Journalism I got a Saturday job on Ninth Avenue, near Forty-second Street, making hero sandwiches at Manganaro's Italian market and sandwich shop. If I was going to wear an apron, I would wear it here instead of the *Times*. I worked side by side with Ernesto, a sad Italian immigrant with patrician features, whose lost dignity I pitied. Behind the Formica counter I could inhale the aroma of espresso, sautéed eggplant, mozzarella, and pungent tomato sauce. The smell lingered on my person long after I had changed out of my beige, brown-trimmed uniform in the dingy beige bathroom, saturated with pink disinfectant.

Here sexism wore no disguise.

"Hey, doll, what are you studying?"

"No kidding!"

Every Saturday, Tony, one of the Saturday regulars who came over for lunch from the garment district, told me, "I bet you're going to be a great authoress someday."

I laughed and said, yes, I hoped so. "But not an authoress, Tony, an *author*, an *author*."

"As far as I'm concerned," he replied in his Brooklyn accent, "you're the best lookin' tomato on Ninth Avenue."

That spring, the publisher of the *Burlington Free Press*, David Howe, and his new son-in-law, J. Warren McClure, came to New York for the annual meeting of the American Newspaper Publishers Association.

Would I be available for an interview?

Yes.

Edgar encouraged me.

This would be a general-assignment reporting job, the two men explained over lunch at their hotel. I would be expected to cover a wide field of subjects, and I would take and develop my own pictures. The weekly salary was seventy dollars, a respectable wage in 1957.

I accepted. It was the first offer I had received that was not on the women's page.

Later my brother would tease me for getting hired by the *Burlington Free Press* when he had not been. Vermont was going to be a way station for me, as it had been for him, he said, before I would go to work on a larger metropolitan paper. My dream was to write for the Paris edition of the *Herald-Tribune*, the *Washington Post*, or the *New York Times*.

While working at the *Free Press*, I met my husband, Dr. Arthur S. Kunin, then a newly appointed thirty-three-year-old instructor at the University of Vermont College of Medicine in Burlington. I was twenty-five. Most of my friends had already gotten married.

I had never doubted that I wanted my life to include marriage, children, *and* a career. Family was important: I wanted to create the mother-father balance I had lost. I had a romantic view of what that life would be, imagining a happy brood of children tumbling over one another, like *The Five Little Peppers and How They Grew*, by Margaret Sidney. I had read all the Nancy Drew mysteries and Gene Stratton Porter's *Girl of the Limberlost*. The heroines of these novels were my heroines. I identified strongly with Elnora Comstock in *Girl of the Limberlost*, whose father died at an early age and who freed herself from her controlling mother when one day she picked up her father's violin and played it against her mother's wishes, revealing a great talent.

"I feel as if you had given my father to me living, so that I could touch him," Elnora exclaims, when she touches the instrument.

As a girl I asked for a violin. On Saturday evenings, sitting in my mother's pink-curtained bedroom, I would take the violin out of its stiff black case lined with maroon crushed velvet and practice in front of her mirror-topped dressing table by the window, trying to tame its strings. I lingered on one long sweet note. Someday I would emerge, transformed and beautiful, like the rare butterflies collected in the great forest by the Girl of the Limberlost.

Journalism promised to be the means of my transformation. The power of my words would propel me into an imagined life. With pencil and pad in hand, I could walk into any room as my brother did. Life would open up to me like a book resting on its spine. I imagined my byline, black and bold at the top of the story, a new medal earned each day.

It was my byline that first intrigued my husband-to-be. He wondered what my real name was, not believing there could be a person named Madeleine May. We met at a dinner party and then again a few days later when I was standing on the steps of the DeGoesbriand Hospital across the street from his office, waiting for a taxi to take me back to the paper. I had a four-pound speed graphic camera in one hand and a three-pound battery to set off the flashbulb strapped into a case, dragging down my other shoulder. He said I looked beleaguered, so he asked me out. It seemed I was being rescued. I was not certain that I wanted to be, just yet. When I found the chance to go to Europe for six months to work as a guide at the Brussels World's Fair, I took it.

On June 21, 1959, Arthur and I were married. As I stood under the canopy in the synagogue and watched my husband stamp on the traditional glass, surrounded by the close circle of our two families, neither of us could foresee what shape our lives would take. I was the happy bride, resplendent in flowing white, he the nervous groom. I smiled at Arthur and took his arm. For one frightening moment, I felt a wave of sadness; had I abandoned a part of myself, here, at the altar? I fought to push such thoughts aside and concentrated on the portrait we formed: bride and groom, arm in arm, walking up the aisle. I had wanted to be married, to be rooted in family and community. His strong love would give my life the center I had yearned for, and I would grow in new ways. But I had felt a tug at my sleeve, the sound of an inner voice that said, Do not abandon the person you dreamed you might become.

We both sensed the dilemma but could not articulate it. Society's expectations overwhelmed us: marriage was the road to fulfillment. How to create separate and shared existences that encompassed two careers and one family was a question that few people then asked, and no one seemed to answer. When I asked it of myself, I felt disloyal and perplexed. Most of my friends had chosen marriage. Those women who hadn't were pitied. Careers were an interim pursuit, before marriage or after. I had discarded that assumption, but I did not know how to replace it with something else.

For the first ten years of our marriage, I was immersed in motherhood, absorbed by the birth of one daughter and three sons. I was generally content with the pattern of my days, which left me little time for reflection. I wove a life that was centered on the family. Satisfaction came from seeing the sunlight illuminate a row of newly canned dill pickles, two dozen jars lined up on the kitchen table. Pleasure came from watching the children cavort under the lawn sprinkler on a hot summer afternoon, and creativity was achieved by sketching, reading, and sewing. I prided myself on making many of my clothes and the children's, matching up the pieces for Raggedy Anne and Raggedy Andy dolls, complete with embroidered hearts. For intellectual diversion, my women friends and I met at the League of Women Voters and gathered in one another's living rooms for the book club.

In our nighttime musings, after the children were in bed, my husband and I talked about the life I had left behind. He understood that our marriage had diverted me from continuing my career and was discomforted with the knowledge that I had temporarily given it up. Perhaps that is why he never made either an overt or subtle attempt to hold me back.

Those who are looking for the formula to combine marriage and career will be disappointed by my revelations. I have no expert advice. Each day we reinvented our lives together and apart as we moved into different stages of marriage, children, careers, and children growing up. Sometimes we happily succeeded; at other times, we painfully failed, and then our lives would diverge, creating a frightening chasm between us that politics widened as it scoured our separate sides. During long periods, we were uncertain of the right course, prompting us to look for new ways of accommodation, again and again. What I gladly share is that my husband was unusually giving of his support to my career. Few other men could have been as generous as Arthur was, not only in rearranging his own life to ease mine, but in taking genuine pride and pleasure in my achievements.

"Are you going to let your wife run for governor?" he was asked one day in the hospital. We laughed about this, knowing that he would never dream of withholding permission, and I would not think of asking for it. But in a sense, this is precisely what he did; he let me run, not by granting his approval, but by giving me courage when I grew afraid, by urging me forward when I wanted to retreat, by cheering my victories and mourning my defeats, and by doing all the small things that made it possible for me to create a political life.

His largest gift was his inner strength, which allowed him to be the companion of a strong woman. Society has little experience with this kind of pairing, a woman and a man. He, too, defied expectations and had to invent a new portrait—of a male political spouse. With good humor he was the first man to integrate the group called the Loyal Legislative Wives in Montpelier, causing some consternation: What would they now call themselves? It was the most spirited debate this organization had that anyone could remember. They settled on Loyal Legislative Spouses, with one abstention.

At the National Governors' Association meetings, he became the favorite of the spouses and privy to the wives' inner circle. He, they knew at once, took them seriously.

Arthur eased into the Kunins' domestic life as I gradually withdrew from it. When I went to Montpelier and the legislature, we gradually shared the cooking. He found a brown bean pot and a recipe for Boston baked beans, his staple until four months later when the children rebelled. Then he discovered a recipe for "stay-a-bed stew," which he shoved into the oven in the morning and took out at night. The turning point in his culinary development came when he took a Chinese-cooking course. Soon, I could no longer compete.

At first I rationalized the change this way: I had assumed the domestic chores for the first ten years of our marriage, when the children had been small, and now it was his turn. But when I was elected governor and my schedule became more demanding, he was doing more than his share. And at the end of a fourteen-hour day in the statehouse, I would return home at night, groping for the light switch, weighed down with my briefcase, fatigued by battle, collapse, and seek the certainty of love in an uncertain world.

Each morning we negotiated the new day, not only planning the menus, but trying to create balance in our lives. After my first term in public office, I felt I had crossed a threshold; I had liberated myself in the Vermont House of Representatives, and I had not been punished for that bold deed. And I could assure both myself and my public that I was a good mother. Ambivalence, however, was never entirely put to rest. At least once a day, I would feel a stab in my chest, thinking I should be at one place when I was at another. I would never slough off that lining of womanly guilt; even when the children grew up, it would always stay inside me. Over time, I learned not to let it overwhelm me, not to let it pull me down, but to carry it as gracefully as I could.

THIS WAS my brave posture when my brother entered the House chamber I had claimed as my own. Ten years after our Mother's Day reunion, I had retrieved a lost part of my life. I should not have been surprised to discover that my choice would be Edgar's choice, too. I had learned what he had to teach, and then took the next step, into public life, by myself.

Now our paths converged because we were, in fact, very much alike, though he came to the political life from a different point on the compass. For me, the legislature marked the beginning of my public life; for him, it was a culmination. He had won the Pulitzer Prize, he had been part of the Washington power elite in the Johnson administration, and he had accompanied Sargent Shriver to his ambassadorial post in Paris. I would congratulate him for each of these achievements from my kitchen, sometimes tucking the telephone receiver between my chin and shoulder while balancing a baby on one hip and stirring tapioca pudding with my free hand. I received the news of his marriage to Louise in Washington from my hospital bed, the morning after the birth of the third Kunin child, Adam.

Here, in this House chamber, for the first time in our adult lives we were seated across from each other in the same official space.

My brother's arrival in the legislature that year also marked a new beginning for him. In 1967 his first wife, Louise, had died in an automobile crash in Springfield, in which he had been severely injured and was hospitalized for four months. When I wept at Louise's funeral, I did not know whether my brother would survive. Every week, I would leave the children with a baby-sitter and take the Greyhound bus from Burlington to Hanover, New Hampshire, to visit him, joining my mother anxiously sitting at his bedside. Months in the hospital had given him time to reflect on the meaning of his life. It was then, I surmised, that he decided to return to Vermont.

I had grieved for him through this painful period and rejoiced with him when he had surmounted it. So his arrival in this chamber was more than a political triumph; it was a victory over the memory of his loss. When we embraced, that is what we silently understood. As I thought about his long voyage, I wondered if he could understand my own. Would he know how my journey had been different from his? The complexity and weight of womanhood gave me less entitlement to a political life, both in my own eyes and, I believed, in the eyes of the public. I wanted him to see my baggage, that heavy, bulging suitcase, filled with baby clothes, diapers, and bottles that I could not leave behind. I had had to stop and rest every so often, afraid that I might never arrive. It had taken great energy to get myself here. Could he possibly know that? Success demanded that I pretend that it had been easy. Here I was, every hair in place, every word out of my mouth correct; the woman who had done it all—children, husband, and a political career. No sweat.

I smiled to myself at this lovely deception, but I was angry, both with my brother and with myself, at my enforced silence. Perhaps I wanted him to do more than understand; I wanted him to leave.

For one awful moment, I envied his attentive, attractive new wife, Judith. They had met in Paris while they were both working at the American embassy, had been married two years ago, and returned to my brother's home in Springfield. When he decided to run for the legislature, they campaigned together door to door, hand in hand. A picture of the two of them appeared after the election in a paid advertisement, thanking the voters for their support. His was the correct boy-girl model.

Stop, grow up! I angrily rebuked myself. This is ridiculous. A fresh wave of guilt washed over me; I hoped no one could read my thoughts. Still, I could not believe there was room for us both.

I WAS WRONG. I retained my position and he gained his. With each new step I took, I was newly surprised that it was possible for us to coexist as civil and loving adults. At times, so was he. Our bond was our mutual affection and the commonality of our beliefs; on most issues we thought and felt alike. Our voting record was so parallel that my brother felt a need to publicly distinguish himself from me. He felt most uncomfortable when there was a roll call. We were called alphabetically, Kunin before May. Whenever we ended up in the same column, which was most of the time, Edgar would hear someone ask with a mischievous grin, "Voting with your sister again, huh Ed?"

One time, before the roll was about to be called, Edgar stood up: "Mr. Speaker, I request that for this vote, the roll be called in reverse." Everyone understood. This was his turn. A vote was taken on whether to reverse the roll call. The ayes had it. The first name to be called was "Zampieri, of Ryegate." Zampieri was nonplussed. He had never had to go first. Having always voted last, he had had the power to either join or defy a trend. Never did he have to start one. Edgar was delighted.

My brother was a persuasive and eloquent speaker. When the appropriations bill was debated on the floor of the House, he successfully took one hundred thousand dollars from the tourism advertising budget and put it into a fuel-subsidy program. As expected, my committee chairman, Emory Hebard, spoke against my brother's motion as something that would unravel the budget. I was in a quandary; should I remain loyal to my chairman or vote with Edgar? I gritted my teeth and voted with Emory. Loyalty first. Immediately I regretted it. I hated voting against my beliefs. Edgar was the hero, and I was in the minority. Back in the committee room, however, I was heroic. Emory knew the significance of my vote. He thanked me. I had won his trust.

"That was a great speech your brother gave. Why don't you talk like him?" a legislator said to me while I was waiting in line in the cafeteria. I shrugged my shoulders and smiled, agreeing it was a fine speech.

Later I learned that after one of our colleagues had criticized my vote, Edgar had vigorously come to my defense. My big brother had protected me. He would always be there when I needed him.

Our political careers continued on a parallel track. In my third term, January 1977, I was named chairman of the powerful Appropriations Committee, the first Democrat and first woman so named. That same year, Edgar became chairman of the Committee on Health and Welfare. The symmetry of our separate positions—sister-brother, Madam Chairman, Mister Chairman, was thrilling for both of us.

That January our two committees held a joint hearing on a Vermont state welfare program we both wanted to protect: one that allowed for payments to indigent two-parent families, called the Unemployed Fathers Program. Vermont was one of twenty-three states that had adopted this optional program. In most states welfare benefits were limited to families headed by single mothers. Governor Snelling had recommended cutting the welfare budget by eliminating payments to fathers.

My committee was sharply divided, and I was adamantly opposed to the change. Eliminating the program would force fathers out of the house for the sole purpose of enabling a single mother to qualify for welfare. Sixty-five percent of the caseload was composed of children; it was they who would suffer.

Maintaining the Unemployed Fathers Program became a personal obsession. (Today I discern the deep personal reason for my passionate defense of the Unemployed Fathers Program; I could never acquiesce to a budget cut that would deprive a child of her father.) It had to survive. Vermont was then a poor state; incomes were well below the national average, particularly in the northern, most rural sections. Poverty was less visible than in an urban slum, but no less harsh for those living in an isolated trailer at the end of a dirt road. Behind the numbers of welfare recipients provided to the committee in computer printouts, I saw the faces of hundreds of listless children, the same children I had seen in the backs of pickup trucks along the parade route on the Fourth of July. But I knew compassion alone would not win my case. I hunted for facts to support my convictions, but after a nationwide search for data, I had only meager results. In the end, I was forced to base my argument on common sense. How could a family benefit if the father was forced to leave home to enable the mother to qualify for welfare payments? Short-term tax-dollar savings would be exceeded by long-term costs.

The joint public hearing on the question was a perfect brother-sister act. As we sat side by side at one long table in room 11, the thrill of sharing the spotlight, of backing each other up at every turn, made me feel that we were perfect siblings. We were sharing. My brother was being generous with me, and I, a mature adult, was treating him with equal respect. As we supported one another with nods and smiles, I felt an exhilarating surge of self-confidence. We were playing a duet, chiming in, harmonizing, each one giving the other some time to show off.

I felt the strength of the new, outer, confident layer of my psyche seeping down into my soul like a warm spring rain; I sat taller, felt warmer, and shed artifice like an old winter coat. I became the person I had rehearsed to be, because the words that came out of my mouth were rooted in the depths of my feeling. The intensity of my defense of the Unemployed Fathers Program made me feel I knew all there was to know on this question, and my recommendation, therefore, became the only possible course—a certainty that would throttle the opposition. Never had I felt so completely in control as when Edgar and I reinforced each other. What otherwise would have been an argument became a truth when our separate arguments converged. And I gained a clearer understanding of the mystery of leadership; it was the power to argue, to persuade, and it resided in an internal space that was shaped by reason and ignited by passion.

But in the end the vote was alarmingly close. Both my committee and his voted 6 to 5 to maintain the Unemployed Fathers Program; the margin was equally close on the floor of the House. Privately, I considered it my most important victory, and Edgar did as well.

In 1978, when I was elected lieutenant governor, Edgar moved over to the Senate. When I was elected governor in 1984 he was appointed chairman of the Senate Appropriations Committee, where he was alternately an opponent and an ally of my administration. Edgar felt increasing pressure from his Senate peers to put distance between us, not only as siblings, but also as the separate legislative and executive powers.

Sometimes the friction between us was obvious. For example, during my first term as governor, I advocated the construction of a juvenile detention center that he opposed. Several years before, in the spirit of deinstitutionalization, the state had closed the old reformatory, but the need

for a small, secure facility had become evident; Edgar and others predicted that the new juvenile detention center would be ineffective, even
harmful.

At one morning staff meeting I shared my frustration over my brother's
persistent opposition.

"This all started," I explained to my staff with a smile, "when I was five
years old and Edgar took apart my blue tricycle. I used to ride it round
and round, in a little park that circled the church steeple. When he
couldn't put my tricycle back together again, I was crushed."

"You never forgave him, right?"

"Right." I laughed. "And that's why we have to win this one now."

The tricycle became folklore: a code word for "sibling rivalry."

"I would never let my kid sister tell me off," Ralph Wright, then
Speaker of the House, told me the next morning. Ralph saw me as beating
up my brother, and Edgar had his sympathy. But every woman who had
a big brother gave me hers. After several fierce battles, some of which I
lost, the detention center was approved. Thereafter, both Edgar and I
were relieved not to have to discuss it again.

My brother's greatest gift to me was that he had chosen to live the life
that I, too, wanted to live. Through his own actions, he legitimized my
tentative course. What might have remained a fantasy without his flesh-
and-blood corroboration became a reality. A political life that would
have seemed out of reach became accessible because he was living it.

My competitive sense had always let me envision myself acting like
him. He was courageous; I would become courageous. He spoke; I could
speak. Even when I spoke first, I sometimes knew that he would follow
with words that either confirmed or contradicted mine. We were sometimes a chorus, speaking in the same rhythm, ending on cue. Sometimes
we argued. That is when I acquired the skills that mattered most. With
my brother as my foil, I learned to disagree, defend myself, and develop
my own voice. I discovered the force of my anger and my capacity to cope
with his. Frightening as such encounters were, their heat did not shrivel
me. They made me expand. My brother inspired sufficient fear and awe
to force me not only to become like him, but to distinguish myself from
him, to develop my own capacities in my own way—to become who I am.
I became emancipated, free to develop into a political woman, to some
degree both despite and because of my brother.

If we had come of political age ten years earlier, our roles might have
been reversed; my brother, I surmise, would have been elected governor,
and I would have been in an ancillary position. Like the yellow-and-black

octagonal street sign depicting the older brother leading his younger sister across the street, we would have conformed to the picture of our time.

Today we both knew that the usual boy-girl sequence no longer was universal. Anything was possible. Older sisters could help younger brothers across the street. And older brothers could allow their sisters to get in front of them. The rigid design of our childhood had been relaxed—in part because of the women's movement, which had allowed us to rearrange our configuration and which made both of us sense the injustice of traditional expectations. Cognizant of the new wave of gender egalitarianism, Edgar did not want to see himself cast in the role of oppressor. Our very closeness told him that my passion for political life was as strong as his and deserved equal expression. His brotherly protective role was not, then, the strong protecting the weak but quite the opposite. His brotherly love made him the protector of my right to achieve political equality.

My brother and I often argued about feminism; many of the recent changes in the relationship between men and women were difficult for him. He had been brought up with traditional views of gender roles, and at an early age had been forced to become the protector of both his mother and his sister. Yet now he relished the excitement of seeing "my kid sister" defy society's expectations.

"I tell you, you're going to win," he told me shortly before I became lieutenant governor. "I met this dyed-in-the-wool Republican at the Legion—an old-time Vermonter—and you know what he told me? He said, 'I never voted for a Democrat before. Never thought I'd vote for a woman, but I'm going to vote for your sister. That's right, I'm going to vote for her. It's about time we had a woman, I say, give her a chance.' That's what he said." My brother repeated, " 'Never thought I'd vote for a woman.' I tell you, you've got it. If he votes for you, anybody will."

No one was quite as proud of me as my brother. When we campaigned together once at the shopping center in Springfield he said, "I'd like you to meet my sister, she's running for governor." And I would chime in, for the few who didn't know him, "And this is my brother, and he's running for the state Senate." We'd both smile with delight—first your turn, then my turn, up and down on the seesaw. Sometimes, I had to pull back. He was so enthusiastic, so overwhelming, that if we campaigned side by side too long, all I did was nod and grin.

By myself, I found my voice again.

*   *   *

IN THE LEGISLATURE I established my place as a member of the Appropriations Committee, where I was ensconced from morning to night. I had accepted the appointment with trepidation; math had been my weakest subject, and like many women students of my era, I was plagued by fear of math. Instead of numbers, I told myself, I liked words. My major at the University of Massachusetts had been history. My master's degree at the University of Vermont was in English literature. I had studied what I had enjoyed. But walking into the Appropriations Committee room on the second floor of the statehouse that first morning was like entering the vault of a bank. These were the guards, each one seated at a long oak table behind a two-foot pile of papers, who had read and memorized every word and number. No one smiled, except for Edward Conlin from Windsor, who gave me a wink. I recalled his civic-minded prisoners and smiled back. We faced the chairman, Emory Hebard, who proceeded to address the three new members like students from another class who had been transferred for poor behavior. The work load would be heavy. Attendance was of prime importance.

"We'll expect you to be here at eight o'clock sharp each morning and count on staying until five or six. This committee works," Emory said, making his disdain for all other committees clear.

The Appropriations Committee was seated on the Mount Olympus of the legislative hierarchy; it controlled the purse. The governor's budget, which he and his cabinet had completed, was sent here, where it was deconstructed line by line. The recommendations of the committee to the full House membership carried great weight. From the House floor, the budget was sent to the Senate Appropriations Committee, where the same process took place. The difference between the two houses was negotiated in a joint House-Senate Committee of Conference, composed of three members from each legislative body.

But the Appropriations Committee's power was not limited to the budget. Every bill that carried an appropriation was automatically sent to this committee, where it could be amended, rejected, or approved. My legislative peers looked at me with new deference—my help might be needed to win passage of their bills.

After a month, I learned to read budget numbers like words and find meaning between the lines. I compared the budget book to abstract art: the longer you looked at it, the more you could see. It took concentration. I learned to compare one budget with another, one year with the next, to look for trends and aberrations. In my search for truth, however, I was disappointed. I had expected to find crisp answers in my new world of numbers. Unlike prose, mathematics was precise. Either it added up or it didn't. No room for finessing.

To my surprise, the budgetary process was less structured than a sonnet. Figures could be moved around the page like free verse, without rhyme or meter. Numbers were like metaphors, open to interpretation. The budget was not equivalent to a math problem with only one correct answer. It was a highly subjective document, hammered together by hundreds of hands, both public and private, each with an imprint of personal preference and public obligation. There was a truth hidden here, but rather than being sharp, it was dull. If read correctly, this gray columned document revealed in infinitesimal detail the cumulative values of its many authors, as well as the labyrinthine structure of state government itself.

Nineteen seventy-five was a recession year; the committee's goal was to produce a level-funded budget, which meant no increase from one year to the next, not even for inflation, which was then running in the double digits. I listened to the chairman's questions posed to all the agency secretaries and department heads as they sat at the far end of the table and anxiously spelled out their budget needs. "Can you live within the governor's budget?"

"How would you handle an across-the-board cut of five percent, ten percent?"

I learned to respect the power of a question, probing, like a surgeon. Those who knew the trouble spots in advance could poke until the patient grimaced. And I tried to pull back the many layers of bureaucracy one by one. What was going on underneath? Always, there was another layer. The committee's questioning and the administration's defense of its budget could turn this into a contest. How many new positions were necessary to run a new program, five or ten? Or could existing staff be transferred and retrained? They would argue for ten, we would urge none, and compromise on five, splitting the difference. With each question I posed, I learned more, building up an encyclopedic knowledge of state government, which I would draw upon when I became governor. Money, I concluded, drove policy.

For the first few weeks of committee hearings, our discussions were hypothetical—a comfortable agency-by-agency analysis. Then it was time to vote: yes or no; give or take away. The numbers assumed new characteristics as tension in the committee mounted: they were either good or evil. To my consternation, the pile of papers I had accumulated contained only a meager collection of helpful facts. Never did I think I knew enough to make a completely intelligent and fair judgment. There was little time to weigh one option against another. The chairman, with a relentless discipline, kept the process moving from one line item to the next. I hated the pace. I didn't want to make decisions in haste. In desperation, I returned to what I knew best, my own judgment about issues that I believed were most important—education, programs for children, the environment—then I would find the facts to back me up. Sifting through geologic layers of information, I was thrilled when I could extract a treasured piece of information and place it on the table: exhibit A. Sometimes my colleagues were convinced, and more dollars were added to education. Other times, I achieved little or nothing except a contrary opinion.

Always, I had my turn to speak. That, I concluded, was my greatest power: to be seated at the table where I was part of the debate, and my greatest contribution was to fight fiercely for what I wanted. Each committee member had begun to stake out his or her territory; I had mine. It took tremendous psychic energy to argue and political skills to achieve results. I had to give if I was to receive. I learned to develop compromises, which sometimes worked and sometimes didn't. Always my private question was, How much should I compromise? When should I hold firm? When must I give up? To my surprise, some winning compromises were more creative and effective than the original proposals I had made.

In addition to meeting my own expectations, I felt the responsibility of acting on behalf of others. As the most progressive member of the committee, I was expected to be the strongest defender of the poor, of women, of children, of the environment. Some expectations I could dismiss because they seemed to reflect narrow special interests, others I wished to meet because they truly reflected my deeply held beliefs. When I first was elected to the legislature, my political portfolio was limited; increasingly, over time, it became more varied and diverse. There was no issue I could abstain from that demanded a vote. Few issues were as simple as they seemed at first glance; neither did they lend themselves to conservative or liberal labeling. Yet having to vote yes or no forced a simplification of the most complex issues and sharply defined my values. An issue had to be abstracted to its essentials for me to cast a vote, but to vote correctly, I had to retain the complexity of the issue at hand, as well as place it in a larger framework of fundamental principles, such as fairness and justice. When I look back, I see that this is how my political philosophy expanded, deepened, and evolved. No doubt my personal history played a part; as a child who emigrated from Europe with my brother and mother at the outbreak of World War II because of Hitler, I knew the potential for the abuse of political power, as well as the possibility of protection and opportunity that the political structure offered. That is what our family found in America. As a result, I believed that government—if it used power correctly—could provide the same opportunities for others to live a better life as it did for me. These were the rays of light that I looked for as I scrutinized the budget and reviewed legislation. But I learned to be tough on implementation; good intentions were not enough; programs had to work. Often the guiding principle was reduced to asking: "Whom will it help and whom will it hurt?"

As we struggled with our decisions, we knew that beyond the microcosm of our committee lay another political hurdle: the members of the House. What kind of legislation would be acceptable on the floor? Emory Hebard reminded us daily that we had to keep the endgame in mind; what did we have to bargain with when we confronted the senators in the Committee of Conference? These were the considerations that guided our decisions. Every number was annotated with a story, a threat, a promise, a possible deal. Coalitions were made and broken, and made again. Trading was open but usually made to look like camaraderie. Was that the real power of being on the committee, having a chit to bargain with? I detested that conclusion, but reluctantly acknowledged its reality.

At the end of each day, exhausted, I felt uneasy about some of my decisions, but I had no time to look back. I had to prepare for tomorrow.

When a nervous administrator of some state agency took the seat at the foot of the table, what we laughingly called the hot seat, I understood the power of this committee. As he faced a barrage of questions from the stern-faced members around the table, I wondered if he hated us for what we could do to him. In his eyes, we were wardens of the worst kind. I vowed not to exploit his captivity by making him squirm.

Yet I, too, was capable of pursuing a line of questioning with ferocity when I sensed a quarry. With shock, I discovered a tendency to show off my knowledge, to play to the press, to flex my muscle. I pulled back, fearing the raw arrogance of my power. I watched Emory. He was quick. I learned from him; he absorbed information and came up with solutions with rapid-fire certainty, some good, some bad. He did not pause for doubt. I had to be alert, ready to agree or disagree with him at a moment's notice, and my skills were honed on the sharp edge of his mind.

Emory Hebard was my mentor, but neither he nor I knew it at the time. He was not a feminist. When he once referred to a fifty-year-old secretary who had worked for state government for thirty years as a "nice girl," I bristled, reminded him that she was old enough to be a woman, and glared at my colleague Jane Gardner, sitting next to me, who trilled, "Oh, Emory, I love to be called a girl."

But Emory was truly gender neutral. He did not see me as a woman first, but as a brain. He fostered my growth. In time, we developed great mutual admiration and trust. He gave me what a mentor must give: responsibility. Without him, I doubt that I could have taken the next step and become chairman of the Appropriations Committee, a position that qualified me to run for governor.

After weeks of painful deliberation, the night we finished marking up the budget I felt a surprising elation. It was done. We had decided. The agony of decision making was over, and this was our reward—this odd sense of completion. We had given and we had taken away according to our collective judgment. No one thought it had been perfect. But a structure had emerged called a budget, creating a semblance of order from the chaos of competing interests and demands. It was satisfying. Unlike life itself, which often meanders lazily around tough questions, the political process mandates that these questions be decided. It provides resolution, illusory as that may be. The finality of decision making offers a momentary but welcome release from conflict and uncertainty. Ironically, only by engaging in battle could I savor its aftermath.

Each day on the Appropriations Committee, I increasingly knew that my tenure here was providing me with an extraordinary education in two subjects: the bureaucracy and the political process that had shaped it. I wondered if I would ever have a chance to use what I had learned.

After a few weeks, Emory had sized me up and decided to groom me to sit on the three-member Committee of Conference that would hammer out the differences between the House and Senate versions of the bill. To avoid partisan criticism, he had to include a Democrat, and I would be that Democrat. He and Douglas Tudhope would hold down the Republican side, although neither man was a staunch partisan.

Emory treated me as an equal. I caught on and I was loyal. He, in turn, was fearlessly loyal to me. There had never before been a woman on the Committee of Conference, and Emory was certain that John Boylan, the conservative Senate Appropriations Committee chairman from the Northeast Kingdom, would be disarmed by the presence of "a lady on the committee." I became Emory's not-so-secret weapon.

The differences between the House and Senate budgets that year were significant. The Senate had cut deeply into the budget, eliminating programs that the House was determined to save. The battle line on the Committee of Conference was clear: we three House members were there to defend our side down to the last nickel.

When I walked into the first meeting of the Committee of Conference on the budget, I smelled a new, gray scent of power. Within the statehouse walls, the freewheeling power of 180 legislators was now concentrated down to six legislators. We three House members took our seats on one side of the table, and the three senators took theirs on the opposite side. We congratulated ourselves that we had won the first draw; the Conference Committee was meeting on our turf, the House committee room. Whatever budget the Conference Committee agreed on would become enshrined in law as the 1976 fiscal year budget of the state of Vermont. The proverbial buck, which we had tossed back and forth in the committee, would stop here. As I sat in my seat, I longed to turn to someone else, a "they" to blame for what might go wrong. I looked behind me, saw a row of lobbyists and legislators, and knew from the looks piercing my back that I was "they." There, against the wall, sat Lorraine and Esther Sorrell, giving me a thumbs-up. They had come specifically to cheer me on.

Only one thing to do, I told myself, fight like hell. We did. Emory made a flat offer—to restore half a million dollars to the human services budget—and caught them off guard with this round number. Boylan turned to Gannett, his right-hand man. We three smiled at one another, waiting for their reply. They would have to think about it. Hurray!

Late the next day Boylan took out his cigar, leaned back in his seat, and lit up. It was a deal. Jokingly, he offered me a puff, which I refused, as expected.

In 1976, Emory Hebard was elected state treasurer. When the Democratic leadership asked his advice, he recommended me to be his successor on the Appropriations Committee. That was not what Timothy O'Connor and Tom Candon had wanted to hear. Of course they knew they had to appoint a Democratic chairman to the committee. The Democratic leader and the Democratic Speaker, blessed with a Democratic majority in the House and given this vacant chairmanship, had no excuse. I was not the ranking member, but I was, according to Emory, the most qualified.

Visibly uneasy, they told me they wanted a private word with me. It seemed more comfortable for them to do this together. Could I join them in the Speaker's office?

"Of course," I said.

After he closed the door behind him, O'Connor said, "Here's the list we're thinking of for the Appropriations Committee."

I scanned it and saw my name at the top.

"Do you think you can do it?" he asked, anxiety etched in every line of his face. He hated to do this. Candon, his buddy, didn't like it any better. But as I saw Candon resign himself to this inevitability, I found myself thinking, He's kind of a nice guy after all.

As soon as my mind processed the fact that he was asking me to chair the Appropriations Committee, I said yes as quickly as I could before I might give in to doubt.

I told myself, Never mind that you're scared shitless. Fake it.

It worked.

I got it.

Congratulations all around.

Politics is fun when you win, I concluded as I sailed out of the room.

Two minutes later, in the corridor of the statehouse, I ran into Jim Finneran, the senior member of the lobbyist corps. He called out, "Congratulations, Madeleine." And then added with a wicked smile, "You know, we're going to be watching you."

And they did. Two things I knew I must never do: lose my temper or cry. I knew what I had to do: hold the committee together; never let them break ranks.

I had noted one name especially on Tim's list: Orrin Beattie, a master of political gamesmanship. I was a delight to him when I sat at his feet; but once I declared my independence and moved to Emory's committee our relationship had become strained. When the House had been controlled by a Republican Speaker, Peanut Kennedy, Orrin had wielded significant power, but now, the tables had turned; with Democrats in control, he not only was stripped of his chairmanship, but assigned to serve under me, his former pupil. I felt uneasy. Orrin might be trouble. (In fact, he was not and accepted his new role with grace.) I would have the help of Lorraine Graham, another member of the committee, whose generous loyalty would be valuable. "You can do it." She smiled the minute she found out I had been chosen.

By virtue of my chairmanship, I became a member of another elite: the Joint Fiscal Committee. This committee, composed of the chairs of the House and Senate money committees, was almost like a mini-legislature with the power to make financial decisions when the full legislature was out of session. The chairmanship rotated between the Senate and the

House. It was now the House's turn, leading me to assume that it would come to me.

I arrived for my first meeting at the appointed time. The moment I entered the room, I knew from the exchange of glances that I had missed something: the private meeting that had been held prior to this one.

"Nominations?" a voice asked.

Without a moment's pause, I heard: "I nominate Mr. Giuliani, chairman of the House Ways and Means Committee, as chairman."

"Second?"

"Second."

"All those in favor?"

"Congratulations, Peter," the boys said, smiling broadly.

"I nominate Representative Kunin for secretary," a member said with a smile.

"I refuse," I said, to my surprise, feeling my color rising.

"Well, if you don't want to do that," Peter Giuliani said, then paused for a moment, "we can make you chairman of the entertainment committee."

I turned beet red. I could not speak. I could only turn to Ginny, the secretary taking minutes, who looked up from her notepad in time for us to exchange a look. Thank God, she understood.

I vowed never to be unprepared again.

A few hours later, I met Peter in the hallway. I asked him to step aside with me. Terrified and furious both, I riveted my eyes on him. "I resented your remark," I said. "It was uncalled for."

He looked dismayed. "I . . . I didn't mean anything, Madeleine."

"It meant something to me. I want an apology."

"Well, sure, if that's the way you feel about it, but honestly, dear, I didn't mean a thing."

I escaped into the ladies' room and mouthed silently, That son of a bitch, that bastard . . . , and then I cried.

My furor was dangerous. I was afraid of myself. I dared not encounter anyone.

It would never end. No matter how far I got, how close to the inner sanctum I came, I would always be vulnerable. My only solace was that I had spoken out, I had told Peter Giuliani how I felt, and he, in turn, tried to understand me as best he could.

"I love you, doll." The note was dropped on my desk by a page a minute after I had given a speech in favor of a motion that had supported Giuliani's Ways and Means Committee. The motion had carried. The note was signed "Peter." I had to laugh. This was the only way Peter Giuliani could talk to me. After I voted against him on the next roll call, I wrote back, "For how long?" He wrote back, "I still love you."

Was this his way of saying he was sorry? Because my anger had been so fierce, I wanted it to dissipate as much as he did.

A week later, I concluded that my feminism seemed to have settled down. I could cope as a woman politician. I had learned to assert myself when necessary without letting sexist incidents divert me from the larger agenda. I felt safe. Just under my skin, however, a subtle feminist pulse continued to beat. I realized it would be there always; it was part of my physiology. Most of the day that hidden pulse maintained a steady beat under my public voice. The slightest stimulus, however, could accelerate it. Then I felt it pump like a huge bellows, certain everyone could hear it throb.

That was how I reacted during my second term in the legislature when I was told that there was a move to rescind Vermont's ratification of the Equal Rights Amendment. How could they do that? We had already fought that battle. I interpreted the move as an effort to put women back in their place, and I took it personally. "I know I am equal, you can never take that away from me," I argued with the imaginary opponent, the idiot.

The motion to rescind, after much effort, was defeated.

The most blatant forms of sexism were easily countered, as when a male colleague looked me up and down, exposing me to his crude scrutiny for the second time. I confronted him: "I don't like the way you look at me. Could you please stop it?"

He looked amazed, stammered something, and walked off. I was exceedingly proud of myself.

It was the nuances that were difficult. In the 1970s, language was changing. The difference between addressing women as "girls" or "women" became the Maginot Line of feminism. In 1974, when Governor Thomas Salmon greeted Chittenden County Democratic leader Carolyn Adler and me at the airport in Kansas City, site of the midterm National Democratic Convention, with "Hello, girls," I did not know what to say. Should I smile and shake his hand or correct him? Carolyn and I discussed the women and girl issue at length in our room. She thought it was an outrage and I agreed.

That evening the governor hosted a cocktail party in his hotel suite. I approached one of his commissioners and said, "Could you let the governor know that we prefer to be called women and not girls?"

Don hesitated. "I think it would be better coming from you."

Just then the governor rose to give a toast and announced that he did not want to be called chairman of the Vermont delegation, he wanted to be called chairperson.

I looked at Carolyn for a signal; this was our opening. But Carolyn had become invisible. Here goes, I said to myself as I stood up. "Governor, I'll be glad to call you chairperson if you don't call us girls. We would like to be called women."

Salmon looked surprised. Before he could respond, Wyn Kernstock, a convention delegate and a professor of political science, picked up the beat. "Madeleine, do you approve of the word 'manageable,' or should it be 'personageable'?"

I grimaced.

Jim Finneran, the lobbyist whom I liked least, took my side. "It's absurd to carry it this far! Leave her alone." I sent him a grateful smile.

Back in the privacy of our room, I agonized over my words. Carolyn congratulated me. "You were absolutely right," she said. I wondered, Where were you, Carolyn, why me?

That night I dreamed that I was standing at the kitchen sink doing dishes at a potluck Democratic dinner. Several politicians I knew were sitting at a nearby table. Suddenly I vented my anger and yelled, "Why don't you help with the dishes, I'm tired of doing this!"

Immediately, I felt guilty. Ah, now they know the feelings I really harbor, all that women's lib stuff, I thought to myself.

"Do you think I've made them angry?" I asked the woman next to me, an old-time party worker who had been doing this for years.

"I think you did," she replied.

One of the politicians at the table turned to me and said, "We'll get some kids to come in and help you."

It was true. I had been doing child's work.

My anger could best be expressed in dreams, but in the daylight, I retrieved my self-control and slipped it over my head like a garment.

I worked hard in the session, during which I chaired the Appropriations Committee, reaching states of exhaustion and emotional fragility that I wished no one else to see. There were moments of elation and times of frustration. When the transportation bill came before our committee, for example, the smell of pork was so strong that it was as if a roast suckling pig had been placed in the middle of the table and every member had reached for the carving knife at once. I was proud that I never lost my cool, but knew that I had come very close.

One floor fight I lost concerned an amendment to the supplemental-appropriations bill—midyear adjustments to the previous year's budget—to fund an addition to the University of Vermont gymnasium. Opponents had reduced the issue to being about "tennis courts for rich out-of-state kids," while supporters argued that the addition would give equal athletic facilities to women and men. A reporter from the *Rutland Herald*, Christopher Conte, wrote the gymnasium "debacle" was a defeat for the Appropriations Committee and that some of the legislators had "thought privately that the reason was dissatisfaction with the chairman."

I was stung. I sought him out, told him his story was unfair, based on anonymous sources. No sooner were the words out of my mouth than I wondered if I had made things worse. For a moment I thought I would cry, and I quickly left. Running into my brother I released my fury to him, grateful for the safe outlet he provided.

I wondered about my thin skin. When would I be able to cope with such exposure and, if so, how? I began to understand the awesome power of the press to define a politician. As a key player, I was an object, vulnerable to its interpretation of my motives, successes, and failures. And the influence of the press would grow in direct proportion to my political success: the higher I got, the greater the heat. The press and I were no longer on the same side, as Mavis Doyle and I once had been, coconspirators against the system, when I was a freshman legislator and she cheered me on. Now I was in the system. Power gave me the right to decide, and it gave the press the right to criticize. Theoretically, I knew this created a healthy tension. Realistically, I responded with almost visceral pain. It was my deepest fear to be regarded as a weak woman, and therefore a weak chairman. I was equally angry about the cowardly anonymous source who would whisper such accusations. I had not achieved total loyalty. I wondered if Conte, perhaps unconsciously, was driven by sex-stereotypical expectations: Did he assume that the first woman to chair the Appropriations Committee would have difficulty in exercising control? Was that what he was looking for?

Stop. You're paranoid, I told myself, and vowed not to be surprised by anything in the press; I should be grateful when they were kind and ignore them when they were cruel. I repeated to myself, You must not respond to unfair accusations. But I knew myself better. I thought I would never build up the necessary calluses. I asked myself, Do I find this more difficult because I am a woman?

Many years later, talking about this question, one woman answered me by describing how her son got ready for his hockey game. First he put on his shoulder pads, then his knee pads, then his helmet, until he had assembled all the protective layers he needed against injury in a fall. He and his mother expected him to get hurt, and were fully prepared. It is these layers that we women had not been taught to wear. "Be careful, don't run, walk, or you'll fall and get hurt," is what we had been told. And when we skinned our knees, we cried.

The night before I was to present the budget on the House floor in 1977, where it would be voted up or down, I acknowledged my terror. What if I lost control of the process? Worse yet, what if there was a move to send the bill back to committee? How much of a partisan fight would there be? Governor Snelling had called a press conference that day specifically to attack our budget, calling it irresponsible. Five minutes later, a reporter was asking for my response.

"He said that?" I asked in disbelief. How could he? The budget, in my view, was a beautifully crafted work of art, the result of months of negotiations. Most of the governor's recommendations were intact, I pointed out. He, of course, focused on those that were not.

This was the usual struggle between the executive and legislative branches.

Three days later, on March 30, the appropriations bill passed the House. "What a relief. It was like having a baby," I said to Lorraine, right after adjournment. "I have never felt so good." Legislators came up to congratulate me. I thanked every member of my committee, even hugged some of them.

In the euphoria of victory, I concluded that the committee had worked well together. Minutes before we went on the floor, I had given the members my before-the-game locker-room pep talk, as I had gleaned it from the movies. Only one member had voted against the bill, and I decided to ignore him. Orrin had stayed with us on the Big One. Happiness was winning the game. Happiness was also maintaining the Unemployed Fathers Program, preserving the welfare budget, and not doing damage to education or the environmental agency.

I took special pleasure in an article published in the *Rutland Herald* in which Christopher Conte, my old nemesis, wrote that I was proving myself as a committee chairman.

I KNEW that as a political woman I was seen as being responsible for the actions of all women. Years before, during an evening public hearing on the ratification of the Equal Rights Amendment (the House had already

passed it and now the measure was before the Senate), the House chamber was packed with people who wished to testify on one side or the
other. While I looked down from the balcony, a woman approached the
microphone with Bible in hand. She wore no makeup and was dressed in
a simple navy-blue Sunday church dress with a white lace collar. She
spoke softly, but firmly.

"It says in the Bible that woman was carved from Adam's rib; that is
God's truth. Those who promote equal rights will suffer for their sins in
hell."

A gasp went up from the women activists seated near me.

"Do you feel there is any need for this amendment to achieve equal pay
in the workplace?" one of the senators kindly asked.

"No, sir. When I need a raise, I just go to my boss and ask for it," she
said with beatific innocence.

An audible hiss was heard in the balcony, followed by snickers.

Danny DeBonis leapt to his feet, came over to me, and pointed his
finger in my chest. "You tell those women of yours, if they make fun of
that girl once more, the Equal Rights Amendment is going down in
flames. If I had another chance, I'd vote against it, right now."

I rushed over to the women. "Keep quiet, you're going to ruin it for us.
The legislators are getting mad," I whispered like a headmistress. Only
later did I ask myself, Why did I accept responsibility for their behavior?
There was no rational reason. I had exhibited a reflex familiar to all
outsiders who want to become insiders. I had wanted to blend into the
environment, so that no one would notice I was there. Laughter and
rudeness are dangerous attention getters. The performance of outsiders
must demonstrate not only that we are just as good as those who have a
historic territorial claim, but that we may well be better. For too long we
have feared that if one woman, one black, one Jew, or one Hispanic
makes a mistake, we will all be punished.

The cure for such paranoia, of course, is to invade the new turf in huge
numbers. Once there were lots of women, it would be hard to keep track.
By 1990, more than one-third of the Vermont legislature was female, as
diverse a group as an equivalent group of men. No one woman would be
asked to control the women.

But as chairman of the House Appropriations Committee, I had no
refuge in numbers. I was alone, the first woman and the first Democrat to
chair the committee. Not only did I have to be competent, I had to be
good enough to open the doors for other women whose faces and names
I would never know. My anxiety increased as a result of the added burden

I had created, but so did my enthusiasm, and as a consequence my performance improved.

Even as I was learning how to become an effective politician, I had to remember that, whether by accident or design, I *was* becoming a role model for other women. After my first year in public office in 1973, Judy Rosenstreich and I were invited to the Eagleton Institute of Politics at Rutgers University to speak to a class on women in politics. At dinner, I sat next to a woman who looked as if she had stepped out of a New England family portrait; her cropped gray hair made her look powerfully prim. She told me her name was Mary Bunting.

"Are you *the* Mary Bunting, the president of Radcliffe?" I asked excitedly.

"Yes." She nodded.

I recalled having read about her when she first was dean of Douglass College at Rutgers University in 1955. I was drawn to her biography in the *New York Times* because she was the mother of five children and married to a physician. If she could marry a doctor, have all these children, and be president of a college, I could do something with my life.

The famous Mary Bunting drove Judy and me to our dormitory, helping us find our rooms and get settled. The next day we each made our presentations to the class. I thought I should reveal my doubts and conflicts, and I told the students about being elected to office despite my hesitations. Judy, on the other hand, exuded the confidence I wished I had. She talked of "changing aspirations." As we described our work in the legislature, I lost my shyness and enjoyed the exchange as I felt the students respond.

A student whom I had met at the dinner right before came up to me afterward and said, "You inspired me." As I looked at her young, eager face, I thought, You will be much better at this than I am. She had told me that she wanted to go to law school. She would plan her career carefully, figure out when to marry and have children, and avoid the conflicts experienced by women like me.

That April, I was invited to participate in another panel discussion at a conference on women in politics at Mount Holyoke College. I had never been on this campus during the four years I was a student at the University of Massachusetts, in nearby Amherst. I felt fortunate to go there, rather than North Adams State Teachers College, where I first thought to go. A one-hundred-dollar scholarship from the local merchants' bureau (enough for the first year's tuition) made the difference. The rest of my college expenses were earned by waitressing summers and holding part-time jobs during the school year, not unusual then for many of my friends at the state university. Mount Holyoke, Smith, and Amherst were the Ivy League. The chasm between us was enormous. I never forgot my freshman encounter with an Amherst student at a party at the Lord Jeffrey Amherst Club. Beer in hand, he approached me with the usual opener, "Tell me, where do you go to school?"

"The University of Massachusetts." I smiled expectantly.

There was a pause. He looked down from his great tweedy height, squinted through his glasses, and remarked in his Brahmin voice, "Oh, how interesting."

Twenty-two years later, I could marvel at Mount Holyoke's manicured campus, where couples were canoeing on a lily-decked pond. I had gotten here not because of money, or family, or rare intelligence, but as a result of the quixotic electoral process. What a great leveler political power was!

The buffet dinner featured a large oval platter of mashed sweet potatoes shaped like a pig. I turned to the person behind me. "Male chauvinist?" We both giggled.

That evening, I met my first woman mayor, Patience Latting of Oklahoma City, population 380,000. She was dressed as plainly as a pilgrim and exuded a quiet strength that I took to be another model of feminism, in contrast to that of Congresswoman Bella Abzug, the woman who had given the keynote address.

Bella had made a theatrical entrance into the auditorium. "So this is South Hadley?" she said in mock disbelief, with her version of a Lauren Bacall voice. This could have been the opening line from a play in summer stock. Bella's eyes quickly surveyed the audience of eager young women. She made herself clear: "I went to another women's college, in New York. It was called Hunter. Some of you might have heard of it." Every word seemed a challenge to the audience to dare take her on. Much as I admired her courage and agreed with her issues, I knew I could never talk like that.

Mayor Latting's quiet demeanor said, It's perfectly reasonable for a woman like me to be mayor, and her confidence dispelled doubt.

A questioner asked her, "What do you do to support other women?"

Without hesitation, she replied, "When I have an appointment to make, I first look for a qualified woman, and if I can't find one, I look for a qualified man."

Applause.

"What was your preparation?"

"I served on the city council for four years. The mayor's position is nonpartisan," she explained.

Listening to her words and watching her gestures, I decided this is how I wanted to be: invincible.

The conference allowed me to be a quiet observer of many other different political styles. Gloria Schaffer, secretary of state of Connecticut, was a soft-spoken, delicate woman who displayed a stylish comfort with power. How had she achieved it? She described how Connecticut was building a tradition of female leadership: Ella Grasso, now running for governor, had been secretary of state; women like Audrey Beck chaired key committees in the legislature. "Ella" buttons were handed out. We loved all it implied: a woman, friendly, and guess what? She's running for governor. I proudly wore mine.

The next day it was my turn to speak. I was on a panel with Carol Bellamy and Karen Brustein, both newly elected state senators from New York, and Ronnie Eldridge, who would become one of the first group of publishers of *Ms.* magazine. The first person to speak was Gwen Cherry, recently elected to the Florida Senate. A large woman with a gospel-sized voice, she drew all eyes to her: "My district includes one-and-one-quarter-million people. I decided to run after the black caucus came and asked me to run and the labor unions asked me to run, and the women's groups asked me to run. . . ."

I despaired. I represented some three thousand people and no group had asked me to run. I bravely followed her, explaining what had impelled me to run—the desire to protect the environment and work for ratification of the ERA. I tried to convey the excitement of political life; the sense that it was meaningful and fun. When I got good feedback on my remarks, I wondered if I had anxiously sought approval and that was why I received it, or had it really been good? I was reassured when Carol Bellamy referred back to my remarks—"As Representative Madeleine Kunin just said . . ." What a new sensation it was to be in a room filled with political women; here I was effortlessly being understood.

The emotional energy I expended functioning in the men's world could only be calibrated when I turned off the switch and relaxed in this comfortable space. Here we fell into speaking in a native language with special intonations, gestures, and looks. This meeting of political women allowed us to look at one another and say, "What we have chosen to do is normal. There are others like us. We are not statistical aberrations." Among these strong, articulate, feminine women, I experienced an internal wholeness, uniting my female and political selves. My political schizophrenia was momentarily cured—I could be both female and powerful.

I returned home fortified as much by the cumulative power of women as by the insights I had gained into individual lives.

At the midterm Democratic convention in Kansas City in 1974, I enlarged my list of political role models. It included Mary Anne Krupsak, the newly elected lieutenant governor of New York; Barbara Mikulski, a newly elected city council member from Baltimore; Midge Constanza, who would later work in the White House; and Martha Griffiths, who had sponsored the Equal Rights Amendment in Congress. Their confidence, energy, and idealism gave me a sense of purpose as well as the knowledge that I was part of a national movement.

TWO YEARS later, I was mesmerized by the closing benediction given by Martin Luther King, Sr., at the Democratic convention in New York City, where Jimmy Carter was nominated.

When he stepped to the podium, he silenced the cheering mob in Madison Square Garden. "Now, you all be quiet, now you don't move and don't talk," he scolded, as if he were speaking to his congregation. No one took umbrage.

"If God is anywhere," he said, transforming Madison Square Garden into a cathedral, "I know that God is in this place." He took a deep breath and pronounced: "It was God that sent us Jimmy Carter."

I believed him. I stretched my face toward him to receive his blessing.

"May the Lord bless you and keep you, and cause his light to shine upon you and grant you peace."

I joined the chorus of "Amens" that reverberated from one side of the arena to the other and back again. And as the convention adjourned, I felt the redemptive power of politics. I floated past the New York City cops, past the garbage cans, past the honking taxi drivers at four-thirty in the morning, lifted by the promise of salvation for the sins of Vietnam, of Watergate, of the murder of John F. Kennedy, Robert Kennedy, and Martin Luther King, Jr.

A young black man in a white suit struck up a conversation. He told me he was a member of the South Carolina delegation, and we talked about the powerful keynote speech that had been delivered by Barbara Jordan. This was his first convention.

"You know, I used to think that I belonged back in Africa, but tonight, I know that I belong in the United States and that the Constitution and the Declaration of Independence were written for me."

As it had for that young man, the 1976 convention enabled me to put myself into a larger political context with a pained history and an optimistic future. I believed that we had put our demons behind us and that a national healing process had begun. Framing my small and separate political life against this large backdrop, I magnified my vision and strengthened my will to achieve it.

THE FOLLOWING YEAR I went to the National Women's Conference in Houston, Texas, sponsored by the United Nations Commission on the Observance of International Women's Year. Abortion, the Equal Rights Amendment, and gay and lesbian rights were the emerging, emotional issues. Never had I seen such a diverse gathering of women, arguing with passion one moment and uniting in solidarity the next. I sat in the gallery and watched the spirited proceedings.

A rally had broken out on the floor minutes before the vote on freedom of choice was to be taken. The Hyde amendment, restricting abortion, had recently been enacted by the Congress. "Choice, choice, choice," reverberated from one section of the coliseum.

"Life, life, life," from another. Each tried to drown the other out.

"Down with Hyde," someone yelled.

"Up with life!" came the reply.

Anne Sonnier of Ohio was in the chair. Her calm, efficient manner reminded me of a League of Women Voters president. She banged the gavel and told the chanting crowd, "I'm going to control this situation for your own good. You work with me, and I'll work with you. I think you'll like working with me and I like working with you. That's how we'll get through this together."

I was in awe of the skill that enabled her to conduct a Vermont-style town meeting with 1,959 delegates and alternates, many of whom were ready to line up at eight microphones to express their views.

When the hall reverberated with boos, she would bang the gavel, chiding, "Stay in order."

When someone yelled out to stop debate, she would pause and ask, "How many people had intended to speak on this issue?" The show of hands was informative. The motion to cease debate was defeated. She exemplified a style of leadership I had not seen before, modifying *Robert's Rules of Order* with common sense.

At the opening ceremony, three presidents' wives joined hands under an enormous banner that spelled out WOMAN. Rosalynn Carter, Betty

Ford, and Lady Bird Johnson grounded the proceedings in respectability. I was grateful for their presence. We were not the radical women Phyllis Schlafly, the leader of the anti-ERA movement, had described.

A group of women superstars was evident in Houston: Gloria Steinem, Bella Abzug, Betty Friedan, and Kate Millett. I also spotted a short, gray-haired older woman in the corridor, using an ornate crook to maneuver her way through the pressing crowd. She parted the waters with each step.

"Who's that?" I asked someone.

"That's Margaret Mead."

I decided to follow her. She led me to a room full of women dressed in native attire; this was the international women's forum.

"The most important thing is that we're all here, considering our extraordinary differences," she said in her speech. She explained that men have less in common as a group than women do because they have been highly differentiated politically and through their careers. (I agreed, but believed that would soon change.) And she challenged the women to exercise political power. "Why have women been so unresponsive to the dangers of nuclear war?" she asked. The antinuclear movement was then limited to a small group.

She answered it herself. "Women have been denied political power for so long that they believe that this is not something which should concern them."

She observed that "women are terrible snobs. Men are basically more democratic. Women have to be very careful that they stand for democratic relationships with one another." I agreed with her and became determined to avoid this trait in myself.

It was in Houston that a substantial number of lesbian women first came out of the closet to join the women's movement. Their isolation and fear were painfully exposed as they released from the balcony thousands of balloons on which were printed: WE ARE EVERYWHERE. Then they chanted, "We were there for you, now be here for us."

For the first time, I confronted the need for civil rights protection for lesbian women. The linkage with lesbianism had been used as a threat against feminism, forcing many feminists like myself into denial of our sisters because we feared the political consequences of that association. Now, I, too, would be there for them.

There was a soapbox in the middle of the exhibition hall where women lined up throughout the day. They had three minutes to say anything. And they did!

Later that afternoon in the exhibition hall I stopped at a booth to find out about a new organization called the Women's Campaign Fund. The organization had limited funds, but had recently been formed for the purpose of getting more women elected. Susan McLane, a Republican from New Hampshire, stood at the booth with me. She was thinking of running for Congress.

"Why don't you run for higher office?" she asked.

I admitted to having thought about it but was far from certain if I would. But if she had the courage to do this, maybe I could, too. And now there was a national organization that could help.

The impression created by the keynote speaker, Barbara Jordan, had emboldened my political imagination. She pronounced the word "democracy" with extraordinary reverence; in her mouth it was holy. Hers was the most confident female voice I had ever heard. "I thank all of you and thank Lady Bird Johnson for an introduction of which I am worthy."

"Of which I am worthy." I put those words in my mouth to try them out. Delicious.

Two days later, while we were waiting at the airport for our plane to go home, a member of our Vermont delegation, Mary Skinner, introduced me to a friend. "I'd like you to meet the most powerful woman in Vermont."

"Mary!" I exclaimed, chagrined, looking down at my toes. Then I caught myself, looked straight into her eyes, and said, "Yes, that's right. That is an introduction of which I am worthy."

We burst out laughing, intoxicated by the female power we had imbibed all week.

7

ON VALENTINE'S DAY, 1974, EACH WOMAN LEGISLATOR IN VERMONT received a red rose from a common secret admirer. Could it have been the Speaker? I decided to stop in Peanut Kennedy's office. The minute I sat down, the phone rang. Peanut picked it up. "You don't mean it. . . . George Aiken?" he said with shocked surprise.

Had Aiken died? No, Peanut's tone was too cheerful. Something else had happened to the venerable six-term senator from Vermont, who had become more icon than politician.

"I'm very sorry that he's stepping down. He will be greatly missed," Peanut told the reporter on the other end of the line. He proceeded to give a one-paragraph official statement exalting Aiken's contribution to Vermont and to the nation.

When he hung up, I knew that everything had changed. Aiken had just tipped over the political chessboard. Every major Vermont politician would make a move. Checkmate was the game. Peanut immediately had it figured out.

"This is going to help Pat Leahy," he said. Pat, a thirty-four-year-old district attorney from Chittenden County, had indicated his intention to run against Aiken months ago, an audacious move verging on the disrespectful. Now it looked prescient.

Vermont's only congressman, Richard Mallary, would move up and run for Aiken's seat. "That'll leave an open congressional seat," Peanut observed and looked at me as if he saw me for the first time. "A woman would have a good chance to run for Congress."

"Really?" I was amazed.

"Have you thought about it?"

I hadn't. Not for a moment. Not even in my dreams. "Well," I said, examining my fingernails, "I've got a lot to learn right here. And besides, nobody knows me."

"That's an advantage. If you stay around too long and get too well known, it's no good either."

Peanut was speaking from experience. He was known as a wily and calculating politician, nothing could polish the tarnished image of the used-car salesman that he was, a bit too slick, a bit too crude, and no one knew this better than he. (When he thought about becoming the Republican candidate for governor in 1976, he had few illusions. "Not even my party backs me," he confided to me. "I like the House, that's where I belong.")

He turned to me. "A woman would have an advantage because people don't trust politicians. And you've been for some 'motherhood bills' like campaign-finance reform and lobbyist disclosure. That'll go over well."

"You've made my day!" I said, laughing. What a nice Valentine! I rose to leave.

"I didn't mean to spoil it," he said dryly. Before I closed the door, he added, "I'm serious."

And he was. Only I wasn't ready. Neither was I qualified.

Six Democrats believed they were, and they stepped forward. (None of them met the qualifications I would have set for myself.) The winner of the Democratic primary was the mayor of Burlington, Francis ("Frank") Cain, a conservative who ran a lackluster campaign against the Republican, former attorney general James Jeffords.

Two years later, in 1976, Esther Sorrell and a group of Burlington Democrats asked me to run against Jeffords. Esther put it bluntly: "You should announce before some stud does."

"Esther, did you say that?" I laughed.

"You betcha."

So on February 29, 1976, I made a list:

Negative factors
1. I might lose
2. Effect on children and husband
3. Loss of position in Vermont House
4. Physical and emotional strain of campaign and of winning
5. Fear of flying
6. Lack of money
7. Lack of knowledge about the issues
8. Incorrect timing
9. Jeffords's strength
10. Liberal image
11. Lack of self-confidence
12. Woman?

13. Lack of support from traditional Democrats in Rutland
14. Inexperience in organizing statewide campaign
15. What can you do in Washington?
16. Larger potential effect in Vermont
17. Future in the Vermont House

POSITIVE FACTORS

1. Experience of running for Congress
2. Support of women in Chittenden County
3. Positive image
4. Accomplishments in the House
5. Ability to speak well
6. Potential ability to organize campaign
7. Support of husband
8. Desire to accomplish something substantial
9. Ability to fight
10. Potential in Congress
11. New life
12. Belief that I could do a good job in campaign and in office
13. Hoped for help, not yet tested
14. Good time for a woman to run
15. Jeffords's weakness among some Republicans
16. Labor support
17. Possible divided Republican party in presidential race
18. Strong Democratic presidential candidate
19. Weakness of Republican party
20. Large independent vote

Jeffords, a one-term congressman whose earlier primary loss for governor in 1972 had been forgotten, was already showing signs of being a maverick, the bad boy of the Republican party, a role that increasingly would stand him in good stead with independent-minded Vermonters. Running against him would be tough.

Esther saw it differently. "If he ever can be defeated, it's now, after his first term. Otherwise, he'll have the seat forever."

I agreed. For a split second, I wished I had taken Peanut's advice and jumped in two years before—I knew I could have done as well or better than those who ran. And now that my head was tempted, my feet refused to move. I could not see myself traveling to every town in Vermont, raising thousands of dollars, asking hundreds of volunteers to help me, giving five or six speeches a day, being out every night, feeling nervous at every dinner, answering hard questions every day, and, most of all, debating my opponent, taking him on face-to-face. I could not envision myself working up the animosity to force him out. As an incumbent, he exhaled omnipotence with every breath.

The *Rutland Herald* carried a background story on Jeffords. My eyes focused on the last paragraph. Jim Jeffords had come from a well-established political family, and his father had been a Vermont Supreme Court justice. The reporter concluded that Jim Jeffords was "destined for a life of politics."

For me, it was the other way around. Nothing in my bloodline contained a drop of political destiny. It was politics that had enabled me to defy who I had been expected to become. Going against expectations had been both exhilarating and exhausting, like swimming against the tide, but I was still catching my breath, uncertain of my long-term endurance. Here in the House, I had mastered the rules of this political environment, its special language, customs, and idiosyncrasies. I was not ready to leave and become a political immigrant once again, a greenhorn. (That is what we had called ourselves after my mother took us to the Easter parade in New York City when I was ten years old. She looked up and down Fifth Avenue for the signs and sounds of the parade. Finally, she asked a cop when the parade would begin. He looked at her with amusement and told her, "Lady, you're in it.")

The Vermont House was where I had served my apprenticeship; my reward was that I had earned full citizenship. Moving from the Vermont House to the United States Congress did not seem to me, at that point, a progression or a promotion, another step to take in normal stride, like climbing a corporate ladder. A congressional race would require a complete reassessment of my goals and capacities, a look down to the ledge below, where I had come from, and up to the next precipice.

The most difficult aspect would be holding the separate parts of my life together: wife, mother, and politician. How would I make time for my husband and children? If I won, and the family moved with me to Washington, my husband would have to find a job, the children would attend different schools, and everyone's decisions would revolve around my needs. If the family didn't move, I would be consigned to a lonely commuting life, and the family would be largely motherless. I could not see a way around this dilemma.

Also, if I became a candidate for the United States Congress, politics would be my career; I would be a professional politician. The phrase made me uncomfortable. As a member of a part-time legislature meeting four to five months of the year with a scattering of committee meetings in between, I was still a relative amateur. When the legislature was not in session, I could slip back into my citizen's role as comfortably as I got into my jeans. I had entered the world of politics not because I wanted a title, privilege, or power, but because I was an active member of the community who had stepped over an almost-invisible line. But running for Congress would be a deliberate, highly visible declaration of political ambition. I was not yet ready.

My LEGISLATIVE YEARS taught me that intelligence and perseverance were not the only criteria for political success. I had always wished for more of each, but now I yearned for more of everything: brains, humor, folksiness, and confidence, especially when, in my capacity as a committee chairman, I was called upon to give speeches.

One March day in 1977 I was invited to speak to the Vermont Association of Realtors at the Lincoln Inn in Essex Junction, near Burlington. Senator Thomas Crowley, the owner of an insurance agency, was the host at the luncheon attended by some one hundred area realtors. His quick humor charmed the crowd. He didn't have to say a word of substance, and they loved him. When it was my turn to go to the podium, I felt like a college professor relying on last year's notes. I had planned to talk about taxes and why we should not reduce them. But the moment I started talking, I knew I was committing political suicide. I tried to rescue myself by explaining that the money was needed for education to produce the next generation of Vermont's skilled workers, something that I hoped would appeal to this business crowd. But as I searched in vain for eye contact, I remembered, too late, that these realtors already knew me as an environmentalist, a supporter of a law they did not like—Act 250, which controlled development.

Scanning the dark-suited gathering, my eyes were drawn to spots of color: a red suit here, a print dress over there. Women were beginning to enter real estate, having discovered they were good at it and could make money. I smiled. There was Joan Hollister, an old friend, married to a minister from Burlington. Nine years ago we had both pushed baby carriages in a march through the streets of Burlington, following the death of Martin Luther King. Her children were about the same age as mine.

The speech went better than I had feared. My discussion about the importance of investing in a well-trained labor force by properly funding education seemed to have kept their attention. I had to convert a skeptical audience to my cause.

Joan came up to me after the speech, beaming. "You were terrific. I agreed with everything you said."

I hugged her, and then wondered, How many in the audience would agree with her? But perhaps it didn't matter; I had the satisfaction of stating what I believed.

That fall, near my forty-fourth birthday, I read Gail Sheehy's book *Passages* and Sylvia Plath's *Letters Home*. Had I made the right choices? I was not the person who people thought I was, mother, wife, and politician, packaged in separate but neatly integrated moving parts. Inside, everything rattled. I was making long lists at night and crossing off the items, one by one, during the day: go shopping, fold laundry, make cookies, write letters, prepare legislation, make telephone calls, clean up the mess in this house. Never did I get everything done. Always there were piles of papers to be sorted, lost socks to be found, dirty dishes to put in the dishwasher, and clean dishes to take out. Life was messy.

Politics imposed an artificial order, a ritual, that allowed me to delude myself into thinking that my life was under control. That was why I liked it. I could close the door behind me and move into another house, into an orderly room, where the countertops were clean, the toys put away, and the schedule followed. Compartmentalized, I felt better. This is who I was, for the moment. But whom had I left behind? I questioned if I would have to deny another, undefined part of myself that I recognized in Sylvia Plath's searing poetry and become, instead, enslaved to meetings, to pleasing others, to becoming someone who I was supposed to be, but was not. Was politics another form of constriction, rather than a liberation? Just as I fulfilled my wifely and motherly duties, was I now carrying out my political functions with similar compunction, molding myself to an outwardly defined model? In Sylvia Plath's poetry she had turned over rocks and uncovered the less manageable and more conflicted emotions that swarmed there. Her life could not contain the passions she had released; one look and I knew that neither could mine. I rolled the rock back.

I found my equilibrium again; if I was careful about compromise and courageous about principle, I could express my inner self in politics. Political action was a creative process, drawing on my emotions and intellect to shape the world around me. I, too, had a vision of what I wanted to extract from my material. Each of us was bound by our disciplines and surprised by our discoveries. And if our creation was not perfect, was that any more illusory than art? Was it not enough to experience the momentary elation when the inner vision and the outer reality converged, when the right word or gesture transformed conflict and chaos into resolution and order? That was what I experienced in the political process when a problem was solved, a compromise reached, a victory achieved. Politics was not driving me into alien territory, forcing me to become who I was not. On the contrary, the political life enabled me to become who I was. Sylvia Plath's rage had no outlet except her own annihilation. My rage could be vented in the political arena, where its expression was controlled and, sometimes, accepted.

If I continued in politics at a steady pace, knowing when to ease up and when to surge forward, I could continue to embrace both my private and public lives like twins, holding one on each hip, shifting my body first to one side and then to the other, as needed. The balance would never be perfect, because I might not sense in time when one or the other needed greater attention. Real life is never as manageable as the lectures we give to ourselves or to others. Throughout these years there have been times of doubt when I asked myself, Is this really worth it? And times of anguish when I found myself surrounded by grasping strangers and wanted, rather, to be held and loved. Occasionally I feared I had lost something, perhaps irretrievably, by some miscalculation, such as standing at a podium giving the commencement address to an auditorium of expectant children when I should have been seated at our dining room table, blowing out birthday candles with my own child.

The podium would steady me, give me a place to stand, to brace my arms, plant my feet, and project. This, too, was reality; not private, not personal, but it formed a connection between me and the audience, which for that moment seemed personal and even, at times, private. I knew it was not love; my senses told me so. These were strangers. And yet, for a second or two, flushed with praise, I abandoned caution and let myself sink into the sound of applause.

MIDWAY through my third term in the Vermont legislature, around 1977, I felt I was ready to run for higher office. I had proven I could do the toughest job in the House; I felt I had learned what it had to teach me. If I stayed there too long, I would become a professional legislator, as much a part of the institution as the people whom I had once been eager to replace. I weighed a race for lieutenant governor, examining the advantages and disadvantages. The position had the prestige of being a statewide office, but its power was limited by both the governor and the legislature. The two prescribed duties were to preside as president of the Senate, and to take over the duties of governor in the governor's absence. Neither shared power willingly with a lieutenant governor, who was an executive-legislative hybrid, part of both branches but attached to neither.

Because the state constitution does not require candidates for governor and lieutenant governor to run as a team, Vermont could have a Republican governor and a Democratic lieutenant governor. That would be the likely outcome if I ran, because Richard Snelling was a strong favorite for reelection to a second term. Snelling had his share of victories and defeats, having first been elected to the legislature in 1959 and then overwhelmed in his bid for governor by incumbent Philip Hoff in 1966. His political future brightened once again when he was elected to the legislature in 1972 and became Republican leader. In the interim he had become a highly successful businessman and brought a dollars-and-cents perspective to government.

The lieutenant governor's race might get more press attention than usual because so far there was no announced Democratic candidate for governor. Whoever stepped forward would be considered a long shot because it was assumed that Snelling was unbeatable. The lieutenant governor's contest was thought to be the only horse race. And Snelling, I knew from our previous encounters, would give me only a minimum of responsibility and visibility if I won; I would not be welcome in the executive chamber, and the Senate, likely to remain under Republican control, would try to exclude me as well. If I won, I might find myself with a title and nothing else.

That was what Mavis Doyle thought and wrote in her *Rutland Herald* weekly column:

> Vermont Democrats are preparing to sacrifice one of their outstanding young members on the altar of the 1978 general election. . . . Some of them [Democrats] still believe in the "stepping stone" method which was standard practice in Vermont until late in the 1950's. In that era a rising politician served as Attorney General, then as Lt. Governor, and then won automatic election as Governor. However the concept was stripped of its credibility during the last two decades.

> Those who occupied this primarily ceremonial No. 2
> post became less involved with crucial issues and in
> effect dropped out of public sight for the rest of their
> lives.

Mavis might be right, I acknowledged, but I wanted to prove her wrong; I would become the spokesperson for the opposition. I had already begun to formulate my differences with the Snelling administration; this office would give me the platform to do it effectively. My political instincts told me I would have to be selective in opposing the governor, because an ongoing feud with him would be unpleasant, not to mention detrimental to the state, as well as bad politics. A well-aimed critique, however, could allow me to test my skills and develop my own agenda. I could concentrate on areas that he did not, such as the environment, energy conservation, and child care, and develop my own areas of expertise.

I might even be able to work at being the governor's understudy. There was some risk; I might never get to play the part. But understudies do get called upon from time to time, and, most important, they imagine they have the part, mouthing the words backstage in synchronization with the actor out front. I thought I needed this kind of rehearsal time. One reason that politicians' wives and widows have so easily stepped into their husbands' roles is that for years they had been standing in the wings, watching every cue and command, knowing precisely when and how to make their entrances. The understudy not only mimics the actor to perfection, but over a period of time, having had ample opportunity to think about it, begins to improvise new interpretations for the role. An understudy has a dual perspective, situated both onstage and off, part of the cast as well as part of the audience. From this vantage point, the understudy can detect better than the actor himself when the performance falls flat and when it soars.

It was Governor Snelling's opposition to the positions I took that, inadvertently, first prompted me to imagine myself doing his job. It happened one moment in 1978 when the House Appropriations Committee had completed its work on the state budget. "Snelling, Kunin Haggle Over Budget" was the headline. For the first time we were billed as equals, and the very fact that I could be a genuine threat to him gave me new self-esteem. He catapulted me to his level and made me equal to the battle, capable of defending myself and launching a counterattack. I knew more about the budget than he did, having scrupulously examined every item for months. I was like a watchmaker with an eyeglass stuck to my eye, familiar with all the moving parts and the tortuous negotiations over tough decisions. I had learned how and when to say no to requests from legislators and constituents and how and when to say yes. Decisions were no longer divided into "good" and "bad"; I had to choose between two equally good proposals because there was only room in the budget for one. No longer was I a special pleader for single causes; I had walked through the entire budget, experienced the trade-offs, seen the interconnections that wove through the system. As chief of the budget-writing committee, I had acquired a broad executive perspective; I knew what had to be done and why.

My conclusions, when challenged by the governor's criticism, were as valid as his. I claimed the budget was balanced, according to our figures. He accused the committee of overspending. The conflict was caused by two different revenue forecasts, one generated by the legislature, the other by the governor. The more he attacked me, the more my views came into focus. His rhetoric worked like a chisel, removing all extraneous material, setting my words in sharp relief. I do not know precisely when that seductive word "someday" began to slip into my thoughts, but it did. Someday, I began to say to myself, someday, I would like to be in his place. I would not do it his way; I would do it my way. My imagination took free flight.

But I forced myself to put my feet back on the ground, knowing I would require a long apprenticeship not only to learn the governor's job, but to recast it. I had to be more than a mime, skilled in illusion. I had to speak my lines as I believed them. That kind of self-teaching would take time. In the office of lieutenant governor, I thought I would be sufficiently out of the limelight to be spared close scrutiny, yet near enough to the action to be a meticulous observer. He and I would share the head table, his place would be in the center, and mine near the end.

Vermont had never elected a woman governor. The people had, however, voted for a woman lieutenant governor in 1955, Consuelo Northrop Bailey. I had not taken her seriously as a role model, for she had been marginalized in her later years as a kind of curiosity. I wanted to be as different as I could be from Connie Bailey; she seemed more club woman than politician, and from another era, dressed in blue draped rayon studded with rhinestones, suitable for the mother of the bride, gushing words that were too sweet for my taste; I pushed them away as I would a rich dessert.

In retrospect I was wrong. Consuelo Bailey was extraordinarily courageous. She became the first woman to be elected state's attorney in Vermont in 1926, and in 1953 she achieved another first when elected Speaker of the Vermont House of Representatives after a lengthy five-way contest—Consuelo against four men. In that postwar period there were forty-seven women in the legislature, and it was the women who held firm for Connie. Both she and her female supporters would have been shocked to be called feminists; they simply thought a woman could do the job.

Consuelo Bailey's portrait hangs in the Vermont statehouse next to the portrait of Edna Beard, from the town of Orange, elected one year after the passage of the Nineteenth Amendment. She had a trying first day. The *Burlington Free Press* reported that when the ritual of seat selection took place at the opening session, no one would take the empty seat next to her. Finally, when a brave male legislator filled the empty seat, the press reported that the hall burst into laughter and applause. I am a sister to Edna Beard.

And to Consuelo Bailey, who helped me make my decision to run for lieutenant governor. The precedent she set made it easier for me, and what her presence in the lieutenant governor's chair had threatened, I would bring about. I would not stop where she had; her barriers would not be my barriers. But for the time being, I could assure myself and the public that this ceremonial post, once held by a woman, was all I wanted.

It was a safe place to begin: the girl would be vice president and the boy president. The familiar configuration was now open to different interpretations: The woman in the secondary role could be content to be there, knowing her place, ready to take her cues from the man in charge. Or the woman in the secondary role could hint at her discontent and her readiness to replace the man in charge. I played to both interpretations. Such ambivalence may have been a necessary preparatory stage before I could overtly seek the governorship itself.

As an active, visible lieutenant governor, which I intended to be, my official presence could begin the critical transformation from the traditional male image of political leadership into a female one. A woman's face in a man's role was still startling, an aberration, and when women play formerly male parts, we go through an unconscious process of translation, like learning a new language. There is an instinctive effort to find familiar words in the language we know. Looking at a woman in a man's role, we focus on the fact that it is a "she" and not a "he." Her neckline, her shoes, the timbre of her voice, her posture, each of her female and male qualities are assessed against standards we know, silently and perhaps unknowingly. The female politician is a new work of art just coming into focus. An element of sexual tension exists: the strong woman playing the part of a strong man is a new variant of the male-female paradigm. Or is it? A female politician conveys an element of disguise, for there is a suspicion that underneath her masculine behavior we would discover a soft and vulnerable woman.

The female politician is unexpected; her presence provokes a brief digression during which the public wanders off into internal musings about how this woman is like a man and yet not like a man. Does ambition fit her, or is it awkward, even unseemly? These distractions become significant when the woman herself cannot be heard or seen for who she really is. Then gender becomes extra baggage, something to be lugged around, adding to the weight of the usual questions and controversies that beleaguer every politician.

Men travel lighter. They only need one suit of clothes, preferably dark blue, and one necktie, preferably red, and two shirts: one blue and one white. With that, they look correct. Women, no matter how often they change their clothes, fix their hair, modulate their voices, are never quite sure if they are properly attired. When I decided to run for lieutenant governor in Vermont, I understood that on some fundamental level, never discussed openly, the voters would have to come to terms with the contradictions that my candidacy would provoke before they could conclude that this new model of political being was as effective as, if not more than, the established one. Given enough time, I believed I could win them over.

As more and more women enter public life, and the female politician becomes almost as familiar as her male counterpart, the distraction of gender may become inconsequential. And if it does not, the consequences may be more positive than negative. In the 1992 elections, women for the first time openly celebrated their differences. And that, combined with their positions on issues that concerned the voters and the availability of open seats, was why they won. Men and women voters both have begun to reject the familiar male models of political leadership, since these have sometimes disappointed them in both style and substance. The anomaly represented by women politicians was no longer a liability; it became an advantage, signaling precisely the dramatic change the public sought. While this marks a clear departure from historic gender restraints for political women, it does not eliminate the gender burden completely. Political women continue to function in a male-defined political environment. Women found it easier in the post–cold war world to gain credibility, a world in which military expertise seemed less important and domestic experience took precedence; should the urgent issues change, as they inevitably will, to ones with which women are less familiar, they will once again have to prove their credentials.

In 1977, women politicians were rare and therefore a curiosity. Only two women had been elected governor in their own right: Ella Grasso, from Connecticut, and Dixy Lee Ray, from the state of Washington. Successful female politicians often acquired stature through the men they were associated with, their fathers, husbands, or mentors. Male leadership qualities seemed to be transmitted genetically or by osmosis. I lacked such instant legitimacy and had to create my own. Could I develop the dual qualities within myself to convey the strength and decisiveness associated with masculinity while being loyal to my feminine self?

Sincerity is vital to political credibility. If I, as a woman, were to create a pretense of a male politician, that would lead to a poor, even comical, performance. Likewise, if I only fulfilled traditional female expectations, that, too, would be found lacking and perhaps laughable. To be convincing, serious, and sincere, I had to meld female and male strengths and trust myself to express both in order to become the political person I wanted to be.

In time, I realized I did not have to presume that male and female qualities were bifurcated. Neither did I have to borrow strength from male models or suppress female emotion. I had inherent female strength, ignited by female passions; both were valid, and together they were amazingly powerful. There was no need for pretense, to become someone else. Quite the opposite, I had to trust and reveal who I was. Eventually, I developed the courage to do that, to release what had been within me all the time.

In 1977, however, I was more practical than prophetic. I determined that the office of lieutenant governor would allow me to become a familiar and friendly figure to Vermonters, known to be reasonable and well informed. After a time, my constituency would not be distracted by the fact that I was a woman. And I could get used to being a public figure. The Appropriations Committee experience had taught me that I could survive conflict, but it was not a skill I enjoyed using. I much preferred the role of mediator. It is possible that I sought the safety of the lieutenant governorship as a reprieve from the Appropriations Committee. I felt I had managed that battleground successfully, but would my luck last? Part of me continued to want to be a nice person, someone who pleased everyone and angered no one. If I presided over the Senate, my responsibility would be to be fair; to make certain the rules of debate were followed to allow all who sought to speak to be heard. Then the process itself, the ayes and nays, would decide. This was a task I felt well equipped to do and even relished. I could be the peacemaker and be spared the battle.

My assessment of the lieutenant governorship was almost correct. I laid the groundwork for a gubernatorial race, more or less as I had anticipated. I gained exposure, confidence, and knowledge. By positioning myself to the side, however, rather than at the center, I failed to hone my combative skills. I deluded myself into believing that controversy and conflict could be avoided if I said the right things at the correct time in precisely the appropriate manner. In fact, what I needed most was to develop my capacity to express my beliefs and manage and survive conflict. I failed to recognize that if I stood for principles conflict was inevitable, regardless of how polite, skillful, or smart I was. It is part of the political condition.

In any event, I gained experience in running a statewide campaign and learned how to build a state organization. This alone was a formidable task. In Vermont, the Democratic party never had a visible organization; there had not been enough Democratic victories to lay the foundation or enough patronage to reward the effort. Most Democrats who got elected had to develop their own organizations, based on personal appeal. The situation did not improve when more Democrats were in power, for the party then lost its minority cohesiveness and began to divide along factional lines. Since I knew I would have trouble winning over some conservatives within the party, it was all the more critical to establish a wide network of supporters.

The opponent I anticipated facing was the incumbent lieutenant governor, T. Garry Buckley, a real estate agent from Bennington. Our first encounter had occurred in 1973 when Buckley was chairman of the Senate Judiciary Committee, before which I was testifying on the ratification of the Equal Rights Amendment. I was a freshman legislator, flushed with victory because the House had recently voted overwhelmingly for ratification, and I was urging the Senate to do likewise.

Buckley had a different idea. Why not hold a state referendum to guide the Senate's decision? he asked.

My heart sank. That would take another year. Besides, Vermont did not have a referendum form of government, and I set out to prove the fallacy of his proposal by asking for the attorney general's opinion on the constitutionality of a public referendum—I had received the opinion that morning.

I informed Buckley, "Senator Buckley, the attorney general concludes that it would be unconstitutional for the Vermont Senate to call for a referendum on the ratification of the Equal Rights Amendment. Referendums are nonbinding and have only rarely—"

Bang! Buckley's fist hit the table.

"The Senate of the state of Vermont can do anything it wants to do, young lady," he roared. "If it wants to paint the ceiling of the Senate chamber red, it will paint it red."

Senator Russell Niquette, a genteel elder statesman, known as the Silver Fox of Winooski, came to the rescue: "I think what Mrs. Kunin meant to say was . . . ," giving me a chance to shift my strategy.

Buckley had been elected lieutenant governor in 1976 over John Alden. The Senate liked him—a good old boy who played by their rules—and the press found him marvelously quotable. When he had beat out John Alden after the legislative vote, defying the popular vote, he commented, "Sometimes even a blind hog finds the acorn."

A year later, however, the public was becoming disenchanted. He seemed a caricature of a cigar-puffing politician, ready to sound off on any subject with astounding abandon. At times, I, too, was stunned by his bravado. It was classic Buckley to propose, as he did when he ran for the U.S. Senate in 1980, to save Pentagon money by equipping domestic flights with bombs.

I had another chance to size up Buckley in 1977 when we both appeared on a panel sponsored by Vermont landlords. I was supporting landlord-tenant legislation, which the landlords passionately opposed. I believed that Vermont could have a balanced law that would benefit both landlords and tenants and win their joint approval. (Only later was I compelled to acknowledge this was a naïve assumption. At another public hearing on the bill, landlords and tenants sat on separate sides of the aisle, glaring at each other as if they were the Montagues and the Capulets at Romeo and Juliet's wedding.) Buckley, as a realtor, was unabashedly on the landlords' side, and the landlords, I noted, were highly attentive to his remarks.

"The less government the better, I say. Settle it with a handshake, best way. That's the Vermont way of closing a deal."

I groaned.

At the meeting I felt triumphant by having met "the enemy," though I knew the audience's assessment of my performance might have been different. It was not the substance of our debate that made me confident that night. It was my response to the exchange, which told me I could take him on. I felt relaxed, free of constraint, able to field questions, and, to my delight, I had discovered I could display a sense of humor. I was not as funny as he was—his outrageous man-to-man humor I could not imitate, and his flamboyance gave him a wide circumference; he could say almost anything, while my territory was more circumspect. Had I tried to keep pace with him, I would have seemed coarse or ridiculous. In a bizarre way, I found him entertaining, even likable. We had one bond: our mutual dislike for Richard Snelling, who had snubbed us both. Buckley enjoyed being a thorn in his side, and I was amused by the spectacle, feeling alternately repelled by and attracted to this man who was my foe. But I felt almost giddy at the end of the debate, so thrilled was I to discover that I could sit at the same table with my enemy, be criticized and fight back, and emerge unscathed. Not a scratch. I was exhilarated. I did not feel beaten. I was not apologetic. And I had not been afraid.

That night, I decided I could run and win. I called it a major decision for a minor office. It would allow me to be visible and enable me to learn. I was encouraged by a *Burlington Free Press* editorial about women in politics that listed me as the most likely candidate for lieutenant governor. It was odd to see myself featured, but I had little trouble getting used to it. I was amazed how easily my ego was won over. I promptly warned myself, Preserve the inner person, whoever she is, for you will need her.

Then I looked in the mirror and said, "Here I come, T. Garry Buckley, ready or not."

At the same time, another candidate was thinking similar thoughts, Peter Smith, the son of a prominent Burlington banking family, who would square off with Buckley in the Republican primary.

THE FIRST TASK I faced in running for statewide office was to find a professional campaign manager. My legislative races in Burlington had relied exclusively on volunteers. Walking out of the statehouse one Friday afternoon, I chatted with Steve Kimbell, who had been the lobbyist for the Vermont Low Income Advocacy Council, which represented the poor. I had trusted his advice in the Appropriations Committee and often agreed with him. Steve was a study in tough love. A tall, tousle-haired ex-marine whose face bore the scars of teenage acne rather than battle, he sometimes seemed rude, but I thought he was merely shy. Neither of us had ever run a statewide campaign, but I sensed I could entrust myself to him. As we walked toward the parking lot, I asked the question, "Will you run my campaign?"

He thought it over for a few minutes and, to my delight, said yes. We agreed that we would launch the campaign officially after the end of the legislative session. This was a commitment; Steve was quitting his job to work for me.

On March 4, 1978, we held our first campaign meeting at my house with my campaign manager and my new finance chairman, Patrick Robbins, a successful Burlington businessman with an irrepressible love for politics. I was pleased with the group we had assembled: Douglas Racine, a young staffer for U.S. senator Patrick Leahy; Mark Kaplan, a state senator; Esther Sorrell; Lorraine Graham; Mary Evelti, who shared the legislative district with me; Marilyn Stout, a good friend; Senator Bill Daniels, considered the brain trust of Vermont's Democratic party; Maurice Mahoney, a young Burlington Democrat; and Nicky Roth, my good friend and neighbor, who had organized my first legislative campaign.

After everybody left, I sat in my empty living room and got depressed. I had handed over the finances to Pat and my schedule to Steve. I was losing control of my life. The top campaign posts were going to men; though my closest confidants were women, I was ambivalent about ceding authority to them. Yet I knew no women with sufficient fund-raising experience, nor had women campaign managers yet emerged. But it is possible that I also needed to balance my female side with a male presence, both for my own sense of security and to make sure that I would be taken seriously. A woman campaigning for office surrounded by women might be considered either threatening or weak.

I grew out of that stage. In 1980, when I felt more secure, I asked a woman, Jane Williams, to be my campaign manager, and we won handily (against a woman opponent, Peg Garland). I returned to Steve Kimbell in 1982, and then in 1984 the manager of my campaign for governor was Liz Bankowski. She and I made the rounds of political consultants in New York, early in the season, and we sought out David Garth, who agreed to see us, we were told, only as a favor to a wealthy mutual acquaintance who lived in Vermont. Garth was then at the top of the list of brilliant political gurus. I introduced Garth to Liz—a tall, striking woman with an abundance of dark hair that refused to fall into place—and told him she was my campaign manager. He invited us to sit down in two black leather chairs facing his desk. I had the feeling that our chairs were especially low and that his was on a huge pedestal.

David looked straight at me and then at Liz and said, "Let me give you one piece of important advice." We knew we were getting for free what most people paid for dearly. "Whatever you do, don't hire a woman campaign manager. It will look like a tea party."

Liz and I winked at each other, thanked him politely, and skipped out. We went on to win.

Looking back, in my first statewide campaign in 1978 I was unknowingly taking David Garth's advice. I had great respect for Steve Kimbell. The relationship of a candidate to a campaign manager, I discovered, is best described as marriage without romance. You are in it together for better or for worse. Steve had gotten to know my strengths and weaknesses by observing me as chairman of the House Appropriations Committee. In my first week as chairman in January 1977, I had developed an incapacitating migraine headache at the end of the day. Prone to headaches, I could usually get rid of them by swallowing two aspirin immediately. This one got out of control. Steve drove me home while I shut my eyes and tried to loosen the vise that had tightened around my head. Nausea was taking over. We had to stop the car while I got sick. Steve had seen me at my most vulnerable hour.

He and I had discussed how a campaign for a woman would be different from a traditional campaign, and we thought we understood how to manage the gender question. I had taken care of the basics: I was confident that Steve had my interests at heart, that he would dedicate himself totally to the campaign. Without that foundation, we would not have stayed strapped to our seats during the roller-coaster ride of the next eight months.

It started the day of our first organizational meeting. Alone in my living room, after they left, I asked myself, What if I am not who they think I am? What if I blow it with some stupid remark, poor gesture, or oversight? I felt the pressure of a public image closing in on me. To add to my concerns, some of my advisers were telling me to run for governor, but I was not ready. I was hopeful that Tim O'Connor, the Speaker of the House, would take that decision out of my hands. Would the group still back me if I just ran for lieutenant governor?

Then, my family. Were they ready for the pressure of a statewide campaign? My husband was supportive, but I asked myself, Will it last? It would be difficult for him to become a more visible political spouse, and to take over more and more family responsibilities. In addition, I would be making more demands on him for emotional support.

My mind switched to the end of the session. All this would evaporate if I botched it in the Appropriations Committee. There was so much work to do. The Friday before, the committee had fallen apart, split on partisan lines. Governor Snelling had been doing his best to recruit Republicans to oppose the budget, and it was having an effect. Perhaps I had been too nice and didn't clamp down hard enough. The recurring question taunted me: Would it have been different had I been a man? Would I have been tougher, and they more respectful? My solace was that while I was having a hard time with the governor, he was having an equally hard time with me.

WE SET A DATE for the announcement: April 28. Five days before that I fell into a slump. Everything had gone wrong. Two weeks earlier, we had sent out 1,080 letters inviting people to the announcement, using a bulk-mailing permit from the Democratic party. Now I learned that the letters were still sitting in the post office because the campaign return address didn't conform with the permit. Someone at Democratic headquarters had forgotten to tell us that the post office had called four days ago notifying them of the problem.

Then I found out that the Democratic mayor of Rutland, Gilbert ("Gillie") Godnick, was supporting Alfred Beauchamp, a Republican businessman from Rutland, for lieutenant governor. He had told one of my Rutland supporters, "I'll support anyone who runs against Madeleine." I could not imagine how I had offended him. I was soon to find out.

I also worried about money. We set a tentative budget of twenty-five thousand to thirty thousand dollars, which seemed like an enormous amount to me, and in the end we stuck close to it, spending thirty-six thousand dollars. We decided to have a few people ask for personal contributions of fifty dollars each. These would be our big donors. And the Women's Campaign Fund had promised me my first major contribution, a check for one thousand dollars. (It was my only Washington contact.) The money was held up, however, because the campaign fund, itself a fledgling organization, had to make sure that Vermont's election laws allowed us to accept its contribution. We were awaiting an attorney general's opinion for the answer. With these delays, would Steve get paid?

Meanwhile, I began to make the political rounds, paying my respects to people whose approval I would need and whose disapproval I could not risk. Most were conservative businessmen, contributors to the Democratic party at a time when it had shared their philosophy but exercised little power.

I got my first taste of local campaigning at a potluck supper in the village of Worcester, near Montpelier, which seemed to be blessed with an inordinate number of enthusiastic Democrats who all lived on the same country road. When I stopped at the general store in the center of town to buy gas, there was a poster tacked up on the bulletin board: MEET MADELEINE KUNIN, CANDIDATE FOR LT. GOVERNOR. I was thrilled. The bold maroon-and-white graphics looked wonderfully professional. (Later I asked Margot Zalkind-Schur, who had designed the posters, to do the logo for my buttons, stationery, and bumper stickers.) When I walked into the community center, it looked like a good party. This was fun. I was going to have a wonderful time campaigning. The next two nights we had huge envelope-addressing sessions to invite people to the announcement. As I was sitting around our dining table with the crowd of friends and neighbors, I was delighted that so many people turned up, that we had such a great time talking and laughing. I was not in this alone.

Then a shadow appeared, threatening my plans. My mother-in-law was dying. We might have to postpone the announcement. It seemed obscene to have to think about this as a problem for the campaign. I was depressed about her illness and the way she was suffering. For the third time, I was witnessing the death of a woman close to me: first my mother, my aunt Berthe, and now Arthur's mother. All the old women would be gone. There would be no other generation to turn to. I shall be that generation.

My mother-in-law died that April. Even as I sat at the funeral service and wept, I knew I was not allowing myself to mourn as I should. The campaign was pulling me into the future; I could not give death its due.

On Friday, April 28, at 12:15 p.m., I walked into room 11 of the statehouse, relieved to see every seat taken and shocked to see the podium covered with microphones. No place to put my speech. The applause lasted long enough for me to set the pages down in a safe nest of wires. Arthur had introduced me. I had wanted it that way. Later, I realized that this was more than a formality: Arthur was giving his public approval; he was letting me go.

"I present to you the next lieutenant governor of the state of Vermont." I kissed him.

"It's with a sense of both excitement and anticipation that I make my formal announcement today to become the Democratic candidate for the office of lieutenant governor of the state of Vermont."

I breathed deeply. Saying so made it so. I turned to my family and introduced them. I had allowed the children to miss school that day, except for Daniel, the youngest, whom we decided to send off and then pick up at school at 10:45. He had run out, and we had then taken off, while I straightened his tie and tucked in his shirt. As we laughed and joked in the car on the way to the statehouse, one of the kids teased, "I'm going to tell Wadi Sawabini [a television reporter] on you."

Wadi was their favorite target. At home, when the children got one threatening look from me, one of them would yell, "Child abuse, I'm calling Wadi." The funny sound of his name, I suspect, was the chief attraction. But I had to acknowledge that my children had discovered a sense of their power; at any moment, they could do me in. As we got closer to Montpelier, the children outdid one another in rehearsing the outrageous interviews they intended to give to the press, getting a delicious shriek from me every time. Daniel was almost nine. Adam, Peter, and Julia were twelve, fifteen, and seventeen.

When we got to the statehouse, I panicked, for I had forgotten my cosmetic kit. Julia went out and bought everything: lipstick, comb, powder, and Tampax. Now the children were seated in the front row next to my husband, neatly dressed, smiling expectantly, and, thank God, silent.

"I am particularly aware of the role that my family will have to play in this campaign. Their well-being will always be of special importance to me, even though in the next few months I may not cook all the meals or fold all the laundry. They've also received their basic training during my three legislative terms, and I'm convinced that the independence and knowledge which our children have gained will help them in their own lives." I said those words and willed them to be true, even as we all knew that our lives would never be the same.

Looking back, I am surprised by the next paragraph. "Some sense of conflict remains for every woman who has obligations outside of the home, but, with a feeling of love and understanding, this can be resolved." I had to acknowledge my conflict openly. By relating it to the experience of all working women, I hoped to reduce its risk to myself. But the moment the words were out of my mouth, they seemed dangerous. I had to quickly assure myself, and my audience, that all this could be "resolved." How certain I was! Or was I?

In my speech, I placed myself in a line of succession; I followed the only other woman who had held high office in Vermont, as well as other Democrats who served in the office of lieutenant governor. "We all remember Consuelo Bailey of South Burlington, who paved the way for women to participate in government . . . we remember John Daley of Rutland and Brian Burns of Burlington, who served as capable Democratic lieutenant governors." I was not yet used to political overkill and chose the word I believed was accurate, "capable," not too little, not too much. As a good student, as well as politician, I acknowledged my teachers, my fellow legislators. "From them I have learned not only to respect but also, frankly, to enjoy the art of politics as it is practiced in Vermont."

I dwelt on my experience: "As Democratic whip, I learned how to function in a legislative leadership position. As chairman of the Appropriations Committee, I received what one might call an advanced degree in government. . . . In that position, I had to keep a statewide perspective and was forced to gain an overview of all of state government. It is probably the position which comes closest to holding higher office. . . ."

I hinted at who I was. "My values stem from a strong belief in the democratic system and a basic sympathy for whose who are sometimes powerless to express their needs. Perhaps I learned to respect our system of government because I came to this country as a child, and my mother transferred to my brother and myself a sense of wonder about this country and a feeling of gratitude, having left Europe during World War II. She also gave us a strong sense of social justice, which I have found to be a good counterbalance to the hard fiscal decisions which must be made in state government."

I was melding myself together, extracting from who I had been and creating who I had to become. The speech was more than a formality; it was a process of self-definition, necessary to me and to my audience. Political speeches are filled with clichés and hyperbole; mine was not entirely exempt. But I needed this language; it enlarged me.

Then I had to act the part. The staff had arranged a perfect, minute-by-minute schedule that would get me to each location on time. The children were driven home, and I took off immediately after my announcement, at 1:15, and jumped into a waiting car driven by my volunteer aide to go to our next stop, White River Junction, by 2:15. We would eat lunch in the car. Breathless with excitement, the aide pointed to the sandwiches sitting in a bag on the floor of the car. There was one for each of us: me, my husband, the photographer, and my campaign manager. Relieved that everything had gone so well, I gulped down a soda and unwrapped my sandwich.

"Ham?" I stared at the pink meat in disbelief.

"Any problem?" he asked.

"It's just that I don't eat ham," I said, wrapping it up again. I was ready to gag. I did not keep a kosher diet, but I had developed my own perhaps equally orthodox taboos. Pork in all forms was one of them. Therefore I would starve. How could these people arrange my life, decide what I should say and where I went, if they didn't even know that I didn't eat ham? I was ravenous and furious at the mismatch. A tuna-fish sandwich, and everything would have been all right.

In between stops, I called the children to tell them how the day was going and make sure they were fine. We stuck to the schedule, were greeted by crowds of supporters at each location, and our mood was upbeat.

Each location had its distinguishing features; for a small state with a population of a half-million people, there were surprising differences. Our first stop on the eastern side of the state, bordering New Hampshire, was in White River Junction at the Coolidge Hotel, where I was greeted by an eclectic group of Dartmouth College professors, longtime Democratic stalwarts, a couple of labor leaders, and a few stragglers from the American Legion down the street. My eyes strayed from the crowd to glance at the dramatic mural, depicting New England life, painted on the walls of the room during WPA days. The occasion seemed more weighty, historic, against this backdrop.

We headed for Rutland, Vermont's second largest city, set in a tight valley, scarred by a shopping center in the middle of town that partially blocks the magnificent mountain range beyond. Rutland Democrats were conservative, suspicious of their Burlington cousins. Mayor Gillie Godnick, who had refused to support me, would not be there. I was grateful that former mayor John Daley handed me the key to the city. People seemed to clap more loudly than necessary when I was introduced, and I suspected it was because of Gillie's obvious absence.

In Bennington the reception was in a motel owned by the leading Democrats in town, Bob and Marie Condon. Sensitive to their far-flung location on the Massachusetts border, they feared being neglected by Montpelier, and I received high praise for showing up. Emma Harwood was there to greet me; she was the most respected labor leader in the state, head of the ILGWU. I hugged her. This was the home of Bennington College and the site of a rural garment industry that Emma fiercely protected. The miles we covered that day, crisscrossing the bumpy spine of the Green Mountains and wending our way south on Interstate 91 and then north on U.S. 7, exposed my expanded universe; I would be responsible for the whole state. The town halls, libraries, gas stations, and general stores that landmarked the highway looked different to me; I felt a surprising proprietary interest. It was as if a layer of skin had been lifted off the face of the state, and I saw things pulsating underneath. I could never again be a casual traveler.

The last stop that night was Winooski, a working-class Democratic stronghold near Burlington that once had thrived on a cotton-and-woolen-mill industry until a forced exodus south in the 1950s. The long, imposing redbrick factory buildings lining the Winooski River bore witness to their former dominance. Now they seemed uncertain of their place, washed up on the banks of the river, silent hulks.

But the crowd in Winooski that night was boisterous. I was thrilled with the exuberance that bounced toward me when I walked into the gymnasium of John F. Kennedy High School. Because I was the only announced candidate, I was the only one allowed to speak. Steve and I congratulated ourselves on our extraordinary luck. And when I addressed the crowd, I had my first experience of being repeatedly interrupted by applause. The words I had already recited four times that day came out of my mouth with a spontaneity I had only known in the intimacy of a living room among good friends, not in a high-school gymnasium with 250 strangers. I ad-libbed, tossed out compliments, joked, and laughed as if I had been doing this all of my life. Had all this spontaneity always been there? I was as amazed as my audience to discover the political personality who had just made her debut.

Brian Burns stopped by to tell me my voice had improved. Had I taken lessons? His wife, Linda, liked my speech; did I write it? Yes, I told her, trying not to be offended by the implication that because it was good, it must have been written by someone else.

That night, I knew I was going to win. Steve was great, Arthur was loving, and the kids were coming through. If it continues like this, how can I lose? I asked myself.

Two weeks later, I watched myself on the eleven o'clock news and hated what I saw. At a press conference I had been asked a question: I was running for lieutenant governor, but there was no announced candidate for governor. Would that be a problem? I had hedged, saying that I was certain that a good candidate would emerge. The six o'clock report had presented this reasonably well, but later that evening my reply was chopped to pieces. After comparing my name recognition with that of other candidates, which made me look like an unknown, the reporter concluded: "Despite this, Mrs. Kunin is waging a strong campaign and doesn't even think she needs a candidate at the top of the ticket."

"That's not what I said!" I shrieked from my bed. It made me look silly. I called up the television studio, and the woman at the switchboard said it was an editing mistake; they were shorthanded. I wanted to believe her.

When I got up at six the next morning, in time to make the kids breakfast and get out of the house by seven, I asked myself, Do I have the stamina for this campaign? Can I remain physically fit and mentally alert? What if I crumble with fatigue? After the birth of my first baby, a friend told me, "You will be tired for the rest of your life." No one had warned me that now I would feel as if I had given birth to twins. I lectured to myself that I must plan my time carefully, learn to take brief naps, and deliberately put downtime on the schedule. Every problem was magnified when I was tired. As Liz Bankowski said at least once a week for the five years we worked together, "Fatigue makes cowards of us all."

I learned to get refreshed by heading for the ladies' room just before a reception or a speech, splashing water on my face, applying fresh powder and lipstick, new deodorant, and a squirt of cologne. This was the equivalent of four hours of sleep. Looking tired was a political liability that I could not afford. Never could I openly admit to exhaustion, or even a headache. I feared my migraine secret would come out.

For a time, severe migraines regularly plagued me. I panicked when I was stricken with an attack. I recall sitting in the car at the curb in front of a house where a campaign reception was about to begin. I had only a few minutes before I was scheduled to walk in. I tried to make myself meditate, to reduce the pulsating pain. It didn't work. Nausea overcame me. We delayed the party while I slipped upstairs and lay prone in a quiet bedroom, praying that the painkillers would subdue my body into obedience. I was mortified. Everyone would know. The telltale signs—dark shadows, slow gait, halting words—would now be confirmed. A half hour later, I thanked God when I recovered. I went downstairs, feeling as if I had been reborn, so grateful was I to be free of pain and to have expelled my private demons, who had whispered to me in that upstairs bedroom that I was not up to this, mentally or physically.

The room was filled with people, smiling expectantly. As I spoke, I felt I was drinking an infusion of kind words: warm hugs and firm handshakes seeped into my bones and made me strong. Over tea I talked with a woman who had gone to medical school more than fifty years ago. She told me how it was to have been the only woman in a class of men. She had made a special effort to come to hear me speak today, she explained as she put aside her cane and slowly seated herself, because she wanted to see a woman elected.

That is how I overcame fatigue, by drawing energy from those around me, imbibing it as if it were being fed to me spoonful by spoonful. Toward the end of a campaign, I drew on reserves I had not known existed. I was living on marrow, not bone.

Externally, no one would know about fatigue or pain. I looked good.

I learned to dress correctly for a political campaign with the help of my friends and staff. I knew I had to be well dressed but not affluent; serious but not stern; feminine but not frilly; masculine but not butch; in control but relaxed, and neat but not dull. The right clothes might not make me into a winning candidate, but the wrong clothes could defeat me.

And I had to be flexible. Whatever the occasion, my clothes had to be appropriate, whether it was a fair, a tea, or an interview. Jackets, therefore, were especially useful; they could be taken off and put on, opened and closed as necessary. One day, I found a perfect ensemble: a flowered-print skirt with matching blouse and jacket, drip-dry. I wore it first to Woodstock and affectionately named it my Woodstock dress. A week later, when I wore it to a Democratic dinner in Middelbury, Colonel Joseph Whitehorne, the town chairman, appraised me and concluded, "You've just won two hundred votes with that dress." He let me know that when Stella Hackel ran for governor, she had appeared at this same dinner in pants. "Turned everybody off," the colonel snapped.

In 1974, when Madeline Harwood had run for the U.S. Congress in the Republican primary, she always wore red, white, and blue. I was sure she would win, but it wasn't enough. When Patricia Schroeder ran for president in 1988, the inordinate attention paid to her ruffled blouses made it difficult to concentrate on her military expertise.

At first, I dressed for the women. It was they who were watching most closely. I had to assure my female constituency that they could be comfortable with me and that I, a woman on trial, would not embarrass them. I had an image of how a woman like me should look, because for years I had been in the audience sizing up women like me. I had been as critical of them as I knew these women would be of me now.

But I also dressed for myself. If I could hold my body together and attire it properly for all occasions, I could hold my life together. Later, I also dressed for the men, either to fit in or to stand out among them, depending on how visible or invisible I wanted to be. Being a visible woman, the one who looks good, is smart, and acts poised, requires constant effort, even if, at times, this is satisfying and even amusing. Years later, when I posed on the steps of the chapel of the University of Virginia with the other governors attending President Bush's Education Summit in 1989, I relished the notion that in my cherry-red jacket I would remind the viewer that, indeed, there had been a woman present. The men, in their dark-uniformed suits, were destined for anonymity.

But earlier in my political career, figuring out how to dress appropriately was an energy drain. Blending in is more relaxing and offers the reward of collegiality. Often I wished for a uniform, something I could put on each day, like a navy-blue suit, a fresh shirt, and a red tie.

What I did not yet know was that it was not my clothes that mattered most; it was my hair. In 1978, my hair was shoulder length, wavy, and brown. When I ran for governor and lost in 1982, it was somewhat shorter, with a few strands of gray. In 1984, when I ran for governor and won, my hair was short, and the effect was extraordinary. Talk about my hair followed me everywhere. I was a Lady Godiva, fully dressed, without her horse. My staff heard of nothing else—until the debate switched to my stockings. "Tell her she can't wear white ones." Finally, the staff got the courage to tell me: nothing fancy or different. Plain, just wear plain flesh-colored stockings.

"You mean they noticed?"

"The phone's been ringing off the hook."

At my first debate with my opponent before a business audience, not an easy one for me to please, I was exuberant after it was over, for I had passed the test, had mastered the material, was quick on my feet, and felt superbly confident.

A middle-aged man whom I recognized as a local insurance executive strode up to me and beamed. He pumped my hand. "Madeleine, you were terrific."

"Oh, thank you, Bill," I said, wondering which cogent point I had made he particularly liked.

"I love your hair. It looks absolutely great."

I blanched. Control yourself, do not kick, do not scream. Smile.

I did. "Oh, thank you, I had it cut," and then I deftly moved away, before I said something obscene.

I tried to analyze the phenomenon. Was it that people didn't know what to say to a candidate, and hair was the first female body part to come into focus that could be commented on? As we note men's ties, which stare us in the face, do we feel compelled to talk about women's hair? Just a conversation starter, I told myself. Accept it as a friendly and irrelevant way to be complimentary. Or was there more to it? When people noted the change in my hair, months, and sometimes years, after I had it cut, was this their way of saying that I had changed and matured, that I now looked like a governor? Was the phrase "I like your hair" code for "I like you; you meet my approval"? Or were people examining my hair to detect subtle signs of transformation, scanning my scalp for tell-tale dark roots? When Roxanne Conlin ran for governor of Iowa in 1982, the front page of the major newspaper had a series of photographs stretched across five columns at the top depicting her different hairstyles at various stages of her career. Not a dramatic difference from one shot to the next, but enough to make the reader examine each one closely. What was she trying to do by changing her hair?

Hair is also sexy. It defines gender. A woman running for an office traditionally occupied by a man has to rein sexuality in. Keep it under control and come up, if possible, with an androgynous style; not wild, not tempting, but coiffed. Something pleasing to everyone. Perhaps that was why in 1984 the press assumed I had made a calculated hair decision on the advice of a political consultant. One reporter asked if it was true that I regularly went to Boston for an appointment with a special hairdresser. When I said no, she sounded skeptical. Just a haircut, with no ulterior motive? Hard to believe.

I BOUGHT my Woodstock dress and had my hair done in preparation for a speech before the Vermont chapter of the National Multiple Sclerosis Society meeting at the Woodstock Inn, owned by Laurance Rockefeller, one of an unknown number of discreet local millionaires. Maintenance was well paid for in this beautifully whitewashed Vermont town with glistening black shutters and an abundance of generous geraniums. The main street had recently been used for a turn-of-the-century movie set. Almost nothing had to be changed for authenticity except for a layer of pigeon droppings molded on a phony fountain placed at the intersection.

I felt dressed appropriately as I surveyed the well-groomed, gray-haired matrons in the dining room, sitting stiffly in their expensive, pink-suede suits. I told myself that if I looked like a lady, they might forgive me for being a Democrat. But were my words well received? Was I being too political for this gathering of charitable, manicured women? A few minutes after I began speaking, three people in the front row suddenly stood up and rushed out. All eyes followed them out the door.

What had I said?

A few moments later, I was told that someone had fallen in the bathroom, and they were the rescue party. As I began to feel I was winning my audience back, I spotted a man in the back row fast asleep. I spoke louder; it did no good. Remarkably, when my talk was over, he came up to the podium and complimented me most generously on my remarks. Naturally, I thanked him.

After the meeting I was scheduled to attend a fund-raiser with a new and enthusiastic supporter, Eleanor Paine, the owner of a beautiful house in the center of town, who was eager to hold a party. She had invited 250 people for cocktails between five and seven o'clock. She was certain we would raise two to three thousand dollars.

By 5:25 p.m., no one had shown up. We bravely made conversation while I tried not to cock my ear for the sound of tires on gravel, a swinging screen door, or even a bark. There were three of us, Eleanor, her daughter, and me. I concentrated on keeping my eyes focused on Eleanor, as if she were holding an eye chart to test me, afraid that my tendency to let my eyes wander toward the door would reveal my desire to cut and run. At 5:45, the first people arrived. We greeted them with an effusiveness I had reserved in the past only for my children after they had been missing for four hours.

Eleanor had planned a cash bar to raise money, but she had been advised that that would be in poor taste; she shouldn't ask people to pay until they got to know me. So visions of the two thousand dollars I had expected to collect melted in the ice bucket. We carried on a conversation that was to become familiar—in infinite detail, we discussed every other event occurring in and around Woodstock that evening and who was likely to be at it, rather than here. We included events that had occurred the day before and would take place the following week; everything was in competition with tonight. Then we itemized who was sick, who had visiting grandchildren, and who should have been invited, but hadn't been. By 6:30, about thirty people, including children, grandchildren, and dogs, were scattered about the dining room, kitchen, back porch, and sun room of this enormous house.

In walked Jack Morgan, the Republican legislator from Woodstock who had opposed my lobbyist-disclosure bill on the floor of the House. "Hi, Jack." I smiled. "I'm surprised, but delighted, to see you."

"Well," he said, trying to explain his presence in this uncrowded room, "I figure you've matured some since we last met."

"You're right, of course," I concurred, with perhaps unseemly gratitude. Then I was introduced to Peter and Jane Jennison, two staunch Democrats and well-known publishers of Vermont humor. They displayed sufficient enthusiasm to make up for the several hundred missing guests. They assured me this turnout was typical, that only about 10 percent of people invited to a Democratic affair ever showed up. Woodstock was a very Republican town, they explained. Of course, in my exuberance that obvious fact had escaped me. How could I, as a Democratic candidate for a minor office, have expected to get a large turnout in a Republican town?

I decided to make the best of the situation and approached a pleasant-looking, tightly corseted woman in her midfifties. She had just returned from Florida, she told me, where she had been robbed three times. I groped for my law-and-order platform. Finally I suggested short jail sentences for young offenders, hoping this would fit her viewpoint and allow me to be true to mine. But perhaps I had gone too far.

"In the East they cut off a hand, and they never steal again," she suggested cheerfully.

"Well, um, yes. A bit strong, though, for Vermont," I muttered, and expressed a desire to quench my thirst.

That night, I got home to Burlington after ten. Two checks were in the mail. One for fifty dollars. Great. The kids were still up. My daughter, Julia, played her new record for me, "Saturday Night Fever." Daniel, Julia, and I danced. He was great, Julia had the step, and I didn't at first. Then I got it, the kids applauded, we laughed ourselves silly, and I fell into bed.

IN EVERY CAMPAIGN, I worried about what effect my political career would have on my children. Would they be hurt to see their mother criticized? Would they understand that political battles were a kind of game that has to have winners and losers?

During a parade in 1982 one of my sons marched up to my Republican opponent, Richard Snelling, and asked point-blank, "Why won't you vote for my mother?"

Snelling explained that we were from different political parties, and that was how the system worked. "I have nothing against your mother personally. She's very nice," he said gently. I called his home to thank him; I was so grateful.

In the lieutenant governor's race, the children dealt with their distress at seeing me attacked by demonizing the poor Republican, Peter Smith, for trying to "beat our mother."

"I got up real close to him, and he has buck teeth," one of the children told me, as if it were inside information.

"And tiny eyes," another added.

All four believed they were helping me when they took Peter Smith's brochures, threw them on the ground, and stomped on them. All the time, I would say, "Now, you've got to be polite."

A friend asked my son in junior high school, "Hey, is Madeleine Kunin your mother?"

Without hesitation, he replied, "No, she's my aunt."

Unfortunately for him, the boy who asked the question was the son of the Democratic state chairman, who promptly told his father that he had it straight from the horse's mouth: Madeleine Kunin was Adam Kunin's aunt.

For a teenager to be singled out in any way is an endurance test. How much teasing they took, I will never know, but from my protected perspective, they passed the test well.

Occasionally, I feared for their vulnerability. The night Julia, then a high-school junior, returned from Girls State, a week-long mock legislative session sponsored by the American Legion, she told us that she had had a glorious time except for one episode. Senator Buckley, the incumbent lieutenant governor, addressed the session and happily announced to the gymnasium packed with girls, "I'm running against a woman. Should I be as tough on her as I would be on a man? I haven't had a lot of experience with women." He winked and added, "Candidates, that is. But I can tell you one thing, you sure all are a lot prettier than she is."

Julia told me guiltily, "I wanted to say something, but I didn't know how." I hugged her close. If Buckley had been within my reach at that moment, I would have clawed him. I vowed to do so in the election, but would I get that chance?*

IN MY FIRST CAMPAIGN for lieutenant governor in 1978, Steve scheduled as many radio interviews as possible. It was free publicity, we agreed. My first noontime talk show was "Comment," on radio station WWSR in St. Albans. I was warned: these guys have no use for Democrats. "Just answer the questions," Steve said, "and you'll be fine."

We pulled into the parking lot two minutes before the show, beckoned in the right direction by the huge radio aerial that rose above the low white wooden building.

The studio, like all radio stations, was constructed for sound, not sight. Three of us sat in the control room, Keith Dunham; David Kimel, co-owner of the station; and I. Keith, a commentator and the older of the two, was paunchy and slightly balding; David was red-haired and lean. Both would ask me questions.

I smiled at Keith. Dave, seeing me looking at his buddy with a plea for

---

* As I was writing this chapter, I received a call from T. Garry Buckley from his retirement home in Florida. Would I support a campaign for clemency for Jean Harris? He believed she was being treated unfairly in part because she was a woman. I agreed to help.

mercy, promptly set me straight. "If you think I'm conservative, he's to the right of Attila the Hun."

"Oh"—I laughed—"I'm sure this will be interesting."

Suddenly Dave seemed more kindly. Yes, he was raw, young, and aggressive, but maybe it was all bravado. On the air he would be different.

David had his regular callers. He knew who they were and how to get them out. "Well, let's talk about abortion," he announced as if he were about to launch a new product. I swore I saw him smile. The red light flashed wildly. Someone was on the line.

"First caller. Hello, this is 'Comment.' You're on the air."

The suspense was killing. Anybody could say anything, and it would be broadcast for miles. So would my response.

"Hi, Dave."

"Hi, Anna. Do you have a question for Mrs. Kunin today?"

"I sure do. Where does she stand on killing babies?"

"I believe that the question of whether or not to have an abortion is a personal decision," I said with measured calm.

"That's murder. You'll never have my vote," Anna said, and hung up.

The light flashed again. A second caller. "Unusually busy this morning." Dave grinned.

"I agree with Mrs. Kunin, the government shouldn't tell women what to do."

"Oh, thank you." I sighed into the microphone, hugging its stem with my hands.

"And besides," she added, "I don't believe in single-issue politics."

Red light. Anna was on the line again.

"Oh no, here she goes again." I sighed.

"I'd like to tell that other woman who just called a thing or two," she fumed. "What she said was sinful, absolutely sinful."

The second caller called back to save herself. Dave managed to get both of them on the line. For about five minutes, I was a bystander at a tennis match, sitting between the two callers as their words flew back and forth. The longer I stayed out of it, the better.

But Dave Kimel was impatient. He shut the ladies off and announced it was time to move to other issues. "Now what about these welfare mothers out there, ripping us off?" he said. "What does our listening audience think about them? I know Mrs. Kunin is anxious to hear from you."

Red light. "I think it's terrible," the caller complained in a tired voice. "I was standing in the checkout line at the store yesterday, and this woman in front of me paid for a bottle of vodka with food stamps."

"Vodka?" I asked.

"That's right," and she proceeded to enumerate a long list of welfare abuses she had personally witnessed.

Dave chimed in. "As far as I'm concerned, these women are just a bunch of professional breeders."

For a split second, I considered my options. Should I walk out or should I stay? Dave's taunt was a punch in my gut. Animals, that's what women were. Nothing I could say would sound right. If I released my fury, I would be punished. If I tried to be reasonable, I would be mocked.

I took a deep breath and found my voice. "I think that's ridiculous, Dave. No woman has children just to collect a welfare check."

Dave smiled. This was a more lively show than usual.

At the end of the half hour, I was exhausted. "Great show," he said as he stood up. "Hope we didn't rough you up too much."

Keith Dunham hadn't said a word.

Steve, who had been listening on his car radio, thought the program was spirited. I had defended myself well. The only problem was that I had said "you know" twenty-one times.

ONE DAY AFTER our one-room campaign office opened, at 12 St. Paul Street in Burlington, former governor Philip Hoff came by to drop off a $250 check. I hugged him. He believed in me.

In the following years, I was often flanked by these two former Democratic governors, who gave me their counsel and their support. When I became lieutenant governor, I asked Hoff to swear me in: he had been my model of a progressive Democratic governor. And when I was elected governor, Salmon, whom I had labeled prematurely as a hackneyed politician, became an ever stronger ally. More conservative than I on some issues, he was quiet about our differences and generous with his support. I grew to value his allegiance greatly.

Phil Hoff, whose philosophy was closer to mine, was far less tolerant of our differences. It became painful at the end of my third term as governor to see my former political idol turn against me. I never explained or understood it, even when I tried to see him as a politician whose ego might be bruised. Despite my efforts to suppress it, the dangerous question surfaced once again: Would my relationship with both these men have been different had I been a man with two buddies instead of a woman with two big brothers?

*   *   *

To avoid the fate of losing, I had to do everything in my power to win, including getting Republican votes. I was delighted, therefore, when that spring I was invited to the Castleton Women's Club annual luncheon. A few miles outside of Rutland, Castleton is a college town with a proud history revealed in the well-preserved elegance of the grand houses that line the main street. The turnout was impressive, and as I scanned the room, I noted that these were the women who had time. They also had power, not as it is commonly defined, but as they exercised it. They controlled everything of significance that happened in their town. It was considered to be a coup to have been invited. I mingled gracefully, bringing up politics discreetly whenever I could, careful not to cause offense.

I was introduced to a Mrs. Altdorfer. "Oh, yes, you're the smart one up there," she said. "I'm glad you're not running for governor. Richard Snelling is doing a wonderful job."

I did not argue.

"I have to tell you, my dear, I don't think Vermonters are going to vote for a Democratic governor ever again. Absolutely disgraceful what that Hoff fellow did." Then she turned to her friend. "How did we Republicans lose her?" Turning back to me, she took my hand. "Now be sure and come back for the Castleton Colonial Day parade. Everybody will be there," she assured me. "Wonderful crowd."

I loved her ambivalence, and I took her advice.

I rushed home that night to get back in time for Daniel's birthday party. I had bought an ice-cream cake that was waiting in the freezer. When I got in the door, I discovered my husband and children had already taken it out and lit the candles. I brought out new candles and made them sing again.

On June 15 I had been invited to be the commencement speaker at Richford High School, in a town not found on any tourist map, with its back up against the Canadian border, fewer than two miles away. Each time the poverty rate was assessed for Richford's two thousand inhabitants, it was the highest in the county. The best-paid jobs were with the U.S. border patrol. This was Pam Greene's hometown. She had been my roommate at the National Women's Conference in Houston. Today, she was my volunteer driver. The first sight I saw of Richford was a high red arch

of rusted metal letters—like MERRY CHRISTMAS strung above a doorway—that spanned the top of the Main Street bridge across the Missis-
quoi River, which cut the town in two. These letters spelled: WELCOME TO
RICHFORD. The *l* in "Welcome" and the *f* in "Richford" were missing.

Elaine Archambault, the Democratic town chairman, had arranged my
day; we would tour all the factories, have dinner at Pam's parents' house,
and then go to the graduation. Elaine met us in front of the cremee stand,
now shuttered tight for winter but the center of activity all summer long
for teenagers who gripped dripping ice-cream cones while they figured
out how and when to make contact with one another. I recognized Elaine
immediately; two enormous maroon-and-white Kunin buttons were dangling from her ears.

"Elaine, you look terrific. How did you make those earrings?"

"I'll be glad to make you a pair," she volunteered.

"They look better on you than they would on me." I laughed, and we
ran through the downpour to our first stop, the Blue Seal Grain Company, which produced two hundred thousand tons of animal feed a year.
Our objective was to catch the workers as they were leaving the first shift
at three o'clock. We would stand in the parking lot and intercept them as
they dashed to their cars. The second shift would be coming a few
minutes later, so we should be able to catch most of the 145 workers. I
heard a siren go off. The men, covered with grain dust, carrying their
lunch pails, hurried out in groups of twos and threes. I had been asked to
stop a stampede. We blocked one or two who couldn't dodge out of the
way. Meanwhile, the incoming second shift figured out what was going
on and detoured a wide path around us. Most got inside unscathed.

Disappointed with our slim haul of voters, we reconnoitered. "Maybe
we should go inside the plant," Elaine suggested. I was game. Once I
climbed the wooden stairs and breathed in the grain-clogged air and
heard the high screech of machinery, I understood why the men had been
in a hurry to get by. After five minutes of exposure, I was talcumed with
dust. We stopped in the manager's office—quiet, clean, sealed off from
the rest of the plant. This was the difference between wearing a white
collar and a blue.

Elaine checked her watch. Time to go. Back to the center of town. In
the middle of Main Street, we stepped down into a basement and entered
a one-room sewing factory. Here a dozen women bent over sewing machines, stitching parkas, pants, and jumpsuits.

"Hi, Lila," Elaine said to one woman, who did not dare to look up,
"we just met your husband over at Blue Seal."

I stopped at the next sewing machine to chat with a woman fitting a zipper into a bright-blue parka. Taped to the machine was an advertising brochure. The smiling, even-toothed, sunburned family in the photograph, clothed in splendid bright ski attire, leaned into one another, like a pyramid, forming a brilliant triangle against a field of snow.

The woman at the machine looked as if she had stepped out of a painting from Picasso's blue period. It was if the brochure were the positive, and the woman before me the negative. Her fingers worked quickly to make the material in her hands look like the garments in the picture. Her hair was pulled back in a ponytail, out of the way, her polyester blue slacks hung loosely over her legs, and her white cotton print blouse remained untucked. The cheerful tempo I had developed of introducing myself, shaking hands, and moving on seemed to make a mockery of her reality. My bright maroon-and-white campaign brochure felt heavy in my hands. Softly, silently, I laid one on her black handbag, on the floor. Our eyes never met. This was piecework, and I was an interruption. She would still be here, long after I was gone.

In my ignorance, I had thought that such working conditions were no longer permitted. This was a time of high technology. I had never stopped to think, when I shopped for clothes and looked through racks of ski parkas, searching for something that would enhance my image, that in such a basement room I would see an exhausted woman sitting at a machine, working with her hands, counting the pieces, the hours, and the money.

Our next stop was a hockey-stick factory. We stepped inside a huge, hangarlike metal structure where the smell of model-airplane glue hit me like ether. I felt I might go under. Take shallow breaths, I told myself.

"How do you deal with the smell?" I asked the first woman standing at the end of a long row, her feet on a rubber mat, her hands raw and red from the wood and glue.

"Oh, you get used to it." She laughed.

I didn't believe her. Some of the women worked ten-hour days on their feet. I walked over to the corner where half a dozen of them were sitting "on break." Fifteen minutes allowed in the morning and fifteen in the afternoon, time to smoke a cigarette, drink a soda, play a fast game of cards, and talk. A pile of soda bottles and cans had accumulated next to the soda machine. The scrawled sign overhead said, CHRISTMAS PARTY FUND. BRING YOUR CANS HERE.

"We've just got time for the furniture factory, they get out in a few minutes," Elaine prodded as I stared at the pile of cans. Is this what there is to look forward to?

Sweat and Cummings was aptly named, I thought as I toured the furniture plant, unable to hear myself talk above the siren of the saws. The logs came down on a conveyor belt, huge specimens with a life force of their own. First they were pushed through a machine that stripped off the bark, then the logs were sliced. The noise was at an excruciatingly high pitch. Only one or two men wore ear protection. When I asked the foreman why OSHA (Occupational Health and Safety Administration) regulations were not followed, I was told, "They want it that way. They don't want to be sissies."

For a moment, politics seemed entirely inconsequential. What could I ever do for them, except force them to wear earmuffs and goggles? I dropped a brochure here and there, stealthily, as if it were a subversive act, and then I began to think there must be a way to change all this, to create better jobs and decent working conditions.

Graduation was a big event in Richford, almost as big as the day each spring when "the ice leaves Richford," Pam laughingly explained.

Everywhere we had stopped on Main Street we had been asked, "Are you going to graduation?" Whether the people had a relative graduating didn't seem to matter. Everybody went.

That June evening in this northern corner of Vermont it was still sweater weather outside. Inside, the air was steamy, as in a locker room. Years of sweat that had dropped to the planks of the gymnasium floor now rose in a mist. A banner was strung across the stage against the maroon velvet curtain. The Victorian letters said, NOTHING IS EVER ACHIEVED WITHOUT ENTHUSIASM.

I sat onstage with the principal, the priest, the president of the school board, and the head of the PTA. The ten-piece band started up "Pomp and Circumstance." Everyone rose from their gray metal chairs. Two rows of high-school seniors started down the aisle. Each girl wore a thin white rayon academic gown and cap, and each boy wore navy blue. The girls clasped long stemmed roses, holding them in front like candles that might go out if they walked too fast. As the class marshals led the procession down the center aisle, they broke through a crisscrossed web of maroon-and-gold crepe-paper streamers. The music stopped. The invocation started. Every head was bowed. The valedictorian stood up to speak. Sitting behind her, I concentrated on her feet; with these shoes she would step out of Richford, one way or another. Her voice broke, but she finished what she had to say as she recalled the best years of her life. When she sat down, she took out her white linen handkerchief and wiped her eyes. Everyone understood.

I was introduced, went up to the podium, and looked at the expectant faces of the graduates. I heard the cry of a baby in the background and wished I could tell the graduates what I had learned that day in their town: Do not allow yourself to be stuck at a sewing machine or to stand in the hockey-stick factory for the rest of your life. Continue your education, get out of Richford.

Instead I said, "It's a great pleasure to be here in Richford on this special day of your lives," and followed the script I had planned. They looked so beautiful, dressed in blue and white. Maybe I had been wrong. Maybe for them it would be different.

Two years later, on a visit to Vermont Technical College in Randolph Center, I was taken on a tour by a young woman student in the first class of women to be admitted into the school's two-year engineering program.

"Where are you from?" I asked her.

"Richford."

"You are?" I wanted to embrace her. "What made you decide to leave Richford and come to school here?"

"I knew I didn't want to work at a cremee stand for the rest of my life."

O blessed girl.

That night in Richford, I promised myself that someday, when I was in a position to do something, I would come back to Richford, and in 1987, when I was governor, I did. At a special ceremony at the town hall, the Richford Board of Selectmen and I signed an agreement for the construction of a new dam, settling a long-standing controversy between environmentalists and engineers that had delayed the project, which would halt damage caused by the ice floe almost every year.

After much study the U.S. Army Corps of Engineers vetoed the project, calling it cost ineffective. Nevertheless, hope was beginning to be felt in Richford in modest amounts; the town had received a grant to restore the post office and turn it into office space and had formed a local development association, the REAC (Richford Economic Advancement Corporation), to attract new businesses to town. As I approached the bridge, I was thrilled to see that every letter in WELCOME TO RICHFORD was in place.

PETER SMITH was a clean-cut, energetic preppy man whom my friends in Burlington remembered fondly as their newspaper boy. He was running in the Republican primary for lieutenant governor against Buckley, so in a sense we shared a common opponent. All summer, Peter and I met at state fairs, and at each one, he would set up shop by wheeling out a huge green canister of helium gas and blowing up blue-and-white balloons inscribed with PETER SMITH FOR LIEUTENANT GOVERNOR. I liked to imagine him with a cluster of balloons in his fist, floating up and out of sight, like Mary Poppins.

I scowled at each smiling kid who went by with a balloon attached to the wrist. I turned to my campaign manager. "Steve, we've got to have balloons." Steve stalled. My anxiety increased. There was no doubt in my mind—because of those balloons, Peter Smith would win.

The first time I campaigned in a crowd, I didn't know where to begin. I stood on a rise looking down at the milling crowd of families who had just dispersed to the fairgrounds after the annual Vermont State Dairy Festival parade in the town of Enosburg Falls, "Vermont's Dairy Center." Every statewide politician had given a speech on the grandstand. I had been introduced, told them who I was, and sat down. The sound system wasn't working. The crowd was eager for the parade to start. I suspected that no one had known who I was.

Now I had a chance to tell them personally. But how could I plunge in? I felt like a swimmer on the high diving board. My eyes followed a column of smoke rising from the chicken barbecue pit. At the base I saw a line snaking across the grass for some thirty feet. That's it! They wouldn't mind if I approached them there. They had no place to go, nothing to do, but wait in line.

If only my brochures had been ready! Instead, I carried a sheaf of purple mimeographed papers that said, "Rep. Madeleine Kunin for Lt. Governor," followed by a short blurb. Definitely amateur.

I approached the last person in line.

"Excuse me. I'm very sorry to disturb you. Uh, I hope I'm not troubling you . . . but I'm Madeleine Kunin, and I'm running for lieutenant governor. I would like to leave this information with you, if that's okay. Okay? Great. Er, um, do you have any questions?" I prayed there wouldn't be any.

Everyone took the paper. Almost everyone smiled.

By the time I had practiced my pitch on a dozen voters, I began to abbreviate it slightly. In a few weeks, I would have it down: "I'm Madeleine Kunin, and I'm running for lieutenant governor. I would appreciate your vote."

I was thrilled with my strategy on the barbecue line until I looked up to find, directly before my face, the tousled head and bright smile of Peter

Smith. He had been working the opposite end of the line, and we met smack in the middle.

As a woman candidate, I was frequently invited to speak to women's organizations, but where could I speak to men? I was delighted to get an invitation to a meeting of the Middlebury Rotary Club. Carl Neuse, a lawyer and a Democrat, asked me to be his guest at the noon meeting.

"Whatever you do, don't talk about politics. I'm the only Democrat here, and they barely tolerate me. I'll just introduce you, and then you can sit down."

I carefully followed his instructions. I stood up, said my name, said I was happy to be there, and added, hoping I was not overstepping any bounds, that I was a candidate for lieutenant governor. Then I dutifully listened to an exceedingly dull speech.

A week later, I was back in Middlebury campaigning on Main Street when a seersucker-suited gentleman stopped to greet me. "Hello there, you're Madeleine Kunin, aren't you?"

"Yes."

"I certainly enjoyed your speech at the Rotary Club last week."

I smiled appreciatively. "Why, thank you."

Never again would I underestimate the power of a few well-chosen words.

Isabel and Bill Farrell, two devoted supporters who adopted me like a daughter, invited me to come to the Newport Fourth of July parade.

"Everybody will be there, we'll make all the arrangements."

And they did. I rode in Bill's 1965 maroon Buick convertible, balanced on top of the backseat next to the mayor, Ken Magoon. Following his cue, I positioned myself in place and kicked my shoes off to save the upholstery and my life, curling my toes into the soft vinyl while making an effort not to look terrified. I clamped my hands over the top of the seat. I looked at the back of the driver's head. He was keeping a steady, slow pace. One sudden jolt, and I'd be dead.

As I waved to the waiting crowd, I wondered how much I looked like an aging parody of Miss Teenage Vermont, whose crown was catching the sun's sparkle in the car ahead of us. I wished that another float had separated the two of us. The band started up behind us. I moved my feet to the rhythm and started to hum to the music, moving my head first to one side of the street and then to the other, hoping that neither side would feel neglected. I tried to pace my movements to the size of the crowd, without looking calculating. I waved, they waved back. Now we were in the heart of downtown, going past city hall, the courthouse, Needleman's Apparel store, and the diner with a huge stuffed polar bear in the window. The crowd was thick. I turned from left to right and back again, wondering whom I had missed.

What a cute baby!

I waved, unable to take my eyes off him. Maternal gravity pulled me in his direction; I beamed at the parents. A young couple was leaning against a tree, holding hands. With each free hand, they waved. My response became bolder. What had started as a genteel Queen Elizabeth–like flapping of fingers now became a full-armed swing. My arm was a compass, swinging in a high arch from east to west and back again. Did they know who I was? Could they read the handmade signs, MADELEINE KUNIN FOR LIEUTENANT GOVERNOR? I dared not look down to see if the signs were still there.

"Hi, Madeleine! Go for it!" someone yelled.

"Happy Fourth of July!" I shouted back.

The adrenaline started to pump. I sat straighter, smiled wider, and waved without pausing to see whom I was waving at. Was I enjoying this too much? I thought of Mussolini. Would I become intoxicated by the crowds? I couldn't stop grinning, even when I tried. My muscles would not let go. Enjoy it, I told myself. Play the part. This is America. This is the Fourth of July.

We were crossing the bridge; the crowd was thinning out. One more red light, and we would have to stop.

Before the parade had started that morning, Isabel Farrell asked that I pay a courtesy call on Beatrice Schurman, the first Democratic woman in Vermont to have sought the post of lieutenant governor, in 1950. Her candidacy, like that of all Democrats in that era, was considered hopeless the moment it was declared. "I am so glad she will see you. She's not well, you know, but you want her to give you her blessing," Isabel said as she fluttered her hands in front of her plump body in nervous anticipation.

The door opened.

There stood a tall, elegant woman, wearing a beige lace-trimmed silk dress, looking more like an aged opera singer than a retired politician. Isabel offered what I thought was a little curtsy.

"Hello, Mrs. Schurman, I would like you to meet Madeleine Kunin.

She's the young woman I've been telling you about who is running for lieutenant governor."

Mrs. Schurman looked down on us and coughed slightly as her eyes adjusted to the sunlight. Emphysema, I calculated as I saw her cigarette in one hand and a white handkerchief in the other.

"I don't want to disturb you," I faltered, glimpsing her frailty through the lace openings of her dress. Her neck was pulled taut by her raised chin.

"Not at all, I'm delighted to see you. Isabel has told me so much about you. I'm proud that you are running. You will accomplish what I couldn't. I know you will win." She smiled. I felt I should bow my head to accept her blessing.

She led us into a darkened, cool living room, heavy with worn brocade and faded silk. It was a room that had been sealed against the outside air, against time. Every wall was covered with framed mementos. There she was, standing with Lyndon Johnson at her side.

"That was taken when I was National Democratic committee woman," she said. She held that post for twenty-five years. For her official trip to Washington, she requested a proper welcome from the Speaker of the U.S. House, Sam Rayburn, and asked that he meet her at the train station, which he did.

"She knew them all," Isabel stage-whispered. "And when she called, they listened."

Here on the end table was a signed picture of John F. Kennedy; on the opposite wall, a large sepia photograph of FDR, and another one taken with Mrs. Roosevelt. She remembered everyone, but only Isabel had remembered her.

When will I receive such a visit, I wondered, from a young woman paying her respects and believing she needs my blessing?

My next parade was in Bristol, a village that the poor could not escape from and the urban refugees of the 1960s had gravitated toward. Local jobs were scarce, and few paid above the minimum wage; those who could commute to either Burlington or Middlebury did. A large lumber mill, still visible by the river from the bridge leading into town, had once employed just about everybody; now it provided a paycheck for only a few. But the town had been spruced up in recent years by a number of young entrepreneurs who had started a couple of restaurants and created a surprisingly lively main street. People from at least a thirty-mile radius came to Bristol for this parade. Steve borrowed his friend's red pickup truck for us to ride in. That would make me look more down-to-earth, he assured me, less like Miss Vermont. We bought rolls of red, white, and blue crepe paper and some tape, and worked feverishly to decorate the truck and make a bold sign that could be read from a great distance. Daniel stood in the back of the truck, popping bubble gum. Just as we were about to start, a huge pink bubble plastered his face.

"It's okay," I said indulgently, knowing I could not reprimand him now. Bonnie, our family dog, decked out in a red, white, and blue crepe-paper bow, gave us a cue with her bark. She had spotted a Dalmatian on a fire truck and was ready to bolt, when Adam held her back with her leash. Julia, keeping a discreet distance from her brothers, stood at the back of the truck and waved now and again.

We arrived shortly after eight o'clock that morning to do some early sidewalk campaigning and get a good spot for the parade. I headed for the town common, centered by a circular green-and-white bandstand and framed by solid redbrick Victorian-era buildings on one side and white clapboard on the other. A perfect New England town. In that early light, I caught sight of a boy who seemed about fifteen years old, holding a beer can in one hand and extending the other straight out for balance, like a tightrope walker, leaping from the roof of one car to another, teetering and tottering as he went, but always landing on his feet. Drunk? At this hour? This was a part of life in Vermont I had not seen.

I paused by a car filled with children. Through the windows I could see little heads and bottoms tossing and rolling about, as if I were looking through the porthole of a tumbling clothes dryer. The two mothers were sitting on the grass, smoking cigarettes. One of the children made an animal sound, something like a sheep. It filled the clear morning air.

"Oh, all right," one of the women said as she jerked open the car door and let the child crawl out. He was retarded and looked around six years old but could not stand up. "Come over here, right now!" the mother yelled. His mouth hung open, weighted down by his wet lower lip. He sat there as if trying to figure out how to respond. He took too long. She lashed out with a smack across his cheek. He screamed. I moved away.

I felt I had stumbled on a secret: the town in the early morning hours as it really was, before the band began to play.

The parade route was instructive. After whizzing by a line of faces, blurred into anonymity, the parade would slow down and a face or two would come into focus. I spotted a woman standing on her porch. Our eyes met, and we exchanged the knowing glances of silent women. She raised both arms in the air. I held mine out and carried her smile like a gift in my hand.

I will do it, I will do it, I said to myself, I will win for her and for me. Again and again I would see those women along the parade route.

Our truck moved through the nice part of town. Lawn chairs with the weight of three generations, Grandma and Grandpa, the children, and grandchildren, lined up in precise symmetry. Iced tea, geraniums, neatly trimmed green lawns. A perfect picture. And then we rode past the tenements. People clustered on a sagging second-story porch, and in the far corner, by herself, a child who looked no more than twelve stood holding her arms straight out as if carrying a tray of glasses that had been poured too full, only she was stiffly balancing the body of a tiny, squealing infant on a white blanket.

Ten years later, when I signed a proclamation creating a task force on teenage pregnancy, my mind was back in Bristol, looking up at that porch and at that child.

MY CAMPAIGN SCHEDULE kept me on the road almost every day. One July day my volunteer driver and I stopped at a mom-and-pop store to buy a soda on our way to Rutland. The radio behind the cash register was on, and as I put my hand down into the cooler, rummaging for the right can, I heard the voice of Mayor Gillie Godnick coming on the air. I pulled my hand out and listened. This was the man who had said he would not support me.

Now he explained why. "When I was at the Democratic convention with her in Kansas City, she was walking around in a peasant dress without her shoes on. She's one of them hippies, a liberal. No way can I support her."

My God, did he say that? What on earth was he talking about? I called my campaign office. It was true; Gillie swore I had been barefoot at the Democratic convention.

We went back to the car to figure this out. I leaned against the door, drinking my soda, and a cop drove by, his belly up against the wheel. He waved and grinned. "Got your shoes on, Madeleine?"

No matter how often I denied it, everyone believed Gillie. On the surface, I treated it lightly and told the press that as "a forty-four-year-old woman, it was quite flattering to be called a hippie."

But I was seething internally. Accusations, I discovered, once thrown to the airwaves take on a life of their own. Repetition creates a reality all by itself. Even I began to imagine this woman at the Democratic convention, dressed in a peasant dress, wearing no shoes. I added hoop earrings, red petticoats, and castanets. In public, the more staunchly I denied her, the more vividly she came into focus. How many Madeleine Kunins will there be, I wondered, in the course of my political life?

When I got to Rutland, I learned that John Mulligan, a Democratic legislator who was angry with my support for the bottle-deposit law, was giving a lunch for Buckley. That night, my dreams were startlingly clear.

I was in a building where everything was cream colored. A door was ajar, and I knew who was behind it, but I wanted to see for myself, so I opened it. There, at a table, sat Buckley and a group of Democratic good old boys.

"Who told you you could open that door?" Mulligan shouted angrily.

"Well, it was open, so I thought it was all right," I said apologetically, wishing I had never walked in.

The same night, I also dreamed I had a six-month-old baby, dressed in a blue stretch suit, chubby and smiling. Was this the world to which my subconscious wanted to return?

My first campaign scare occurred on August 3. We received a call from an aide to Governor Snelling warning us about a story that was about to break. Lenore McNeer, an enthusiastic supporter of mine, had obtained the mailing list of the Governor's Commission on the Status of Women and she had used it to send out fund-raising letters for my campaign. This was apparently illegal, it being against state regulations to use state lists for political purposes.

My vulnerability as a candidate hit me; many people were now working on my behalf, and how could I control them? My campaign had cast a wide net; I would be responsible for everything that happened, whether I was personally involved or not.

At any time, any place, I might get a call from the press, asking me to respond to an event or a statement. What I said or did not say could make all the difference. Could I trust my instincts not to overreact, to be thoughtful, to be informed, to minimize damage and protect my candidacy, no matter what happened? The fear of a surprise attack would create undercurrents of anxiety in this and every other campaign.

I had been careful throughout the campaign not to base my candidacy on gender. I was running not because I was a woman, but because I was qualified. But whether I acknowledged it or not, gender was ever present.

The point was made for me at the Swanton lumber company, when one of the two brothers who owned the store volunteered, "It would be good to have a woman. Maybe women could do a better job than the men."

I politely demurred. I had heard that these brothers were solid Republicans and any indication that I was a feminist would certainly put them off. "Well, we'd like to blame the men for the way things are, but realistically, we can't," I said as agreeably as I could.

"Oh yes we can," an elderly woman standing right behind me protested. "If we were in charge now, they would blame us, wouldn't they?"

I looked at her, astonished. "Why, why, yes," I agreed, "I guess you're right."

These sudden outbursts of feminist anger from strangers were not uncommon on the campaign trail. Usually they would be preceded by denials. "I am not one of those women libbers," a woman in a grocery store informed me, as if that disclaimer would protect her, and then promptly launched into a tirade against men. "Whenever women do something, they do a better job. Now I don't have a college education, but I know I am a lot smarter than my husband." She clapped her hands over her mouth and looked around. "Maybe I shouldn't have said that."

My campaign touched these women in ways I did not fully understand; it released their anger, raised their hopes, and increased their fears. If I succeeded, I would confirm the best they could wish for themselves; if I failed, I would confirm the worst. We had to move on, I was reminded, as I looked at the schedule and got back to the car.

We passed the lumber store once again. There in the window was a mannequin dressed in a Victorian gown in honor of the store's fiftieth anniversary. In her gloved white hand, she held a maroon-and-white Kunin brochure.

THE SUSPENSE of the campaign became unbearable. How could I last until November? Each morning when I woke up, I would either be refreshed with the optimism of a good night's sleep or exhausted from the anxiety of bad dreams. I counted the days on my fingers, as a child counting the days before a birthday. This would end. Much as I dreaded the election night answer, the outcome would be a release.

The Women's Campaign Fund had lent us a campaign consultant from Washington, Audrey Sheppard. Methodically, she told us what must be done, step by step. We needed more money, staff, and organization. How could everything get done? The campaign process was so amorphous; so much was beyond our control. Audrey's quiet, earnest approach seemed to create an overlay of order. I was grateful not only for her flip charts but for her showing us that there could be a structure to a campaign.

THERE WAS another part of my life. At Adam's bar mitzvah on September 14, he looked angelic and recited his haftorah perfectly. For the other children's celebrations, I had always done the baking myself, enlisting friends a week in advance to help with preparations. This time, the event was catered. I was relieved that only I seemed to know the difference. As I looked around the synagogue, I told myself, This is what is real and important—the familiar ancient prayers and music, the smiling crowd of friends and relatives, my husband, our children. Was I threatening to crack this beautiful picture with the force of my own ambition? I could not allow myself to probe further. I had chosen this course; there was no alternative but to win.

TEN DAYS LATER, I was standing in the middle of the field of Catamount Stadium, before an eager crowd of seven thousand stock-car-racing fans, cautiously placing my hand into the lower depths of a brown plastic garbage bag, reaching for what I hoped would be a dry, perfectly formed, easy-to-throw cow chip.

Steve had signed me up: a cow-chip throwing contest for politicians in the town of Milton, once a farming community and now a working-class bedroom town of ranch-style houses and trailer parks near Burlington. But people came down from Canada and across from western New York State to watch the races at Catamount, which attracted well-known stock-car drivers.

"It'll be great exposure," Steve insisted over my protests.

Why had I let him do it? This was more than undignified; it was gross. This was the Roman forum of Vermont, and for the first time, I felt like a Christian in the lion's den. (Years later I saw it differently, when I had the fun of starting the Governor's Cup Race by announcing over the loudspeaker, "Gentlemen, start your engines!")

While the motors were revving up in the pits, our motley band of politicians and tagalong spouses lined up, alphabetically, ready to march out to center field. The moment the band struck up, Arthur and I were to follow Jerry Diamond, the incumbent attorney general, and his wife, Candy; Marie Dietz, the Right to Life candidate for Congress, and her husband; and bringing up the rear would be my Republican opponent, Peter Smith.

Should we carry signs or not? Is it better to be incognito? Will I lose votes or win votes, I wondered, by this crass behavior? Arthur reminded me that the purpose was simply name recognition. I relented.

We paraded out into the field, and I held a stick with my poster tacked to it bravely flapping in the wind. I was glad I wore jeans; maybe that would make me look as if I belonged here. Certainly my casual attire would help me find the proper athletic stance for cow-chip throwing. Now that I was here, there was nothing to do but hold my head high and grin. I was being a good sport.

But, as I knew only too well, lousy at sports. I had never won anything. Not even a place on the girls' softball team. Please, God, let this be over as soon as possible. "Ladies and gentlemen, we are about to begin the third annual Political Cow-Chip Throwing Contest. This is the moment we have been waiting for. In the lineup we have . . ."

The organizers of this annual event were in no hurry. Each of us was given a complete introduction, followed by an extended drumroll. I shifted from foot to foot, looking up, around, and down. What would happen next? I was totally at the mercy of the voice coming over the loudspeaker and the cheering of seven thousand bloodthirsty stock-car-racing fans. I took Arthur's hand.

The crowd fell silent. Suddenly, a new drumroll erupted. Down the field, I could distinguish a portly, elegant man in a tuxedo. He looked like the headwaiter from a fine French restaurant who had accidentally walked through the wrong set of swinging doors and found himself in this stadium. A bad dream. What was he carrying? Something sparkled in the light; it was a trophy-sized silver bowl. He held it in both hands with extraordinary care. Over his right arm, he had draped a crisp white towel. The bowl, I discovered when he came to a full stop in front of me, contained water. Here, he explained, delicately, is where we would wash our hands.

"Of course," I said, appreciatively.

The crowd, getting the message, roared.

Up stepped the judge. It was Bob Bannon, a local radio disc jockey, more familiar to me for his political banter than for his judicial skills.

Today, he took his job seriously. Bannon pointed to a white-painted tire, lying on the grass about fifteen feet away. The test, Bannon explained, would be accuracy, not distance. I brightened. This way, I could throw underhand.

The cow chip I had blindly selected from the bag was perfectly round, flat, and dry—a good one. As I held it high in the air like a discus, it gained immediate approval from the crowd.

I stepped up to the starting line, bent my knees, said to myself, I'm going to beat that son of a bitch Peter, and tossed.

Bannon stepped up to the microphone, to the tune of "Hail to the Chief."

"Ladies and gentlemen." He paused significantly. "The winner of the 1978 annual Catamount Stadium Political Cow-Chip Throwing Contest is none other than Madeleine Kunin, candidate for lieutenant governor."

Peter Smith's face fell.

He knew, and I knew, this was an omen. I would win. I had psyched him out, in front of this crowd.

Worse yet, I was a girl.

I was near hysterical with happiness, holding my golden-bull trophy high in the air. Back in the stands, I was surrounded by the press. A microphone was stuck in my face.

"What do you think this means, Mrs. Kunin?" a reporter questioned, with mock seriousness.

"I guess it means that women can throw it as well as men." I giggled.

Minutes later, I watched Peter Smith working the crowd in the stands. He moved quickly, smiled easily. He was taller than I had remembered. I hated having to run against him. Too bad we couldn't have remained on the same side, as we seemed to have been when we both were campaigning against Buckley.

But now he was my opponent, having achieved a surprise upset by trouncing Buckley in the primary that September. I found myself in the unenviable position of having to campaign against a nice, clean-cut young man.

I discovered how tough the race would be while sitting in my car before going to my appointment at Guys' Coiffure and listening to the news on the radio. Every hour on the hour, the radio station had released a section of the Naramore poll taken right after the Republican primary. They had already announced the results for governor, congressman, and attorney general. Now, at two o'clock, they would reveal the numbers for the race for lieutenant governor.

"The Naramore poll, released today, shows that Republican Peter Smith would beat Democrat Madeleine Kunin two to one. The surprise victor of the Republican primary, who defeated the incumbent T. Garry Buckley by a large margin . . ."

Click.

My mouth felt dry, my cheeks flushed. I wondered if I would slump over the wheel as in a grade-B movie. Instead, I looked at my watch and asked myself, Should I keep my hair appointment, for which I am already late, or stop at my campaign office, just around the corner, first? I headed for the office; Steve hadn't heard the news. He put his arm on my shoulder and advised me to keep my appointment. It was as good a place as any to recuperate, perhaps better than most: a woman's space where I could feel warm water pouring over my head, firm hands washing my scalp, and the warmth of the dryer near my face.

Back at the campaign office, I was informed that the radio station had called for my response and so had the newspaper. It would be best if I talked to them myself, Steve suggested. "Try to be upbeat," he said, as he held his hand over the mouthpiece and handed me the phone.

There is only one thing to do, I told myself, fake it.

"No, I'm not at all discouraged by the poll. It was to be expected that Peter Smith would experience a surge of support right after the primary. After all, he defeated an incumbent. But his lead will fade away, and I am confident of victory in November."

I hung up and hoped that God would not punish me.

The night before the election I prepared myself for defeat. I was going against a strong Republican tide. Governor Snelling was heading for a landslide victory. My chances would depend on heavy ticket splitting.

We had one break. In an offhand comment to a reporter traveling with his campaign, Smith was asked, "What do you think will be the impact of running against a woman?"

He replied, "Oh, all the broads will vote for Madeleine."

The reporter included this remark in her story, and a few days later "Broads for Madeleine" T-shirts and buttons appeared all over Vermont.

I was amazed at the response.

"Hey, here's another broad for Madeleine," someone would shout to me from across the street.

The remark was picked up by the press, seized by women, and continued to dog Peter wherever he went. I tended to dismiss it with a laugh. But I realized later that his mistake may have tilted the election. It brought to the surface a factor that we had both scrupulously ignored: gender. And it mobilized my constituency, putting Smith on the defensive.

For election night I decided that, rather than renting hotel space, I wanted to hear the election returns at home. Brian Burns thought it a terrible mistake. "You'll never get rid of people, if you lose." But I wanted the comfort of home, win or lose.

By nine-thirty I knew I would win. The phone was ringing incessantly with returns and congratulations. (The final results were 62,372 votes for me and 58,171 for Smith.) At ten o'clock, I picked up the phone in my kitchen and because of the crowd couldn't understand a word. I yelled into the phone, "I can't hear you. Could you please hold on a minute while I go downstairs and pick up the other phone?" I put the receiver on the counter and wended my way downstairs, chatting along the way. Finally, I got downstairs, picked up the phone, and asked, "Who is it?"

"This is Jimmy Carter," said the voice. "How are things going up there?"

I was aghast. I had kept Jimmy Carter waiting! Recovering my breath I said, "UPI has just declared me the winner."

"That's why I called. Congratulations!"

I blurted out, "I can't believe you're really calling me." I wanted desperately to say something profound and could only come up with "It's great to be a Democrat, Jimmy." Immediately, I wished I had said "Mr. President."

The kids, downstairs in the playroom, overheard the conversation. They chimed in, "It's great to be a Democrat, Jimmy!"

The next day, the *Free Press* story carried the headline: "She's Somebody's Wife, She's Somebody's Mother, and She's Our Lieutenant Governor." A television crew came to my house to film my reaction. I was pleased that they could see the red roses, just sent, and the clean tablecloth I had fortunately had time to put on the table.

8

I HAD CHOSEN A BOOTH IN THE REAR OF THE NARROW CHINESE RESTAU-
rant, where soy aromas swam over the glossy black tabletops. My eyes
sought darkness like a bat.

This is where I wanted to meet for lunch with my husband and the
children. It was noon, November 3, 1982. I wanted to show them how to
be a good loser, but the gummy, translucent sweet-and-sour sauce on the
chicken leg stuck to the roof of my mouth; it was hard work to swallow.

A shaft of light cut into the floor. Its compass needle came from the
front door. A couple was being escorted to a nearby table. "My God, I
think I know them."

I riveted my eyes on my food and prayed they would not see me. I could
not bear it—having to smile, fearing to cry. I curled down in the booth;
my feet hit the table pedestal.

Forgive me, I have lost. I ran for governor and I lost.

I truly had believed I would win.

I have made a fool of myself.

Everybody had known what I didn't: that I would lose. My son Adam
confessed to me years later that sometime that fall the children had had a
private discussion.

"Hey, you know, Mom's going to lose."

"You think so?"

"Yes, but we can't tell her."

And they didn't.

My last campaign stop had been at Simmonds Precision Products, an
electronics plant with more than a thousand employees, located in Ver-
gennes, twenty-two miles south of Burlington. I had been taken through
the plant by the manager himself—Joe Kerr—an avowed Republican.

I was thrilled with the VIP treatment he gave me. "Meet Madeleine
Kunin," he said, calling over the workers on the factory floor. "She's
going to be the next governor of Vermont."

Manic with day-before-the-election hysteria, I believed him. Like a

reckless lover, I abandoned all caution. The screen I had carefully erected
to filter out political hyperbole fell. I was like a stripper, throwing my
clothes to the audience, piece by piece, until I was down to almost nothing. They had yelled for more, and I gave it, all of it. I laughed, joked, and
pirouetted my way through the plant. I shook dozens of hands in the
business offices, moving from gray cubicle to gray cubicle with an ecstatic
grin on my face. This was not the plastered-on campaign smile, but the
smile of a drunk, reeling with visions of victory. I reached for each hand
as if it were a pillar, eager to hold on, sorry to let go.

They had known, of course. All that time, while I was gyrating, they
knew I looked silly—worse yet, pathetic. Oh, God, what had I revealed?
Why hadn't anyone told me to cover myself up? Defeat had made my
performance ridiculous. Victory would have made it momentous.

"I shook the governor's hand the day before the election. I knew she
would win."

Everyone would have remembered the winner.

Blessedly, they would forget the loser.

But I had not imagined it all, had I? All those people who waved back
at the traffic intersection yesterday at six in the morning? There we were,
a Jack-in-the-Box with a cluster of supporters on the street corner, jump-
ing up and down, Kunin signs puncturing the air, bodies in constant
motion to keep warm, to keep laughing.

Seventy-four thousand votes, 44 percent, the morning paper had said.
That was real.

"Go for it, Madeleine!"

"Right on!"

The race had been tough from the start. I had declared my candidacy
after Richard Snelling decided not to seek a fourth term. Early in January,
an editorial appeared in the *Burlington Free Press* urging him to run
again. As petitions asking him to run accumulated on his desk each morning, he took time to let the momentum build, but then gave in. Yes, if the
people really wanted him to run once more, he would serve. From one
day to the next, my political prognosis changed—what had been considered a race I was likely to win, turned into a race I was expected to lose.
But I could not pull out. I had made a public commitment, and privately,
I did not want to be a coward, intimidated by Snelling's reemergence.

Public reaction was immediate. My friends urged me not to run. People
who had looked me in the eye and shaken my hand as a future governor
now shifted their glances downward because they did not know what to
say to "poor Madeleine." Never had I felt more lonely, because I could

not share my distress. Outwardly, I had to rally my troops and proclaim that Snelling's reentry into the race "made no difference," while inwardly, I knew it made all the difference in the world. I would lose.

But over the course of the campaign I had shed much of that anxiety, and the outer confidence I had displayed adhered to my form, not like a cloak, but like a skin.

At last, I had become who I had wanted to be: the thumbs-up campaigner. My entire body was committed. For five unremitting months, I had pushed my weight against the wall of a dangerously sagging campaign. Whenever I eased up, the wall pressed against me, threatening to bring me and everyone else down with it—my family, the campaign staff, and the people in the crowds. Having carefully portioned out my feelings so that I'd be sure to have some left for the end, in the last week I became careless. With one exuberant gesture, the seed corn had spilled to the ground, leaving not one grain in reserve.

In those final days I became hard with muscle, and everything bounced off; nothing hurt. Like an Olympic athlete I was poised to sprint at the sound of the gun, ready to give a speech, recall a name, give an opinion, and fight for my political life. Go!

Stop!

It's over.

What do you mean, over? I looked at the flabby skin drooping from my upper arms.

It happened so quickly. Sitting on the off-white sofa in the hotel room at nine o'clock on election night, I reached for peanuts and waited for the early returns.

The radio was the oracle. Vince Naramore was the voice.

The first Burlington machine result was from Ward 6: 106 for Snelling, 96 for me.

"Considering it's a Republican ward," I said, "that's not bad."

Vince called it a poor showing. I hated his self-satisfied certainty. What did he know? What gave him the right to decide my fate? Why was he out to get me?

The second returns were from my own Ward 5, which showed me ahead by only a few votes. Not a good sign. Could Vince be right? No. Wait.

At 9:18, Vince Naramore called the race for Snelling.

I felt punched.

"Over, already?" I asked, placing my splayed hand on my bruised chest. Impossible.

But Vince's catechism of defeat was unrelenting. "She did well in Ward Three, but that's to be expected from a heavily Democratic ward. She would have had to do much better here, to make a showing statewide."

I don't know what I expected. But it wasn't this voice, oozing clinical satisfaction in response to every change in my condition.

The morning after we went to the bus station with Peter, who was going back to Williams College in Massachusetts. I was wearing sunglasses on a dull day. A familiar woman turned to me, clasped my hand, and said, "I'm so glad you ran."

Absolution. I felt the tears rising in my eyes. Oh, no. Get away, before you drown this woman with pathos. "Thank you," I whispered, and escaped.

Of course I had known all along that it would be bad the morning after a defeat. Knowing didn't help. Knowing something theoretically and experiencing it emotionally are two very different things. Of course, I knew that, too.

I cringed when I recognized what I was doing: blaming others. If only so and so had worked harder I would have won. And where were X, Y, and Z when I needed them? Ducking for cover.

Was this one of the three stages of grief? Denial, anger, and, finally, acceptance? I had not reached the final stage.

In exhaustion and despair I dragged myself through a list of what ifs.

What if I had been stronger, smarter, and fought harder? For the final push, we had recorded a five-minute television commercial during which I talked in my own words, looking straight at the camera, about why I wanted to be governor: a soliloquy about improving education and creating a better standard of living for all Vermonters. I represented change, I told the listeners, and my opponent, the status quo.

I sat alone on a stool, making my direct, personal appeal to the voters. The problem was we had only enough money to air the spot twice. As it was, we had had to borrow twenty-five thousand dollars from the bank. I was in debt. But if we had had more money, if everyone had seen me, I might have won.

If we had developed a different campaign strategy, who knows? We had relied heavily on position papers to win. Every other week, John Dooley, a legal aid lawyer who did issues work for my campaign, had produced a lengthy paper based on the cumulative wisdom of his research, aided by an advisory group of experts. One after another, we had churned them out—economic development, agriculture, education, environment, law and order, social services. I made dozens of proposals—

enterprise zones for rural areas, an agricultural-products marketing plan, state aid to education reform, criminal-code revisions, tougher child-abuse laws, and expanded child-care services. Dooley pulled it all together; he was the smartest person I had ever known. If brains could win elections, we would have won. The press dutifully showed up for the unveiling of each opus, yawned, and gave it a paragraph. The only satisfaction was that Dick Snelling eventually felt the need to produce a few position papers of his own.

What if we had handled the nuclear-waste issue differently? By chance, we had discovered that high-level nuclear wastes had been regularly shipped through Vermont from Canada en route to a nuclear-waste disposal site in South Carolina. The issue had fallen into our laps.

I accused Snelling of giving permission for the shipments without informing the public of the risks. What if there was an accident?

Steve obtained the date of the next shipment and released it to the press. The governor accused him of endangering security and charged me with hysteria. It was obvious I could not govern in a crisis.

A week later I got a call from Abbie Hoffman at my house. He had been barricading the roads against nuclear-waste shipments in upper New York State.

I panicked. "No, I don't need your help, Abbie. But thanks anyway." Would the press ever find out he called? God, I hoped not.

The nuclear-waste issue had become the focus of our television ads. Everything was staked on it. I was against shipments for safety reasons. By implication, Snelling was endangering the public. But it wasn't enough.

What if we had developed the issue differently? Too late, I discovered that controversy, not facts, brings a campaign to life.

I stopped the what-ifs and took solace from the popular wisdom that told me it was impossible to beat a three-term incumbent. I accepted this for a few hours. Then it wore off. I would have to medicate myself with old adages once again.

During the campaign, on the average of once a day, a well-meaning supporter would tell me, "Don't worry, this is a good dry run for next time."

I controlled myself. "Oh, no, I'm running to win. The campaign is going great. The polls are wrong. I'm getting a terrific response wherever I go." Silently, I yelled, Do you think I'd be crazy enough to pour my guts out for a dry run?

For election night I had prepared two speeches but practiced only one:

victory. Defeat had been a white piece of paper with words on it. Now, under the hot lights, I had to say them—with meaning. I knew what I had to do. Be calm. Be kind. And think of the future. I wanted to rage, mad like Lear against injustice, against my opponent, against the entire world.

Instead, I breathed deeply. Oxygen. In, out, swallow. Once again. Look in the mirror.

"You look great."

"Thank you."

I smiled. My staff smiled back. Our visions shimmered. "A concession speech is the first speech of your next campaign," Steve Kimbell whispered to me as I got into the elevator to go to the ballroom, to walk the mile to the podium.

Bad news does not draw a crowd. A few friends, mostly press. I had done them a favor. It would be an early night, just as they had predicted. I was grateful I did not have to face all of my supporters.

Surrounded by my family, I said, "I've just called Governor Richard Snelling and congratulated him on his victory. I know he will be an excellent governor for the people of the state of Vermont and will serve us well for the next two years."

Applause.

I felt as if I had just lifted a two-ton truck single-handedly and set it down, gently. Nothing got damaged.

"I want to thank my husband, and my children. They have been so generous, helped so much. I could never have done this without them."

I dared not look into their eyes. We all looked out into the floodlit void and smiled.

Inwardly I said, "I'm sorry I lost. But it's okay. We're a good family. I am sorry you have to go through this. Be brave. We'll make it." I squeezed the silent words into hugs, one for each child, and a separate one for my husband.

This was the first of my campaigns in which the children had been heavily involved. Both Julia and Peter had taken time off from college to work in the campaign; Adam and Daniel had tagged along with me whenever they could. Arthur was with me many weekends and evenings. Whenever they joined me, I felt rejuvenated; the separate parts of my life, thus connected, released a surge of energy and made me glow with well-being.

I called Steve up to the podium. "I want to especially thank Steve Kimbell for the outstanding job he did as my campaign manager. You were terrific, Steve," and I hugged him.

Break away. Stand up, face front.

I called up the entire campaign staff. "Come on up here, you were wonderful, I love you all."

At last, it was over. In a strange way, I was relieved. The emotional roller coaster of the last week had been terrifying. First I had been hit by a new Naramore poll: 66 percent for Snelling, 33 for me. It couldn't be right.

On top of that, the *Free Press* endorsement of Snelling was devastating. Down I went. Then up, after a debate with Snelling on WNCS radio in Montpelier, when I felt sharp enough to cut through glass.

Steve called me first thing next morning. "Hey, listen to this. We got our first endorsement. From the *Brattleboro Reformer*."

Terrific. I had always suspected that Norm Runnion, the editor, was brilliant. He hated Snelling. Loved me. I didn't know yet how fickle such political love could be.

A week later we received another endorsement, from a columnist for a Middlebury weekly. His rhetoric was less vituperative, making it appropriate to distribute. We had five thousand copies made.

Two days before the election a woman working a Windsor radio station called the office to tell us that a listeners' poll had me ahead, by 10 percent. The staff at a weekly newspaper took a straw vote: 5 for me, 4 for Snelling.

My sister-in-law Judith called from Springfield. She was doing get-out-the-vote calling for us, and the response was strongly in my favor, she reported. I did not dwell on her generous lack of objectivity.

Straws. I grasped at every one of them.

The night before the election, I was lying in bed, going back and forth between opposite scenarios. Win/lose, win/lose, I rehearsed each scene.

"You'll survive either way."

"No, I want to win. I can't help it. That's all I want. I think I can do it." And with a childlike prayer, I added, "Please, God, make me win," and fell asleep.

"Gracious" is how the press described me the morning after defeat. I was a gracious loser who had made a graceful exit. Ballerina words. But was I being too good, a good little girl leaving the stage without a fuss? What words would they have used had I been a man? Strong, perhaps. Brave.

Which was how I would feel when I began to recover. I had run. I had staked my claim. I was a future contender. I had achieved a respectable loss. To my surprise and satisfaction every postelection story about the governor's race of 1982 included the phrase "in a closely contested election." I got points for doing better than expected.

And I had freed myself from the chafing bonds of being lieutenant governor. As soon as I had announced, I felt released, free of Richard Snelling, free of the legislature, free of pretense. No longer did I have to subdue my ambition; my hidden agenda was out: I wanted to be governor. It was as if I had been hunched down for a long time to fit my body into a small space, and now, in the open air, I stood up straight and stretched. Everything inside me expanded. I discovered a new clarity in my answers. I was thinking like a governor.

At the end of the first week of the campaign, I began to feel my persuasive powers. As I barnstormed around the state, I literally pulled people out of the doldrums and moved them to higher ground through my own physical strength. One by one, I lifted them up.

"Yes, I can win. I feel it in my bones. Help me, and we'll do it." I would not let them avoid my eyes.

Each night, I was exhausted with the effort. But it was worth it. In the process, I moved myself. This was not a suicide mission. This was a winnable race.

Some days, it was easy.

The *Rutland Herald* story on my announcement-day visit to Springfield was a gift: "Kunin has them singing in Birdland," the reporter wrote (Birdland was the name of a housing development) and quoted one compliment after another from people I had met on the door-to-door campaign stop.

And that night at the Democratic dinner in my honor, in Springfield, there was lots of spaghetti, music, and a good-sized crowd. I giggled when I discovered there was a duck at the Duck Inn, a portrait set in a linoleum square in the middle of the black dance floor under the turning ball of blinding strobe lights. Was my announcement just an excuse for this gaiety, or were all these people here for me? Who cared? I gave a rousing speech. My brother loved it.

Other days were harder. On the schedule for the next morning, in fact, was a press conference and breakfast with local supporters at the Andrews Inn, a newly renovated historic building in the center of Bellows Falls. But as we headed for the car, Edgar handed me the morning paper. A raid on the Andrews Inn. Yesterday. They had broken up a homosexual prostitution ring. Here, in Bellows Falls, Vermont. Children might have been involved. Out of Boston.

"This is where I am having a press conference?" I asked my press secretary in disbelief. Why hadn't he known?

Edgar was worried. "Just get in and out quickly," he advised.

Should we cancel or shouldn't we? No, I couldn't back out.

The dining room at the Andrews Inn was quiet. Former governor Tom Salmon showed up. The hotel staff and my supporters were delighted to see us. No hint of trouble.

The fact that we kept to the schedule raised me a notch in Bellows Falls's esteem, Salmon told me. The gay and lesbian community was appreciative. I had trusted my instincts and stuck to my commitments. At the end of that first whirlwind tour around the state, I knew I had made the right decision to run for governor. The position of lieutenant governor, while comfortable, was beginning to limit my growth. I had achieved a careful if precarious balance; I had declared my independence from the governor without being disloyal to the state. When I ran for reelection as lieutenant governor in 1980 against Margaret ("Peg") Garland, I was still happy with my work, and Vermonters approved of me: I received the endorsement of every newspaper in the state.

Even the conservative Northeast Kingdom *Caledonian-Record* was unusually enthusiastic (this did not happen again):

> Despite our long tradition of Green Mountain Republicanism, we are splitting our ticket for at least one Democratic candidate this year. We are casting our ballot to re-elect Madeleine Kunin Lieutenant-Governor of Vermont.
>
> We didn't support the Burlington Democrat's bid for the second highest office in our state in 1978. But we have had occasion these past two years to observe Mrs. Kunin in action and we think one good term deserves another.
>
> Madeleine Kunin is known in Montpelier and throughout the state as a highly able presiding officer of the Vermont Senate, respected by legislators of both parties. . . .
>
> Mrs. Kunin's GOP opponent, another Burlington resident and former State Environmental Board Chairman Margaret Garland, has chosen to campaign on the issue that Governor Snelling needs a working Republican partner as Lieutenant-Governor. But despite our usual political preference for the Grand Old Party, we can see a serious flaw in Mrs. Garland's argument.
>
> Unlike certain other states, Vermont voters are able to split their tickets by voting for candidates of different parties for the respective offices of governor and

> lieutenant-governor. And Vermont voters have indeed
> demonstrated a tendency to split their tickets in recent
> years . . . we are voting for the incumbent Democratic
> Lieutenant-Governor who has demonstrated that she
> can do an excellent job in that post regardless of which
> candidate is elected governor.

I did not relish running against a woman whom I respected. I had known Peg Garland through the League of Women Voters; when I was a member, she had been state president, which gave her enormous prestige in my eyes. Later she became chairman of the State Environmental Board, where she continued to gain respect. But now, she wanted my job.

Her candidacy challenged my claim to the office. As the incumbent, I had to justify who I was and what I had done. Gone was the polite neutrality of the League of Women Voters.

She said it was "utterly ridiculous not to have the governor and the lieutenant governor working cooperatively," and accused me of building an empire. She would be loyal; I was not.

She had no ambitions of her own; I did.

She was the good daughter; I was the rebellious one.

Her charges, regardless of their political motivation, made me question my ambition. *Was* I overreaching? I could not put her challenge in perspective. The polls were strongly in my favor. I had not only to win, but to win big. I was the incumbent.

By the middle of the summer, I felt the strain. The family began to rebel. In the heat of the campaign everyone's daily schedule revolved around me, and every weekend there were parades, fairs, and festivals to attend. They all objected to the schedule, my days and nights away from home, the demands on their time. And the schedule was not the only problem. I was asserting myself not only in the public arena, but at home. How could I transform myself the moment I walked into the house from the aggressive campaigner back into considerate mother and wife?

"You aren't governor here," I was told as I stood at the kitchen sink, asking why no one had emptied the dishwasher.

"I know, I know," I replied, and I bent down to hide my anger.

Politics, by its very nature, is an obsessive, selfish, single-minded endeavor. Can it ever be done in moderation? Can it truly be shared, so that everyone gets the glory? I knew the answer. So did my husband.

Therefore, should I slow down, or even stop? Was I going too far, too fast? I retreated to reading novels, engrossing myself in Joyce Carol Oates's new book, a wild fantasy called *Bellefleur*. A reviewer had commented that her characters had discovered they could not retreat into solitude; they had to get back into the flow of life. I, too, was caught in the flow of life. Should I perhaps have expressed myself in the fantasy of a fiction rather than attempting to live it?

I counted the days before November 4. Could I sustain the physical demands of early morning hours, missed dinners, long days on the road, and nights away from home? I started to develop ulcer symptoms. I stopped drinking coffee. No wine. This helped, but the migraine headaches returned, terrifying me with their power. No one must know. Yet the loss of physical control rendered me helpless. The fatigue made me wonder, Is it worth it? I thought I was not made of strong-enough stuff. Face to the wall, cold cloth on my head, knees curled up to my chest, I was barricaded in my pain, alone. The next morning, the pain gone, I felt reborn. Was it the absence of pain that made me happy to be alive, or the assurance that I could, in fact, go on?

A few nights of sleep in my own bed and eating dinner at home restored me. Election night, 1980, I quit smoking. My son Daniel gave me a beautiful certificate of congratulations, bought in Woolworth's, which I taped to the refrigerator door.

The day after my decisive reelection victory the *Burlington Free Press* printed this story, headlined "Democrats View Kunin as Party Leader."

> Eight years after she first won a seat in the state House, Democratic Lt. Gov. Madeleine M. Kunin awoke Wednesday morning the leader of her party in Vermont.
>
> As a Republican tidal wave crushed strong Democratic contenders for Governor and attorney general, Mrs. Kunin walked away with 59 percent of the vote in her race—as strong a showing as Gov. Richard A. Snelling's.
>
> The GOP landslide robbed Democrats of the attorney general and secretary of state offices, leaving Mrs. Kunin the only Democrat in state office.

In a morning-after interview with a Burlington reporter, I hedged. "Certainly I will be viewed as a spokesman for the party. But I don't see that as my major role. I couldn't be an effective lieutenant governor if I pursued it on that basis."

Former governor Phil Hoff told the reporter that I could not "escape" my new leadership role. "Although she must put her office first," he said, "whether she likes it or not, she has this mantle, too, just as the governor does." He saw me as the spokesman for the have-nots, the poor, the children, the elderly.

I was not sure I wanted to wear the mantle Phil was putting on my shoulders. Could I satisfy his expectations and become a forceful party leader, simultaneously keeping the allegiance of other Vermont citizens, like the complimentary editor of the *Caledonian-Record*?

Democrats in Vermont, in 1980, had to have bipartisan support to get elected. The Democratic party alone could not muster sufficient votes to elect a candidate, and the independent vote was increasingly pivotal.

Or was Phil asking for something else? As a spokesman for the have-nots, was I expected to take another kind of risk, to speak up for those who had no voice? That was why I had become a political person in the first place, after all. For a time, I had deluded myself into thinking that I could float above the fray by satisfying everybody's expectations; I could be a strong party leader, spokesperson for the have-nots, and lieutenant governor of all the people of Vermont. It was only a question of skill.

What I did not see then was that it was also a question of courage.

The reporter had poised her pencil in the air for a moment before asking the tough question. I was being charged by some, she said, with being too wishy-washy. What was my response?

"My political style is more low-key than some," I answered. "I like the consensus process rather than division. My style is not confrontational." That was how I got things done.

But the reporter was astute, and her story concluded: "Whether she can balance her style with her party's expectations and turn her re-election into a base for higher office will be decided in the next two years."

I believed I answered the question in 1982. When I announced my candidacy for governor, I told my supporters:

> I am prepared for a strong campaign and I intend to win. . . . This campaign will be most important for the people who are not here today. For the young man who has just been laid off, for the young woman trying to figure out how to pay for her college education, for the elderly widow being moved into a nursing home, for the welfare mother who has just lost her job, and for the factory worker trying to improve his skills and increase his take-home pay.

But the 1982 campaign also released me from the self-imposed constraint to be nonconfrontational. Four years as lieutenant governor had revealed both the strength and weakness of my political strategy. I was comfortable, but I had moved away from the center and to the margins. I had become more of a commentator than an activist. A careful, commonsense approach had established my credibility and electability—I was a good lieutenant governor—but that alone would not enable me to become governor. However strongly I believed that the less combative skills of mediation, negotiation, and consensus building could resolve most controversies, my experience had proven otherwise.

From the start, I was engaged in battle.

As the newly elected lieutenant governor, I met with Governor Richard Snelling on November 29, 1978. I was alone. He was accompanied by his secretary of civil and military affairs, Chuck Butler.

"What do you want?" the governor asked when I stepped into his executive office.

"I wanted to meet with you because we're going to be serving together for the next two years, and I want to discuss how we can work together." I had run on a platform which boasted that I could work with a Republican governor, and after I won, the press had asked me if I wanted to attend cabinet meetings, and I had said yes. The governor had been incensed. Under no circumstances would I attend cabinet meetings, he warned.

Today, I chose not to pursue that subject. But I aroused his fury when I looked at the tape recorder on the corner of his desk to see if it was on. He noted my glance and asked testily, "Do you think I would put it on without informing you?"

I smiled nervously.

His color rose. A large man of hefty proportions, he puffed himself up like a frog.

I looked him straight in the eye.

My neighbor Elizabeth Bernstein, a student of psychology, had told me once that the best way to deal with aggression was eye contact. I glared. It worked. His glance went down.

"Let's find some mutually agreeable way of keeping me informed," I suggested. "I don't have to attend cabinet meetings or be privy to confidential or controversial information. But I do need to be kept up-to-date."

He called me an adversary, an opponent, since I was the titular head of the Democratic party. Looking back, I was unduly shocked. When the tables were turned six years later, and I was a Democratic governor elected with a Republican lieutenant governor, his argument made more sense to me, but now I righteously countered, Haven't we both been elected by voters of both parties, and aren't we here to serve all the people of the state?

When I found he could not tolerate anything I said, I made no further effort to answer or interrupt. He did all the talking. "How can you expect trust on my part if you accuse me of manipulating the revenue figures?" He pulled out a news clipping, lines of type marked with his yellow high-lighter.

I said nothing.

He returned to the subject of cabinet meetings. He took a backseat at cabinet meetings, he explained. "It's very difficult to be governor. When I first got here, I had no idea what the job was about. You couldn't learn it by sitting in on cabinet meetings, anyway. I let my commissioners have total say in all decisions. I simply accept them as they come across my desk."

I tried to look as if I believed him.

"At any given time, two or three things are not under control in state government, and anyone could use that information politically. That's why I can't share that information."

I nodded. But it was not until I sat at his desk that I understood what he was talking about. He was not simply paranoid. "I will inform you the same way that I would inform any legislative leader."

"But I have more responsibility than any legislative leader," I interjected. "I have to be capable of taking responsibility."

He took a sip of ice water from his coffee mug, which was coated in sweat.

"I'm not going to do anything to promote you, but I won't do anything to hurt you. I'm not out to get you."

I let a soft thank-you escape.

It was the voters who were at fault, he explained. "They didn't know what they were doing when they voted for two people from different parties. It can't possibly work. I'm going to do what I can to change it, change the constitution. I may not be listened to the first three or four times. But eventually they will understand."

Obstinately, I gave it one last try. Could we end the meeting with a mutually agreed-upon statement from both of us to give to the press?

"I haven't got time for that." He looked at his watch. "I've already spent too much time with you. That's an indication of how much time it would take to brief you each week." He stood up.

I walked out. My real crime, I saw, was that I had won my election. For that, there could be no forgiveness.

Bob Smith, a radio reporter, was waiting in the lobby. "Was it that bad?" he asked.

I changed the look on my face. "No, no, not at all." In the last half hour my confidence had been shaken. But I knew my effectiveness would be compromised if I told the truth. I could not emerge from my first meeting with the governor depicting myself as a victim of the governor's wrath. To save myself and, to some extent, him, I did what women have always done; I remained silent.

As I walked down State Street to the parking lot I was met with friendly greetings. "Congratulations. Glad you won."

"Thank you." I smiled, taking the compliments and plastering them over my fresh cuts. I felt fraudulent and, to a degree, guilty. My public image and my real self had been fractured, and I thought the fault was mine. Had I been more diplomatic, I might have mollified him. Four years later, I would know better. It was impossible to achieve both goals simultaneously: to get along with Governor Snelling and to pursue my own ambitions. Gary Nurenberg, a reporter from WCAX-TV, had heard about the meeting. He called me to ask how it was.

I lied. "Fine," I said.

That evening, to regain my equilibrium, I talked to a few friends: Lorraine Graham, Esther Sorrell, and Brian Burns. They warned me about what people were saying: that Bennington's Democratic legislators were jealous, that Lorraine shouldn't be on Appropriations again because she's "Madeleine's girl," that Althea Kroger shouldn't be whip because "she's one of Madeleine's people."

What nonsense! The petty, mean-spirited nature of politics appeared like an unexpected rash, and suddenly I was being quarantined, set apart, by virtue of my new office. Whom could I trust? Not many Republicans and not all Democrats.

Still, I had won.

Well-wishers told me so.

At a Christmas party, I turned bright pink in the glow of so many congratulations. When I sat down in a corner to relax, a friend pulled up a chair and asked, "Tell me, are you knitting your life together?"

His question caught me off guard. How did he know that success had its dark side?

"Yes," I said, "I am."

I RECALLED the exuberance of election night just a few weeks earlier, when the house was packed with well-wishers and the television lights lit up every corner of the room. In the following days I tried to piece it all together; to reconcile the public image of the triumphant victor with the woman who was the mother of four, the keeper of her house. With each political victory, I experienced a similar jolt from having landed in a new place, requiring me to readjust my balance and seek solid ground.

Role model that I had now become, I was considered an expert on the question. But I knew, and my family knew, that I had to reinvent myself at each stage. The age-old tension between family and work tightened the threads in the fabric of our lives, leaving puckers that had to be pulled straight with both hands. The week after my election I looked through my file box of three-by-five recipe cards. I baked bread. As before, the kneading helped. So did the offering.

I told a reporter who asked how I managed my family responsibilities, "I feel much better on the mornings when I make vegetable soup." She didn't laugh. She wrote it down.

So during my four years as lieutenant governor I eased into an increasingly demanding public life while my children grew up. My duties were flexible. When the legislature was not in session for roughly seven months of the year, I could write my own job description. In retrospect, I see that I chose to run for the office in part for that reason: I would not have to leave my family. At the time, I did not acknowledge to others that I made this compromise. Successful women were expected to work out the conflicts between home and work completely, in their own way and on their own time. Maternal and family activities could not be undertaken on company time. Only by preparing the next day's dinner at midnight, if need be, did we believe we could obtain permission to lead our daytime professional lives. If we failed, that was our fault. I accepted that bargain without questioning. Later, I had to learn to change, to allow my husband to take over more of the mothering role, which in time he did. I had to take the risk of being called a bad mother, and he risked becoming a new kind of father, who cared for the daily needs of his children. That would happen when the children were older, in high school and college. But not now.

I was interested to see that the lieutenant governor who succeeded me, Howard Dean (he succeeded Governor Snelling upon Snelling's death while in office in 1991), openly talked about wanting to spend time with his two young children. That is why he did not schedule breakfast meetings, he explained, and why he had not run for governor until 1992. The presence of his children at official functions was lauded; this was the sign of an exemplary father.

But in my first race for lieutenant governor in 1978, political consultants advised female candidates not to ever include family pictures in their campaign brochures. Whether or not to be seen with the children in the 1970s was a subject of serious discussion for women in politics.

I decided to follow political tradition. If men could show off their families, so could I. The family photo sessions for which the entire Kunin family had to smile became both a trial and joke. My children were hardly enthusiastic. We tried to capture both the cat and the dog for the picture. See how human we are? The dog enjoyed it; the cat did not. (One year, our son Peter wasn't available for the family campaign picture and Bonnie, our dog, took center stage. The caption continued to read, "Madeleine Kunin, her husband, and four children.")

I concentrated on issues that the governor did not. With the help of student interns, a part-time consultant, and a ten-thousand-dollar federal grant, I appointed a citizen's energy advisory committee, and we issued an energy conservation report with a list of legislative recommendations. I oversaw the production of an energy handbook designed for distribution to town energy coordinators, positions established in response to the energy crisis. I conducted a study of the child-care fee-reimbursement system, which concluded that many needy families had been denied benefits because income requirements had not kept pace with inflation. The study supported a legislative initiative to expand child care to more low-income families. And that winter, Vermont had an extraordinarily high level of highway fatalities. I was determined to examine the cause and issued a report suggesting highway structural changes as well as more state troopers on the road. As soon as I launched these initiatives, the Republican secretary of state and the governor's secretary of administration accused me of executing a "blatant political maneuver," while the Republican party chairman considered that I was "overstepping the bounds" of my office for political gain.

I held firm. In some ways, the governor's isolation made me a ruler in exile. The studies linked me with important constituencies as well as with the legislature. Invitations for speeches arrived regularly, and I became a familiar figure at Rotary Clubs, the Jaycees, the Lions, women's organizations, and various interest groups.

I moved at a comfortable pace. But the lack of pressure stymied my growth. Just as I could edit my schedule, I could also limit my exposure to controversy. As second in command, I could avoid the divisive issues, pick and choose where I wished to make my mark. Little more than advocacy was expected of me, and sometimes simple compassion would prompt gratitude.

I became a good listener. Constituents tell stories to lieutenant governors, I discovered, that they do not tell to governors. Through me, the public had access to an elected official; being close to the source of power appeared to provide relief for some complaints.

I listened as neutrally as I could when some constituents told me how arrogant Dick Snelling was. Then I watched what happened when he walked into the room. These same people would walk up to him, smile, shake his hand, and say, "Glad to see you, Governor. You sure do honor us by your presence."

I marked this down for future reference. Remember, just because people sometimes fawn over you in public life does not mean you have won their friendship or respect.

How could I tell whether people meant what they said? After I was a private citizen again in 1991, I began to understand that it was truly impossible to know. I was riding in a taxicab from Boston to Cambridge following my appearance on a television program where I commented on President Bush's State of the Union address. I thought about what I had said and wondered how it compared with the opinion of the man on the street. The reporter in me had returned.

"What did you think of the president's speech?" I asked the taxi driver.

He thought plenty. It was a sham. The president understood nothing about the problems of real people. "But what can you expect from a politician? They're all out for themselves."

I slid a little lower into my seat.

"Throw them all out. That's what I say. They're all a bunch of crooks. The best thing would be term limitations. That would take care of the ones that have gotten too comfortable and ripped off working stiffs like me. Look at the S and L crisis. Millions down the toilet."

His voice became louder as his words bounced into the backseat of the cab. "Get rid of them, every damn one of them. The sooner the better."

He paused for a moment, turned around, and asked, "Lady, what do you do?"

I hesitated. Out with it. "I'm, er, I'm a politician."

"No kidding?"

"Well, a former politician."

"Were you very high up?" His voice had moderated.

"Umm, you might say so. I was governor of Vermont."

"Holy shit! A governor! I never had a governor in my car before. What state?"

"Vermont."

"Vermont, beautiful state. Beautiful. I can't believe this. What an honor. Hey, would you mind just autographing this piece of paper here, before you leave?" He ripped a piece of lined paper from a spiral pad. "For my granddaughter. She just turned five. Cute as a button. Jesus, I can't believe this, a governor, in my car. What a night."

We pulled up to the curb. I reached for the handle.

"Let me open the door for you, please. Allow me, thank you, thank you, Governor."

It isn't that people dissemble, I concluded. It's that they are ambivalent: they both love and hate politicians.

While I was in the position of lieutenant governor, the scale tilted toward love. I could not be blamed for what was wrong because I did not have the power to make it right, and I was still a quasi-outsider, both because of my title and because Snelling's rejection pushed me into the arms of the voters.

"Don't you ever get tired of listening to other people's problems?" I was asked at a public hearing in the town of Lincoln, called to hear local reaction to a proposal to place a large windmill on Lincoln Ridge. The townspeople were united in their opposition. The merits of producing clean, renewable energy were laudable in theory, but not here, not in their backyard.

I appreciated the question, but I demurred with an incomplete answer: "No, I always learn something."

True. And I learned to categorize complaints into levels of seriousness—some required only a nod, while others needed personal intervention. But what I did not admit was that I was tired of listening because I felt constrained by lack of power. I wanted to do more than listen; I wanted to act. The only way to do that was to become governor. The lieutenant governor's office had begun to feel cozy, like an overheated room. It made me soporific. A newspaper commentator, Scott MacKay, pinpointed its politically debilitating effects, which at the time I disputed; in the *Burlington Free Press* on August 1, 1982, he wrote:

> In the Statehouse, she is known as a decent politician who knows how to forge a compromise and whose easy-going personal style has generated few enemies. Politicians of all stripes will describe Kunin as a nice person. . . . Yet beneath the veneer of her candidacy, there is the nagging feeling that Kunin has not given voters an adequate reason to oust Snelling.
>
> No overriding issues fuel the Kunin campaign. It is

a technocrat's campaign so far, one with little soul or
substance.

On many issues, she masks her positions in clichés
and picayune criticisms of Snelling's performance. On
some issues, she seems misinformed.

Much of this may stem from her job. Being Lieutenant Governor, a part-time post where the only real
duty is to preside over the sleepy state senate, gives a
politician a lot of time to campaign and meet people
and little experience in making difficult decisions and
choices.

When I read that, I thought I already understood the requisites of
power, the need to make tough choices that do not please everyone. I had
learned that as Appropriations Committee chairman. But the words still
sounded more like a schoolgirl's recitation than a woman's political reality. The desire to please had flowed in my blood from birth. It was
impossible to tourniquet it. That is how I had been taught to survive.
Causing displeasure was dangerous and, therefore, had to be avoided.
Not until I was governor did I fully understand what the phrase "tough
choices" meant. That is when I knew *how* to govern. In the meantime, I
learned *why* I wanted to govern. One Sunday in June 1979 I attended the
annual Community Action Agency meeting at the fairgrounds in Barton
in the Northeast Kingdom, the poorest area of Vermont. Tom Hahn, the
flamboyant and controversial head of the organization, a holdover from
the War on Poverty era, had aggressively dueled with Snelling about who
in Vermont should control several millions of federal antipoverty dollars.
In this obvious power struggle, neither wanted to be the first to back
down. It was clear that this cheering crowd loved Hahn, a larger-than-
life, rabble-rousing evangelist for the poor, who aroused other people's
hatred with equal passion.

It was not a pretty crowd. These were the families not often seen at
public events, and never in such large numbers under one tent. These
were the people stranded at the end of the dirt road on those mornings
when the car won't start, stuck in a trailer set on a patch of dirt, cluttered
with things that other people throw away. Now they were assembled in
one place; it was impossible to drive by quickly and move on.

At the start of the meeting, I watched a woman in tight maroon stretch
pants, dragging her weight in her hips as she walked to a folding chair in
the front row. Was her size a statement of power, the only one she could
have? "You gotta see me, whether you like it or not."

She was surrounded by a cluster of skinny kids and seemed capable of either caressing or crushing them. One child's clothes were too big, another's too small.

A mother called out to her seven-year-old, "Johnny, stop that, come over here this minute, or I'll get your hide." Her mouth opened, exposing eraser-red gums and no teeth. When her lips closed, she had the stitched mouth of an old woman.

A dozen elderly men and women maneuvered their wheelchairs to one corner on the left of the podium. A teenage boy wheeled his chair around like a hot rod, muscles flexing on his upper arms, cruelly dramatizing the lost potential of his stick legs. There were other disabilities I could not see but could only guess at: generations of incest, abuse, retardation, and neglect. Now Tom Hahn got up to speak.

"Dick Snelling ain't nothing but a porky flatlander," he dared.

The crowd roared. They despised the hand that fed them. Acknowledging dependency would mean another loss of self-respect, piled on top of everything else.

I wondered which of these children sitting cross-legged on the ground, watching the show, would make it out of here. One or two were bright-eyed. Many seemed almost too well behaved—it was not that they were controlling their energy; they had given it up.

I tried to provide encouragement in my brief speech, stressing my support for programs created to help Vermonters find their way out of poverty, like Head Start, adult education, and job training. After I stepped off the makeshift stage, I was relieved to have won the crowd's approval not so much for who I was, but for what I represented: an official who seemed to care. But I felt oddly depressed. What good had I done? What could a politician do to truly change their lives? Was there any hope of softening the harsh lines of poverty, visible on every face?

Does anything really work? I don't know, I confessed. But I am not ready to accept things as they are. There must be a way to change things, but it isn't through nice-sounding words. (Years later, as governor, I would expand prenatal care services and begin to provide health care coverage for all Vermont children. By 1992 Vermont boasted the lowest infant mortality rate in the nation.)

My public life allowed me to walk into rooms that would have remained closed in my private life. I would not even have known of their existence. People who would have been strangers allowed me to become one of them. It was an extraordinary gift, and I tried to accept it politely and gratefully. It taught me things I did not know. As an elected official I had a grand tour of Vermont, going to out-of-the-way places and meet-

ing people at every social and economic level; I became an invited guest
who could sit down at the table and join in. I was served a banquet of
courses, all laid out according to ceremonious rituals marked on the calendar: birthdays, holidays, celebrations, dedications, demonstrations,
ground breakings, and deaths. At these events I touched hands and looked
into faces. At funerals I cried; at celebrations I laughed. When asked to
say a few words, I would lean forward at the podium, extending my body
to the crowd, opening my arms wide, palms open, foreshortening the
distance between me and the audience as much as I could. As I absorbed
the meaning of the moment it became concentrated to a sharp essence,
which I then expressed.

In December 1980, I gave opening remarks at a workshop on domestic
violence sponsored by the Governor's Commission on the Status of
Women, in Montpelier, and then stayed to listen to the first speaker.
Martha read an essay about her life as a battered woman. She loved her
husband, she explained. The first beatings had occurred two months after
their wedding. She described her trips to a counselor, her hope that her
husband would change, and her recurring feeling of worthlessness. Again
and again, she returned to him, hopeful that this time would be different.
The pattern was repeated, love and violence slapping each other in rapid
rhythm. "Then I escaped to the crisis center, and later got an apartment
of my own. I was beginning to come alive again," she told the audience.

She visibly came to life before our eyes. Her tear-streaked face, which
a moment before had looked pathetically frail, blossomed into that of a
strong, laughing woman. She could see who she was and was glad of it. I
was awed by her transformation. The private experiences of pain and
healing were publicly shared in her storytelling. Years later, when a budget request came in for state funds to establish crisis centers for battered
women throughout Vermont, Martha's story flashed into my mind.

One reason I love politics is that the political life is so rich in experience
and emotion. Like art, political action gives shape and expression to the
things we fear as well as to those we desire. It is a creative process, drawing on the power to imagine as well as to act. The driving force is a vision
of an ideal. Like artists and writers, politicians try to construct order out
of chaos, contain evil, and identify good as they fill the canvas. And like
artists, they must transform reality with their expressive powers. In the
process, they discover things they did not know or understand before. As
a politician, I can stand on a stage, give my soliloquy and define reality as
I see it. The public expression itself helps to ease despair, end isolation,
and engender hope. The problem, whatever it may be, has been framed

and thereby contained. The next step is to solve it. Transforming internal fears into external actions may be illusory, facile, and eventually disappointing, but for me, it is a way to restore equilibrium, as well as a way to change the world.

Inaction, contrary to its reputation for being a refuge, is neither safe nor comfortable. Perhaps the difference between politicians and other people is that they have a certain restlessness combined with recurring optimism, the persistent belief that good, when put to the test, will be stronger than evil. I have felt optimism's pull as a physical force holding my head above water. One difference between art and politics is that artists explore despair, while politicians may acknowledge it only briefly and then must search immediately for alleviation.

Martha's story left me digging for solutions like a gardener, on my hands and knees, looking for dried bulbs. I had to produce answers that could flower into solutions, not only to meet public expectations, but also to fulfill my own. I had been moved by her story. I could not bear to leave it unfinished without a happy ending. When years later I approved a piece of legislation, I knew full well that I was not solving the entire problem of domestic violence; I was only taking a fragment of it; looked at from a blurred distance, it was minuscule. But seen from Martha's viewpoint, it was large. The Marthas of the world may still suffer, but, I could tell myself, they wouldn't have to tell their stories to strangers in a room alone.

I KNEW there were no blueprints for governing, either for men or for women. I understood the basic requirements: knowledge of the facts, an understanding of people, a vision for the future, a desire to solve problems, and the courage to make tough decisions. Yet the work itself remained a mystery. Why, then, the compulsion to strive for it? Politicians often frame their personal ambitions as responses to other people's demands rather than their own. I would like to think that was not the case for me, but at times it was. Voices I once dismissed as unrealistic now received my attention during my years as lieutenant governor. "When are you going to move upstairs?" I was asked when visitors came to my ground-floor office and pointed to the governor's office up above. And I smiled when I was introduced at meetings as the next governor of the state of Vermont. Running for governor would not be overreaching, I told myself. I would be fulfilling expectations. I was creating the assumption that I would run for governor, just as I had wanted to. I had reversed the tradition set by Consuelo Bailey that women go so far and no further.

I was also creating expectations for myself, assisted by my curiosity about whether I could do the job. It was easy to think of politics as a game at which I wanted to test myself in order to see how good I was. And public expectation tugged me forward; I did not have to do all the pushing myself.

"You make me proud to be a woman," an elderly woman told me after a speech. I shook her hand. And believed her. I was doing this for her.

The egomania of politics, which I feared would contaminate me, was only buttressed by thinking of each campaign as a cause larger than myself. Self-sacrifice and self-promotion became meshed in intricate patterns that I cannot sort out. A strong sense of self is, of course, essential for public life for both women and men, and so is the ability to subdue the self in order to understand others and be sensitive to their needs. A desire to succeed in politics is propelled by these two seemingly contradictory forces, which frequently change places and sometimes coexist: to save others and to save oneself.

As a state legislator, I had become concerned about improving the quality of nursing-home care after I intervened on behalf of a friend of my mother's who I suspected was being abused. I vowed to redouble my efforts as lieutenant governor and readily accepted an invitation to visit a nursing home during National Nursing Home Week, but I also frankly considered my visit to St. Albans a campaign stop and hoped to get press coverage. I had been to many nursing homes in my political career and knew what to expect: the smell of disinfectant, the occasional mad outburst from a strapped-in patient, the dead look in wide-awake eyes. These visits always left me depressed, and I would wish to myself that I would not live that long.

Some thirty women and a sprinkling of men, half of them sitting in wheelchairs, had been assembled in the living room. Every woman had had her hair done in pretty silver curls by the same beautician. In the center of the room a young woman with long blond hair who seemed to be quite pregnant was strumming a guitar, but her lilting sweet voice could not penetrate the sad silence that rose from the mute rows of women.

"What's the average age here?" I asked one of the aides, while I glanced toward the door, waiting for the television camera to arrive.

"In the mideighties. Gladys over here is a hundred and four."

Gladys was slumped in her chair, fast asleep. I reached out for the hand of the woman next to her, who stared at me, transfixed. She grasped my fingers and clamped on them like a lock. When I pried them off, one by one, she began to cry.

What a terrible thing to live like this, I told myself, without your mind, with only your body, and not even that.

The folksinger picked up her tempo. Connie Depot, the activity director, helped one of the women patients get up from the sofa. She had trouble standing, but Connie took her left hand, put an arm around her waist, and positioned her to dance. The woman could not move her feet, but she swayed to the rhythm of the music. And then she smiled. Connie smiled back. Then the woman lifted a foot from the floor, then the other. They both laughed. Her tremors stopped. Her terrible face softened. Her body acquired grace. This couple was in a ballroom somewhere among hundreds of people, moving across a marble floor under crystal chandeliers while the orchestra played a waltz.

"That's the last thing that goes, their hearing," Connie told me when the music stopped. I thanked her for letting me come.

The television camera never arrived. I didn't care. How could I have been so crass as to think that was the purpose of my visit? Connie and her partner had acted out a scene that I would not forget; they had given me a gift of extraordinary generosity. I would keep it for a long time.

OF THE MANY PEOPLE who influenced my political life, I single out Lenore McNeer. On June 18, 1981, I attended her funeral in Montpelier. As I sat in the church, I wished I had told her what she had meant to me. I first got to know her in 1972 when I became a state legislator and she chaired the Governor's Commission on the Status of Women. It was she who mobilized a massive women's town meeting in Vermont in 1977 and organized the delegation that attended the National Women's Conference in Houston. At the time of her death, she was fifty-nine; I was forty-seven. I tended to look at her as a senior adviser and myself as one of her protégés.

Lenore's life had followed a pattern that by all outward appearances was successful: marriage, a family, and an academic career. Her unexpected suicide made me question every assumption I had made about her life, except one—her generosity. She seemed to know what other women needed and gave it to them in abundance. At times, her effusive compliments and overdone lengthy introductions had been embarrassing. When

I spoke to her class of women students each year at Vermont College on what she called "The Real Political Trade-Offs," she would start by saying, "Here's a woman who is a political insider, tough, knowledgeable, and a lady." I would squirm, but she knew, as few people did, how hard it was for women to be both tough and ladylike. Her words acknowledged the risks I had taken and legitimized the choices I had made when others' silence failed to. And the fact that she saw there were trade-offs showed a rare sensitivity. After a grueling week in the legislature, an encounter with Lenore was healing. Whether I wanted to believe it or not, I greedily drank her praise.

Manic-depressive, some said, to explain her inexplicable act. I wondered if I harbored these same tendencies. With each campaign my moods were so mercurial. The day before yesterday, for example, I had been high as a kite after speaking to the Girls State convention. One young woman had asked if I was considering running for governor, and I had said, "Yes."

A cheer went up from the varnished gymnasium floor. Hundreds of sixteen-year-old girls stomped and cheered, sending up the dust from between the floorboards. They stood up, some on their chairs. Whoops and yells showered over me like confetti. Amazing how they understood.

But at my next stop at a Retired Senior Volunteer Program (RSVP) lunch, things had been different. When I walked in the door, doting grandmothers at every table, looking up from their red Jell-O melting on the green lettuce leaves, beamed at me. I reminded myself, They do that for every politician, watch it, watch it. But I didn't watch it enough. An AP reporter, Chris Graff, came up and asked for my reaction to a poll that had just been released, pitting Governor Snelling against me. It showed him winning 2 to 1. Suddenly the smiling faces looked like masks. The flower centerpieces were made of plastic.

But I am the same person, I told myself, regardless of what the polls say. How can I tell what is real? Was it the happy applause in the dining room a moment ago, or the black crawly numbers that Chris had just dropped in my lap?

"It means nothing," I said. "Nothing."

That afternoon I had serious doubts about my capacity to survive the wild political ride without injury, praised and damned, uphill and down, moving at a terrifying speed. If I steeled myself against both criticism and praise, might I lose my capacity to feel, to think, to understand? Lenore McNeer's life and death had served as both inspiration and warning.

* * *

As I BECAME more politically seasoned, I learned to sustain optimism in small ways by participating in the ordinary events of everyday life. In 1985 I accepted an invitation to be the speaker at the Memorial Day ceremony in Orwell, a town of just over a thousand inhabitants, precisely fifty miles south of Burlington. As my husband and I approached the town on a brilliant blue-sky day, every house looked freshly painted, every lawn neatly trimmed, reminding me that life could be neatly organized, death and decay kept in check. In the heart of the town, on the common, there was a bandstand patterned as prettily as a paper doily, its waist draped in splendid patriotic bunting. A white-columned redbrick Greek Revival church with a weather vane atop the belfry graced one side of the common, next to it was the town hall and the school; the other side of the green was balanced with the library, a fortresslike Gothic Revival bank, and some fine Italianate houses with Queen Anne decorative wooden flourishes. The symmetry of the common anchored the town to the green earth.

I was handed a corsage of red, white, and blue carnations, tied with a ribbon. I happily attached it to my shoulder, as if the corsage would pin me to the town.

There was a problem with the program, the master of ceremonies explained. Frank Phelps, ninety-four, who was to be presented with a special hand-carved cane, the annual Oldest Citizen of the Town award, unfortunately hadn't been able to make it. His daughter was supposed to bring him, but first he needed a shave and then he had needed a nap. Everybody was sorry.

"He's a real fan of yours," Mike Audet, the chairman of the school board, told me. "And a Democrat." Mike should know. He was one of two self-declared Democrats in the town; his brother was the other. Together, they managed a seven-hundred-acre dairy farm with two hundred cows, eighty milkers.

"Well, I'll take the cane to him!" I exclaimed.

"That'll make Frank happy, that's for sure."

We drove the four miles on a dirt road out to the Phelps house, a typical old Vermont farmhouse with cracks in the plaster ceiling and dark-walnut kitchen cabinets. The house smelled clean, like fresh butter and milk. There Frank was, surrounded by his daughter and a bunch of grand-children. He took the cane, stood, and posed for a picture with me and his family. I think the event might have made his day. It was hard to tell. But I knew he had made mine.

This Memorial Day vignette was more than postcard perfect. The town of Orwell was a family, and I wanted to be adopted by it. I loved the brass band, the speeches, the tricolor bunting, and the hospitality of the ladies who served cookies and lemonade under the shade of a maple tree. When the master of ceremonies read the names of the townspeople who had died in the past year, one by one, it was here that I wanted to be buried. Each citizen was mourned under the hot sun. This was more than a perfunctory Memorial Day service to which a politician had been invited. This was a privileged ceremony, which I had been allowed to attend. These were the town's rituals, created to honor the dead and celebrate the living.

When, during my second campaign for governor, I went to a candidates' forum sponsored by the Vermont Association of Snow Travelers, I paid careful attention to my opponents as they addressed the crowd. Clearly, they were pandering to this group, promising them everything they wanted. So when it came my turn to speak, I was friendly, responded to their questions, and told them that if I were elected, my door would always be open to them. As chair of the House Appropriations Committee I had helped them get their first line item in the budget for trail maintenance, and I reminded them of that. Was that pandering? My opponents, had they stayed to listen to me, would no doubt have said yes.

Yes, I wanted their votes, but I also liked them. I had traveled on Vermont's back roads and seen snowmobiles parked in almost every yard, either in front or in back of the trailers. I knew why men working in the lumber mills and women in the sewing factories bought snowmobiles "on time" and sped, after work, through the woods. It was an escape from the grueling monotony of their working lives.

As I was ready to leave for my next campaign stop, one of the men came over to me, pressed my arm, and gave me a smile. "This time," he said, using the metaphor he knew best, "I think you'll slide right in."

As CHAIRMAN of the House Appropriations Committee, I had been asked to visit the Waterbury State Mental Hospital, built in 1905. Its round towers, high peaked roofs, and thick red-stone construction would have made a fine movie set for a gothic thriller, but the state had other plans: to convert its thousands of square feet of empty space into offices. A facility that once housed three to five thousand people—the senile, the bizarre, the retarded, the homeless, the depressed—now held about fifteen hundred: deinstitutionalization and new drug therapy had made the exodus possible.

Our entourage of a dozen bureaucrats and legislators paraded through dayrooms, dormitory rooms, and, finally, the secluded padlocked rooms.

The rooms were empty. Absolutely still. I imagined the sounds that these walls had absorbed. For the first time, I understood how drastically treatment for the mentally ill had changed. I knew that prior to his death my father had been briefly hospitalized for depression. Renovating these empty rooms for another use seemed to permit him to be transformed from illness to health.

"How soon can the renovations begin?" I asked the state buildings director. Cover the scars with whitewash, take down the bars, bring in fluorescent lights, take the locks off the doors. Thousands of people had been institutionalized here because there had been no place for them to go. Now many had returned to the community. When I became governor, I would make certain that they would be well served. When I took office, Vermont's state hospital could not meet certification standards. Over the next six years, we reduced the size of the institution, brought it up to a high standard, and established an effective community mental-health system to provide more humane and effective care close to patients' homes. At the end of my governorship Vermont was ranked first in the nation in the care of the mentally ill by the National Alliance for the Mentally Ill.

In 1981, plans were made to close yet another section of the hospital, housing a school for severely disturbed children. The director asked me to visit, for she was lobbying to keep the school open.

She took me to the gymnasium, where a boy was sitting on a mat in the center of the floor. His name was Peter, and he looked about the age of my youngest son, twelve. The therapist told him, "Stand up, Peter."

Peter did.

"Sit down."

Peter did.

"Good boy, Peter," his teacher said.

Peter held his hands flat in front of his chest like a bunny. He was given a cracker and chewed it with apparent satisfaction.

A fat boy rushed at me in the hall. He was older than Peter, fourteen perhaps, and stronger. He flung his arms around my neck tightly. The counselor jumped toward me and pulled him away. I was scared, but embarrassed that I had shown it. What had shocked me most was his facial expression. It was absolutely blank.

"He's been difficult this morning. Sorry about that."

I asked her what she knew about these children. "Many don't have parents. Some have been beaten. What you see here is often the result of poverty, abuse, and neglect. For others, we just don't know."

I thought of my own good fortune—four healthy children—an accomplishment I had almost taken for granted. Now I felt fresh gratitude and could not accept these children's fate as inevitable. "There are things we could do, aren't there?" I asked her, pleading for an affirmative answer.

"Yes, alcohol has a lot to do with it. If we could provide better parenting skills and more family planning, that would go a long way."

I filed her words and my impressions away and vowed to retrieve them when I could follow through. In time, I found ways to do so—we established Parent-Child Centers in every county of Vermont, where young parents could obtain child care and learn parenting skills. And I strongly supported access to family planning.

As I PREPARED myself to run for governor in 1982, I searched for ways to make my political voice stronger and more succinct. I sometimes found it hard to give short, direct answers because I wanted to be the good student who knew everything. At other times, I equivocated because in fact I saw both sides of the issue. That was how my mind worked: I looked at a problem from every perspective, testing various hypotheses before reaching a conclusion. Sometimes I spoke too soon, while I was still working through the problem, and I described the process rather than the conclusion, when that was all that would have been required.

I rebelled against the distortions of the clever one-liner. Sometimes language dictates thought, rather than the other way around. But some questions, I learned, have to be answered with brevity because the subjects demand it. Once I made this discovery, I relished the clipped sound of one-syllable replies.

"Do you believe in the death penalty?"

"No."

"What is your position on abortion?"

"I am pro-choice."

On some subjects, I, as a politician, was no different from other people: I had no opinion on them, a state of mind that is normal for an ordinary citizen but, I feared, would be intolerable for a public figure. In a rush to fill the void, I sometimes erred. It took me a while to have the courage to say about some issues "I'm looking into that" or "I don't know."

(*Above*) Entering the
legislature to take office
as Vermont's first woman
governor, 1985; First
budget address, 1985

Photos: Toby Talbot: AP

(*Left*) The first tap—the official start of the maple-sugar season, 1985; (*Below, left*) Signing the kindergarten bill, 1985; "Greening Up" with the Cub Scouts, 1985

Photos: Toby Talbot: AP

Receiving a call during a press conference from the Department of Energy announcing that Vermont was not on the list of possible nuclear waste sites, 1986; Fly fishing for the first time during a promotional fishing expedition (I caught two rainbow trout), 1986; Showing that Vermont's deficit would be paid off by the next day, 1986

Yesterday: $ 403,527,000
+ overnight   +   174,000
+ Today's deposit +   1,880,000
                   _____
Today: $ 405,581,000
Needed: - 405,669,200
                   _____
To Go: $ -   88,200

Photos: Toby Talbot: AP

Toby Talbot: AP

(*Above*) Taking second-
term oath of office, 1987;
Family gathering at second
inauguration, 1987

Donna Light

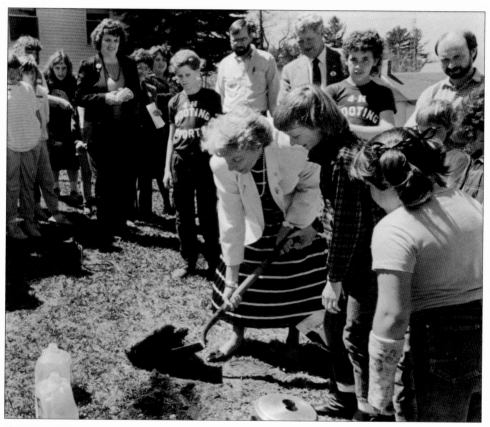

Craig Line: AP

Tree planting with
the Mountaineers 4-H
Club, 1988

(*Above*) Greeting a well-wisher
at the Barre Housing Authority;
With brother, State Senator
Edgar May, at the statehouse

Photos: Toby Talbot: AP

Vyto Starinskas: Rutland Herald

Tears and toasts: Announcing that I will not seek reelection to a fourth term, 1990. Caught with a Kleenex at the podium during a speech and toasted the same day, leaving the statehouse with Kathy Hoyt, chief of staff

oby Talbot: AP

Farewell to a packed Vermont
legislature after six years as the
state's chief executive, 1991

Political language is different from conversation. The words I said and the words that reporters quoted me as saying frequently seemed unrelated. Disembodied, they were transformed. Placed alone on the page, without introductory clauses or the usual pauses, they became either monstrous or petty. Spoken by a television commentator, they seemed distorted by his lips. Even when they came out of my own mouth, I felt my words begin to detach from my body. Rarely did my answers to questions conform to my intentions and behave like the wise, good words I wanted them to be.

At the end of an hour-long interview at a Middlebury radio station the news director told me, "You seem to reveal your philosophy more than the usual politician."

Did I? What had I said?

"Maybe it's because you're a woman," he added.

I didn't know. I felt suddenly exposed. I should wear more protective layers. If I said nothing, I would be accused of being vague; if I said too much, I would offend. I must learn to accept the reality that no matter what I said, I would never be able to please everyone.

My equanimity was short-lived. The same radio reporter excerpted a comment from my interview about my position on Vermont's purchase of Hydro-Quebec power. It was on the news wire that afternoon and a headline story the next day: "Kunin Supports Snelling Position on Hydro-Quebec." Had I said that? What had happened to my qualifying clauses? I supported the purchase if it proved to be a good buy for Vermont consumers, if the power sold to Vermont came from existing hydroelectric sources, and if the environmental impact was adequately assessed. (When I was governor, that was the basis of my approval.)

Logically, I knew it was impossible to give universally pleasing answers. Still, I thought it possible, if only I used the right tone, the precise words.

The desire to please persisted. As a result, I was sometimes called wishy-washy. I rebelled angrily against the charge.

A reporter for an alternative weekly coined the name "Straddlin' Madeleine." I hated it.

How could he have said that about me?

I had taken positions on everything. And on several issues, such as choice and protection of the environment, more forthrightly than other politicians, for which I received criticism from other sources. Yes, I had expressed myself carefully. But that was my style. That was who I was. Was it my tendency to give long answers that made him think that his nickname was both apt and funny? Was it that I was polite, soft-spoken, and, yes—a woman? If I had pounded my way through a speech, saying the same words with a deep voice and aggressive gestures, would he have said that?

Didn't he know that I was trained to be polite and pleasant? The peace-maker at the dinner table, who stopped the children from fighting and exercised control with a firm, calm hand. The good mother, who knows she must avoid anger, if only to show the father how it should be done. Or was my desire to be pleasant an animal survival instinct, the only one I knew? Not physically stronger, I had to use what I could—my smile, my words, my psychological strength—to fend off attack.

I believe my desire to avoid controversy was also prompted by a sense that I should counterbalance with moderation the radical choice I had made to live a political life. I had combined the roles of mother, wife, and politician—in itself a rebellious act. I wanted to assure my public, as well as myself, that despite this aberration I was normal, that I had not abandoned my feminine self. This sense that I should soften the impact of being a political woman, which had a strong influence on my political style, was not calculated: it was a reflex.

I was also conscious that gender was not the only part of my political biography that was nontraditional. I was a Jew, an immigrant, and a progressive Democrat. Each label could thrust me beyond the confines of political acceptability. Ironically, the same experiences that had politicized me now endangered me. As a feminist, an immigrant, and a Jew, I was perhaps too different from the average Vermont voter, yet it was this identity that inspired me to enter public life and shaped my values. I responded to two contradictory demands. I could not be too different from my constituency, but to qualify for leadership, I had to distinguish myself from others by standing for what I believed. Experience would teach me that this dilemma was more significant in theory than in practice. Still, fault lines of fear remained about being Jewish, the result of thousands of years of ghetto anxiety passed down to many Jews. The only way to be safe was to make oneself invisible. Don't draw attention. I had done just the opposite. Public life made me highly visible.

When I ran for governor in 1984, a reporter called my campaign manager, Liz Bankowski, to tell her that he was planning to do a story on my political liabilities. He named them: I was a woman, a Jew, and a Democrat.

Liz paused. "Has anyone said anything about Madeleine Kunin's religion being a liability?"

"No, but—"

"Then it isn't a story, is it?" Liz said.

He did not agree.

Liz called the editor to squelch the story, and she succeeded.

In 1982, my staff picked up snippets of anti-Semitism here and there on the campaign trail, but these rarely reached me. I like to think that Vermonters are unusually tolerant. In fact, it is more likely that few voters knew or cared what religion I professed. That in itself is an astounding achievement for a person who came to America in response to Hitler's anti-Semitism.

I WAS, HOWEVER, moved when Father Raymond Giroux, the priest most often called upon to say grace at annual Democratic dinners throughout Vermont, looked at me, bowed his head, and said, "In the name of Jesus Christ and the great God Jehovah."

Thank you, Father.

On one occasion I felt the direct influence of the Holocaust experience on my public life. Legislation that would establish higher penalties for attacks or assaults motivated by religious, racial, or gender bias—called hate crimes—had been introduced into the Vermont legislature but received scant attention until a vicious beating of a homosexual prompted a public hearing in the spring of 1990. A large crowd gathered in room 11. I had never personally testified on pending legislation as governor. But this time I did, and to my surprise, I felt unusually emotional when it came my turn to speak.

> When there is violence against any person in society, because he or she is different, it threatens us all. Only by speaking out are any of us safe. We cannot tolerate the abuse of homosexual and gay Vermonters under any circumstances. This law, while not perfect, allows us to make a statement of conscience, to reaffirm our values, and to counter the evil that surfaced in a dark alley. I urge its passage.

Only afterward did I understand that my wish to testify on the bill had stemmed from my childhood connection with the Holocaust experience—one reason for my family's exodus from Europe. I could not, in good conscience, remain silent.

Gender, unlike religion, was always present as a topic of debate. Was being a woman a liability, and if so, to what extent?

It is impossible to assess the precise impact of gender on a political race because one cannot separate it from other factors, such as experience, timing, and incumbency. I could tell little from the voters' response because I rarely heard a voter say he or she wouldn't vote for me because I was a woman.

There was one exception. In my first campaign for governor, I was being led through a senior citizens' housing project in St. Johnsbury by a group of volunteers when I heard some yelling from the next apartment. The advance team had sprinted two doors ahead to check out who was home.

"I won't vote for a woman. No way. Never," the voice of an old woman blasted down the hall.

"She's demented," my friend kindly explained.

"Not necessarily. She's just being honest." I laughed.

Polling results indicated that older men and older women had greater gender bias. Younger working women were most favorably inclined to women candidates. Younger men were next.

But I learned to keep my answers simple in response to any gender questions, since talking about gender as an obstacle would make it so. It also sounded like an excuse, which I did not want to use. "It's hard to assess the impact of my being a woman on the race" was my stock response. "I suspect a number of people won't vote for me because I'm a woman, and another group will vote for me for the same reason. They probably cancel each other out."

The complete answer was more complex. I had given it when I lost the election in 1982, and I had immediately regretted it. "Kunin Says Sexism Played Role in Her Defeat": the headline made me cringe.

"No, no, that's not what I said!" I yelled at the breakfast table, to anyone around.

Then I read the article, which was not all that bad.

> The electorate is more skeptical of a woman candi-
> date's leadership potential, particularly when the
> highest political offices are at stake, Lt. Gov.
> Madeleine Kunin said Tuesday.
>   Reflecting on her Nov. 2 defeat in the Vermont gov-
> ernor's race, Kunin said sexism was a factor but not
> the leading one.
>   "I don't attribute my loss to being a woman by any

means, but it did make a difference," the Burlington Democrat said.

I had said that Snelling's incumbency was the main factor; that principal argument appeared in the next-to-the-last paragraph of the article.

> "Very few people would admit today that they wouldn't vote for a woman—we've moved beyond bigotry—but it comes down to who is believed when complex technical subjects are discussed, or who is perceived to have managerial ability," Kunin said.
>
> She said men are welcome to take up feminist causes, as when Gov. Richard Snelling was applauded for calling for a state constitutional equal rights amendment. Women, on the other hand, have to struggle to be taken seriously when speaking on subjects such as hunting and fishing policy and state finances, where the views of men have been dominant. . . .
>
> One of Snelling's main campaign strategies was to stress his managerial credentials and invite comparison with Kunin's background. Virtually no women in Vermont could match Dick Snelling's background—women simply haven't had the opportunities.

Well, that was true. Snelling was a millionaire CEO of his own company. Women in Vermont inevitably had different life experiences. The female candidate for an executive position has the burden of explaining that these differences might qualify her equally well for the job, but there was no way for the voters to make a clear comparison. Female leadership credentials therefore seemed less effective. Mother, volunteer, teacher, legislator, did not add up to the same thing as CEO of a corporation.

> She charged that the news media treat women candidates as a separate class and have helped perpetuate the belief women are more emotional and less rational in decision-making.
>
> As an example, the Lieutenant Governor cited a *Free Press* editorial endorsing Snelling for re-election. In it the Governor was praised for having stood up to "the hysterical cries that you should be doing more about the shipment of nuclear waste through the state." Kunin said the word "hysterical," which derives from the Greek word for a womb and refers to an irrational emotional response, would never have been used had Snelling's Democratic foe been a man.

I had granted the interview shortly after returning from giving a speech to alumni at Harvard's Kennedy School of Government program for state and local officials. That was on November 8, six days after the election. My wounds were fresh. I could not help myself. I poured it out, expounding on the subtlety of bias against women that made it hard to talk about and deal with.

I shared my most poignant discovery. "To be liked is not the same thing as to be given power."

It was true that all along the campaign trail in 1982 I had felt signs of affection that I mistook for approval. "For men, I surmise, there is less need to be liked. Power alone is enough," I told my Harvard alumni audience.

"Women, men believe, do not need power. They can be placated by compliments. I recall walking into a television studio and chatting with the host, Jack Barry, a longtime friend. In my heart, I'm with you, he said. It wasn't his heart I wanted. It was his vote."

I told my audience that even when men and women take identical positions, their comments are perceived differently, because they are seen and heard in a different context. I recalled the man who came up to me after a debate during which I had attacked Snelling, and said, "Do me a favor, stop picking on him. You remind me of my wife."

In my vulnerable postelection condition, I expressed my frustration at losing the argument over the shipment of nuclear wastes.

> In a situation where there is conflict, where there are opposing versions of the truth espoused by different candidates, we must ask, Whose views are validated? Who is believed?
>
> Winning is not determined by mastery of the facts. The candidate who wins or loses is the person who captures the issue, who wins over the press, who gains credibility for her or his side. It is, in the end, a power struggle, plain and simple.

Later experiences only deepened my sense of this truth. Women have more difficulty in winning a close argument on the facts when they go toe to toe against men because, with few exceptions, they have not been taught how to debate, and they believe, like the good students they are, that the facts alone will prevail. Moreover, men are encouraged to show bombast, emotion, and outrage when they fight. These qualities are not considered appropriate in women. Neither is modesty an effective approach. There is not yet an acceptable model for women to follow in defense of the truth, as the nation witnessed in the Anita Hill testimony during the Clarence Thomas confirmation hearings.

The day after she made her charges of sexual harassment against her former boss, newspapers across the country gave identical space to Anita Hill and Clarence Thomas. Headlines asked, "Who Is Telling the Truth?" It seemed an equal contest. And when Anita Hill and her supporters told the Senate Judiciary Committee that she had passed a lie detector test, they thought they had the ultimate weapon. The truth would decide. Instead, her opponents chose to question the reliability of lie detector tests.

Clarence Thomas had the freedom to exhibit outrage, emotion, and anger; Anita Hill did not. Neither emotional expression nor emotional control seemed fitting; either way her behavior was judged inappropriate to truth telling. Neither was she believed to be speaking for herself; her opponents on the Senate Judiciary Committee easily made her the pawn of special interest groups or, worse yet, the victim of devilish incantations in the novel *The Exorcist*. The immediate reaction to Anita Hill's testimony taught us that women must continue to invent themselves as they prepare not only to articulate the truth, but to defend it. The belated understanding and respect she earned indicates that perhaps new models of female truth telling—based neither on male nor on female traditional behavior—may be emerging.

More than a decade after the 1982 campaign, when I look back at both the speech and the interview, I second my conclusions, but at the time I was chagrined that I had expressed them. I thought I had exposed myself and spoken more from pain than reason. In fact, I had spoken the truth as I saw and felt it. But my self-incriminating reaction epitomizes the danger that women face when they speak of the effect of gender on politics: dangerous because misunderstood. Explanations of subtle, complex issues of sexism in politics become excuses for failure placed in screaming headlines, "Kunin Says Sexism Played Role in Her Defeat." I had inadvertently fallen into the trap of victimization, precisely what I had worked so hard to avoid by running for public office. Gender, related to politics, counted for everything and nothing, but rarely could it be discussed to any advantage.

Still, being a woman made subtle differences in how I experienced routine events as a politician. For example, as lieutenant governor, I had been invited to a St. Michael's College summer day-camp program for community children, operated under a federal grant. It required that they invite a public figure to provide "cultural enrichment," and on this particular day, I was the enrichment.

Some two hundred children, aged ten to sixteen, were herded into the school auditorium on a beautiful summer morning. The children made it clear, by their fidgeting, that they would have rather been somewhere else.

I kept my remarks short and asked for questions. A dozen hands shot up.

"How old are you?"

"How much money do you make?"

"Do you think there will ever be a woman president?"

"Do you have a bodyguard?"

The questions continued until the counselor called a halt. Enrichment time was over, but a bunch of kids lingered. I found myself encircled by a bevy of little girls who stood by me, as if I were the only tree in the forest. Not a boy in sight. Breathlessly, they wanted to tell me things. I had to know that:

"I visited the United Nations."

"I saw the Statue of Liberty."

"I saw the president on TV."

"They never asked questions before," the counselor observed. "They must be comfortable with you."

I gave each girl a hug. That is why I was there. That is what being a role model meant.

The first time I crowned a beauty queen I had difficulty placing the crown on her head, not because it wouldn't fit on her head but because it didn't fit with my feminism. It was the time of the annual agriculture show in Barre, when all the agricultural organizations in Vermont gathered and farmers surveyed new equipment and technology. Some three hundred Future Farmers of America (FFA) were holding their yearly banquet, and for the first (and only) time, Governor Snelling had given me a proclamation to read at the event. How could I sanction a beauty pageant? But how could I, as the governor's representative, not do it?

Music blared from loudspeakers on either side of the stage. The beauty-queen candidates and their frozen escorts marched in. Each terrified young woman was wearing a long, homemade, pastel taffeta dress, cut from what seemed to be the same Butterick pattern. The judges first announced the winner for third place. The girl pretended to be thrilled, but what she really wanted, of course, was to have been last, which in this case meant first. I tried not to show my disapproval of the whole thing.

The judge left time for a suspenseful pause. The second-place winner was announced. She smiled dutifully and stepped aside. The winner, a tall red-cheeked girl with long permed hair, stood alone. The other two embraced her on cue, like Cinderella's sisters.

It was my turn. I held the crown in my hands and at the appointed moment placed it on her head. As I bent toward her, I whispered in her ear, "Don't forget, you can use your brains, too."

Perhaps she thought I was crazy. It was hard to tell. She continued to smile.

AFTER my 1982 defeat, when the question of whether to run for governor again interjected itself into my thoughts, I put it off. I was not ready to face that decision. Cross-country skiing with my husband one day in late March 1983, we moved in a linear pattern through the silent, snow-covered woods. It might be the last snow of the season. I tried to take pictures with my eyes, saying, Remember this. Everything was white—above, below, and around, like the surface of the moon, only soft. The wall of a red-striped rock jutted up from the snow, green lichen crocheting the surface. I would never see this if I could not ski here now, pause, and look.

Why leave the safety and privacy of this space, with the two of us exploring this terrain, to step out into a dangerous and uncertain political world again? I shivered. This carefully laid-out trail with pressed parallel tracks as straight as knitting needles told us exactly where we had been and where we were to go. Everything on either side could be touched, seen, and understood.

Beyond these woods, nothing would be clear. My feet and fingers would tell me little. Yet, could I stop here? I imagined other possible scenarios, and my sense of adventure returned. I felt I was standing on top of a hill with my ski tips over the edge, looking down. I had to make the descent. I could not back away. Go, before you think about danger. Go, before you're tempted to stay on the trail you know so well.

Then I remembered how it was when I fell, a jumble of arms and legs groping for realignment. I stood up unsteadily and brushed myself off, getting rid of the evidence. Everyone who passed by here would see the gouge in the snow. Here, they would note, is where someone had fallen. Only with the thaw would it go away.

Could I do this again? Take the risk? Lose twice? I doubted it.

*　　*　　*

ON THURSDAY morning, January 5, 1984, I was working on the text for
a corporate report, my first technical-writing assignment. As I typed at
the kitchen table, my mind wandered toward dinner. What should we
have? I had been out of office for a year and had started to construct a
new life, writing, teaching, and hosting a radio talk show. I had spent a
semester as a fellow at the Institute of Politics at the Kennedy School of
Government. I had been inordinately grateful for that; Harvard had given
me an identity, a community, a life of the mind, and, most important, the
stamina to consider running again. I had not yet settled on a new career.
That was yet to be defined.

I struggled with the second paragraph. It was eleven o'clock in the
morning. I had been working for an hour. Then the telephone rang—
another interruption. I would have to answer it.

It was my sister-in-law Judith, calling from the statehouse in Montpelier. "Did you hear the news?"

"No, what happened?"

"Snelling's not going to run. He just announced it during his State of
the State address. I wanted to warn you. You might get press calls."

"Are you kidding?"

"No, I just heard it, I was sitting up in the balcony at the statehouse and
ran down to call you."

I jumped in the air. My stomach fell. In a second, everything had
changed. My cocoon was unwinding. It whizzed around uncontrollably,
like the spool of a kite caught by a gust of wind. I held on fast.

"Is it really true?" I asked, stalling for time.

"Turn on the radio. Hear it for yourself."

I did. "Governor Richard A. Snelling, in a surprise announcement, said
this morning that he will not seek a fifth term. A stunned audience . . ."
the announcer's voice said.

"It's Over," the *Rutland Herald* headline shouted.

It's begun, I said to myself.

A split second, and I knew. I would run. That's all it took.

I tried to control myself in public. I would take my time before making
a decision, I told the press. Maybe I would run for governor, maybe for
Congress.

Peter Welch, the Senate president pro tem, coveted the Democratic
party nomination. Because he had criticized Snelling over the budget during the past session, he thought he deserved it, but I would not let him
push me aside.

The phone did not stop ringing.

"It's your turn, Madeleine. Go for it. You paid your dues."

"Thank you, it's great to hear from you. I'll need your help."

"You've got it."

They were right, after all—those people who had seen 1982 as a dress rehearsal. I had to run and lose in order to run and win. The only way to redeem 1982 was to win in 1984.

But why did I risk another loss? And on intuition? No poll, no meetings, no detailed analysis. That came later, after I had made up my mind.

I was convinced that this time I would win. I had to do it for my children, to show them that loss is reversible; for my constituents, to prove that I was worthy of them; and for myself, to discover renewal.

There was another reason. I had to exorcise the loss. It had to be removed surgically and be replaced with victory. That was how, at last, I would heal.

9

Lattie Coor put his arm around me. He and his wife, Ina, were giving a party at Engelsby House for university faculty and trustees. I had never had such proximity to the president of the University of Vermont before. A few months ago, in 1983, I had sat opposite him in a bloodred leather chair in his mahogany office to discuss the possibility of teaching a course. I was hoping to find a niche in academia. He had listened politely.

Now, in his white living room, he laughed uproariously at my jokes. Was I really that funny?

George Ewins, a Republican businessman, was less discreet. "Since you might be our next governor . . ." he said, and then proceeded to give me some economic advice. I was now worthy of it.

Everything at the party was different, now that Snelling was out, and I was in the running. When I walked into the room, I was greeted like one whose arrival had been long expected: my coat taken, my glass provided. No more awkward moments standing in the doorway at a safe distance from the crowd, sizing up the situation, looking for someone to talk to, a corner to claim, a topic to discuss, the latest movie, book, or the weather. When I was pregnant with power I was given solicitous attention. My place was prearranged. Always a hand at my elbow to lead me to the center, where important people waited to draw me in. Seeing a circle of light fall at my feet, I stood taller, smiled broader, and spoke my lines more distinctly to the first person whose hand reached out for mine. In a few minutes, I was released, as gracefully as I had been captured, expected to move on, to reach for the next hand and the next, not too fast, not too slow. *My* rhythm controlled the tempo in the room. Only the gauche expected me to linger. If caught by a harangue, I would be rescued by someone whose duty it was to do so. I had to circulate.

Politics popped up in colorful bursts in the center of conversation, like sparklers on the Fourth of July, drawing a curious crowd.

Eye contact was different. No one looked through or past me. Everyone looked at me. Neither men nor women allowed their eyes to stray toward someone more interesting, important, or fun. It was me they wanted to talk to. And it was they who wanted to be heard.

Remember this, I warned myself. It will evaporate like rain in dry heat.

The night following Snelling's announcement, I had discussed the possibility of the race with my husband and children. Could we do it again? Ironically, a campaign has a dual effect on families: the excitement and tension of the race bring husbands and wives closer together, even as they threaten to separate them. I felt a new closeness as we embarked on the adventure—so much to do, to talk about, to plan—but I also knew I would be asking for more than I could give in return. A campaign was egomaniacal. As the candidate, I would become the center of our campaign universe. But this universe is finite; it begins with the campaign and ends with the election. Then what? I would be alone. Ultimately, the aftermath would be mine, be it victory or defeat.

I was afraid of the swings of the pendulum, drawing us together in happy conspiracy one moment, pulling us apart in separate anxiety the next. How could I keep it steady? Could we maintain the pose of the family in the photograph, neatly cropped for happiness, like a Christmas card framed in red? Like other families' portraits, our picture was not deceptive; it just did not tell everything.

I turned to my typewriter and wrote my campaign vows in capital letters:

—NOT TO GET UPSET WITH THE PRESS THE SAME WAY—LET IT RUN OFF, EXPECT IT, HUMOR IT AWAY, WAIT FOR THE NEXT GOOD STORY.

—TO STAY CLOSE TO ARTHUR AND THE CHILDREN. TAKE TIME OUT FOR THEM, INCLUDE THEM.

—NOT TO FEEL A SENSE OF CRISIS WHEN THINGS GO WRONG. TO PUT IT IN PERSPECTIVE. DO NOT DWELL ON IT.

—TO BE POSITIVE ABOUT WHAT I THINK AND SAY. RECOGNIZE THAT SOMEONE IS ABOUT TO BE PISSED OFF AND ACCEPT THAT.

—TO BE BOLD IN SPEECH, IDEAS, AND ISSUES. AND BRIEF.

—TO PACE MYSELF, FIND MORE TIME TO TAKE OFF.

—TO BECOME LESS OBSESSED (BUT I AM ALREADY, I DON'T KNOW HOW NOT TO BE) BUT FORCE MYSELF TO REMOVE MYSELF FROM IT PHYSICALLY AND EMOTIONALLY FROM TIME TO TIME.

We had a meeting of an emerging kitchen cabinet: Liz Bankowski, Pam Greene, Beth Baldwin, Althea Kroger, Steve Kimbell, and John Dooley. After Snelling announced he would not run, I picked up the phone to call Liz, who was studying for a degree in public administration at Harvard;

she would have to take a leave of absence to run my campaign. Selecting Liz as my campaign manager and, later, as my chief of staff was the most important political decision I made. Would she do it?

"Yes."

"Great!"

Few in Vermont knew who she was.

"Where'd you get her?" my brother challenged.

"You'll see, she's terrific."

But after I made my decision final, I was left alone in the living room. Fears recurred. Could I do it? Have I got the brains, fortitude, humor, and energy? I won't be perfect. I will be criticized. I greeted an obvious insight like a revelation: everyone in political life gets criticized. So don't be surprised. The key is not to avoid criticism, but to survive it.

"Bankowski: The Woman Behind Kunin," the headline in the *Rutland Herald* soon pronounced. And there Liz was, with her long, thick hair streaming beyond the frame of the photograph. Liz and her husband had moved to Vermont the year before from Washington, D.C., where I had been introduced to her in the office of the Women's Campaign Fund. She had been a staff aide to Father Robert Drinan, the Jesuit congressman from Massachusetts. The first time I met her I sensed that this was a woman who understood both politics and feminism. What she didn't know about Vermont, she could find out. Father Drinan told the Vermont press, "She's just sophisticated and savvy. She knows where the votes are."

Liz and I were close, excellent but not intimate friends, perhaps deliberately so. She understood, more clearly than I, that she needed to maintain perspective. Too much intimacy would have endangered it. She had to be able to tell me what no one else would, things I did not want to hear. Usually, I listened. I could always trust her advice. No matter how harsh her words might be, I ultimately forgave her because her motive was unquestionable: to protect and enhance her candidate and enable her to win.

She understood the nature of the struggle I faced as a woman running for governor because we had an unspoken bond: our common experience as political women infringing on traditionally male territory. The campaign, we both believed, would not only make a political statement, it would affirm the purpose of our own lives and those of other women. Winning would provide more than victory; it would be a stunning metaphor of new female strength. This was the passion that drove us.

As a campaign strategist, Liz was thoroughly pragmatic. She knew precisely what we were up against: the wall of history. And she knew what had to be done to break it down: to show her candidate catapulting over the barrier of precedent by virtue of her experience and vision.

Liz had earned a local reputation as a political genius in just one year after having managed a state legislative campaign for Julie Peterson, a thirty-one-year-old counselor working in a shelter for battered women, who, in a stunning upset, defeated the sixty-two-year-old incumbent, the former lieutenant governor of the state and town moderator for the annual town meeting, Jack Burgess.

"We called ourselves the termites," Liz later confessed. "We took nothing for granted. No one knew we were there until the outcome was certain."

Liz mapped out my election battle at every level, the top layer of old-fashioned politics as well as the underlayer of new feminist politics. She was a go-between for the two, never underestimating the significance of either. Most important, Liz's experience validated my sense of reality. She saw what I saw and felt what I felt; her nods and assents confirmed my responses to the political world where we both functioned as relative strangers. In a myriad of overt and subtle ways she seconded my interpretations when I needed affirmation and could find it nowhere else. When I was pushed back by the odd look, the joke, the snicker, either real or imagined, I would be reassured by a woman who knew precisely how I felt. She would also, through her comprehending presence, provide a safety valve for my anger. I could kick the chair without fear of inflicting damage. No explanation was necessary. My isolation was reduced. I was not fighting single-handedly; there were two of us, learning the language and customs of political men whose power we wanted to appropriate for our own. Together we deciphered the political code and figured out its contradictory signals from one day to the next. On one hand, "Welcome, girls, everybody's invited," and on the other, "What in the world are you doing here?"

The first year I became a member of the National Governors' Association, in 1985, I attended the annual meeting in Washington, D.C. At the first session my fellow governors and I were waiting for the arrival of the president of the United States and members of his cabinet. I surveyed the marvelous proportions of the gold-draped East Room of the White House, with the balanced portraits of Martha and George Washington and two fireplaces on either side. I read my own nameplate with fascination. I belonged here! Someone had set my place at this table: a White House notepad in the center, a pencil at my left, and a glass of water at my right. Edwin Edwards, the governor of Louisiana, was seated at my left. I introduced myself. He looked at me with the curiosity he might reserve for a rare insect, and said, "I didn't know there were two of you."

There were. Martha Layne Collins, governor of Kentucky, and me.

Liz and I formed a club of two to make up for their club of many. We knew that this structure called politics was not our creation. It was built by them, for them. The men knew where each nail had been driven, both straight and bent. We had to feel our way along the walls with our hands, like blind women.

As I worried about maintaining the tenuous balance between my political and family lives, I wondered how Liz would manage hers. She was of a different generation, ten years younger than I, with different expectations and, I thought, new answers. When we first strategized over coffee in her kitchen, her son, Joshua, was in diapers, crawling between our legs on the kitchen floor. Her daughter, Sarah, was three. She prided herself on going back to work two days after each baby was born.

(When Joshua was six years old, Liz took him and Sarah to the Shelburne Museum near Burlington, where the highlight was a walk through a refurbished railroad car. Joshua noted a dummy propped up in the plush red velvet seat.

"Who's that?" Joshua asked.

"That's a governor," Liz explained. "This used to be the governor's private railroad car."

Joshua said, "Don't be silly, Mommy. Men can't be governors."

Liz, like a good mother, replied, "Well, someday they will, Joshua.")

The first thing the campaign had to achieve, Liz argued, was to keep Peter Welch out of the race. Making the rounds in the halls of the statehouse, she quietly corralled support for me and eroded his. "It was not that hard," she later observed. "The timing for you was right; you were the heir apparent. But it was important to avoid a primary fight. We couldn't afford it."

The next thing—our first positive aim—was to establish my credentials. That was the burden of the gender question, revealed by the polls. I had to earn credibility, though in public, Liz dismissed the "Are we ready for a woman?" question. "This election has nothing to do with Kunin's being a woman. There is a sense that she has paid her dues, that it's her turn."

Our first television ad was simple; it was in black-and-white print, line by line:

Experience
One candidate for Governor chaired the Legislature's
   Appropriations Committee
Managed state spending in good times and in bad
Spent ten years in state Government . . .
Experience

At the end, the screen went dark and a photograph of me flashed on. "Madeleine Kunin for Governor, for Vermont."

Surprise! This experienced candidate is a woman! Both Liz and our pollster-consultant, Tom Kiley, were certain that had they flashed my picture first, the text would not have had equal effect.

Once we established my credentials, we needed to prove that I could govern. I would not know whom I would face in the general election until the Republican primary election was held in September—a choice between Attorney General John Easton or a political newcomer who had made his mark in the private sector, bank president Hilton Wick. Easton, considered the early favorite, was the man we believed we had to beat. He used leadership as his campaign slogan. Emblazoned on every poster was: THE DIFFERENCE IS LEADERSHIP. His handsome square-jawed visage implied that leadership was what men could deliver. But Easton felt handicapped by the lines of privilege interspersed in his biography: a bachelor lawyer who lived in the well-to-do ski-resort town of Stowe. To make amends he had garaged his sports car for the fall and rented a sedan. He had to do more. He discovered a campaign strategy employed by Senator Bob Graham when he ran for governor in Florida. Easton called it "Working with Vermonters." A headline declared: "Easton to Take 16 Jobs!" Each week, the Republican candidate for governor would spend one day at a different site on a construction project or factory floor. Liz and I sat staring openmouthed at the front page of the newspaper one morning. There was John Easton, muscles bulging and chest bared, lifting a piece of timber up over his head. We called it the Adonis picture.

"What can I do to match this?" I asked the staff.

"Nothing" was the answer.

Why not? I had to be a regular person, too. Waitress, hairdresser, secretary?

Wait a minute. You're running for governor. I had to become gubernatorial. Becoming gubernatorial required more than image building: what would count most was the image I carried with me in my head. Nothing about the campaign could indicate that I was a pretender, acting out parts without proper conviction. I had to stake a claim on gubernatorial territory as if it were rightfully mine, as if women had always owned it.

But what exactly did being gubernatorial mean?

The 1982 campaign had told us what it did not mean. It did not mean having citizen task forces producing detailed position papers on every major subject. That approach would not only be unnecessary, but could be detrimental if the papers were thought of as substitutes for my taking strong stands myself. Whatever I said in this campaign had to be concise and decisive. And better than saying things, I had to demonstrate what I believed by taking specific actions.

Easton, Liz observed, had the luxury to be thoughtful, even, at times, undecided. I did not. I would be held to a different standard, not because of gender bias but because of gender assumptions. "Leadership," "gubernatorial"—these words contained the subliminal afterimage of a man. Thousands of years of history had made maleness synonymous with leadership. We had to stamp that image with an alternative in freshly inked black letters that spelled "woman." Every gesture, word, and response would be critical to our success. Was I being gubernatorial? To answer yes, I had to start from within, by seeing myself as the governor.

The man who understood that best was John Dooley, the author of those position papers in my previous campaign. John, who had the capacity to analyze any issue with extraordinary clarity, knew that this time facts and reason would not be enough. I had to have command of the issues, to lift them off the page and marshal them into action. I had to prove that I could not only spout ideas, but fight for them. Discussing a problem with John and forging a solution were stimulating experiences that cleared my head, like an hour of vigorous exercise.

But John brought more than intellect to my campaign. He was a feminist and a humanist, drawn to the cause of helping a woman get elected by his personal sense of justice. John provided a moral and ethical bulwark for the campaign and, later, for the administration. (It was with great reluctance that four years later I appointed him to the Vermont Supreme Court. This was where his intellect belonged, but I hated to let him go. I surmised then what I now know, that his contribution on the court would be more lasting than all his accomplishments in state government.)

Both John and Liz were unorthodox choices. Both served me extraordinarily well. If there is a lesson to be drawn here it is simple: when running for public office choose people who understand and believe in you, who share your values and your zeal, who are highly competent, and in whom you have total trust. Everything else can be learned.

Organizing a gubernatorial campaign the second time around was, from a tactical standpoint, easier. The rudiments of a grass-roots network were already in place. Personally, I felt stronger. I had not intended to learn by losing, but circumstances offered me no choice; I was strangely buoyed by the knowledge that I had already experienced the worst. Never could I forget the face of defeat. All power, it whispered, is ephemeral. Fame, honor, status, are fragile things, thin as ice freezing over moving water. Its momentary solidity is deceiving. Watch for a change in the current or a rise in the temperature. The gray film will shatter into thousands of sequined crystals, making a tinkling sound. I have seen it before, and it will happen again, as inevitably as a change in the seasons.

I found solace in the thought that if I lost a second time, it would hurt less because it was familiar. And if I won, victory, the great redeemer, would obliterate the memory of defeat. Defeat without a sequel would remain chiseled in my record like my name on a tombstone. Defeat followed by success would become a footnote, easily eroded by time. Envisioning victory became the font of my healing, the source of my courage.

On January 13 I made my announcement that I would be a candidate for governor.

> In the last few days, I have received encouragement from people all over the state, affirming my conviction that participating in the political life of this state is the most worthwhile thing I can do with my own life. It is the only way that I know to change things for the better.

To my delight, I provoked laughter when I told the audience:

> I have enjoyed a time of introspection, time with family and friends. Time for writing, exploring new ideas and endeavors. I believe it's important for people in public life to break out of the political rhythm from time to time. Dick Snelling, I'm pleased to say, has reached that same conclusion, and I wish him well. . . .

And I held the audience's attention when I said:

> As I thought about what I would say today, I tried to define what it is about Vermont which makes it different from all other states in the nation.
> We know it is different.
> That is why we live here.

That is why we proudly call ourselves Vermonters, whether we're fifth generation, or whether we just took a wrong turn off I-89.

I concluded that what is different about Vermont is that here each person counts.

We notice each man, woman, and child. There is enough light, there is enough space in our landscape for each one of us to form our own silhouette. That sense of respect for the individual in Vermont has given us a sense of shared responsibility. We care about one another and we let it show. When a farmer's barn burns down in the night, his neighbors are there the next morning, ready to raise the roof beams.

That's not a picture in *Vermont Life*. That is life in Vermont. It is that barn-raising spirit that I believe we can bring to state government.

Because here in this state, when a man or woman is laid off in Springfield, we feel that man and woman's hardship in Burlington. When an elderly woman loses her Social Security, she is not a statistic to us. She is a woman we know, a woman we help. And when we hear about a child who has been abused, anywhere in the state, we feel love for the child, and we hold out a protective hand. We feel a sense of individual responsibility for one another's welfare, and don't believe that only the experts can solve our problems. . . .

As governor of the state of Vermont, my highest goal will be to invite the full participation of all Vermonters.

We can make Vermont a state where children receive the finest education, where adults have rewarding work that pays a decent wage, and where all share an environment that makes life enjoyable.

Happy applause filled the room like bells. Supporters spilled in to offer their congratulations.

The announcement had fallen into place quickly; this time, I was not weighed down by labored phrases like shopping bags pulling on each arm. My words flew out as if they had been waiting for this signal to be released.

Neil Davis reported in the *Burlington Free Press* the next morning: "Projecting self-assurance and good humor, Madeleine Kunin told one hundred supporters and reporters Friday afternoon what they already knew: she will reach a second time for the governorship. During her well-orchestrated announcement ceremony, she drew two standing ovations and several other rounds of clapping and cheering."

"Well-orchestrated"? I made no effort to correct him. When the press erred in my favor, I would accept it with grace.

It was more difficult to maintain my perspective when they erred the other way. The night before I had turned on the six o'clock news on WCAX-TV, and I watched as the television reporter, microphone in hand, superimposed his words over mine. None of my speech could be heard; the only voice was that of the reporter concluding that I had said nothing of substance. I wanted to scream, "Go away and let me talk!"

The journalistic practice of substituting the reporter's interpretation for the candidate's words is frustrating not only for politicians, who feel manipulated, but it is equally annoying for the public, deprived of the right to form its own conclusions. The extraordinary power of the press to shape my reality never ceased either to awe or to anger me.

By April 18, the date of my first public forum, the three candidates were portrayed by the press as equally positioned at the starting gate, despite Easton's statewide recognition, which far exceeded Hilton Wick's, a late entry in the race. He had been president of the Chittenden Bank for fourteen years and had served as the chairman of every significant board and charity drive in town. Easton was the favorite, but Wick was the beneficiary of history. Vermont had had a successful businessman-governor from 1969 to 1973, Deane C. Davis, the former head of the National Life Insurance Company in Montpelier. He had walked straight from retirement into public office. Hilton Wick, who had never held prior public office, was thought by some to be capable of following in Davis's footsteps.

The *Boston Globe* had reported on April 15:

> A three-way debate on Wednesday in Burlington could set the tone of the campaign. Meeting in public together for the first time will be Democrat Madeleine Kunin, 50, a former lieutenant governor who lost to Snelling two years ago; Republican John Easton, 40, the state's handsome and low-key attorney general; and Republican Hilton Wick, a 64-year-old lawyer and banker with no political experience but many influential friends.
>
> And the issue each candidate is likely to tackle will be: Who can best take the reins from Snelling's firm hand.

The night of the forum, Richard Snelling appeared first on the evening news. Then the camera switched to the candidates' forum. The reporter was correct: we were all running against Richard Snelling.

My opponents had one obvious advantage: they looked like governors. In their portfolios they carried traditional gubernatorial credentials. Wick's lack of political experience did not dismiss him from serious consideration. His skills from the private sector were considered transferable to public life.

"What the state needs now is a chief executive with fiscal-management ability," he said. Faced with this competition, I would have to convince the public that I had the capacity to act on *my* vision of the future—a good economy, healthy environment, and better education—because of my experience in state government and a passionate belief in the issues that mattered most to Vermonters. To help figure out the strategy we hired Tom Kiley.

In May, Tom came for a day to brief me, the staff, and a handful of advisers on his polling data. I had already been told the raw figures, and they were good. If the race were held today, I would win against either Republican opponent, Easton or Wick.

In a Kunin-Easton contest, I would get 49 percent of the vote; Easton, 32 percent; with 19 percent undecided. In a Kunin-Wick contest, my margin of victory would be 30 points. There was a clear gender gap: 46 percent of the men supported me and 52 percent of the women. Also an age gap: half of those under the age of thirty-four would vote for me, but only 36 percent of those sixty-five and older.

Despite the good news, I did not look forward to the session with Tom. More than any other activity in the campaign, discussion of polling data would turn me into an object; something to be dissected and diagnosed as I lay on the examining table. Everyone joined in with chilling dispassion. My closest friends forgot who I was. Steve, my former campaign manager, and Liz, who now held my fate in her hands, bent over me, poking me like a cadaver. Memories of two years ago, when I was found to be badly wanting, surged back. I could not bear to go through it again.

The numbers, black and white, indisputable, killed illusion. I could not count on people's smiles, handshakes, or kind words. They were just being nice or, worse yet, lying. Here—under the clear plastic cover of the polling report—was reality.

"The numbers are good, but the race is not at all assured," Kiley, a former Jesuit, said. I felt his verdict came straight from God.

"The most important target group for the Kunin campaign is men. Only forty-six percent of the men say they intend to vote for her. If she can maintain this level of support . . ."

She? Hey Tom, oh Tom, I'm over here.

I stayed quiet.

"However, in 1982, the gender gap grew as the election neared and Kunin became more aggressive. Men ultimately voted in overwhelming numbers for the male candidate, Richard Snelling."

Oh, was it that bad? Was I too aggressive? Should I be different now?

"We are convinced that Kunin must overcome a special burden of proof with male voters in particular. She will be required to demonstrate decisiveness and a capacity to handle the difficult management choices she will confront as governor."

Decisiveness, yes, I promise, absolutely.

"We believe the key target group could be narrowed down to middle-aged, independent men, between thirty and fifty. Perhaps in August or early September we could probe further to find out what reservations or doubts they may have about her as governor."

Probe further? Please don't.

"Although she is in a commanding position now, Easton is not nearly as well known as Kunin, and he can be expected to close the gap as he attracts additional voters."

Here today, gone tomorrow.

Liz examined John Easton's strong points.

"Liz, do you have to?"

She did not hear me.

"I see Easton is generally perceived to be doing a good job. Most of the voters see him as capable and professional, taking strong stands and having the courage of his convictions.

"Under Madeleine's 'Unfavorable Impressions,' the first one I notice is 'wouldn't be strong enough, not pushy enough, a little wishy-washy, doesn't make her stands clear.' "

"But, Liz, that's only four percent of the voters. Look on the other side of the ledger. Eleven percent think I am 'well informed, have everything under control, and would make a good governor.' "

I looked down the list of "Favorable Impressions of Madeleine Kunin," page 44 of the report. "Hey, look at this. 'Gutsy, has backbone, speaks what she feels, stood up as lieutenant governor'—nine percent!"

No one paid attention.

"We've got a lot of work to do."

"WHERE'S your campaign?" I was asked repeatedly during the dog days of summer. "We don't see it."

"Where are your issues? Why don't you speak out?"

I wanted to scream, "I'm on the road every day and night, and we've issued hundreds of press releases. What can I do if the press doesn't print what I say?"

Liz urged patience. The campaign was not focused on me because I was unopposed for the Democratic nomination, and press interest was geared to where the action was: the Republican primary.

At midsummer Liz arranged for me to have lunch with the two former Democratic governors, Phil Hoff and Tom Salmon. She knew precisely what she wanted to produce: a photograph of me with the two of them, as their equal. They would give me their blessing. I felt like a schoolgirl, but I did as I was told. The picture was terrific. The boys were my buddies.

While the campaign may have looked dormant on the outside, it was frantic with activity on the inside. Liz had a phone growing out of her ear. When she tired of listening, she put the receiver in the top drawer of her desk and let the person on the other end keep talking. Five minutes later she'd take it out, and as expected, the voice would still be talking. Liz would interrupt with an "uh-huh" and stick the receiver back in the drawer.

Some mornings I would wake up exhausted and ask myself, Is this worth it? What a crazy way to spend six or seven months of my life!

"Kunin for governor" was what the voice said to me when I called the campaign office phone. It still startled me. How much am I putting myself in that position, and how much *am* I that person?

I told myself that I was more gubernatorial than last time; less forced, more natural. And I knew that my opponents, Hilton Wick and John Easton, were also rehearsing a part they had not played.

My dreams pictured my anxieties. One morning I woke up with two in my head: I was at home and couldn't find the things I needed to get dressed: no shoes, stockings, or clothes. I was scheduled for a nine o'clock radio program and should have been at the station ten minutes before airtime. At 9:10 the phone rang. I knew it was the radio station. The voice asked, "Where are you, Mrs. Kunin? We're waiting for you."

"How could I have allowed this to happen?" I asked. "Why on earth didn't I leave earlier?"

In the second dream two friends, Bill and Alice Daniels, were supposed to pick me up at a certain time at my hotel, but instead I was on the street in traffic, looking for their car. It was getting late. I didn't see the car. Then I realized I was in the wrong place. I should have been at the hotel.

How could I get them a message to tell them I was somewhere else? Now I wouldn't get where I was going.

I woke up, looked at my watch, and fell back asleep.

At the candidates' forums, I was usually given the honor of going first. Wick inevitably followed and did what opponents dislike most: he agreed with me and stole my lines. The next day's headline read "Wick and Kunin Agree on Telephone Rates."

I had staked out this issue, making the three-hour trip to Brattleboro to testify against a telephone rate increase before the Public Service Board on the night of my wedding anniversary, June 21, a trip I had been most reluctant to make. Liz considered this a perfect demonstration of our strategy; instead of issuing a position paper, I would take action by testifying on behalf of the consumer. The coverage was fine down south, but only a brief report appeared in the *Burlington Free Press*. The guilt I felt in not being with my husband that night added to my exasperation. I reread my campaign vows. But despite the lack of statewide coverage, my testimony had been effective—I had put myself on the record by testifying in person and could refer to my experience throughout the campaign.

I remembered the lessons of 1982—stick to basic themes, and keep it short. Education, jobs, the environment, and good fiscal management were the central themes I repeated in speech after speech.

Vermont was a poor state with a low per capita income. More highly skilled, well-paid jobs were needed to raise the standard of living. When I was asked by voters how we could achieve that goal, I told them the answer was education. Good schools, I believed, would be the best form of economic investment. We would aim for a good early beginning, with kindergarten for every child; raise teachers' salaries (Vermont ranked forty-ninth among the states); improve vocational education to provide a useful education for non-college-bound students, and promote adult retraining.

I made other promises: we would invest in infrastructure, create rural job zones in low-income regions, and form a Vermont Venture Capital Corporation to assist small-business growth.

The environment and the economy became intertwined themes. "In Vermont we can achieve a balance between the goals of making a decent living and enjoying the good life—we can ensure that they reinforce one another." I continued to adhere to that principle throughout my terms of office and, later, as a private citizen.

We knew my experience was weak in the one area in which the attorney general was strong: law enforcement. If the chief law-enforcement officer of the state should attack me on his turf, I would be vulnerable.

Crime, according to our polling, ranked third in the electorate's priorities, after "improving the quality of education" and "creating new jobs and industry." ("Preserving the environment" ranked fourth.) But Easton, to our enormous relief, chose not to play his law-and-order card.

Not only did we hone the issues this time around, we targeted our votes. In 1982 I had received 74,393 votes, or 43.95 percent of a 54.4 percent turnout.

In 1984, a presidential year, nearly 70 percent of Vermont voters were expected to turn out. That would project to 220,000 to 240,000 votes cast, and Liz calculated we needed 120,000 votes to win. "We need to target 50,000 votes to win this election," she wrote in her campaign memo. "How will we reach them?"

This is how Liz analyzed the electorate:

> Independents and moderates will dominate the election. Two-thirds of this group are under 50, and we will need at least 60 percent of them to win.
>
> One of every four voters lives in Chittenden (county), concentration in Burlington (one-third of all voters in county). Must carry Chittenden. MK received 45.1% of vote there in 1982. Target areas outside Burlington: Essex, Colchester, South Burlington. Many young professionals in these areas . . . should be ours, John Easton may appeal to them.

Down the list we went, targeting Franklin, Washington, Windham, Windsor, and Bennington counties. Six weeks before the election our efforts paid off when we began a massive get-out-the-vote effort by telephoning all registered voters in the target areas. I will never know if this effort made the difference between victory and defeat, but in a close election, the adage "Every vote counts" became a reality.

On the campaign trail, I did not allow one voter to escape. Traveling north from Bennington on U.S. 7 that summer I stopped at Lindholm's Diner, in Rutland, to campaign. It was lunchtime. I parked in the rear lot and entered via the back door, making my way from booth to booth, stopping to introduce myself at each one. "Hi, I'm Madeleine Kunin and I'm running for governor. What a beautiful day. Where are you from?"

I was getting a friendly response. No one minded the interruption. Then I looked up. There was Hilton Wick, coming down the aisle, giving out little yellow-cellophane-wrapped hard candies with "Wick for Governor" on each one.

We laughed, crossed each other's path, and went on. I assessed the situation. If he was only tossing handfuls of candies on the table, and didn't stop to chat, I would win. I stayed in the diner a half hour longer, forcing myself to take my time to tell the customers in their booths that I cared about them. Unlike Hilton Wick, I was not just passing through. I would remember them.

The desire to become a real person on the campaign trail through a few short exchanges made me want to open up my life to strangers with one instant revelation: a look, a word, a handshake, or a smile. See, I am not the one-dimensional cardboard cutout of a politician you thought I was, propped on the sidewalk, ready for you to take a picture. If only people could know who I was, then they would understand why I wanted to become governor.

But sometimes even a small gesture could be misunderstood. On our way to Rutland, I had asked Arthur to stop the car. We had just passed a gas station with a pretty shingled roof overhanging a large bulletin board cluttered with notices and campaign posters. I had spotted one for John Easton, and I thought I should put mine up. It would only take a minute.

"Okay if I put up a poster?" I asked the man at the cash register as the screen door slammed shut behind me.

"Sure, put it up," he said genially.

"Great, thank you," I said. I never knew what the response might be. Some people would only hang up posters for Republicans. Others would hang none, afraid to antagonize any of their customers.

The bulletin board was crowded. I'd left my thumbtacks in the car. I was in too much of a hurry to go back and get them, and besides, the kids were getting restless.

"Come on, Mom, hurry up."

"Just a minute, I'll be right there."

I took some thumbtacks off another poster, brought two corners together under one, and managed to squeeze mine in between in a perfect spot: eye level.

The man from behind the counter had come out to watch me, and I could see a look of total disgust on his face.

"You mean you don't even have your own thumbtacks?"

I blushed. I thought I might laugh my way out of it. "Seriously," I turned to him, "does this really bother you?"

His face was his answer. There was no way I could make amends. I was just another cheapskate politician ripping off his bulletin board. How many people, I wondered, would I offend, with no malice intended?

*　　*　　*

THE CHALLENGE to create common bonds with people who were very different from me was sometimes formidable and often revealing. I vowed to widen my circle, make myself understood, and broaden my understanding of other lives. On a July day in 1984, I stepped into Francis Howrigan's farm kitchen in Fairfield at six-thirty in the morning. Francis was the state senator from Franklin County, and that was when he said I should be there. Franklin County was an important Democratic stronghold. Francis's approval would carry it. Was this a test to see if this city woman could get up in the morning at a decent hour? I vowed to win him over. But the question was, How can I communicate with Francis? In the statehouse, Francis was taciturn. It was hard work to get more than a yes or a no from him. Sometimes I had settled for a shrug.

He was sitting at the table eating breakfast with two of his sons.

"Good morning, Francis. Thanks for agreeing to show me the damage." The idea was to have him show me the flood damage caused by a recent downpour, which I would then discuss on a radio program at noon in nearby St. Albans.

He barely looked up from his coffee cup. I saw the sinews in his back and arms and thick sunburned neck; he was an ox of a man who had fought with age and at sixty-seven was still winning. His face was set into hard lines that could move either way, like slats on a venetian blind, closed in a scowl or open in a grin. One was as scary as the other. I decided to be patient.

Francis looked up. "Want a cup of coffee, piece of toast?"

"Yes, thank you."

His sons didn't say a word. Was this the shyness of the country? His daughters had gone the other way: they had left home, got educated, and had careers. The sons had come to the kitchen to get their instructions for the day's chores. Francis was the lord of the manor; he knew everything.

His wife, Neva, entered. In Montpelier, she often sat silently at her husband's side, trying to disappear as best she could. What she seemed to fear most was the inquiring eye of a stranger. Here she greeted me happily, wiping her hand on her apron before taking mine.

"I'm so glad to see you, Madeleine," and she poured me a fresh cup of coffee. She led me by the hand into the living room, where across the length of an entire wall she had hung the graduation pictures of all twelve children, five sons and seven daughters. Each photograph had the same colored tint, the same light gloss, and the identical expression: bright-eyed and wholesome.

Neva beamed. This was her world, where she was secure and happy. I had badly misjudged her.

Here, in his kitchen, his house, on his land, Francis's words fell into an easy cadence. "Let's get going. I'll show you around. Want to see the damage, do you?"

"Yes, I'd like to see it for myself."

We got into his car. As he opened the window and leaned his elbow out, I began to relax. He was at home. We went down the dirt road a half mile and made a right turn.

"That's my farm over there," he said, pointing to the newly painted hay wagons, tidy red barns, and a small green-shuttered white house. "Run by a hired man."

I commented on the hay wagons, gleaming like new toys.

"Always keep everything in good repair. Makes all the difference. If you ever see a farm with a broken-down hay wagon, you know the fellow's gonna have to sell out, this year or next."

I nodded.

The 1978 blue Chevy took another turn. "And that's my farm over there," Francis repeated, pointing to the other side of the road. The phrase was to be said again, many times. When Francis's father had come to Vermont years before, they had had nothing. He had worked the land by hand, removing each stone to clear the fields. Now Francis was a wealthy man. His twelve children would inherit eleven farms.

That evening, the Democrats held their annual dance at the Sheldon Springs Casino, a building that looked best at night. A string of Christmas lights hung over the entrance year-round. I sat next to Francis at a long picnic table while the band struck up a polka. It was BYOB (bring your own booze), and every couple had a cooler. Francis offered me a cold beer. I thanked him for having given me a wonderful day. I had learned a lot, I told him.

"Book learning isn't everything," he said. "You have to know that the snow falls off the roof sunny side first."

I laughed. That is how he saw me. An intellectual. A woman trying to do what women are not supposed to do. And I had seen him as a shrewd but uneducated man. As I had watched him that morning, his foot kicking a stone out of our path, and followed his long gaze stretch over his perfect fields, I understood him better. But could he ever understand me? My mother had cleared her first field, lifting one stone at a time, and with no husband to help her. I wished somehow that I could tell him that.

About a month later, on July 27, I was the commencement speaker at the Fanny Allen Hospital School of Nursing in Winooski, near Burlington. Jeannie Howrigan, Francis's daughter, had invited me; she was the director. We embraced.

"I'm thrilled that you could come. These women are special," she confided.

Thirty women were about to get their degrees in practical nursing. She pointed out a middle-aged woman in the back row. "She's got four kids and commutes from Waterville every morning, two hours each way. Gets up in the middle of the night to study, goes back to sleep, and gets up at four-thirty to make the pot roast. She's never once been late to class. She's got a husband, but he's been out of work most of the winter. She was just determined to make it."

Jobs would be scarce, Jeannie said. And the pay wasn't great, $4.65 an hour. I wouldn't have known it. Each woman graduate stood tall, her uniform brilliantly white, perfectly pressed, her cap neatly placed on her head like a crown.

A CAMPAIGN ENCOUNTER could sometimes tell a story in an instant, flash a picture that would endure. At a street fair in Morrisville, hundreds of people had congregated in the center of town, strolling back and forth. There had been rain, but it had stopped; the stars were out, and fireworks would soon begin. All the grim statistics I had known about Morrisville—high unemployment, low wages, and persistent poverty—were obscured by the colored lights, strung happily from one lamppost to the next. I stood in the middle of the closed-off main street, with the local state representative, Stub Earle. He had agreed to campaign with me, and it had caused a stir. Stub, campaigning for a Democrat? He relished the mischief. I was thrilled that I was meeting everybody in town; this was a substantial political harvest.

I stopped to shake hands with a large, muscular man wearing a tight, over-the-belly maroon T-shirt, short sleeves rolled up to his shoulders. His left arm exposed the telltale outline of a pack of cigarettes, tucked under the sleeve for ready access. His right shoulder bore a tattoo. His hand miniaturized mine in its grasp.

"Boy, am I glad to meet you!" he said. "I've seen you on TV. Wow, Nancy, come on over. Guess who's here. Madeleine Kunin."

He brought over his wife and three kids, the youngest asleep in a stroller. The wife held back while the two children grasped the stroller on either side.

He couldn't stop talking. There were things he had to tell me. A couple of weeks before he had gotten his high-school diploma in an adult-education course, studying at night while doing construction during the day.

"That must have been hard to do," I observed.

"Yeah, it took me a long time. Thought I'd never make it."

"Your wife and kids must be proud of you."

His wife broke into a smile so bright that it lit up this corner of the night. One of the kids gave way and exposed his missing front teeth. The other looked up at his dad. Never had I seen pride so dazzlingly portrayed.

THE CASTLETON COLONIAL DAY parade was held each summer, and I had worn comfortable flat white shoes and a red, white, and blue outfit; the day seemed perfectly coordinated—every time I waved to a face in the crowd, I got a warm greeting in return. After the parade was over, I worked my way back to the main street of town and stopped to shake hands with two couples, sitting side by side at the edge of the sidewalk in their matching green-and-white lawn chairs. One couple now lived in Florida, they told me, the other in Vermont. The Florida couple complained about Vermont's long winters and dark days; they were glad to have retired to winter warmth. The other couple had also moved to Florida, but then decided to come back to Vermont. This was their tidy house right behind us, and their perfect lawn under our feet.

"Yes, we moved back. We didn't think we would, but we came back here," said the elderly woman, looking down at her neatly polished white shoes. "There was a FOR SALE sign at this house, and we knew exactly when it was built and who had built it in 1930, so we just bought it. We don't want to go to Florida in the winter, we really love Vermont. We always get out, all winter long. And we have a nice garden in the back, and the church is across the street, and we have a lot of old friends nearby."

Her lipstick had bled a bit beyond the outlines of her mouth, but she was perfectly content. Everything they wanted was right here on this street. That's why she loved Vermont.

*   *   *

WHEN GERALDINE FERRARO received the Democratic nomination for vice president in San Francisco in July, almost everyone I met on the campaign trail talked about her.

"What do you think of Gerry?" I'd be asked.

The vision of Mondale and Ferraro together at the podium had been dazzling on television. Why the fascination, even among people who would never vote for her? The idea of having a woman on the ticket was exciting because it was unexpected. Suddenly every woman could imagine herself there, if only for a moment. But what did it mean for the election? I found myself looking at Geraldine Ferraro as I knew other people looked at me. I examined her clothes, her hair. How does she decide what to wear, when does she get her hair done? Is it bleached or natural?

Here is a picture of her with her family. I gazed at it for a long time. "Now that's a happy family, devoted husband, wonderful kids." Of course I knew that every family had its problems, but I could not help studying hers intently and wanting to believe that it was perfect.

When Gerry brought her campaign to Vermont on Saturday, October 21, 1984, the crowd was estimated by the police at between six and eight thousand. The paper reported she was greeted with "exuberant cheers, stomping feet, and waving signs."

Planning for her visit had caused her staff and mine a problem. How should these two women politicians greet each other? Should they embrace or hold their arms high in the air in the traditional victory sign? The moment we both got on stage at Memorial Auditorium, in Burlington, the crowd went wild, and without a moment's hesitation our joined hands shot in the air.

The sight of us together seemed to cause an explosion. Our double image, in one stroke, shattered tokenism. Power had long been given to one lone woman at a time, standing onstage by herself. When she left, it would be gone. That, in part, was why power could be given to one woman; it would be easy to take it away. But the sight of two women reinforcing each other was a revolution. Suddenly the room had become ours.

Fathers brought their daughters to see us, carrying them on their shoulders, holding them in their arms, leading them by the hand. "I want her to see this, to know this, so she'll remember," a man said as he asked a bystander to snap our picture together: Gerry Ferraro, Daddy, the baby, and me.

"Such a beautiful sight," an elderly woman said. "I thought I'd never live to see the day." I was embarrassed by her gaze and bent over to hug her.

WOMEN, I KNEW, would in the end make the difference in my election. The gender gap would enable me to win. Indications that the women's vote would be powerful had first appeared at a fund-raiser in April at the Ice House restaurant, in Burlington: the draw was an appearance by Gloria Steinem. When I mentioned to my brother that Gloria was coming, he looked worried. "Gloria Steinem? You'd better be careful. You don't want to be branded a feminist." And when my good friend Elaine received her invitation to the event, she wrote back to me, "You already have the women's vote." The implication was that Gloria would not be helpful.

The reception, arranged on a week's notice, attracted 150 people. "Wow," I exclaimed when I entered the packed room and pushed my way toward Gloria, now barricaded behind the podium. Everyone was moving in the same direction, craning to get a better look at the woman with flowing hair and studious glasses. Her beauty took the edge off feminist outrage, gave it a sheen that drew the crowd. She was a sensation because she achieved what all of us wanted for ourselves: to be strong, beautiful, and angry without fear of punishment or rejection.

Gloria gave a rousing speech, joking that women used to be elected only when their husbands died and they became widows. "The men found this was too hard on them. That's why they've become feminists."

She opened up her checkbook and asked each person in the room to recall her last charitable contribution. "Your checkbook, just like the federal budget, is a reflection of your values."

Heads nodded while pens were fished out of shoulder bags. Forty-five people signed up to volunteer. The campaign had come to life here in this restaurant. Gloria's words had released the energy in the room; it bounced off the walls and made us laugh and cheer with a fervor we didn't know existed. Every woman there felt a new sense of her own power and turned to share a piece of it with me.

How could I have thought to deny the existence of this hidden weapon, which I had known was there but was not certain I could use? Yes, overt feminism would anger some and intimidate others. This was a real danger. But I could not cut myself off from feminism at the root; this is what fed me when other sources ran dry. Among groups of women like this,

whose ambivalence I shared and whose hopes I projected, I would redis-
cover why I was living a political life. And they, by their presence, would
tell me that I was not living it alone.

Only once did I feel abandoned by women. It was during my reelection
campaign in 1986, when I faced two opponents: Bernard Sanders, the
independent socialist mayor of Burlington, and Peter Smith, the Republican lieutenant governor.

It was a difficult campaign, for I did not relish the attack from both the
left and the right, placing me somewhere in a muddy middle. One evening
when the three of us were imprisoned in an oppressive, airless radio studio for a candidates' debate, I found it hard to breathe; their bombast had
sucked up all the oxygen in the room, and their joint attacks felt like body
blows.

Two weeks before the election I heard a rumor, hard to believe, that a
friend of mine in a women's group that had explored the ramifications of
feminism and religion was supporting Bernie. I called her; it was true.
Bernie, she explained, was better on Nicaragua. And he was a feminist.

"Don't you understand," I pleaded, "anything about the journey?" I
tried to explain. My rise to power was different from his. So were my
issues and my style. As a woman, I could never sound and act like Bernie,
whose daily diet consisted of vitriol.

She was regretful, but firm. I had lost her.

He would be a better feminist than I, Bernie proclaimed the weekend
before the election at a rally in City Hall Park. I had done nothing for
women, he shouted. When my husband, there as my surrogate (I was
scheduled to speak elsewhere), rose to speak in my defense, he was booed
by the crowd. Arthur's red-faced anger became the children's horror story
of the campaign, which they embellished in the retelling—our private
macabre joke. That night I was grateful that the television reporter on the
WCAX-TV evening news did all the talking over the image of my husband shouting silently in the background.

That same year a referendum was on the ballot to ratify a state Equal
Rights Amendment. In the final weeks, a negative ERA campaign was
unleashed that led to its defeat. I sensed my support was eroding on both
the right and the left, as my candidacy became a flash point for the anti-
ERA vote on one side and the Bernie Sanders antigovernment vote on the
other. As the incumbent governor, I was now a political insider, and
Sanders did his best to tag me with responsibility for all the things that
people hated about bureaucracy. As a feminist, however, I remained
somewhat of an outsider and became a visible target for the antiabortion,

antifeminist vote. I had assumed—with my first victory as governor—that feminism in Vermont politics had been safely mainstreamed. Not so. The potential for backlash was there, and the ERA referendum brought it out in the open.

When I was elected to my third term, the Sanders supporters returned to my fold. Bernie was not in the race, and my record on women's issues was hard to dispute. But a lesson remained: no group, regardless of its commitment, would remain loyal forever. And women, even those who regarded themselves as feminists, could be won over by the traditional rhetoric of men who promised to speak for them on their issues more effectively than a comparable woman.

Gloria Steinem's message was different: it was time for women to speak for themselves by electing women. This was the ultimate goal of feminism, to change the values and priorities of our country, not through surrogate male representation, but directly. If women wanted this to happen, they had to do what the men had always done, she explained; they had to support women by giving money to their candidates.

Large campaign dollars, I discovered, were still predominantly raised by men. Most candidates have a few angels who take on their cause. I felt fortunate to have found one by 1984: a partner in a Wall Street brokerage house whom I met when we served on a nonprofit board together. John Rosenwald had only one agenda; he enjoyed being around politicians—it did not matter to him whether they were Republicans or Democrats—and he particularly liked supporting women. There would be times when I felt exceedingly uncomfortable with political fund-raising, but not with John. He always kept his word, and he never gave a hint of asking for anything in return.

He promised to arrange a Wall Street campaign lunch for me on April 24. This was the first event of its kind for Liz and me. We were about to enter the world of the corporate elite, as foreign to us as any we could imagine. John had assured us he would invite friends who would be happy to contribute to the campaign of the next governor of the state of Vermont. We could expect to raise about ten thousand dollars.

From La Guardia Airport we took a cab to the financial district, near Wall Street, arriving half an hour early. The first snack bar we found had a two-dollar minimum, but all we wanted was a cup of coffee. Neither Liz nor I could bring ourselves to indulge in such extravagance. We went to the employees' cafeteria in the building, thrilled to get a cup of coffee for twenty-seven cents.

In the main lobby we looked for the elevators that went to the fiftieth floor. I had called John that morning to tell him Liz was coming with me for the lunch, and he had called out to his secretary, "Put some more water in the soup, Joanne." But the soup, it turned out, had no water, only cream. And the view from John's office window encompassed all of New York harbor.

"More people live right here than in the whole state of Vermont," I told John. I unwrapped my gifts: a small jar of maple syrup for each guest, and a big one for John.

John's guests filed in, one by one; two women were included. One man, a New York lawyer, was a good friend of my brother's and had known my mother: my disparate worlds were joined when I saw him. He made me wish my mother could see me now, and I hoped he would report to my brother that I was handling myself well. Sibling approval was still important.

I was proud of us; Liz and I handled our knives and forks as well as our conversation, as if we had always eaten on the fiftieth floor of an executive suite. But glamorous as the attention was, I knew that people wrote checks to my campaign because of John, not me. He was collecting his chits. I felt an obligation not to disappoint him. In my remarks about my campaign, about Vermont, I wanted to make John proud of his investment.

What if I lose? I asked myself as the waiter set down the peach melba floating in raspberry sauce, decorated with snippets of mint leaves arranged in perfect symmetry. I dared not disturb the pattern. I pushed the thought away, but it edged back in. Will they still love me? Or will they want their money back?

Terrible question, I answered, and turned to the gentleman at my left. I concentrated on his gold cuff links and wondered how much they cost. Perhaps he wouldn't miss his contribution, after all.

As John began to introduce me, I rehearsed my lines. I aimed for a *Wall Street Journal* approach, illustrating my points with humorous Vermont anecdotes and lots of solid statistics. The Vermont economy depended on a sound environment and high educational quality. A number of the guests had vacation homes in the state; they nodded their assent. When I sat down, John gave me a thumbs-up!

The two women who attended the lunch stayed on to chat afterward and proposed an idea: Why not have a breakfast sponsored by the women on Wall Street? Two months later it happened; this was the first time that women had reached out to network among themselves in the same manner as the men had always done. Our success in raising money from women on Wall Street was one indicator of the changing status of women in both finance and politics.

Money raised from women seemed less tainted; we were helping one another achieve a common goal—equality for women. Yet, regardless of the source, fund-raising was difficult and always carried risk. Would I ever be totally free of obligation once I was elected? I vowed that I would be, and I took pains to make certain that I was. Still, there was uneasiness. I could be sure that I would not make any public decision based on political contributions, but what about phone calls, lunches, friendships, and other forms of access?

"Liz, couldn't we run a low-budget campaign and dispense with all this fund-raising? What if we set a limit and only accepted small contributions?" I would have been much happier.

Liz was not.

"We've got to raise the money to run a professional campaign," she insisted. Reform was a luxury we could not yet afford. But we were very careful.

I was invited to attend a high-donor Democratic cocktail party in Washington.

"Be sure to collect business cards," I was advised by the young woman who was sent along from the National Democratic Committee as my guide.

I knew I had to be bold, walk up, and introduce myself and tell people about my campaign. It seemed inordinately crude, but I was assured that people expected it. One by one, I stashed the cards away in my purse, hoping I would remember who was who. I wondered, Will any of them remember me? And how does one actually ask for money?

"You can do it in a follow-up letter, and enclose a packet of information with it," the woman coached.

I saw a huge man, identified as a Texan, staring down at me with his small eyes, habitually half-closed, I surmised, against the glaring sun that saturated his ranch. Or was this the squint of avarice? The outlines of his massive body and bigger-than-life features seemed to have been drawn by a disrespectful caricaturist. I looked up at his burly chest and followed the pattern of his tie straight up from the point at his belly to the knot around his neck. I detected the pattern of a Texas monument topped by a huge gold star. One arm was resting on the shoulders of a slim, mild-mannered man in a brown suit and green tie. The Texan introduced the man he held in tow, turned him toward me, and proudly said, "That's mah congressman."

I had no doubt he was.

I told him who I was and what I was running for. He told me about oil and gas. He listened attentively to my story and ended the conversation with the words, "I want to do a little something for you. Just go ask Susie over here," and he pointed to his female assistant, dressed to kill.

I was introduced to a man who fulfilled the promised definition of "mogul": his fortune was in real estate. The word was he was very close to Mondale and had been flying him around in his private plane. I chatted with him for a few minutes; something about him told me, "This man is wearing a very expensive suit." I did not have to touch it to find out.

"When our committee gets together, we'll do something for you," he said and moved on. I was left holding his card.

"He's built most of Washington, you know," someone clued me in.

"Go talk to that man over there," my guide advised. I speculated why a foreign importer would contribute to American political campaigns. Months later, I was told he had been indicted. Good thing I didn't try harder.

As I said good-night to one man who had a blue star on his name tag, signifying "major contributor," he held on to my extended hand and fingered my wedding and engagement rings. "Where's your husband to-night?" he asked. The tone was both seductive and accusatory.

I decided to treat it lightly. "Oh, he's home taking care of the kids." I laughed irreverently, and immediately felt both foolish and guilty.

As I put on my coat and reached in my pocket for my gloves, I became angry. Why did I have to answer his question? A man in my position would not be asked, "And where is your wife tonight?" Nor would he have to explain who was taking care of the kids. Nor was there likely to be any sexual innuendo connected with his fund-raising. A political con-tribution would be as matter-of-fact as a business deal. Men were accus-tomed to receiving large sums of money; most women were not. Whether I liked it or not, being female would always make a difference.

None of the men I met that night sent me a contribution. Only one person, whom I happened to chat with on my way out the door, later became a contributor and a friend who would follow my political career with genuine interest. In part, I was relieved. The feelings I brought home with me from that party were queasy. Did I really want to play this game? Would I have talked to these people at all, under other circumstances, if they had not worn their little stars on their name tags?

I told myself it was safer to raise money in Washington as a candidate for governor than it would be if I were running for the U.S. Senate or

House. I was grateful not to be in that susceptible position, where something could be asked of me in return. There would be few favors these people could request from Vermont. Undoubtedly that is why only one person, who was free of self-interest, contributed.

WOMEN SUPPORTERS became my strongest fund-raising allies. I developed an effective fund-raising network of highly dedicated women in Washington, New York, Boston, and, eventually, California. Some were introduced to me through the Women's Campaign Fund. The Women's Political Caucus, the National Abortion Rights Action League (NARAL), and the National Organization for Women (NOW) also raised money for women. When we added up the total contributions at the end of my 1984 campaign, we were surprised to discover that as much money had come from women's organizations as from labor unions, the Democrats' traditional source of support.

Gender was not the only influence on fund-raising. I was running for a statewide office when most national political action committees were not interested in contributing to governors' races. Environmental and education groups, my natural allies, were almost exclusively focused on Congress. EMILY's List (Early Money Is Like Yeast), formed by Ellen Malcolm in 1985 in response to the fund-raising difficulties Harriett Woods had in her losing Missouri Senate race, took the same position, not supporting Democratic women in state races until a policy change in 1990.

Individual women, however, were extraordinary in their commitment and generosity. Without them, it is doubtful that I could have been elected.

In 1982, I had raised and spent $250,000. Liz proposed a goal for 1984 of $350,000. That budget would support the cost of five full-time staff, media buys, polls, equipment, telephones, and office space. Our contributor list looked distinctly different from my opponents'. Individual contributions were smaller; the number of contributors, larger. I took some solace from the fact that we raised more money in small amounts. Yet, as I look back, I would not want to engage in political fund-raising in the same way again. The system is in dire need of reform. Despite the vows a candidate may make to herself to deny favoritism, the relationship between special interests and the candidate is established once a check is written. The danger is not so much outright corruption, which is rare, but too much familiarity, which is common. The outlook for reform was briefly enhanced when Jerry Brown ran a presidential primary campaign in 1992 with a promise that he would only accept contributions of one hundred dollars or less, and for a short time the formula seemed to work, until both his fund-raising and his campaign collapsed. The outlook dimmed once more when the Federal Election Commission announced that 1992 congressional campaign spending soared 43 percent over 1990. Some of the increase was attributed to a greater-than-usual number of vacancies, but spending per congressional seat also reached a record high of $5.4 million. The assumption that women are disadvantaged in raising money was denied when the two top Senate fund-raisers were women— Barbara Boxer reported $10.3 million and Dianne Feinstein, $8 million.

In the final weeks of my 1984 campaign, female supporters did more than raise money. Many gave the campaign total commitment. Trudy Boyles made hand-sewn banners of maroon-and-white felt to hang at strategic locations in her town, and then suddenly they began to appear everywhere. From one end of the state to the other, the banners multiplied by magic. Each time I saw one, I felt a thrill. "There's another one! They're springing up everywhere." I was going to win.

Anna Bloom and her husband hammered together wooden car-top signs and started handing them out to their friends.

"Thanks, Anna. Thanks."

"It's nothing, darling. For you, I'd do anything. Tell me, are you eating?"

Her eyes had the combined look of a Jewish mother and a Christian zealot.

Instinctively, the women seemed to know what we all did, but dared not articulate: we were making history, and making history would not be easy. Everyone would have to help. Nothing could be taken for granted.

When we analyzed our fall polling data, the gender gap emerged as a two-edged sword—we were winning with women, but we were losing ground with male voters.

"We've got to change the schedule," Liz concluded. "Where can we find male voters?"

"Rotaries."

"Yeah, Rotaries, Lions, chambers of commerce."

"Okay, okay, schedule me, I'll go, I'll do it," I agreed.

I had begun to divide up my audiences into two sections: women and men. I would speak about women's issues to one group, and economic issues to the other. It had become expected that I would talk about family and work issues when I addressed a women's group and focus on economic issues with men's groups. But why not vary the pattern? If the women's agenda was to be mainstreamed, it would have to be championed by men as well as women. And women were equally entitled to the hard economic facts and figures I had usually reserved for male audiences.

Today I found myself at the Barre Rotary Club. As soon as the bottom layer of vanilla-fudge ice cream had been spooned out of his glass dish, the president of the Barre Rotary Club hit the bell. I jumped.

"Now it is time for our speaker. Jules Chatot will make the introduction."

Jules had taken me through the granite sheds two years ago; he had been one of my early supporters. Almost everyone in this room had some connection to granite, either making it or selling it or providing services to those who did. Jules's daughter, Judy, was one of the few women to work in the business. Perhaps he would approve of my speech. Last night, I had made the decision: I was going to unveil a day-care platform at the Barre Rotary Club.

I kept the attention of the audience for the full twenty-five minutes. Then they plied me with questions and, to my surprise, some answers. One man stood up in praise of child care. He had employed five women in his drafting business; when four got pregnant the same year, he couldn't afford to lose them, so together they established a child-care program on the premises that had worked beautifully. He didn't have to train new workers, and the women could keep their jobs, as well as take care of their babies.

"Kunin Tells Barre Rotarians Child Care Is Good Business," the August 16 headline read in the *Barre-Montpelier Times-Argus*. "Madeleine Kunin told a nearly all male audience that the need for affordable child care for working couples and single mothers is as important an issue for men as it is for women."

"It's been proven that employee-sponsored child care decreases absenteeism, reduces turnover, and increases productivity," I told the audience.

"We are strengthening our economy by strengthening our families." To my delight, the men were pleased to be included in this "women's issue." If we could join forces here, would it be possible to bridge the gap between women and men elsewhere? I, too, had made gender assumptions that were subject to change.

A poll taken after the September primary showed Easton in the lead. I reminded myself of my first lieutenant governor's race and the 2-to-1 lead Peter Smith had enjoyed immediately after the primary. Relax, I told myself. This is the bump to be expected for the victor of the primary campaign. Easton had handily defeated Wick.

Still, the campaign seemed stuck. The race was missing a compelling theme.

On September 13, it fell into our laps.

John Easton had told a reporter that the next governor would not be able to make many changes in his first term because he would basically have to "be a caretaker."

The word "caretaker" leapt from the page. We carefully lifted it off, framed it, and stuck it on the wall.

This was it. John Easton would be the caretaker; I would be the governor who would create change.

On September 14, I shared the podium with Easton at a forum sponsored by the Eastern Milk Producers Cooperative. "I don't buy that concept of what the governor is," I told the audience. "Being a caretaker is not my job description for the governor of the state of Vermont. The next governor should offer new ideas and new initiatives. You have to approach the job with a sense of excitement and a sense that change is possible."

If Easton had fought back, we might have lost. Instead, he plodded on, politely. The race was heating up. "Kunin Fights Gender Liabilities," the headline read on September 17. I would be making history if I won; I would be the fourth woman governor in the history of the country to be elected in her own right, following the precedent set by Ella Grasso in Connecticut, Dixy Lee Ray in Washington, and Martha Layne Collins in Kentucky, all within the past few years.

On September 19, I decided to top John Easton's proposal for a 10 percent increase in funding for Vermont public schools. I countered with a proposal for 20 percent.

He said we couldn't afford it.

I said we had to, and that I would cut other programs if necessary to do it. I was carving out my territory: I would make education and the environment my top priorities.

Three weeks before the election, the *St. Albans Messenger* carried an editorial, reprinted by the *Rutland Herald*.

Easton Comment Haunts Him Now
It's hard to say why voters pick one candidate or the other. Neither candidate has been able to latch on to an issue so identified by the voters. Neither candidate

has really caught fire in terms of disproportionate press coverage. Many voters have been caught mumbling under their breath that it just isn't going to be the same in Montpelier after Dick Snelling leaves. But among the less apathetic Kunin seems to be bringing one thing to the campaign that may be making a difference. Early in the campaign Easton made the comment that the next governor would be a caretaker governor. Kunin has not let him forget it. It was a mistake by Easton because Kunin has used the comment against him to portray a directionless campaign and the prospect of a "do nothing" term as governor.

The truth is that the next governor will not light Montpelier afire with new programs. The state cannot afford it. But Vermonters like to hear someone talk about doing a better job with what we have, and Kunin seems to be getting that message across. Vermonters, like all Americans, like to hold out for the prospect of something better. Turns out it's also good politics.

The issues that I had been spelling out all spring and summer now came into focus. I would be the activist governor, representing change. John Easton represented the more cautious and less optimistic status quo.

The rhythm of the campaign shifted into fast tempo in the last month. While I was seeking out as many interviews as possible and shaking every hand within reach, the campaign focused on targeting. Phone banks were fully staffed every night with twenty to thirty volunteers calling key areas.

In the final weeks, Liz sensed something was missing in the campaign: a visible male presence that would give us a shot of political testosterone. Much of the staff, except for the press secretary, Michael Wilson, and our field organizer, Gary Schaedel, was female. The daily campaign meeting was overwhelmingly peopled by women.

In the spring, I had formed a kitchen cabinet that included men who represented different points of view and had access to opinion makers in the business community that we did not. They gave us feedback, provided a funnel to their constituencies, and had helped with debate preparation. Jim Guest, a former secretary of state and now candidate for Congress, played the part of John Easton during our mock debates. We used a room in the Superior Court to make the setting as formal as possible. I would stand at the podium and answer hypothetical questions for our rehearsals prior to each debate. My answers were videotaped, played back, and analyzed.

When the actual round of final debates began, I was like a boxer anxious to get into the ring. Not only did I have the answers, I wanted to fight.

Appearing in the television studio, I felt superbly confident; my hair had been done that morning, my suit was the perfect blue, and the answers I needed were at my fingertips. The exchange between Easton and me had a rhythm; each time he gave an answer, I could toss it back. I did not search for the right word, tone, or position; I knew it. No longer did I debate whether to be passive or aggressive, cautious or decisive. I had found my stance, my voice, myself.

The informal kitchen cabinet of male advisers was helpful in enabling me to reach this point; it also gave important balance to my campaign. What we needed now in the final weeks, Liz observed, was a *public* male presence; a man who could connect with the boys and demonstrate that we were intent on winning.

"I've got it," Liz exclaimed. "We'll get Joe. Joe Jamele."

"Joe?" I asked. "Are you sure?"

Joe and I had worked side by side years ago as young reporters at the *Burlington Free Press*. Joe was a political pro, and a hard hitter. Now he had achieved both maturity and respectability as Senator Leahy's press secretary. He was the first person I had ever heard referred to as a "spin doctor." Leahy agreed to lend him to our campaign, and Joe relished the idea of coming aboard for the final push.

It is impossible to know how much Joe's presence helped my victory, but I am certain that he did a lot to relieve the tension. The first day out, he made a statement immediately picked up by the press. He compared John Easton to Boy George, a controversial rock star, questioning indirectly the candidate's masculinity.

"Liz," I called frantically from a pay phone after I had picked up the afternoon paper, "first day out of the box, and Joe made the news. This is terrible. John Easton may sue us."

John Easton, fortunately, let it pass. Liz put Joe on a shorter leash. He did not have to go far, it turned out; he just had to stay close to Easton, whom he drove crazy with worry. Each time he came near him, Easton suspected Joe was up to some of his tricks. In the meantime, Joe schmoozed with the press, dropping hints here and there about what they should be covering in this race.

During our final television debate, Joe came along as my coach. Throughout the debate, he stood behind the cameraman making faces. When I gave an answer, he grinned; when Easton spoke, he frowned, took out his notebook, and wrote everything down. To my surprise, no one carted Joe away.

Election night the returns swung wildly, first in one direction, then another. My mood followed the same meteoric rise and fall; I was hugging my husband and kids for joy one minute, and cautioning them with apprehension the next. At 8:35 p.m., with 7 percent of the vote in, I was ahead, 54 to 45. By 9:40, my lead had narrowed to 50–49. Our family watched the returns from an upstairs hotel suite; the growing crowd, anxious to celebrate, was waiting below. At 10:30, I had a one-vote lead, with 31 percent of the votes counted. It was time to go down and speak to the crowd so we all paraded downstairs together to make an interim announcement—it looked good, but it was much too early to celebrate victory. My lead had narrowed because the larger Democratic towns had given me a substantial early margin. These votes came in first because the cities voted by machine. But when the rural towns, which voted by paper ballot, started dribbling their votes in, my advantage began to erode. By 11:00 p.m. Easton had pulled ahead by 165 votes. At 1:31 I picked up 685 votes in Brattleboro.

A campaign is a wild thing and cannot be controlled. Months of planning, spending, and manipulating seem irrelevant on election night, when this beast develops a mind and spirit of its own. What I saw on display that night was a composite of quirks, moods, snippets of information and misinformation, prejudices, paranoias, hopes, and fears, all put into a meat grinder and churned out as votes. I would simply have to wait for the machine to finish its work.

At three o'clock in the morning, 95 percent of the vote was in, I had 48.7 and Easton 49.7. I went down to the hotel lobby and had a final press conference, standing on the stairs, looking at the tired but patient press below. "It's time to call it a night. We still don't have final results. It looks good, and I am hopeful, but we'll have to wait until morning. Go get some sleep. That's what I'm going to try to do." I smiled and said, "Good night."

The next morning we assembled at the campaign office. I had had two hours of sleep. The returns continued to come in, a handful at a time.

"Who's that in the corner?" I asked.

"That's a state trooper. Jim Dimmick. He's here because they think you're going to be the governor-elect."

Would he stay? Was he watching my every move? All our comings and goings, each person who bombed through the door asking, "Hey, what's up?"

"Easton's going to hold a press conference at noon. Turn on the television, quick," Michael Wilson yelled. Everyone huddled around, and there was John Easton, big as life on the screen, making a concession speech.

"The other night I said I smelled victory in the air," he said. "What I didn't anticipate was a small zephyr that blew in the wrong direction." And then he offered me his congratulations. I noted that he was extremely gracious.

The moment the words were out, we fell into one another's arms and laughed and cried, all at once, all together. Emotion—held in check for so long—spilled out messily, covering everything and everyone. We slobbered to our heart's content.

"The press wants a statement," Michael interrupted.

"Yes, of course. Give me just a second."

And off I went to dry my eyes, comb my hair, and gather my thoughts. This is how it would be. Always, at any moment, on camera, on the record.

Jim Dimmick followed me, discreetly waiting outside the bathroom door. He managed to look as if he had just noticed something important that had slipped to the floor and was about to pick it up.

I smiled. He'd be okay. He would give me my space. And he would protect me.

I gave my statement and thanked John Easton for conducting a good campaign. Minutes later, I couldn't recall a word I had said.

"Time for lunch," my brother shouted, and we gathered the family together for a private celebration: my husband, the children, and I.

As we walked out the door, a reporter stopped me short. Her car had just pulled up. "Hi, I'm from the *Philadelphia Inquirer*. Can you tell me who Madeleine Kunin is?"

"She just left," I said as I grabbed Arthur's hand and took off, giggling every step of the way.

10

As I stand here before you—the solemn words of the oath of office echoing still in my mind—we know that we have opened another chapter in the proud and independent history of the Green Mountain State.

I am the first woman to serve as governor of Vermont, the third Democrat since the Civil War, and the second governor of European birth.

But I do not stand here alone.

I stand with my husband and children, with members of my family who are a source of my strength—and my joy.

Their love and support are essential to me. I stand with the memory of members of my family who are no longer with me—my mother, my aunt, my grandmother—the strong women who could never have dreamt I would be in this place on this day, but who, through the courage of their own lives, give me the stamina to stand as tall as they did in their time.

When I raised my right hand to take the oath on January 10, 1985, my eyes were riveted on the ruddy-faced, black-robed, visibly nervous man standing three feet in front of me: the chief justice of the Vermont Supreme Court, the Honorable Frederic W. Allen. He did not read the oath of office, but recited it from memory. Midway he abandoned the printed text and improvised. After each pause, I repeated whatever he said. The words were familiar, but the order was not. He was moving in circles, instead of in a straight line. At last, he caught the last sentence: "So help me God." I repeated, "So help me God" with enormous relief. Had anyone noticed our digression? No one had.

It was our portrait, not our words, that held the public's attention. The two of us with our hands raised, he robed in black, I dressed in white, had created a startling image: gubernatorial power was being transferred to a woman. I was the same, and I was different. This had always happened, and it had never happened. Tradition had been continued, and it was being broken.

From my place on the podium, I looked out on the House chamber. On the center aisle sat my husband and four children and a cluster of relatives. They were flanked by former governors and their wives, who had been escorted down the center aisle one couple at a time.

I had been escorted to the podium by a legislative delegation led by my brother, Edgar. Our blood tie allowed us to communicate with the squeeze of a hand precisely what it meant for us to walk down this aisle together, as senator and governor, brother and sister. We were propelled forward by the crowd, lifted down the aisle by pressing hands, shoulders, and waves of rising and ebbing applause.

A small chamber group played Handel's *Water Music*. The invocation was given by Rabbi Max Wall, who had performed Arthur's and my wedding ceremony, had blessed each of our children when they were born, and had presided at my mother's funeral.

Here, in the Vermont House of Representatives, Rabbi Wall paused before speaking, reached into his vest pocket, took out a black yarmulke, and placed it on his head. How easily he did this, here in this bareheaded chamber.

When I took the oath, I put my left hand on a stack of three family Bibles held by my husband. The thin one, printed in 1828, with a brown mottled cover, had belonged to my grandfather Gaston Bloch. The small square Bible was a women's prayer book, designed to fit into a handbag, that had belonged to my grandmother Aline Bloch. The third, the heaviest, had been given to me by my aunt Berthe and had belonged to my great-grandfather Isaac Bloch, a teacher and cantor in Alsace, who had received it from his father, Aaron, born in 1800. The hand-cut, uneven pages, embroidered in Hebrew lettering, felt like linen, and the air that escaped from between the covers smelled of hands. As my palm rested on the family wedding cake of books, I felt their power filtering through my fingers.

I looked at the members of my family who were here now—my aunt Irmel, the only surviving member of my mother's generation, there with her son Eric and daughter-in-law, Roz. There was my eighty-four-year-old cousin, Ferdinand Kahn, and his wife, Elsa, from Brattleboro; he had met my mother, my brother, and me at the pier when we arrived in New York harbor in 1940.

I imagined my grandfather and my grandmother Gaston and Aline taking their places in the front row. Their three daughters would have sat next to them. First, the youngest, my mother, Renée; then Alice; and finally Berthe, the oldest.

Aline Bloch died the year before I was born. The only words that I know my grandfather Gaston Bloch said to me were spoken when he gazed down at my crib: "It is as if Aline has come back to us again." For years, I traced my political roots to this grandfather. When I look at his photograph, into his intense eyes focused on a distant point, he seems poised to stand up and speak. He had forbidden his family to attend his political speeches, but the *Israelitisches Wochenblatt Für die Schweiz* (*Israel Weekly for Switzerland*) recorded that he had twice been a candidate for the Zurich city council in the sixth district for the Freisinniger party. His platform was decidedly progressive, advocating universal health care and old-age pensions for all, long before such policies were adopted. In a speech in the Tonhalle, the largest auditorium in Zurich, in May 1933, the year Hitler rose to power, he spoke at a rally of the National Front; "in front of some one thousand people, most of whom were not friendly to the speaker, Gaston Bloch spoke strong, courageous words, which we all will remember," said the paper.

Not until 1983, when I discovered a lost branch of Texas relatives, did I learn that I also inherited political genes from my grandmother's side of the family. Her niece, Jenny Goodman, had been appointed postmistress of Laredo by President Roosevelt. No doubt Jenny had delivered the votes. Her feminism was discreet; she signed herself "J. R. Goodman."

My grandfather had been a man in search of a better life, and in his youth he moved from place to place to find it. Born in Huningen in Alsace, he made two attempts to settle in the United States before finally making his home in Switzerland. The first time Gaston Bloch came to America, he went to San Antonio, Texas, where he married his childhood sweetheart, Aline Brunschwieg, who had traveled to San Antonio with her parents to visit two brothers.

My grandparents had sat next to each other in my great-grandfather's school; he was head of the Jewish community in Hapsheim, Alsace. According to the marriage certificate, the Holy Union of Matrimony was performed in Bexar County, Texas, on October 17, 1890, by Rabbi Moses Jacobson, "minister" of Temple Beth.

In this rugged frontier state, which had joined the Union only forty-five years earlier, my grandfather and grandmother established a dry-goods store in Laredo. When I look at the brown-tinted photograph of his trim white beard, balding high forehead, and delicate, strong white hands, it is difficult to imagine this man on the dusty streets of Laredo, strolling among a group of bowlegged, pistol-packing cowboys.

Gaston Bloch was involuntarily initiated into the law of the Texas frontier when—on more than one occasion—a couple of cowboys smashed the windows of his store and helped themselves to the goods. He told the story of how, at a nearby saloon, the same bunch regularly flung open the swinging doors, took aim at every liquor bottle, and cleared the shelf.

Then there was Bloch's horse. "We laughed until we cried," my aunt Berthe would recall, "when he told the story of Bloch's horse." Grandfather had a stubborn horse that would not, under any circumstance, cross over a bridge. A crowd would gather as the horse stood his ground, winning the battle against my grandfather's gentle but vain entreaties every time.

My grandmother's two sisters, Serette and Carrie, stayed in Texas, married, and prospered. My grandmother was prepared to settle in America, like her sisters. She enjoyed the excitement of this new country and admired the independent spirit of its pioneering women. But my grandfather wanted to go back to Europe. After two years in Texas, they crossed the ocean, holding their nine-month-old baby daughter, Berthe, in their arms; she had been born in San Antonio on August 14, 1891. My aunt Berthe, a woman who was the personification of a lady, was to spend almost her entire life in Zurich and London. Whenever she had an opportunity to mention her birthplace, however, she was delighted to let it be known that it was Texas.

One year after my grandparents returned to Europe, they once again crossed the Atlantic, sailing on the passenger liner *The City of New York* from Southampton. My aunt told me her first memory was of standing on the ship's deck, wearing a red-and-white coat with a collar made of swan's down. This time, they went to Pittsburgh, where a second daughter, Alice, was born. I know nothing of why they went there and can only imagine how grim this steel-mill city must have been in 1893. And a year later they returned to Europe, this time to settle in Switzerland. In Zurich, my grandparents opened a clothing and textile store. My grandmother was the businesswoman in the family. "She was very, very clever," Aunt Berthe recalled. On buying trips to Paris, she bought fabrics, copied Parisian fashions, then designed the clothes and cut the patterns herself. The sewing was done by women who worked at home. I felt flushed with pride when I was told that I took after her. *Sehr tüchtig* was the expression: "very efficient."

"She was very modern in her thinking," Aunt Berthe told me. "She said she had been brought up too strictly. To me, she never said an unkind word. Once, when I first learned to write, I had written my name all over the wallpaper in my room. When she saw it, she only said, 'Les noms des foux se trouvent partout.' ['The names of fools are found everywhere.'] You see, that touched my pride."

In the last years of her life, my grandmother took to her bed, propped up on enormous pillows. Not one wrinkle marred her flat white sheets. Was it a heart condition or depression that made her withdraw to the silence of her room? Or was this simply how women then responded to exhaustion, disappointment, or grief?

In a photograph of her in her early forties, she is seated in the center of her family, an elegant woman in a black taffeta sequin-trimmed gown. The high black lace collar is filigreed with light from an ivory silk lining. Her jutting chin is softened by her hair, piled loose and high on her head. She is surrounded by her daughters—Renée, Alice, and Berthe—wearing lace-trimmed, flounced white dresses with identical Gibson girl collars, and white ribbons falling from their long dark hair. They look pensively at the photographer as if he were the future. My grandfather stands behind them, the dark-suited patriarch surrounded by sumptuous womanhood. My grandmother, ramrod straight in her chair, knows she is the center of her universe. It is a dream picture, staged against a painted studio backdrop: gossamer drapes, a light-filled window, and spires of candelabra. The eye moves effortlessly from silk to glass to silver. The family is enclosed in comfortable bourgeois elegance. I dare not disturb them; I cannot enter that room, much as I would like to touch the golden bones of the glossy gilt chair in the corner, where Berthe's white hand pretends to rest.

I turn to another family photograph. This is a postcard sent in 1912 by Jenny Goodman from Texas to Switzerland. She is wearing an ankle-length white suit, holding a pretty little handbag on a chain. Her hand is resting on a rough-hewn chair made of logs. I see the peeling bark and feel the splinters. This painted studio backdrop portrays the frontier; sawed-off tree stumps are at her feet and fallen trees are in the background, which fades into a vast Texas sky. These are the two worlds my grandparents spanned.

My grandfather Bloch returned to America on business more than once with his sons-in-law—my father, Ferdinand May, and his brother, Salli. With them he formed a partnership to import BallBand rubber boots from Mishawaka, Indiana. One of their trips to America becomes real to me when I look at a formal dinner invitation that the family saved:

> Complimentary Dinner, honoring Mr. Ferdinand May and Mr. Gaston Bloch, Zurich, Switzerland, given by Mishawaka Rubber & Woolen Mfg. Co., Mishawaka, Ind., U.S.A., in their private dinning room in the Company Restaurant, May 6, 1930.

Also saved was a picture of my grandfather about to throw a horse-shoe, and another—surrounded by his American hosts—chopping wood.

He was comfortable on both continents, fluent in German, French, English, and Italian. His role was to serve as interpreter for his sons-in-law.

Both in Texas and in Switzerland, their households echoed with sounds of French, English, and German, often a mélange of all three. I can imagine their voices slipping from German to English to French, as my mother and brother and I did after our first months in America, moving out of one place into another and back again, until eventually, our words, like ourselves, became ensconced in America.

"Isn't it funny," Aunt Berthe observed years later, "one part of the family started out in America and then lived their lives in Europe. And you were born in Europe and lived your life in America."

Dual citizenship was my heritage. I had always known about the United States, just as my mother had from listening to the stories told by her parents. It seemed inevitable that we would come here. It had been foretold. This was the country where one could reinvent a life. That was the promise of America: new wealth, new identity, in a new land. My grandparents, setting sail twice, had been drawn across the sea by that force.

Today, as the newly inaugurated governor of Vermont, I held up my immigrant past like a red, white, and blue banner, stretching it across the balcony of this House chamber. I was the personification of the American dream. The phrase, like all clichés, both described and distorted the reality. But I wanted to pay homage to my mother, to bring her into the chamber with me, to feel her presence, and the only way I could do so was to tell her story.

> It was my mother who, as a widow, came to America with two small children, aged 6 and 10, in 1940, as war was spreading over Europe. In addition to a limited knowledge of English, she carried with her to these shores a limitless dream of what this country could offer her and her children.
>
> And she talked to us about the dream, but it was not until many years later that I fully understood her. Her dream enabled me to strive, to reach and to touch some horizons I was certain were beyond my grasp. That dream must continue to beckon the next generation.

My mother believed it, pronouncing, with a sense of wonder, the words "Anything is possible in America."

The reality of the dream was more powerful than the rhetoric because we believed it without question. That is what my mother gave me. Optimism. Despite the tragedy of her life, she refused to be defined by it. Her faith in America was infectious: never would I be able to be cynical about this country. It had saved us.

Not only from war, but from self-denial. We could grow up to become anything we wanted to be. This was not fantasy; this was America, the country in which the old restrictions of social class and religious bias did not count.

History would not decide our fate—we would. In this country, no questions were asked; no doors were closed. Whether it was true or not did not matter. What mattered was that we were propelled by the power of the myth—this was the gift that enriched me.

My relatives sitting in the audience looked like an ordinary gathering of visitors, not the descendants of wandering Jews from Germany, Alsace, Switzerland, England, and Russia. I looked at my husband and his three younger brothers and wondered what his father would have felt today, had he lived long enough to walk down the aisle and take his seat here.

He was born in the town of Gomel near Kiev, where two-thirds of the population was Jewish, and they were largely artisans, watchmakers, goldsmiths, and merchants. One side of the street was Jewish, the other Russian. Poverty afflicted them both. "Plain people would drink tea out of a saucer. The fancy tea glasses with silver handles were for the rich. In some places they drank only hot water and dreamed of tea," my father-in-law recalled.

"Dreamed of tea"—the words called up images of a Chagall painting where dreams swirl over rooftops like cream. Gomel was earthbound, and being Jewish defined where you lived and how. "In Gomel we could not own land. I figured out that we rented the land that our house was built on. If the 'goy' who owned it decided not to renew the lease, then the house was his. Whenever a policeman came to the door, the first thing you did was bring out the Sabbath schnapps and give him a drink."

That was the world Eli Kunin left to come to America when he was fourteen. Like his father before him in Russia, he opened a kosher butcher shop in the Brownsville section of Brooklyn. But his real life was elsewhere—the blood-splotched hands that wielded a butcher knife by day were purified at night to wield an artist's paintbrush. On canvas his children and grandchildren appeared as the miracles they were. Everyday he read the *New York Times* and the *Jewish Forward*. He was not a believer, but he was a Jew. And he dreamed, not of tea, but of a life of the mind; if not for him, then for his sons who would never have to remove sawdust from their shoes—two doctors, one lawyer, and, the youngest, an art historian. Would my father-in-law, had he been sitting here, have thought now is the time to bring out the Sabbath schnapps, just to be on the safe side, or would he have smiled the smile he had for the grandchildren, knowing that, here in America, anything could happen?

On this day, I wanted to pay homage not only to my family but also to other women. They were like caryatids under the balustrade, holding me up.

> As the first woman to take the oath of office of governor of the state of Vermont, I recognize that I was able to raise my right hand before you this afternoon only because so many women had raised their voices long before my words were spoken.
>
> It was Susan B. Anthony, after all, who told us, "Failure is impossible."
>
> I stand here because of the women who worked in the mills in Winooski, who taught in the one-room schoolhouses in Alburg (as my mother-in-law did), and who entered this hall of the Representatives in Montpelier before me.
>
> Clarina Howard Nichols, the first woman to speak in this chamber . . . Edna L. Beard from Orange, whose portrait hangs outside these doors, became the first woman to be elected to the House of Representatives. . . . I, and the forty-four women in the House and four women in the Senate, stand here in the shadow of Consuelo Northrop Bailey, the first woman to be elected lieutenant governor. . . . We all paved the way for one another, knowingly and unknowingly. I do not stand here alone.

The women in my family had helped prepare me for this day. The difference between my life and theirs was that I was born in a different time and a different place, a time when the definition of womanhood had expanded and the benefits of citizenship were being granted. What I did not know was that I, too, was not yet fully emancipated; my dilemma was different from theirs, less obvious, less acute, but I was not free of the tangle of ambivalence that greets every woman who enters the male-built labyrinth.

My mother became a widow when I was almost three years old and my brother was seven. She was thirty-six. I have no recollection of my father except through photographs. When I was a child and would ask what had happened to him, my mother told me he had died of a heart attack. Not until I was in college did I learn he had committed suicide. The pain of his death was unspeakable. Each time I asked my mother to tell me more, I felt I was picking off a scab. She pulled away. Its silent legacy accompanied us always, enshrouding us in embarrassed, deprived silence.

My father's death made my mother a widow as other people might become a teacher, a doctor, or a nurse. Underneath every bright outfit, I spied her mourning clothes. She did not remarry.

In our family there was a lack of balance but not a lack of love. We leaned heavily on one another. Always there was an effort to compensate—my mother to us, and my brother and I to her, to suture the bleeding gash of loss.

She took us to America in 1940 to escape the threat of Hitler. Now I understand that she may have had a second reason: to escape the stigma of tragedy. My father had been hospitalized on June 16, 1936, for depression at a private psychiatric clinic near Zurich. In 1991 I obtained his medical report and read it as if it were written yesterday, devouring the words like a hungry child. The aftertaste was bittersweet; it told me more about my father than I had ever known.

I want to drown out the institutional voice echoing from the typewritten pages, but I cannot. To rid itself of guilt, the report points at my mother.

July 20: The doctors warn her that he is in danger of committing suicide. She denies it. She refuses to have him placed in a secure room for his own protection. They recommend around-the-clock private supervision. No, she won't have it. After much discussion, she concedes to having a private nurse for one hour a day to take him on walks.

July 28: "Today there was a visit from his wife, who found her husband doing well, believes she is simply fulfilling the wish of her husband when she says she wants to take him home from the sanatorium on the thirty-first. He will stay several days in Zurich and then they will go together to England for a few days of vacation. The wife is not in agreement with the suggestion that he stay here a few more days, following electroshock treatments. She insists that her husband come home primarily so that he does not have to celebrate the First of August [the Swiss national holiday] here."

I cannot read the rest without crying—for her, for him, for my brother and me. For the first time, I know her pain.

July 30: "At eight o'clock, when the nurse went to see him, he said that since it was sunny weather, there was no point in staying in bed longer . . . at a quarter to nine the patient left the grounds to take a walk. Until now, the patient always had been accompanied on walks; today he was alone. At nine, the patient rented a boat at Bendlikon for one hour. He paid one franc fifty in advance. After about ten minutes the person who rented the boat to him noticed that some three hundred meters from shore the boat was floating without an occupant. He went immediately to the spot, but found that no one was in the boat. An attendant who was called brought the boat to the dock, and found in it several letters, a jacket, and a wristwatch belonging to the patient. On the bedside table of the patient was found a letter to his wife. . . . We notified the police."

They searched the lake for four days. They never found the body. Three months later, on October 22, Ferdinand May was officially declared to have drowned; a death certificate was issued, based on the suicide note, in which "he bade farewell to his wife, the children, and other relatives, with the plea that they forgive him for taking this step. He can no longer live like this."

I hold the piece of paper in my hand like a shard, newly dug up, the dirt still clinging to the rough edges. I wonder how to place it in order to reconstruct the bowl of his life.

My aunt flew from London to Zurich the next day. "It was terrible," she said. "Let's not talk about it. What can you do, you can't change anything."

Because there was no end point, no memorial service, no marker, my father was difficult to put to rest. As a girl I had not been expected to feel the loss of my father. "A boy needs a father" is what people said, and for a long time, I, too, believed this, until I opened up, as a woman, to grief.

How did this man, whom I did not know, shape me? The few memories my mother gave me were strewn with roses: he was generous, hardworking, kind, and successful. A poor German-Jewish boy who had wanted to study law, he became a wealthy businessman in order to support his widowed mother, three sisters, and younger brother. He established branches of the May and Company shoe business throughout Europe: London, Zurich, Paris, Amsterdam, Budapest, Luxembourg, and Frankfurt. He traveled to Finland, Russia, and America to buy shoes and rubber boots. He was generous to a fault.

The perfect father, I imagined. He never interfered in my life or told me what I could not do. For years, I entertained the fantasy that he had not really died; he had gone on a trip, gotten lost, and would come back. When I learned he drowned, I imagined that he swam to another shore.

My cousin Irene remembered a different man. One rainy day she lied about having worn her rubber boots to school, and my father found her boots hidden in the hallway. When she got home, he slapped her, hard.

I never knew that father. I gazed at the photograph of this handsome man and adored him. He was self-educated, spoke many languages ("even dialects," my cousin Fred told me), took care of his brother and sisters, had a premonition of the Holocaust, and brought most of his family out of Germany to safety in England. He had a sense of humor, loved to waltz (so do I), and called my mother *Spatz* (sparrow). Sometimes, when his good looks drew too many flirtatious glances, he made her jealous.

I see their world through photographs. A picture of my mother, father, brother, and me, touching one another, arm to shoulder, hand to knee. We are a family. I stare at it and cannot believe it. How could this have been, when there is no memory?

Here they are in the Alps, faces sunburned, all lined up in a row, their black skis sunk in white snow, about to slide into the camera: my mother, my father, my grandfather, my uncles, and my aunts. My father, the joker, sits on a cousin's shoulder. There's another photo of my mother on my father's shoulders; both their arms are stretched out for balance, forming double symmetrical wings. Here they stand, hugging each other in the snow, standing sideways, smiling at the camera; no light separates their silhouettes. There he is, standing behind my mother in a field of deep snow, both arms raised, holding his jacket over his head, peekaboo. The white grin stands out in the darkened face. She, looking ahead, smiling, hand on hip, oblivious to his prank.

That world has remained frozen, like a subterranean layer of my being. I am drawn to it with a terrible longing to awaken it with my hot breath. The photographs are like frames in a silent movie, asking me to lip-read the actors' mouths, their eyes, their hands.

It is a private world, only revealed when the light falls on their faces; otherwise, they are entombed, in albums, in boxes, in the backs of dark closets.

Other parts of my father's life were not exposed to the camera's eye. In 1914 he had been drafted into the German army and fought on the western front until 1918. He was poisoned by mustard gas, "friendly gas," from German troops. They left him lying there for dead. He survived and returned home an Orthodox Jew, insisting on a kosher home, which my mother, dutifully but not convincingly, kept. Aunt Berthe believed that his depressions stemmed from these nightmare years.

His father, Elias, died suddenly of a heart attack, at the age of fifty. His mother, Babettchen, supported her five children by taking over the family dry-goods store in Geinsheim am Main, near Frankfurt. Her portrait shows her seated in a darkened room, with specks of light bouncing off pewter plates in the background. Her face emerges in the light: her hands are thick and knobbed; they hold a prayer book.

My father's death left my mother restless, in search of something she never quite found. My father's business success had produced a small inheritance. This is what we lived on, augmented by my mother's uncertain income. We moved from place to place. First we went to London to be with my aunt Berthe and uncle Daniel. She rented a flat at 43 Windsor Court, Golders Green Road, but then—for reasons unknown—decided to return to Zurich, where at first we lived in a small hotel. There was no family home to return to because my father had decided, in January 1936, to emigrate to Canada because of the threat posed by Hitler; he had sold his business and given up our apartment.

When I was five, and excited about starting kindergarten, we moved from Zurich to a small town called Hergiswil on the Lake of Lucerne. There was no public school; starting kindergarten would have to wait, much to my disappointment. My brother attended the Catholic school and I stayed home. My mother chose Hergiswil because she believed it would be safer in the country, in case the Germans invaded Switzerland. The list of Jews, we were told, was ready.

Weekly, we went to the American consulate in Zurich to inquire about her visa. The Banque Federale wrote her a reference: "Mrs. Renée May, pension Dolderberg, is personally known to us as a highly respectable lady and she is in possession of sufficient means to enable her to meet all living expenses."

World events soon outwardly expressed my mother's inner turmoil. In the *Israelitisches Wochenblatt*, a July 31, 1936, editorial posed these rhetorical questions: "Is a new war ahead? Is the future of Switzerland at stake? Will the world go up in new flames, with all the horrors a modern war can bring?"

The same paper carried a story, "The Wandering Jew," reciting the following figures:

> 93,000 Jews left Germany between April 1, 1933, and April 1, 1936.
>
> 15,600 went to Belgium, England, Holland, and France.
>
> 3,000 went to Switzerland, Austria, Italy, Czechoslovakia, and Yugoslavia.
>
> 1,000 to Scandinavia.
>
> 2,000 to Spain and Portugal.
>
> 18,000 to Poland, Eastern Europe, and the Balkans.
>
> 31,000 to Palestine.
>
> 9,500 to the U.S.

4,500 to Brazil.

2,000 to Argentina.

600 to Chile.

3,000 to South Africa.

We, too, had wandered. When my parents married, they lived in Frankfurt; after a few years they moved to Switzerland, then back to Germany, and finally back to Switzerland in 1928, the year before Edgar was born. My father's sister Minna, his brother, Salli, his nieces, nephews, and cousins left Germany for England; other cousins went to America, and two to Palestine; my cousin Milli went to Holland, where she married. She and her daughter were hidden separately by a succession of courageous Dutch families and survived. Milli's husband was arrested in Amsterdam, sent a postcard home from Auschwitz, but died in Dachau. Other members of the family stayed in France or Germany, and in Alsace-Lorraine. My grandfather's brother, Gabby, remained in Nice with his wife. "We are French. No one will harm us." The day his son came home on leave from the army, they were betrayed to the Gestapo. They died in a concentration camp.

My father's sister Augusta, who did not want to leave Germany, was taken away. Her sons never forgave themselves for not getting her out. My Parisian cousin André and his wife, Mimi, tried to find refuge in Switzerland, but were turned back at the border. He escaped to a small village in France, where he painted pictures under an assumed name. Both survived.

On the day of my birth, September 28, 1933, *Die Neue Zürcher Zeitung* reported on Hitler's declaration of "intentions" for the benefit of Switzerland, Holland, Belgium, and Denmark. "No serious person in Germany even entertained the thought of making other countries subservient to it," the announcement stated. The Swiss accepted this interpretation of Hitler's rise to power with relief.

On June 10, 1940, the day Italy entered the war, we arrived in New York.

My mother, brother, and I, laden with gifts of chocolates, had said tearful good-byes to our friends two weeks earlier at the Zurich railroad station. My responsibility was to carry the chocolates, a whole bagful, which I left by mistake on the train.

I remember lying on the lower bunk of the berth and the touch of the rough, scratchy blankets on my cheek, the taste of hot chocolate sipped from a thermos cup on my tongue. The sounds of things clanging in the night, men shouting, and dark shapes rushing past the opaque window made me scrunch my knees up to my chest and hug myself until the rocking rhythm of the train soothed me to sleep. I was not alert to danger.

My brother remembers when German soldiers came through the train, demanding to see everyone's papers. The conductor, who accompanied them, knew my mother because he used to be a conductor on the route from Hergiswil to Zurich. Giving a barely perceptible nod to her, he told the Germans, "Nothing to worry about. She's not a problem." They moved on.

We remained in Genoa for several days. I remember looking out the hotel window and seeing Japanese soldiers parading in the square below. My mother pulled me back.

I felt enormous excitement the day we finally boarded the SS *Manhattan*. My mother was dismayed that our "private" cabin contained five other occupants, including a baby, but I was thrilled to discover shuffleboard and amazed by the sight of apple pie à la mode. Each day we had lifeboat drills: out came the clumsy, thick orange life vests. Then one night, we were awakened by a loud bang. We jumped out of bed and ran to the upper deck, hurriedly fastening our life vests. A German torpedo had grazed us. No damage. Back to bed.

Years later, my brother obtained the manifest of the ship. Across from "May, Renée," in a column headed "Race, or People," was written "Hebrew."

Only later did I understand what we had escaped and how accident had spared us from becoming victims. We were the lucky ones. My father had left Germany, my mother had left Europe, and we had come to America. But other members of my family had not; six million Jews had not. On some level that I do not yet fully understand, I believe I transformed my sense of the Holocaust into personal political activism. This was the source of my political courage. I could do what the victims could not: oppose evil whenever I recognized it. The United States of America would protect me. I lived in a time and place when it was safe for a Jew to be a political person, to speak, to oppose, to stand up. What my grandfather so courageously had tried, I could do. Never had Jews enjoyed that privilege. For thousands of years, Jews had been forced to live apart, silent, and hidden—for so long that they themselves equated safety with invisibility.

"Shhh, don't speak so loudly" . . . "Don't let anyone know"—that is how we were supposed to survive. That had been the message of history and the message from my own childhood. If one Jew got into trouble, we would all suffer. Therefore, stay low, keep quiet, and we will be safe.

The Holocaust had proven that there was no protection in silence. The only defense against evil was to oppose it. And I, I lived in a time and place that gave me this privilege. Therefore I had to use it and do what they, the victims, could not. Victimization, either as a woman or as a Jew, could be avoided only through the expression of individual and collective strength. A political life opened that possibility. That is why I chose it. That would be my form of atonement for the sin of survival. Political action, viewed in this light, became a lifesaving compulsion, not a courageous act.

The morning the SS *Manhattan* pulled into New York harbor we had gotten up early to catch a glimpse of the Statue of Liberty. Oohs and aahs from the crowd seemed to rock the boat from side to side. We assembled on the pier next to our trunks under the letter *M*, since we were May.

"There they are," my mother shouted excitedly as she recognized Fred and Irene, my father's cousin and his first wife, walking toward us. He had come to America in 1926, worked as a dishwasher, and now was headwaiter in a fancy hotel, the Trianon, owned by Harry Schiff. Irene was dazzling. I had never seen anyone like her. A short, stocky woman in sling-back platform shoes, with a circle of rouge on each cheek and lips that smacked a perfect print of lipstick on my face, she wore red—red dress, red shoes, red handbag, red gloves, and red hat with a red feather on the brim, waving like a flag.

Her first words to me, as she looked critically at my straight blond bob, were, "Mudlin, you've gotta have coils. In America, all the goils have coils."

For years after, burlesquing her Bronx accent, we would break into helpless laughter again and again. We were as innocent as she was brazen; that was what was so funny.

But the dream was real. It had swept me not only to these shores, but also onto this podium, where I could swear my allegiance to the Constitution of the United States of America with the fervor felt by those who welcome citizenship as a sinner does atonement.

The day my mother took her oath of citizenship, July 20, 1949, she was extremely nervous, memorizing, down to the last minute, every sample question in her American-history book. The questions, it turned out, were easy—too easy, she said afterward. And she joined in relieved laughter when the judge told the courtroomful of new citizens, "The difference between you and other Americans is that you became citizens with your clothes on." I repeated that story years later to newly sworn-in citizens in Vermont, and they laughed just as she did.

The message my mother's life conveyed to me was ambiguous, one of both her female vulnerability and her female strength. I wanted to reject one and claim the other. After my father's death, she had reinvented her life; perhaps not totally to her satisfaction, but she had courage and the strength to survive. And she had created a family, even if we were not like other families; we were loved.

In our family of three, each person's feelings bounced off the others' and ricocheted back. There was no room to scatter emotion about, as one might in a larger, more symmetrical family. My brother was not only the son but also became the father and protector. And I, the daughter, was child, companion, and confidante, exposed always to the undiluted intensity of my mother's need.

The desire to escape her widow's vulnerability gave me resolve. Energetically, I determined at an early age that I would do everything to escape her fate. She taught me who I could become as well as who I did not want to be.

On this day, taking the oath of office affirmed my sense of place. I was no longer a fatherless immigrant, a wandering Jew. I belonged in the inner circle, not on the periphery like my mother. I had become governor of a state. What greater legitimacy could there be? Someone who spoke for others, for a whole people, not someone who had to plead with others for protection, for recognition, for life itself.

I was not the woman my mother was, the woman who added up figures at night with her fountain pen, wondering how long her money would last. Nor was I the child embarrassed about wearing the wrong socks, shoes, hairstyle; anything that betrayed me—a lunch box—could be wrong. The first time I invited a school friend to our apartment for lunch, I insisted that my mother prepare exactly what her mother had served me: peanut-butter-and-jelly sandwiches on white bread, divided into four perfect triangles with the crusts cut off. And potato chips, in a tidy heap, placed over on one side of the plate.

Today, I, too, had done everything right. Tradition had been meticulously followed. As governor, not only could I adhere to the standard, I could set it.

My mother would not have expected this. Not from me. The American dream had cast my brother in the starring role, the boy who could become president.

Edgar fit the description, showing Horatio Alger tendencies at an early age, to my mother's delight. He was determined to make money. As a boy, he delivered meat for Grossnass, the kosher butcher on Queens Boulevard in Forest Hills, sold magazines on the street corner in Los Angeles. He was innovative. He sold fresh eggs to neighbors, shipping them from a farm in New Jersey where we had gone to summer camp. This was America. Each day, something new. Sibling rivalry made a contribution. Why should I not be allowed to reach for the American dream as my brother did, just because I happened to be a girl?

As my mother talked about Edgar, I eavesdropped. His stories became my possibilities. I borrowed them, dressed them up in different clothes, and made them mine. My mother had envisioned a different future for me; my happiness was equated with a traditional marriage and a career "to fall back on." But unwittingly she had taught me how hard that fall could be. She should have known that I would learn more from one page of her life than from all her admonitions.

She herself seemed to grasp for the dream again and again, and when she didn't find it in one place, she tried another. After a year in New York, where we had settled into an apartment in Forest Hills, she packed us up and we boarded a train for California.

Our life in Beverly Hills did not follow the script. We were isolated in a little white-stucco bungalow with a red-tile roof on North Carson Road, for my mother did not drive. Unlike New York, where immigrant groups formed clusters in every neighborhood, Los Angeles seemed to be a place where we were the only people on our street who spoke English with an accent. My mother became ill and had to have surgery; my brother came down with scarlet fever and was quarantined for six weeks.

The day of Pearl Harbor is so vivid in my mind I don't know if it really happened that way or if it was a movie. At noontime on December 7 an open, plank-sided truck, painted green, careened down North Carson Road, barely missing the palm trees in the median. Bundles of newspapers were piled high, falling this way and that. I can see the newsboy, standing up in the back of the truck, leaning dangerously over the side of the wooden panels, waving the newspapers high in the air and yelling at the top of his lungs, "Extra, extra, read all about it. Japanese invade Pearl Harbor." I ran into the house to tell my mother.

The Japanese gardener who mowed our lawn once a week disappeared. When she went shopping, my mother carefully examined the stems of apples, to check if they had been poisoned by Japanese spies. That was the rumor. When she learned that her brother-in-law Salli and his family were moving to New York from Canada, she decided to go back East. It was better to be near family.

My mother tried many different jobs. Her family and the courses she took at the University of Zurich had given her an appreciation of culture but not the skills for a career, and her need for financial independence had never been considered.

In New York, she had brought piecework home in the evenings to our apartment in Forest Hills: she sewed bright-red and green sequins on the fat black-felt decorations of hat pins. I handed her the sequins, one at a time. A few months later, she gave that up and took a job as a nanny; she had to leave the house before breakfast to arrive at the home of the two psychiatrists who were parents to twins. Her instructions were never to let the babies cry. She lasted three months. Later, I had to give up my room when we took in a boarder. She was sixteen and had numbers tattooed on her arm—a survivor of Bergen-Belsen. She could not stop eating, hardly talked, and read vociferously. I shared my mother's bedroom, occupying the other twin bed, dreaming of the life we might have had had my father lived. My mother had brought one prize possession with her from Europe. It was a Gobelin, a tapestry that hung above the sofa in the living room. Lack of space had forced my mother to leave behind the heavy gold frame in which it had once been displayed. She rolled up the tapestry and fit it into the trunk. Wherever we went, it found its place of honor. The scene is Versailles, where an elegantly attired couple is performing a courtly dance. She, her pretty face framed in yellow curls, wears a pink satin dress, pinched into a V-shaped waist. How did she breathe? She did not need to. Her partner wears a purple-and-gold cape draped over one shoulder and extends a languid white hand toward hers. Her ivory bosom swells. She waits. Their seduction is observed by the musicians seated on a parapet. The tiny tapestry stitches blend from a distance into brush strokes—the folds of her dress are soft, his cape, seamless—but up close, I see the pocked pattern of single stitches.

My mother told me that my father had bought the tapestry one night from an old woman on a street corner—was it in Budapest or Bucharest? Five women had worked on it for five years, and by buying it from the woman on the spot, he rescued them from starvation.

The Gobelin my mother saved and brought to America is a stylized parody of the Old World, and it pulled me into an imagining of a place that might have been, of the apartment in Zurich where it once had hung and where a mother and father had lived.

The Gobelin caught the eye of the surgeon who made a house call when I had appendicitis at the age of thirteen.

"That is very beautiful," Dr. Nissen said, with a hurried glance at the wall as he bent over to pick up his bag from the sofa. Then, before my mother could reply, he walked out the door. For weeks, she worried that the Gobelin would make him think we were rich; what would she do with the bill?

In 1950, the Gobelin was packed up again when we moved to be near cousins in Pittsfield, Massachusetts. Life outside New York City would be easier. My mother lived there until the final years of her life, when she moved to Vermont to be near her children and grandchildren. She died in 1969, at the age of seventy. I wished she were here today.

Of my European relatives, only Aunt Berthe and cousin Irene had seen this statehouse. Aunt Berthe had been here on October 16, 1975, and had sat in the balcony, looking down at her niece and nephew in the Vermont House of Representatives.

My brother began: "Mr. Speaker. It gives me great personal pleasure to introduce to you the senior and most revered member of the May-Kunin family, a lady who comes from the Vermont of Europe: Switzerland.

"And now, Mr. Speaker, chivalry, courtesy, and the fact that I am the junior member of the family coalition require me to ask your permission to yield to the member from Burlington."

I rise, and exaggerate protocol with pleasure.

"Thank you, member from Springfield. Mr. Speaker, I believe this is the first time that one member of the House has yielded to another in order to make an introduction. We are both very pleased to have with us today our aunt from Switzerland who has been a source of inspiration to us both. It gives me great pleasure to introduce our aunt, Mrs. Bendel."

She rises and takes a bow in response to the applause, as if she had just finished singing an aria from *La Bohème*.

Music was her true love. In 1911 her parents had allowed her to study singing at Dr. Hoch's Conservatorium in Frankfurt. Her Zurich music teacher had arranged a secret audition by Dr. Andrea, conductor of the Tonhalle orchestra, who unbeknownst to her had sat in the next room listening. He had agreed she had a great talent and absolutely must study in Germany.

"My parents were considered very broad-minded to let me go," she said. To permit a daughter to leave home and go on the stage was highly unusual for a middle-class family. There were certain conditions: she could sing *lieder* but not opera. "I did sing arias from operas, just the same," she confided later.

There was no doubt that Berthe was the most beautiful of the three sisters. (My mother, the youngest, was in awe of her all her life. The middle sister, Alice, suffered from being in her sister's shadow. Alice died of childbed fever, five weeks after giving birth to a healthy girl—my cousin Irene.) Today, we would describe Berthe's magnetism as "presence." The light in her eyes reflected a vivacious spirit, and her deep-throated laugh verged on the raucous. Nothing held her back when she was amused.

Her photographs tell me she knew how to pose, stretching her body its full length, one foot forward, eyes into the camera's lens. Each picture is staged. There she is, bare shouldered in a simple black satin gown and a string of pearls; here she looks serious, seated in layers of lace and silk, with a rose pinned to her bosom; and there, on skis, the Alps in the background, she stretches her legs forward and leans her body back to let the camera record every detail of the elegant long knitted jacket and jaunty matching cap.

Here she is at a costume ball. In each group picture, crowded with clowns and queens, peasants and jesters, I can pick her out. Her face catches the light; she is the one in the center, the one who won first prize.

Among the possessions she kept, carefully wrapped, was a four-inch-wide, three-yard length of red silk grosgrain ribbon embossed in gold, with pretty flowers and the words "Dem Singvogelchen" ("The Songbird"), an award she received at a performance on March 19, 1910, in Zurich. The ribbon was saved in a box along with two letters, one from her mother and one from her father, written to "Mein Liebes Berthe" on September 12, 1912. (Another letter, from 1911, was addressed to "Chère Berthe." Was German preferred for authority?) After several pages in which my grandmother thanks her daughter for sending the beautiful photograph, which is both "artistic and very natural," she makes her point:

> Now, dear Berthe, I come to a subject that dear Papa and I have spoken about for a long time. It is the following: It is sixteen months since you, dear Berthe, have been at home. We would all very much like to have you with us at home again, at least for a time while you are still single. We, too, want to have some time with you. Your studies in Frankfurt are not yet ended, as you still have some months to complete. Our thinking is as follows: You will now come home for about two weeks, let your voice rest a while and then you

can take private lessons with Maria Phillipe in Basel. We think you have had enough training in the conservatorium. . . . Dear Berthe, I hope that you understand me correctly and know that we only want the best for you.

She ends the letter with descriptions of two fur and velvet jackets; which would Berthe prefer? They will order either one as soon as she gives the word.

When my aunt recalled the letter, she said, "Then, if parents asked you to do something, you just obliged. Today, I would have asked Herr Leimer to write to my parents and tell them no." Giving up her career "was a pity," she said, "but you never know, I might have married, stayed in Frankfurt, and with the war, that would have been the end."

Leimer would have told them that he was about to have her perform, that she had a great talent. "Sie Können alles machen," he told her, "opera, lieder, alles." ("You can do everything—opera, songs, everything.")

He was not equally generous to all his pupils. When someone did not do well, he snapped, "Wenn sie so wieter singen, Können sie heim gehen und strümpfe stopfen." ("If you go on singing like that, you can go home and darn stockings.") "But I was never afraid of him. If you showed fright, he only got worse."

Throughout my childhood I heard Berthe's story: what she gave up, first to please her parents, and then to satisfy her husband. A year after her return to Switzerland, cards were sent out announcing that on December 12, 1913, Berthe Bloch was married to Daniel Bendel, in Baden, Switzerland. She later said she met her husband "through friends," but I surmise that my grandparents arranged it. My first and last recollection of Uncle Daniel is of his gray spats. Children were not within his line of vision. If I had expected my uncle to be a surrogate father, I was soon disappointed.

He had had a severe childhood, having run away from home in Romania at the age of fourteen, earned his passage to South Africa, and found his way to London. When my aunt met him, he had become wealthy and had settled in Zurich. Daniel did not want Berthe to sing. At first, he did not allow her to have a piano. "She was like a beautiful doll; he wanted to keep her under lock and key," my mother told me. She once left him and then came back. Divorce was unthinkable and seldom talked about.

Her memories of the man who controlled her life were kind. He regretted, she said, that he had not taken her along on a visit to Romania in 1932 to tend to his parents' graves. Instead, she stayed with business friends in Berlin. But he brought back an embroidered Romanian folk costume for her, which she later gave to me. Its colors remain unfaded; only the thin linen of the blouse is fragile to the touch. She must have looked splendid in it.

She kept a photograph of her visit to Berlin. Three elegant women are walking toward the camera on a street that may be Unter den Linden. They smile at the camera, holding their fur-collared coats closed; my aunt wears a cloche hat and pearls. Even in this smart trio she stands out, her carriage confident, her smile like a model's. The deep perspective and the street's grainy texture make the photograph look like a painting, complete with feathery trees and watercolor brush strokes of two men, one wearing knickers and a cap, the other carrying a briefcase. There is an intruder in the picture in the lower right-hand corner. He does not belong there, but a piece of his flapping jacket, white hand, bent leg, and swinging cane is caught in the frame: an old man intent on his mission, as oblivious of the ladies as they are of him.

The certainty of their rhythmic stride, the clarity of their black silhouettes against the gray street, give them a remarkable unity—women sharing laughter, secrets, pleasure. I look at the photograph through the lens of the future, knowing what awaits them here in Berlin. The man with the cane will trip them, they will fall, and he will step over their bodies. What happened, I wonder, to the other two women walking in step with my aunt?

The locus of her marriage to Daniel Bendel was a mansion, one of the most beautiful houses in Zurich, which he built in 1924 high on a hill on the Hadlaubstrasse, overlooking Lake Zurich. Here she now had a music room and a piano. I do not know if he permitted her to sing outside these walls. "We lived in it for twelve years. He wanted it, and he had such a *strong will*," she said. Her great regret was having to sell it. "It's terrible when you have to give it up, not nice." But they sold the house during the recession of the 1930s, when they moved to London shortly before my father's death.

Both house and grounds were professionally designed. The rose garden, where I learned to walk, was enormous. "We had a hundred and fifty rosebushes; my job every morning was to work in the rose garden and cut the flowers. Every room had a vase full of roses," Aunt Berthe recollected.

There is a photograph of me walking on a gravel path; at my right are roses, bordered by a low hedge, and behind them is the white-stucco house, with triangular lead stained-glass windows crosshatching the rounded arch. One plump stockinged leg is set back and the other forward, and I am wearing a white cotton frock with tiny rosettes, white-

and-black-patent laced shoes: my hands are held out chest high, fingers curved down and extending slightly forward for balance.

"You were so proud, you can see it. You were so glad to walk, and so fair, so fair. . . ," she remembered.

My mother and her sister were unusually close; because of the age difference of seven years, Aunt Berthe treated her more like a daughter than a younger sister, and my mother responded in kind. She looked up to Berthe as the model of perfection. The older sister had the effect of forcing the younger child, years later, to turn around every so often to check and see if her seams were straight.

The house was Aunt Berthe's masterpiece. Fifteen large photographs documented the furnishings in every room. Turning them over, I linger on the details, moving quietly from room to room. My eyes follow the geometric pattern of the parquet floors, the plush Oriental rugs, the ornate carvings on the fireplace, the silky patterned texture of the bedroom wallpaper, the gleam of the wooden headboard, the layers of gauzy curtains filtering light from the window, the crystal chandelier throwing silver splashes on the oil painting behind it, and the symmetrical arrangement of four Biedermeier chairs in the living room, waiting for someone to come in.

No one does.

My aunt recalled the details: "Every door was mahogany. The music room, the one with the bay windows, had lovely mahogany paneling. The *Herrenzimmer* was done in Florentine Renaissance style. We had a sideboard on the veranda that was paneled in cherry wood. It was used as a sun parlor. The dining room had blue silk on the walls, Adam walls. When we had a party and used to dance, we opened all the doors, and you could move from room to room."

"You had parties?" I asked.

"Yes, when foreign visitors came. Upstairs, there was the bedroom, a spare room, and a *Kleidezimmer*, in Versailles style. Two maids' rooms were on top, and a bathroom."

"Two maids?"

"We needed them in that house. On the top floor was another small living room and a sewing room. It had the most beautiful view of the lake and the whole city."

Is it memory or fiction—did I skip from room to room, not daring to touch the polished tables, or leave a fingerprint on the silk wallpaper? "Shhhh, quiet, don't run, wash your hands."

Irene had other memories. "When I stayed at Berthe's house and played in the garden," my cousin remembered, "Uncle Daniel would run after me wherever I went, holding a little rake and smoothing out the gravel path."

And did Aunt Berthe, hearing her footsteps echoing from floor to ceiling, placing roses in the vases, humming to herself, long to let her voice burst out with the raw gusto unleashed in her laughter? Was her morning walking tour restricted to the stage of Ibsen's *Doll's House?* My mother, the younger sister, less bound by beauty and more freed by tragedy, thought it all a terrible mistake: "She should have never married Daniel. He was the wrong man for her."

And love, what about love? I wondered. She kept, until her death, a photograph of a young man. On the back she had written his name: Adolphe Gresson. His white collar is slightly rumpled, his tie broad and somewhat flamboyant, and his head, undeniably handsome, crowned with blond hair that refuses to be combed. His eyes are open to laughter.

All but four pages of Aunt Berthe's brown, leather-bound, locked diary are torn out. A small, folded paper is saved among a box of letters. I open it up; it is a flyer from Tea-room Matter, a resort café, featuring that evening "Vivere." At the very top, she has written the year: 1938. When I return the paper to its familiar folds, two blue-ink inscriptions appear, face up. "Fidèle pensée et amitie éternelle, Adolphe."

Just below, she has written, "Après 33 ans, ceci est toujours vrai! Berthe."

So fresh, I feel the words pierce like a thorn.

Oh, Berthe.

Your spirit was silenced, first by loving but firm parents, and then by a proud and domineering husband. It was as if they had killed you by placing an exquisitely embroidered satin pillow over your head. And you never said a word.

Never, never, would this happen to me. What remained trapped within her would within me be free. Berthe's great tragedy was her self-denial, which she bore without a trace of self-pity. I vowed that I would use my voice, practice every day, run up and down the scale over and over until I overcame stage fright and could stand up in front of everyone, under the lights, and perform.

I TURNED to the next page of my speech:

> My immigrant roots, while more recent than most, are not extraordinary.
>
> It is the immigrant spirit of hope which I wish to bring to state

government—a spirit which instills in our children the belief that anyone can achieve anything in this country with hard work, an education, and a fair chance.

It doesn't matter where you came from. It matters where you are going.

I believed every word. I stood here, flanked by the American flag and the Vermont flag. I had prayed, and I had recited the Pledge of Allegiance; I was American. The sad pages of my diary were ripped out. Only these remained.

I look forward to the challenge of leadership which Vermont has placed before me.

I have faith, not only in my ability and in yours, but in our mutual resourcefulness. In Vermont, we have grown up with the knowledge that nature indeed may be harsh and unpredictable, but also with the assurance that each season brings its own renewal and each year follows a certain rhythm. We know it is not only possible to blend austerity and optimism, it is part of the human condition, and it is essential to our survival.

I thought of my family and how they had crossed the sea again and again, each time certain what they sought could be found.

I reached the last lines of my speech:

With your help, and the blessings of the Almighty, we will succeed.

Let us begin.

The applause receded.

I was ready to be escorted into the executive chamber.

11

I STOOD UP AT THE ALTAR BEFORE THE OPEN TORAH SCROLL TO SAY THE blessing that preceded the reading. In ten days I would be sworn in as governor of the state of Vermont. Now I was reading the Hebrew words before the congregation, as worried about making mistakes as I had been as a child in Hebrew school. But I pronounced each syllable clearly. This was not a time to mumble.

Rabbi Wall had invited me, my husband, and each of our children to accept the honor of taking an Aliyah.

After the Torah was wrapped and put away, he announced to the congregation, "Governor-elect Madeleine Kunin will now give a few remarks."

He motioned me to come to the pulpit, to stand where he had been.

"I never thought that the heirs of the Jewish patriarchs, Abraham, Isaac, and Jacob, would allow me to speak to the congregation. Perhaps I am also speaking for Rachel, Sarah, and Rebecca." I smiled.

"When we think of the immigrants who first settled in this community more than one hundred years ago as a group of itinerant Jewish peddlers we realize how far we all have come. They could not imagine Jews owning land or running a business. How could they have envisioned a Jewish community like ours, so confident of its place in society that it could celebrate the election of a Jewish political leader?"

Afterward, Adam said he thought my talk was "awesome," but Daniel was embarrassed. "Why should we be so important?" he asked.

"It's not that we're important," I tried to explain, "it's that the rabbi wanted us to have some spiritual guidance."

Daniel slipped lower in the pew.

I followed the familiar Hebrew refrains with renewed concentration. I did not want to lose my place in the prayer book. I wanted to believe. "God, give me strength. Always let me see right from wrong. Make me charitable." And, with a glance at Daniel, I added, "Do not let this go to my head."

I felt the presence of the congregation behind us, bodies turning toward one another, heads nodding approval. Their glances warmed my shoulders and the back of my neck. I sat up straight. Suddenly, I slumped down with Daniel.

"I'm not who they think I am. I spoke well, but my words are just a facade. There's nothing underneath."

The anointment of victory had not worked its miracle. I would have to do it myself.

I tried to place myself in the context of more recent history, recalling newspaper headlines about the deeds of governors.

None of them were perfect. Ordinary mortals do this job, I reminded myself. You are an ordinary mortal; you can do this job. Compare yourself with the others. Davis, Salmon, Snelling, they all made terrible mistakes. You have some strengths they didn't have and some weaknesses they didn't have. We're not talking about patriarchs here. We're talking about governors. Stop being in a state of wonder. Get to work.

"Governor Kunin?" a voice said as we walked out of the synagogue.

I gave myself a shove. That's you.

Had anyone noticed the two-second delay? "Yes?"

How long would it take for me to answer to the title, so that I would radiate from the inside out, rather than wear my title like a jewel, pinned to my lapel? Perhaps if I said the word "governor" in my sleep it would take hold, like a new language. I would begin to "think governor," as one thinks in French or Spanish.

Years later, Gretchen Morse, my secretary of the Agency of Human Services, recalled her first day on the job. Like several women in my administration, she had little past experience that had specifically prepared her for her new position.

"On my first morning I sat in my office and asked myself, How do I begin? The phone rang. I stared at it for several rings, waiting for something to happen. The secretary was on a break. I had to pick it up.

" 'Hello,' I said. 'This is secretary of human services, Gretchen Morse.' If I said it often enough, that was who I would become. By the end of the day, I got used to it."

My new identity was interpreted in a variety of ways, depending on the source. In the Jewish press I was the "Jewish governor of Vermont," and in the Swiss press, I was my native country's "beloved daughter." My mother would have been thrilled to read in the *Aufbau*, a German-language weekly to which she had subscribed, that I was the "immigrant governor." The AMA newspaper played it big: "MD's Wife New Governor of Vermont." In the body of the story I was "Republican Madelaine [sic] Kunin." What else would a doctor's wife be?

On the television shows "Good Morning America" and "Today," where I appeared during my first week as governor-elect, I was treated like a curiosity. How on earth did this happen? Bryant Gumbel's questions implied. I wanted to set him straight, to say, "I won because I was better than my opponent." Instead I gave him a Mona Lisa smile.

The first day in our new transition office, I discovered the meaning of true power: my phone calls were immediately returned. "Let me try to get Mr. —— out of his meeting. It's no trouble. No trouble at all."

"*Out* of a meeting?" I repeated. "Until now, people were always *in* meetings."

Traveling home on the interstate at eleven o'clock one night in December, I felt safe; the trooper assigned to me as my "security" was at the wheel, and I fell asleep in the front seat. When the car suddenly slowed down, I woke up to see blinking blue lights moving up from behind us at a rapid clip.

"Uh-oh," I said. "This is it."

Then, as suddenly as they had appeared, the blue lights veered off, as if they knew my wish, made a U-turn in the median, and headed the other way.

"What happened?" I asked the trooper.

"I told him this was Vermont One."

Vermont One. That was my code name, what I had coveted when I had been Vermont Two, lieutenant governor.

I took a deep breath. "That's power," I said.

I felt both a thrill and a shiver. I was the boss; the state police, like all of state government, was now under my command.

"Careful, careful," a voice said. "Never act as if you were above the law."

I hear you.

"Could you slow it down a bit?" I asked, more out of duty than desire. I liked driving fast, and with the trooper it was safe. Now I could flirt with danger while simultaneously being protected. That juxtaposition was difficult to resist.

MASTERING A NEW PROTOCOL was a learning process, both for the troopers and for me. On our first trip to Boston, Sergeant Jim Dimmick had arranged for Liz and me to be met at the airport by the Boston police.

The moment we got to the curb, up pulled a black-and-white patrol car, lights blinking. Liz and I looked at each other, shrugged our shoulders, and got in, folding our knees up to our chins while inhaling a heavy dose of air freshener. Two scented cardboard strawberries were dangling from the front mirror.

"I guess this is how it's going to be," we communicated to one another.

Sergeant Dimmick sat in front, next to the uniformed Boston cop.

Two motorcycles, sirens blaring, led the way.

Each time we stopped at a light, the crowd of pedestrians waiting for the light to turn green craned their necks and stared into the backseat.

How can they tell that I'm the governor? I wondered. I didn't know I had that much recognition in Boston.

Then it dawned on me. We were separated from Jim and the driver by a steel grate. There were no handles on the doors.

My heels pressed down on the rubber floor mat. "Oh my God, Liz." I burst into laughter. "They think we're under arrest. A couple of middle-aged hookers, maybe?"

The next time we traveled to Boston, Jim spent an hour on the phone with the cops ahead of time: "No grate, no patrol car. Just a plain sedan, you guys, you hear?"

Jim had five sisters. Liz and I could put on our makeup in the back of the car, comb our hair, discuss our clothes, take our shoes off, and giggle whenever we felt like it. Nothing fazed Jim, not even when he was greeted as the governor.

"Over there," he'd signal, as we went through airport security. "She's the governor."

I had won the election, but not automatic recognition. When my husband and I picked up our credentials at our first National Governors' Association meeting, the woman behind the table who was checking off our names did not bother to look up: she stuck her hand out; the governor's white-ribboned, gold-lettered name tag went to my husband; the guest one went to me.

In conversation, when I was introduced, I noticed that people didn't hear the word "Governor" before my name. They smiled and nodded, as they would to anyone who had just joined the circle, and promptly resumed their conversation. They had not heard the word "Governor" because their eyes had not prepared them for it. This woman, experience told them, is at best an adjunct to power, a wife, an aide, or a hanger-on. Their eyes did not allow the possibility that she might be the source.

Sometimes I ignored the slight, playing at being eavesdropper, mischie-

vously plotting to surprise the person later. Other times, I would feel
compelled to try again. If I was introduced loudly, slowly, and clearly for
the second time, it sank in. "You're the *governor*?"

But I realized that their responses could have been mine. The reactions
weren't prompted by deliberate gender bias, but conditioned by years of
accumulated information as deeply ingrained as the genetic code; men
were governors and women were not. Only Liz's son, Joshua, had been
taught otherwise, and that is why he had provoked such laughter.

Even after three terms in office, I learned that I still had to explain who
I was. Once I was standing on the lawn in front of the White House after
a group of us had finished a meeting with President Reagan. Clusters of
press had gathered around individual governors for interviews. Michael
Dukakis, then a presidential candidate, was the center of attention. Having concluded an interview with a Vermont reporter, I walked over to
listen to Dukakis. A White House aide motioned all spectators to move to
the other side of the sidewalk, including me. "This area is reserved for the
governors."

"I'm a governor," I replied, suddenly feeling stupid.

"Let me see your identification."

Like an idiot, I showed it to him.

The women from the White House staff standing by gave me knowing
looks. How often, I wondered, had they had to prove who they were?

At an earlier governors' conference, Representative Daniel Rostenkowski, chairman of the powerful House Ways and Means Committee,
was about to address a plenary session. This was my second governors'
conference, and I was cheerfully confident, compared with my first year.
I worked my way to my place at the table, after exchanging first-name
pleasantries with a dozen of my fellow chief executives. I was greeted like
a buddy.

The chairman banged the gavel. Everyone was seated.

"Gentlemen," Rostenkowski began as his eyes swept the ballroom.

I looked across the room to Martha Layne Collins, governor of Kentucky. Had she heard it? She was too far away for me to read her reaction.
Had anybody noticed?

An African-American staff member, sitting quietly behind Governor
Bill Clinton, gave me a wink. I wanted to run up and throw my arms
around him. I winked back.

I tried to concentrate on Rosti's words, blotting out the shadow of his
powerful hulk. I was in agreement with what he was saying, but that
didn't matter. He was talking to them, not me. Why is this so goddamn

important? I interrogated myself. This is just a man who is used to talking to men. No harm intended.

But he made me invisible, I countered. And I can't stand that. I am here at the table, and yet I don't exist.

I wanted to wave my arms wildly and make a scene. Yoo-hoo, here I am.

Applause. The power broker rose and worked his way past the standing line of governors eager to shake his hand. I watched him go by, his eyes focusing deliberately ahead, his body identifying the exit well in advance.

The next speaker was being welcomed to the podium: Senator Robert Dole from Kansas. He greeted the governors. Then he paused and made special reference to Governor Martha Layne Collins and me.

I beamed. Elizabeth, his wife, had surely made him aware.

Two years later, again at the National Governors' Conference, I sat as a member of the National Governors' Association Energy and Environment Committee. Governor Arch Moore, Jr., of West Virginia was the chair. I had come prepared to do battle on acid rain. Moore, from a coal-mining state, had every intention of denying me that chance.

This was his second time around in the executive suite. He had made a comeback in 1985. The sound of his soft Southern speech was hardened by his eyes, wary as a turtle's head poking out of his shell.

"Gentlemen," he said, banging the gavel. "It's time we begin this meeting."

Two governors turned in my direction and shook their heads. I thanked them with a nod.

At the end of the meeting, I went up to the chairman. "Governor, I hope you take no offense, but it bothers me when you address the committee as Gentlemen. I would appreciate it if you would acknowledge the fact that there are two women governors in the room."

Governor Moore looked nonplussed.

Before he could reply, I turned and left, executing a small leap in the air on my way out. I'd done it.

When the meeting resumed in the afternoon, Moore recognized me. "Will the gentlewoman, gentle lady, gentle person. . . ."

Laughter erupted in uncontrollable spurts from various corners of the room, not certain whether to shut itself off.

"What is it you want to be called, did you say, young lady? Would it be Governess?" he queried mockingly, pressing on the last syllable until it hurt.

C-Span is filming. Keep cool.

"I would like to be called Governor, just like you, Governor Moore."

Each word was heavy on my tongue. Enunciating was such effort. If only I could have been witty, making him laugh before he knew he'd been struck.

Armed with a title like "Governor," I had believed, gender questions could no longer harm me. After all, I had won over a male opponent. The answer was self-explanatory. Was there anything more to discuss?

Yes.

And no.

Most of the time, during my three terms as governor of Vermont, I functioned as any other governor, and that is how I was judged. But in a sense, my gender made me different from the start, and while the difference often faded, it never went away. The precise effect, however, was difficult to measure because boundaries blurred. It was impossible to draw a line between my womanhood and other inherited characteristics. Being a woman was a part of my being, but it was difficult to say which part. Were I a man, I might also have been soft-spoken and inclined toward compromise. But behavior that we readily accept in a man, we may tolerate less well in a woman, and vice versa. The deeper one explores these gender issues, the more difficult it is to reach conclusions. Most gender generalizations are inevitably flawed, because, like all generalities, specific experiences will frequently contradict them.

That does not mean that we cannot make them, however. Everybody does, constantly. If I did not make gender generalizations about myself, others would make them about me. I could not help reacting. Each day, in a myriad of small and often quickly forgotten ways, I was acutely conscious that I was a woman carrying out a job that had traditionally been performed by a man. The net impact was both draining and exhilarating in almost equal measure. I saw my life through a double lens of gender assumptions, one layer made by me, the other by everyone else. At times the woman figure became abstracted, and I was compared with this "other woman," whether I liked it or not. Sometimes the two of us got confused—me, the individual, and she, the archetypal woman. I was forced to defend her, whether I knew her or not. Sometimes I stood up for her, and other times I disavowed her. There were days when I wanted to rip her poster off the wall, and there were days when I saw her face in the mirror.

A few months into my first year in office, an article appeared in the *Burlington Free Press*: "John Dooley, the Little Governor." As secretary of administration, John was my frequent spokesman.

We had established a daily routine. Each morning began with a staff meeting at which John and I and five or six other members of my immediate staff would plan the strategy for the day. John took great pains never to take a position on a question without first discussing it with me and getting my approval. Most often, we agreed. When the "Little Governor" story came out, he was deeply embarrassed. I tried to be amused, but John and I knew what had happened. Power was slipping from its unaccustomed female height to find its natural level: the male behind the throne.

Some forms of gender bias were subtle, relying on tone and language to make the point: men are strong, and women are less so. In the fall of 1990, when Dick Snelling was governor-elect once again, a headline above a story describing budget problems read "Snelling Eager to Get Back in the Ring." A few weeks earlier, I, facing similar news, had been "beset by budget woes." He was the fighter, whereas I had been the victim; active male versus passive female, each of us true to our gender stereotypes, reinforced by our acquired image and actual experience. He was the businessman, with his shirt sleeves rolled up. I could not roll my sleeves up to the elbow.

Certain adjectives are attached to women regardless of their individual temperament. "Hysterical" and "strident" are most common. Less than a year after I left public office, and Governor Howard Dean had succeeded Richard Snelling, Dean announced a reduction in revenue estimates and proposed midyear budget adjustments. An editorial concluded that "In similar circumstances Madeleine Kunin would have been shrill with anxiety. . . ."

I nearly became shrill when I read it. How could they describe me that way? In my eighteen years of public life, I had been scrupulously self-controlled, sometimes to a fault. If anything, I had been charged with being too distant, even cool. No matter. The writer had plucked the adjective from his subconscious and put it in the sentence where it fit: woman/shrill. I speculated whether the writer was reflecting a yearning for the "take charge" father figure following the uncertain single parenthood of Mom. I would never know.

There were times, however, when I was confident that gender stereotypes had been laid to rest. I and the female members of my staff had proven, had we not, during six years in the executive branch, that the experience of growing up female was not a political handicap to be overcome, like a stutter. No longer did we have to decipher another code in order to speak the language. Now when men walked into our meetings, they had to decode us.

I don't know what Tom Salmon thought the day he made an appointment to see me in my office to discuss a matter of interest relating to Green Mountain Power Company, of which he was chairman of the board. I surmise that in a prior strategy meeting, a colleague might have said, "You go, Tom. As a Democrat and as a former governor you can talk to her."

When he stepped into my office he was greeted by three women: Ellen Fallon, my legal counsel; Liz Bankowski, secretary of civil and military affairs; and me. We sat on one side of the room; he sat on the other.

The question he posed was, What kind of role does the state intend to play with the utilities and Hydro-Quebec? The utilities were eager to sign their own agreement with the Canadians and regarded the state's involvement unfavorably. My goal as governor was to assure that profits from the sale of Hydro-Quebec power would accrue to Vermont rate payers, rather than exclusively to the stockholders. Potentially, Vermont could be a conduit for low-cost electricity to southern New England and thereby reduce Vermont utility costs. Ellen played bad cop. I played good. Liz kept the dialogue moving.

I paused midway and photographed the scene: three women hanging tough; the man was doing the asking, we were giving the answers. A first for us; a first, no doubt, for Tom Salmon.

AFTER I LEFT public office, a woman lobbyist I knew expressed her regret. "You know, we were much in demand while you were governor. They felt they had to have a woman up front. Now we're no longer needed. The guys are back."

The ripple effect of a woman in a governor's office is ultimately a powerful catalyst for change in the lives of many, many other women. Not only could women envision themselves in a variety of new roles, women who before might not have thought of a career in state government could now see themselves there. The high visibility of a woman governor had instantly enlarged the applicant pool for positions. Women who may have been in the habit of screening themselves out of top jobs because of their perceived lack of credentials became more willing to take chances.

The result was that we had a very big reservoir of female applicants for positions all over state government.

When I made appointments, I took the approach that any chief executive officer would take: I was determined to find the most competent people to serve in state government; I relied heavily on the informal network of people I had worked with, gone to school with, and knew personally. The appointment of a transition team, and the voluntary efforts of several corporate personnel directors on loan to Vermont, extended the search beyond the perimeters of my experience. Nevertheless, the network mattered.

My network was different because it stemmed from my circle: instead of the Old Boys, we were the Old Girls. The difference between how I made appointments, compared with my predecessors in the executive office, was subtle but significant.

Sallie Soule, commissioner of the Department of Employment and Training, was the ringleader. "The men have looked out for one another for years; we've got to do the same thing," she earnestly proclaimed.

Sallie had been born into comfortable affluence, but would not settle for the life of a Smith graduate of the class of 1950. She had been expected to be content with days on the golf course and evenings at charity balls, but Sallie's social conscience made her ask for more. It never failed her. She shared it generously with me. A successful businesswoman who had devoted much of her time to volunteer activities, she considered running for the Vermont state legislature in 1976. We discussed the pros and cons of her decision one spring afternoon at a leisurely ladies' lunch in our friend Priscilla Welsh's kitchen. Admiring Priscilla's beautiful flower arrangement while tasting her chilled pureed-carrot soup, we women looked as if we were enjoying a typical ladies' lunch. But instead of the recipe for carrot soup, we were figuring out the formula to get Sallie Soule elected.

The table agreed she should run. Sallie had high standing in the community and was refreshingly outspoken. She would have no problem getting elected, even as a Democrat in a solid Republican district.

"Do it, Sallie," I had urged. "You'll be great."

And she was. Sallie was elected to her first term the same year I was elected Democratic whip. She reminded me, years later, that thanks to my intervention, she had gotten the appointment she wanted on the Ways and Means Committee.

In 1984, I had asked her to be the cochair of my campaign for governor with Tom Salmon. The day after the election, she became a key member of the transition budget-writing team. By then, she had served two terms in the Vermont Senate, where she had held a seat on the Appropriations Committee. Five months later I appointed Sallie commissioner of employment and training, where she won national recognition for reorganizing the department.

In 1978, Sallie ran in the same two-member district as did Gretchen Morse, a Republican and former social worker with two school-age children. This was Gretchen's first run for public office. The two women ignored their different party labels and campaigned together.

I served with Gretchen, too, in the legislature; her seat was directly in front of mine. I watched her grow from a curious freshman to an authoritative leader who could steer complex state-aid-reform legislation through the General Assembly. Her success was due in part to her impressive and unusual alliance with her conservative committee chairman, Peter Giuliani.

Six years later, I would be looking for a secretary of the Agency of Human Services. I narrowed the list down to two people: one candidate had worked for state government in Massachusetts; the other was Gretchen.

Sallie lobbied. "Gretchen would be terrific. She understands all the issues, she'll work well with the legislature, and she'll give you total loyalty." Sallie's judgment reinforced my own. So I matched Gretchen up with a seasoned deputy, Jim O'Rourke, a member of my transition team who had held a number of management positions in the Agency of Human Services for eleven years. Would he mind being second in command to Gretchen? No, on the contrary, that arrangement would suit him fine.

I wondered, Will this marriage work? In fact, the two became inseparable, each providing strengths for the other. Under the old rules, of course, their roles would have been reversed.

I asked Sallie Soule to team up with Kathy Hoyt, a woman who had been in and out of state government for several years and had taken the last five years off to take care of her two young sons. Now she was ready to return to work. Sallie was delighted to work with Kathy and became her mentor. When Sallie left state government after three and a half years, Kathy succeeded her as commissioner. In five years, I appointed Kathy secretary of civil and military affairs to replace Liz Bankowski.

Susan Crampton, a partner in a CPA firm, had twice volunteered to be the treasurer of my campaign. I was impressed with her professional competence and sought her out after my election: Would she be interested in a position in state government? Her first answer was no. Then she called back: "Yes, I believe I would." She became the first woman to head Vermont's Agency of Transportation.

Patricia Thomas and I had shared an office thirteen years before when we both were part-time instructors at Trinity College in Burlington. I had organized a panel discussion on how women can manage to combine family and career at which Pat was one of the speakers. When she applied for a position in state government, I knew immediately who she was: a woman whose career had evolved as mine had. Since we had left Trinity, Pat had gotten her Ph.D. in public management. She looked good on paper, but could I take the chance that she could transfer her academic skills to state government? She assured me that she could. The entire Trinity College network was behind her, including two Sisters of Mercy who were the past and present presidents of the college. So I appointed Pat Thomas director of the Department of General Services, where she did an outstanding job. When Kathy Hoyt became secretary of civil and military affairs, I appointed Pat to succeed her.

Jeanne Van Vlandren, an analyst in budget and management, had worked in state government for ten years. Not until I interviewed her for director of labor and industry did I discover that she did not have a college degree. She had dropped out of college and was self-educated. I was concerned whether her limited formal education would enable her to handle an administrative position. She was certain she had the skills to move on; this was what she had always wanted and she promised not to let me down.

I talked it over with Liz.

"Let's take the chance. She's got the drive and dedication. Labor and industry, always headed by a man, and usually a lawyer, is nevertheless a small agency with seventy-five people to supervise."

"It's sort of a starter agency," Liz observed.

I agreed.

In no time, Jeanne began to shine.

Ellen Fallon came recommended as my legal counsel by John Dooley. She was the best-qualified lawyer he knew, soon to be president of the Vermont Bar Association. Ellen was not keen on serving in state government, but she was excited by the prospect of working for the first woman governor of Vermont. That is why she said yes. In two years, when Ellen returned to private practice, she was succeeded by another woman, Jeanne Baker, who decided to work in state government for similar reasons.

Any governor has his or her natural allies, people who are drawn to an administration because of personal allegiance or a shared cause. I had mine. The difference, I felt, was that in my case we attracted a network of women and men who might otherwise not have envisioned themselves in these jobs, a group that had rarely been sought out before. Many had policy reasons that inspired them to serve, including a strong commitment to education and the environment. And they shared a common excitement about working in a woman-led administration.

My timing, as I look back, was fortuitous. Ten years earlier, recruiting women into state government would have been more difficult, and there wouldn't have been such a large pool of competent women candidates. But a new wave of talented women had gone to law school or medical school and pursued their careers in the 1970s, and they had accumulated the credentials to assume management positions in the 1980s.

Mollie Beattie, for example, had enrolled in the graduate forestry program at the University of Vermont several years after working as a newspaper reporter and for Outward Bound, the women's movement having motivated her to enter a nontraditional field. So she had the credentials that enabled me to appoint her to a position never before held by a woman: director of forests, parks, and recreation, the first woman in the country to hold that job. One of her male predecessors, Jim Wilkinson, enthusiastically backed her appointment, for he considered Mollie "outstanding."

The appointment that gave me the most personal pleasure was of more modest proportions. Teresa Randall, a British war bride, had for years worked in the food line at the statehouse cafeteria, dishing out breakfast and lunch to legislators and staff. From the snippets of conversation I had with her as I waited to reach the cash register, I was sure that Teresa had potential for a better job. Her well-groomed appearance and bright-eyed sparkle made me think, frankly, that she belonged on the legislative side of the counter.

Shortly after my election, I asked her to be the governor's office receptionist. Teresa worked at that job for less than a year before she moved on and up to become assistant sergeant of arms at the statehouse. Every time I saw her, we exchanged knowing glances: her career was a clear example of how so many women can assume much more responsibility if they are given the chance.

Women were earning their credentials, their resumes were filling up with graduate degrees, but when placed head to head with male competitors, they sometimes still lost out because they had not followed the predictable career track. Gretchen Babcock, whom I promoted from deputy director to director of the Department of Banking and Insurance, could not decide between two strong candidates vying to be the department's legal counsel. She decided to run them both by me, and I interviewed each of them. One was a young man in his midthirties who was working in another area of state government. Beads of energy erupted with his every gesture.

"Do you think you could transfer your skills from that department to this?" I asked.

"No problem. The work is very comparable. I have no doubt I can do it."

"Even though the fields are different?"

"Yes. I'm a quick study."

There was no doubt that he was. His competitor was a pleasant-looking woman in her forties who had recently completed law school in Washington, D.C., with honors. I noted a fourteen-year gap between her graduation from Radcliffe College and her entry into Georgetown Law School, and I filled in the blanks. Married, two children, several years of unpaid activities, mostly volunteer. I knew this woman. Her life could have been mine.

She explained that she had worked in a related field in Washington, but she took great care to specify that "it wasn't precisely in this field. So I can't tell you that I have the required expertise to do it."

Her recitation of her qualifications was agonizingly precise, not allowing one assumption of her competence to be made that could not be sustained by the evidence. She was the good student who had gotten every question right by dint of hard work and meticulous attention to detail. She drew a clear line between what she knew and what she did not. Honesty did not permit her to cross it even when what she wanted was just on the other side.

The young man had been tutored differently. He had learned to reach beyond specificity, to imagine himself where he wanted to be, and then get himself there. There was no demarcation line between who he now was and who he could become.

Had I been a man interviewing these two candidates for the job, I imagine I would have recognized my earlier self in him: a bright, ambitious young fellow on the way up. Somewhat overreaching, perhaps, but why not? That's how I was at his age: cocksure. The woman? Qualified, perhaps, but not enough confidence. I need an aggressive person for this job who can take on the big boys in this business. His resume moves up in a straight line, uninterrupted, from college, to law school, to work, and it shows serious intent, commitment, and ambition. She took time off to have a family. Now I fully understand that. My wife did the same thing. But it slowed her down. She's lost ten years. She'd be well qualified to work somewhere in the department, but not at this level.

I read her resume differently. The ten years she "lost" were for me, judging from what I had done, when she "found" valuable experiences. As homemaker and volunteer she had gained useful organizational skills, as well as important insights about how other people live, what they worry about, and what they aspire to. That she went to law school after raising a family reveals a special kind of ambition. It requires tremendous drive to succeed while meeting the demands of both family and school. If she gets this job, she will see it as a new beginning, a delayed fulfillment, more motivating perhaps than immediate success would have been for the man. Something tells me that she will give this job her all.

And she did. In four years' time, she became commissioner of her department. (Her predecessor, Gretchen Babcock, had followed a similar route, clerking for her law degree after her children were enrolled in school.)

Not everyone always agreed with my assessment, of course. When I named state representative Amy Davenport to the newly created position of family-court judge, two lawyers vehemently opposed her. Representative Davenport, they wrote to me, was not qualified. The only reason I had appointed her to this position, they claimed, was because I was returning a political favor; she had helped win passage of the family-court bill, which had created this new judicial position, and this was her reward. She had insufficient litigation experience.

I replied that Representative Davenport had met the qualifications set by the Judicial Selection Committee, which had included her name along with others on a list of candidates from which I would make my choice. And she had extensive experience in her private practice, which specialized in family law. In addition I knew her to be thoughtful and intelligent, and I was confident that she could learn what she needed to know. Her own life experience as a divorced parent, now remarried, would be valuable to her on the bench. Most significant, she had a judicial temperament: she would be fair. Yes, her qualifications were not entirely traditional, but for this new position, her skills were precisely what was needed.

The concept of "different but equally qualified" would not be immediately appreciated, but within two years, Judge Davenport was receiving universal praise for her work on the bench.

It is difficult to measure the full ripple effect on a state that comes when a woman chief executive takes command. I knew that the concentric circles had reached another shore when I received a letter from a fifth-grade girl. In her best cursive writing she wrote: "My friend and I wanted to let you know what we are going to be when we grow up. I'm going to be Governor and my friend is going to be President."

For another ten-year-old girl, who happened to get a ride with me in the back of the convertible in a parade, just meeting a woman governor was clearly a thrill. "What an exciting week it's been," she bubbled. "Here I am riding with the governor and last Tuesday my cat had kittens."

In the first few months of my administration, I realized that my public presence alone had a powerful effect, regardless of who I was or what I said. "You have become public dream property," a woman wrote to me, years later.

One practical consequence for my administration was that women continued to move up through the ranks of Vermont state government, sometimes encouraged by me, often by one another. Patricia Walton, having first served her internship as a budget analyst and then a deputy, became director of the Office of Budget and Management; in turn, Patricia encouraged her deputy, Margaret Maxfield, to apply for her position when she moved from budget and management to the legislative side of the aisle to head the Joint Fiscal Office, the equivalent of the Congressional Budget Office.

No longer were women managers in state government isolated examples of success. They became a trend. The change was apparent in the statistics: in my second term, women composed approximately 40 percent of my appointments, including boards and commissions. When I made my appointments, I never considered a quota system, nor did I have a personal target in mind. If I had announced a strategy to appoint more women in state government, I would have risked being accused of unfairness. But I did reach out.

I'd be handed a list of ten men to serve on a commission, and understand that once, perhaps, this had been normal. I would scan the names and know that, now, it was not.

"Where are the women?" I would ask.

"Sorry, Governor, we couldn't find any qualified women to serve on the Science and Technology Advisory Committee."

"I'm sure if you go back, make some calls, and go beyond the usual network, you'll find some."

And they did. But it took the second try. Established power circles are small and tight, and people in government and business go around and around tapping the same people again and again. The women and men who are left out are not necessarily less qualified, but are simply not in the loop. The qualifications for most jobs have been designed by those who hold them, and their main purpose is to perpetuate one another by appointing people who best fit their own image. It's not that there is a male conspiracy at work to keep women out; it simply happens that those in power are more comfortable with people who resemble themselves.

Adding women to the circle does not lower the standards, as is sometimes claimed, but only makes the inner circle larger and enables women, when they reach the top, to do the same thing: to appoint and hire people like themselves.

The change in the numbers of women in my administration does not tell the whole story. Over six years, a subtler change occurred; we began to note a difference in the established political culture. It manifested itself slowly and discreetly—indeed it was barely recognizable—until we were about to move out. But one commissioner identified it early on. When asked what it was like to work for a woman governor, she told an interviewer, "No more little jokes about women; not even the deference paid to women in that lovely, gentlemanly way. Nobody does that in state government anymore. You just walk into a room and you realize what the difference is. Nobody dares make even those wonderful, warm statements about a woman being in charge, or a woman's opinion. It is just now taken for granted, and it really is different." For at every top-level policy meeting, women were present, not at the periphery, but in the center. And this pattern became the norm.

The men in my administration rebelled when, in the final weeks of my last term, I hosted a "women's lunch" for the writer Jamaica Kincaid. In retaliation they jokingly requested a "men's lunch." So I invited another Vermont author, a man, to a similar lunch, but he canceled just before the soup was served. Was it his absence or the all-male table that made the conversation lag halfway through?

"Hey, this isn't any fun," Tom Menson, secretary of administration, noted.

"It seems so odd, it isn't normal," Mike Wilson, the press secretary, chimed in.

An air of self-consciousness weighed down the conference room. Without realizing it, perhaps they had gotten used to having women colleagues around. "I'm beginning to think this was not such a good idea," George

Hamilton, head of the Office of Policy Research and Planning, said, with his eye on the clock. We soon adjourned the lunch.

Ironically, the shift in the power balance between men and women in the administration sometimes helped to *avoid* controversy rather than create it. For example, a policy for pay equity for men and women working in state government was implemented with little rancor. A study had been ordered by the legislature the previous year that had recommended specific salary changes throughout state government, raising some salaries and lowering others. Liz later told an interviewer when she looked back on our successful implementation of this controversial policy, "This is a phenomenal task in every other state that has tried it. It almost happened without anyone noticing it here. I began to think that this was due to the fact that not only did Madeleine set the climate for doing that, but we have so many women in top management positions to effect it, that it happened here . . . without a whole lot of wringing of hands."

The *policy* impact of a large number of women in a state administration is more difficult to assess. Male appointees shared my legislative goals with the same enthusiastic tenacity as the women did, and several—like Tom Menson, George Hamilton, and Jonathan Lash, secretary of the Agency of Environmental Conservation—became close and important confidants. Gender did not make a visible difference most of the time, yet it influenced the shape of the agenda. It seemed that a different gravity was at work: certain issues rose to the top that otherwise would have sunk to the bottom. My political priorities stemmed from various experiences and observations, and they expressed the totality of who I was and how I had lived my life. In that respect I was no different from any other politician. Each one of us extracts policies from the mosaic of our lives. The distinction was that I ended up with a somewhat altered list of priorities than my male counterparts. I claimed no exclusive hold on any of the "women's issues" on my agenda, such as protecting the right to a legal abortion and advocating for children; a number of male governors espoused the same causes. What was distinct, however, was the intensity with which I pursued certain of them. As a woman I had lived with the absence of power, and the issues that aroused my fiercest passion and strongest commitment were related to that core of my female vulnerability. Instinctively I was determined to buttress the weak wall of the female experience that had depended for centuries on the beneficence of men.

The certainty of law, I knew, could release women from that precarious dependency. Reproductive freedom provides an example. The question of a woman's access to a legal abortion is so explosive because it is central to a woman's ability to live her life without having to first obtain male protection or permission, which may or may not be granted. Rather than pleading for protection as a child would, it must be given to her, as a right, by law. During my tenure as governor I took a strong position on the right of a woman to choose to end an unwanted pregnancy. My first test regarded Medicaid funding of abortions. Prior to my administration, Vermont had been sued for not funding abortions and a district-court judge ruled against the state. The choice had to be made whether or not to appeal the decision to the Vermont Supreme Court. By accepting the verdict, Vermont, with my tacit agreement, was required to fund Medicaid abortions, and it continues to do so. In my third term I became active at the national level in defense of maintaining *Roe* v. *Wade,* the 1973 case that made abortion legal. When the U.S. Supreme Court handed down the *Webster* decision on July 3, 1989, giving states more latitude to restrict *Roe* v. *Wade,* I debated the pro-choice position on television opposite pro-life governors several times. I recruited nine other governors to file an *amicus brief* before the Supreme Court on a case that would have required abortion clinics in Illinois to meet standards similar to hospitals, further restricting access to abortion, especially for poorer women. (The case was later settled out of court.) And that spring I linked arms with the pro-choice marchers in Washington.

In 1992, after I had left public office, when I testified at the Senate hearings in opposition to the confirmation of Justice Clarence Thomas, I appeared along with a panel of three other women: Faye Wattleton, then president of Planned Parenthood; Kate Michelman, president of NARAL; and Sarah Weddington, the Texas lawyer who had argued *Roe* v. *Wade.* At one point, Senator Alan Simpson of Wyoming expressed his impatience with our panel: "But I think you know, you who worked so hard for this cause of choice, that I agree with you on this issue and have all my public life." Then with obvious frustration he asked, "When will somebody cut the high drama that this is the end of the earth if this happens one way?"

For Senator Simpson, choice was one issue on a long list, and he had checked it off with his vote. But for the women testifying it was central to the dignity of their lives. Without the ability to control reproduction, we could go back to being "kept barefoot and pregnant."

When we gathered outside the Senate chamber after the hearing, I was surprised by my need for emotional release. For a moment we four hugged one another. None of us was a political neophyte; we were all experienced, confident women. Yet, lined up face-to-face with the Senate Judiciary Committee, we had felt powerless. We were pleading a case that the men on the committee had the authority to decide. The inequity of the power structure between rulers and subjects was heightened by the inequity of gender—men on one side of the table, women on the other—and the scale tipped farther when weighted with the subject matter. Had the committee been discussing the military budget, I suspect we would not have felt so angry, because that has been a traditional male bailiwick. But the committee was making a decision about an issue that exposed our continuing vulnerability to male overpowerment. Perhaps that is why we embraced when it was all over.

Intensity is a critical factor in politics, where almost every issue has competitors vying for equal attention. Each politician has priorities, and they are promoted with various degrees of energy, depending on accumulated values and personal experience. The issues that survive the competitive weeding-out process are those that have the fiercest defenders.

(The power of passion in politics was demonstrated in the summer of 1993 by Senator Carol Moseley-Braun when she opposed Senator Jesse Helms in his effort to pass an amendment that would have renewed the United Daughters of the Confederacy's patent on the Confederate flag insignia. The senator attacked racism head-on, forcing the senators to jettison the time-honored decorum that had wrapped this issue in senatorial courtesy. The result was a highly unusual reversal of a prior vote, and a victory for Senator Moseley-Braun, 75-25. As an African American and as a woman, she was an outsider who brought her raw life experience to the Senate floor with a force that exposed the ugly truth of racism and allowed it to be voted down.)

While many male politicians have been strong advocates for child care, few of them have known themselves the agonizing choice that many women must make every day between their obligation to their family and their work. Nor have they known how difficult it is to find good care for their children, and neither have they experienced the financial and spiritual poverty endured by women who have been abandoned to raise children alone. That is why many female elected officials support policies for child care and family leave so strongly. A study by the Center for the American Woman and Politics at Rutgers University concluded that women legislators were more likely to give top priority to "women's rights policies" and "public policies related to their traditional roles as caregivers in the family and society—e.g., policies dealing with children and families and health care."

It is not surprising then that the establishment of a new family court rose to the top of my agenda. The institutions that govern families had been largely created for women by men. But now we had the extraordinary opportunity to redefine them, to reshape them, on the basis of both women's and men's experiences.

My agenda sometimes differed from that of my male colleagues for another reason: as a woman I had fewer commitments to the existing power structure and more in common with those who lived outside it. Not being connected, either financially or socially, to powerful lobbying interests, I, like many women, was more of a free agent, and it was natural for me to take a citizen-consumer position, rather than a corporate one, on questions such as protecting upland streams or setting standards for development. More recently these issues have become less polarized as the public has demanded a higher standard of environmental consciousness, and both the business and environmental sectors have moved toward mutually agreeable solutions on many fronts. But to be an effective advocate for fundamental change, some detachment from the establishment is necessary, and perhaps that is why some women politicians tend to align themselves with the more progressive causes.

What is generally referred to as society's "power structure" is, in fact, a large, amorphous system with no definable parameters. Men have traditionally occupied every corner of that system and have naturally collaborated to influence it. Women, to have an equivalent impact, must be similarly scattered throughout the power structure in strategic positions. Perhaps that was why the influence of women on policy decisions in my administration was greatest when we supported one another's priorities from individual key positions in various sectors of state government and advocacy groups.

On some issues, such as expanding subsidized child-care services for working parents, I saw a powerful coalition taking shape. Two key commissioners, Sallie Soule and Gretchen Morse, were strongly supportive, for both of them saw increased child-care funding as a solid investment that would enable Vermont families to become financially more secure. Further backing for child-care funding came from the legislature, one-third of which was composed of women. And public support emanated from a now-enlightened constituency with a record number of women in the work force, many of whose working lives were dependent on safe, affordable child care. And many employers, now dependent on women workers, supported the trend. Early in my first term, I sponsored a conference on employee-supported child care that was widely attended and helped disseminate the value of family-friendly policies in the workplace. The cumulative effect was powerful: my use of the governor's bully pulpit, my commissioners' enthusiasm, the legislators' support, and the public's understanding allowed us to mobilize what was already there and give it a focus. In the 1990 legislative session in my last term as governor, the full power of strategically located women became most vividly apparent in the debates over the family-court bill, which would change the existing fragmented system—divorce proceedings were handled in one court, adoption in another, and abuse and neglect cases in yet another—into a single system in which one judge would handle all matters that pertained to families.

For twenty years, various proposals to establish a new family court had been debated in Vermont. Always there were good reasons for the bill not to pass. A group of assistant judges objected because they feared they would lose power under the new arrangement, a group of lawyers objected to the new procedures they would have to follow, and legislators did not want to alienate either group. Neither did anyone know how to fund it. Others questioned the necessity for change: Would a family court really help families? The old legislative adage "When in doubt, vote no" was applied. The status quo, ancient and heavy as an elephant, lowered itself down on the bill once again.

But in 1990 the elephant got up and walked away; the family-court bill became law. Why? Several factors converged to make it happen. For the first time, the family-court bill had received the endorsement of the governor, the Vermont Bar Association, and the judicial branch. Never had there been such unanimity among the key players. A moment before I signed the bill into law at a ceremony in my executive office, one of the professional advocates for the family court said to me, "We knew that if we were ever going to do it, it had to be this year, while you were in office."

The federal government inadvertently gave the legislation a boost by demanding that states adopt tougher child-support regulations. A changed judicial structure was needed to implement the law effectively. (Figures released in 1992 ranked Vermont the number-one state for the collection of child support.) Our reward for compliance would be additional federal funds that could be used to change the current system over to a family court. The rest of the money would be generated by increased court fees.

With this broad coalition, we formed a phalanx around the bill, protecting it from each assault. All complex and far-reaching pieces of legislation run into trouble in their final hours. The bill's survival does not depend on the merits at this point, but on the skills of the rescue party there to save it. In 1990 each time the family-court bill fell into a coma, someone came to its aid.

"We need new language. The assistant judges are furious with what we've got. They have enough votes on the committee to kill the bill," the three women House members of the Committee of Conference, bargaining with senators over the bill, reported to me in my office. So they wrote new language. The Judiciary Committee chairman, Amy Davenport, rallied her members, and Sally Fox chaired the Conference Committee. Both women had practiced family law. The next day, a new problem threatened. "There's not enough money in the bill to fund the new positions," the conferees reported.

"We'll find it," rejoined Pat Walton, head of budget and management. With pencil and paper and a keen eye, Pat found the money.

New technical problems arose almost every hour. Gretchen Morse and Jim O'Rourke, secretary and deputy of the Agency of Human Services, established virtual residence in the back room of my office, guiding the bill through more than a hundred tense revisions. Four women senators rallied their male colleagues' support in a close vote. Their firsthand accounts about the effects of divorce on families countered the filibuster of another senator, now divorced, who feared the family court would threaten fathers' rights. The bill's strict child-support provisions were also hotly debated.

The quiet but determined collaboration among the women in the House and Senate and within the administration was not planned. Nor did it exclude men, many of whom were enthusiastic supporters of the bill and worked hard for its passage. But this core of intensely committed women fought fiercely to keep this bill alive because, for them, the family court was not another issue tagged on to a long list of issues. A maniacal intensity propelled this legislation forward because of the high hopes that lay behind it: that a family court would equalize the balance of power between men and women within the judicial system by recognizing the vulnerability of women and children when they were at the most fragile point in their lives.

One provision of the family-court law was the appointment of four new magistrates to decide questions of child support. Based on the requirement that candidates have experience in family law, I appointed four women. When the appointments were announced, one lawyer commented, "I don't know why she couldn't find one qualified man." What

I could not tell him, because of the requirement for judicial-selection confidentiality, was that only one man had applied, and he was less qualified than the female candidates. I would have preferred to appoint more men, but I surmised that so few applied because the salary was lower for magistrates than for judges—one of the less successful compromises in the bill.

On September 26, 1990, I swore in these four new magistrates in Vermont's Supreme Court chamber. The high walls of this austere room, which customarily deflected whispers, now resounded with noise, for a dozen children and babies had taken control. Two three-year-olds were chasing each other over and under chairs, one was playing peekaboo behind the empty row of high-backed chairs reserved for the justices, and another tested the microphone. "Hello everybody, my name is . . ." he announced before his mother grabbed him. Nobody was very well behaved, but it didn't seem to matter. A small table in the center of the room reserved for lawyers' briefs today was spread with coloring books and crayons. Two little ones were busily at work, oblivious to their surroundings.

The chief justice tripped over some kid who had stepped on his robe and gotten under his feet.

I swore the women in, one family group at a time. They had debated— should they wear their robes in their new positions or not? Like many judges, both male and female, they wanted to break down barriers between the public and the court, but they also wanted to retain the respect granted to the judiciary. After much discussion, robes won out.

Patricia Whalen was first. Her baby son in her arms grabbed the beads around her neck, and when she pried his fingers loose, he cried. She repeated the oath, word for word, with minor whimpers of interruption.

Lori Valburn took her oath with her daughter, husband, grandmother, and great-aunt at her side. The grandmother was too feeble to get up and join her at the podium. Lori moved the ceremony over to where she sat.

"Raise your right hand," I instructed.

And she, and her little daughter, did.

"Please repeat after me: 'I shall be true and faithful to the state of Vermont, and the constitution thereof.' " Line by line she recited the words back to me in a clear loud voice that filled the chamber. This woman believes that this is as important as being sworn in as chief justice of the United States Supreme Court, I said to myself.

Chief Administrative Justice Stephen Martin watched from the sidelines. When he first met with the new magistrates, he had instructed them to choose a chief judge from their ranks whom he would deal with. They had said no; they would all function as equals, and administrative tasks would be handled collegially.

A five-year-old boy stopped short in front of Chief Justice Frederic Allen. "Could you please tie my shoe?"

The gray-haired judge knelt down, and his black robe spilled to the ground like pools of ink swirling around him.

This merry scene was a crazy, happy chaos that only families with little children could create. What better way to inaugurate the new family court? And who could understand it as well as these laughing women balancing babies on their hips? This was a revolution. Four women had stormed in together, and now they celebrated together, their womanhood, their motherhood, and their love of justice. It was as if the stoic blindfolded figure holding the balance scales in her hand for thousands upon thousands of years had set her burden down. Enough! I'm tired of being a symbol. And with that, she took her seat behind the bench.

I enjoyed a feast of celebrations around the opening of new family courts in every county. These were my parting gifts.

On October 1, 1990, for example, District Judge Shireen Fisher inaugurated the new family court in Lamoille County. At the start of the dedication, she thanked "the Lamoille County Bar Association for providing the balloons."

Balloons? When had a bar association last been thanked for balloons? I wondered. Bunches of colored balloons flapped their loud approval against the courthouse pillars. It might have been a birthday party.

One hundred children sitting in folding chairs on the lawn cheered happily for the Vermont Bar Association. They had marched to the courthouse from their redbrick elementary school situated just beyond the other side of the town common in Hyde Park.

Judge Fisher began her lesson. Earlier, she had invited the children to tour the courthouse. "Some of these children have already been in court as a result of divorce or abuse cases. Many were afraid to come today," she told me. "I wanted to make the court familiar to them, a place where good things can happen."

"How many of you know who the highest elected official of the state of Vermont is?" she asked from the podium on the courthouse steps.

Thirty hands shot up.

"The governor!"

"Right, and here she is."

I stood up, and they applauded.

"What do you call the number-one judge in the state?"

A tense moment for the chief justice.

One hand rose into the air. "Is it the chief justice or something?"

"Right, and let me introduce him."

Justice Allen looked visibly relieved.

At the ribbon-cutting ceremony for the Windsor County family court that afternoon, Magistrate Patricia Whalen approached the symbolic red ribbon stretched across the room with reverence.

"I'd like to think this is the umbilical cord I am about to cut, and we are giving birth to a new child in the judicial family . . ."

A few eyebrows went up.

"There were painful birth pangs, but . . ."

Patti did not stop. She continued with her best metaphor.

No more touchdowns! I exclaimed to myself. How many sports metaphors had I sat through, trying to comprehend the game?

Later, balancing a glass of punch in one hand and shaking hers with the other, I commended her on her courage. She laughed. "This is our language, they might as well get used to it, umbilical cord and all!"

On December 3, 1990, I had the pleasure of swearing in the first woman to be appointed to the Vermont Supreme Court. Until then, few women had met the necessary qualifications to serve on the state's highest court. With a vacancy that year, I had a solid pool to choose from, and when I announced Denise Johnson's name, it generated wide approval.

She had prepared her remarks carefully, incorporating a quotation from Abigail Adams when she had reminded her husband to "Remember the ladies. . . . Do not put such unlimited power into the hands of Husbands. Remember all Men would be tyrants if they could." Her words were wonderful, but it was the image that dazzled; the first woman governor swearing in the first woman to the Vermont Supreme Court. Each of us was wearing red. When Denise took her place across from me, an exchange of glances knotted our individual excitement together. The power of bequeathing power may be the greatest power of all.

Denise's two-and-a-half-year-old daughter, Lily, wearing a red flowered dress and white lace collar, was restless. She wandered back and forth between her mother, her father, and her grandparents, too busy to decide where to sit. Halfway through the oath, while her right hand was raised, Denise reached out and took Lily by the other hand and kept her at her side. That seemed to do the trick. She liked being in the center with her mother.

The retiring justice, Louis Peck, ceremoniously helped Denise put on her new black robe. Then, according to protocol, she took his seat at the bench. Lily came over and sat in her lap.

There the justices were, all in black, posing for the photographer: four men, one woman, and Lily, sucking her thumb.

EARLY in my first term I learned that the feminine traits of mediation and consensus building were not always appropriate to the political task at hand. At the end of my first year in office, for example, I became engaged in a heated battle with Vermont's major ski area, Killington. The owners expressed their dismay with me before I took office. During the campaign, Killington's developer, Preston Smith, had backed John Easton, the candidate from the ski resort of Stowe, and when I won, the Vermont Ski Area Association made no effort to hide its disappointment, maintaining a steady diatribe against the people I appointed and the policies I pursued. They consistently objected to the permit process required for building new trails and condominiums, for drawing water from streams for snow making, and for building sewage-disposal systems. When I appointed Jonathan Lash, a former activist in the Natural Resources Defense Council, as my commissioner of water resources (later he was promoted to head the environmental agency), Killington fumed that I was appointing too many "environmentalists." I was confident that once I was in office, Killington would recognize that my administration played by the rules. Certainly, then, they would too.

Governor Snelling, a probusiness governor, had also dueled with Preston Smith. During his administration, signs had been posted at one of the Killington ski lodges blaming the state of Vermont for blocking expansion.

In May 1985, Preston Smith announced that Killington would lay off two hundred workers, which he blamed on the effective freeze on expansion projects attributed to the state-permitting process. I challenged his figures, saying that the layoffs were seasonal and routine: "This is a phenomenon that usually occurs in these months, and it's called the snow melting."

At the same time, Killington reported that it wanted to make snow from treated wastewater. Bumper stickers appeared—KILLINGTON: WHERE THE AFFLUENT MEET THE EFFLUENT. An editorial cartoon in the *Barre-Montpelier Times-Argus* by Jeff Danziger showed two skiers riding up the chair lift carrying toilet plungers with the caption "Uh-oh. Looks like the snowmaking machines are clogged again." A Killington employee who slapped a bumper sticker on his car was sued by the ski area, but subsequently won the case on the grounds of freedom of speech.

On December 30, 1985, David Dillon, Killington spokesman, announced that the owners of Killington and Mount Snow would invest $8.6 million outside Vermont because Vermont environmental regulations made it too difficult to expand. "We go where states are willing to work with us instead of against us," he announced. I reminded him that ski-area expansion had proceded smoothly at three other ski areas: Stratton, Ascutney, and Bolton Valley. I accused Smith of trying to bully the state of Vermont, requesting favored treatment, and embarrassing the ski industry. My final salvo was to call the Killington group "whiners and complainers."

Most newspaper editorials took my side, and the mail ran 4 to 1 in my favor. Never, since I had won the last election, had I received such a response, and I was amazed by the reaction. I had fought back, and it felt good. Plain old outrage had its place. Everywhere I went, I heard, "You give it to 'em, Madeleine. We're with you all the way." Protection of the environment, I discovered, was not an elitist issue. The workers on the shop floor at GE cheered me on; the hook-and-bullet crowd wanted to keep land open so they could hunt and fish.

By getting angry I had become a heroine.

"Not a bad thing to do," Liz observed, "from time to time."

ON MARCH 18, 1985, I issued my first two pardons. In doing so, I had been exceedingly careful. Other governors had gotten into serious trouble by pardoning criminals who became repeat offenders. In six years, I granted few pardons, none for sexual offenders or drunk drivers. Immediately after I had affixed my signature to the pardon document, I called each man on the phone to give him the news myself.

"Hello, this is Governor Kunin speaking."

A voice at the other end said "Yes, Governor."

I tried to picture him, the man about to be absolved of his sin. I only knew his record, typed on a tidy form, to which were clipped letters of recommendation.

"Gratitude" was a word I thought I understood. But I hadn't until now.

"I want to let you know that I have reviewed your request for a pardon and, after careful review, have decided to grant it."

"Thank you, Governor, thank you."

I felt an urge to command him to live a good life, as if my words alone could make it happen.

Granting a pardon, forgiving another human being for his crime, is a great power. No doubt the privilege had ancient origins, once granted only to the king.

IN CONTEMPORARY political life, the hold on power is never constant, I discovered soon after I took office. Others were quick to vie for it. The most eager contenders were the newly elected senators of my own party, who for the first time held a majority in Vermont's upper house. Every proposal I made required their approval, and they did not give it without a struggle. Then on the House side, the newly elected Speaker, Ralph Wright, flexed his political muscles for daily exercise.

The success or failure of my legislative agenda weighed heavily on me. I knew my legislative scorecard would be more carefully tabulated than that of previous governors because I was the first woman and also the first governor to have a Democratic majority in both houses. Each day was filled with meetings with key leaders, committees, and individual legislators. After the morning briefing, I would send my lieutenants into the field to testify before committees and fight for our agenda. Each night, they reported back. I both loved and dreaded the process, depending on the hour, the day, and the results. Negotiation and compromise are at the heart of the legislative process, and a legislative body is the ultimate instrument of consensus building. When it worked, I was euphoric. When it failed, I was miserable.

Looking back, I believe my six-year record for new legislation in Vermont was good; I got my agenda through approximately 90 percent of the time, and achieved a great deal of what I had promised, but only as a consequence of constant attention and enormous effort expended working with individual legislators, committees, and outside constituencies.

One by one, legislators would be invited into my office when a tight vote was imminent. Whole committees would be invited in for lunch. Strategizing on how to get a bill through, and in what form, and when, gave me the concentration of a chess player. When needed, the Speaker would go to work on the floor of the House, lining up votes, one by one. He knew how to count. Usually he won, and most of the time, he agreed with my agenda. When he didn't, he left no doubt.

The mercurial highs and lows of the governor's job were different from anything I had ever experienced or could imagine. Only a summer storm would bear comparison; emotions clouded and cleared quickly, only to change back again, without warning.

On March 26, 1985, I signed my first contract with the state employees' union, representing some seven thousand workers. The executive director of the union and his committee, seated around the oblong wooden table, were all smiles for the camera, pens poised in midair above the document, ready to sign. But the day before, the same man had held a dart between his fingers, and the bull's-eye had been me. Now we sat side by side; having fought the battle, we could declare the peace and feel we had earned it. Never had I run the course so quickly from warfare to reconciliation. The beauty of political conflicts, I knew, was that they got resolved. Solutions emerged because they had to, by a certain time. The illusion of closure, confirmed by joint signatures on a document, was extraordinarily satisfying.

In early January 1986 an opinion poll was published. Good news: my favorability was up from 73 to 76 percent. Common sense told me not to place weight on the improvement, but my psyche refused to listen. Having fed regularly on complaints and problems, the daily bread of politicians, I craved this delicious reward. I kept the news on my tongue like a lozenge, letting it dissolve slowly.

Each day was different, but a reconstruction of an ordinary day conveys the mood and tempo of governing. First thing in the morning I concentrated on a Republican attack on my property-tax-reform proposals, which had led the evening news and were headlined in the morning paper. They were the subject of discussion at our morning staff meeting as we sipped coffee, turned pages, and tossed our reactions on the table. Why had the Senate Democrats, whom I had counted on for help, offered no rebuttal in my defense? They had been difficult from the start. Life had been considerably more interesting and they had gained bigger headlines when there was a Republican governor to attack. Working with a governor of their own party was a hard adjustment. Was that why no one came to my defense, or was it due to a mix-up in my schedule? I had planned to notify key legislators about the property-tax proposal during the regular Thursday-morning legislative reception. If I had gotten to them first, before the press did, maybe they would have been loyal. I found out that my legislative liaison had put the notices in the mailboxes too late in the day for them to pick up before they headed home. No time to dwell on it now, because it was eight-thirty and we were already a half hour behind schedule. Whom was I keeping waiting?

The pace of a day in a governor's life is difficult to chart. As for many executives, the day is broken into five-, ten-, and fifteen-minute segments—some planned, many not—and a half hour on one subject is a long time.

We went through the list of priority bills and checked out their status: Where were they in the process, what were the chances of success, and what needed to be done to move them forward?

"I don't know if we have the votes to pass the drinking age," my legislative liaison, Mary Ashcroft, reported. I had campaigned to raise the drinking age to twenty-one. The House had passed the bill weeks ago. The Senate now balked. I would have to talk to each of the holdouts once again.

"How bad does it look?"

"Close, we might get Gillie, but I don't know. Without him, it'll go down."

Mary had more bad news. My proposed increase in state aid to education was being threatened. "Too much money is what they say. The towns that aren't getting an increase will fight to the death against it."

"We have to mobilize at the grass roots. The towns which will benefit have to get the message out that they desperately need the help," I said. We would have to gather a coalition of education groups to plan the strategy, and I asked Mary to sound them out today.

Meanwhile, my secretary reminded me that I was keeping a candidate for a judgeship waiting, a call from an important town Democratic chairman was on hold, and a radio station wanted me to go on live for the ten o'clock news. Liz informed me that Ralph Wright refused to speak to her until he got the board appointment he wanted for a constituent in Bennington.

That afternoon I was scheduled to go to Springfield to visit a school, and that evening to talk to the Chamber of Commerce. The next day, I would visit the elementary school in Norwich. When would I have time to prepare my remarks for all these places? "Can someone get me talking points for the Chamber? And I need the statistics on state aid for Springfield and Norwich," I told Liz. "How much aid they're getting now, and what they would get under the bill."

The group that had been scheduled for a policy session on a complex utility question had already arrived. A half-hour discussion to sort out the options had been scheduled. "Could you pull out the memo they sent over?" I needed to read it before the meeting. "Ask them if they mind waiting, while I interview the judicial candidate first."

"Before you get started, I just want to remind you that the probate-judge vacancy has to be filled by the end of the week. How many people do you want to interview?" my legal counsel asked.

"The top three. Put the list in my reading material tonight, and I'll let you know in the morning."

The press secretary slipped in. "Have you got time for a quick television interview this afternoon?"

"What do they want to talk about?"

"The drinking age."

"I should do it. It'll give me a chance to push it and put the heat on the Senate."

A little while later Mary returned, after having made her Senate rounds. "I think if you talk to Gillie and one or two other senators, we might pull it off."

"Okay, why don't you ask them to stop by right after lunch, before I leave for Springfield."

"Hate to tell you, but one hundred kids from Bennington are standing in the hall outside waiting to see you. They've been there for half an hour. Tim told them he was sure you'd have a minute. Just to take a picture. They have to get back on the bus before noon."

"Oh, no! How could Tim do this?"

Representative Tim Corcoran had campaigned with me in Bennington. After walking half a block down Main Street with him, I realized I was in the company of an extraordinary political IQ. Tim knew everybody's complete name, the street where they lived, whom they were married to, how many children they had, where they went to school, whether anyone in the family had died in the last year or had a stay in the hospital, and—most important—whether they had voted in the last election. (I suspect he also knew how.) The day after any new person moved into town, Timmy was on their doorstep, voter registration form in hand. No son or daughter turned eighteen in his district without Timmy noting his or her birthday. Not one senior citizen missed the opportunity to vote absentee. The day I was with Timmy, he dropped off some fresh zucchini and squash at the Senior Center, and the ladies were all over him, patting his hand gratefully for his sweet generosity. As I wondered what in the world to do about Timmy's kids in the hall, I remembered the early morning hour on election night in 1984 when Timmy and Ralph Wright had called me at election headquarters from Bennington. "We've got two thousand votes for you, just what you wanted; it'll put you right over the top."

And it had.

"Bring the kids in," I relented.

The children rushed through the door as if it were a fire drill, exuding a mixture of smells usually found on the insides of lunch boxes.

"Everybody just take one little step toward the center, and we can get you all in," my press secretary, who doubled as photographer, instructed.

I was in the center. I was grateful I was tall. That way I could breathe.

"Say cheese!"

"Cheeeeese!" we sang together.

I could not resist giving the group a mini-lesson in state government. As with all school groups, I knew that this was the only chance I would get to make democracy a reality in their lives. So I pointed out to them the portraits of the two women in the statehouse: Edna Beard and Consuelo Bailey.

I looked at my watch. I was way behind schedule. I'd have to cut short the interview and go to the briefing unprepared, reading the memo while the group made its presentation. And when would I have time to prepare for my weekly press conference? It was scheduled for tomorrow at 10 a.m. Anything could be asked at a press conference; no subject was off-limits. I would have to have all the facts at my disposal.

Lunch was brought in from the cafeteria and eaten at the conference table with Tom Menson, my secretary of administration, and Liz Bankowski, my chief of staff, as we went over difficult budget choices. Revenue estimates were shifting once again. How would we explain the change to the legislators, and how should we adjust the budget?

A visit from the Canadian consul, during which we shared pleasantries and exchanged beautiful, personally signed picture books, was followed by a photo with Miss Teenage Vermont, a sweet-looking child with a smile that never relaxed, accompanied by her very eager mother. "Haven't I just done one of these?" I discreetly asked my scheduler as we positioned ourselves between the Vermont and American flags. She shook her head. "No, that was Miss Pre-Teen Vermont."

As the three of us grinned into the camera, the trooper appeared in the doorway with my coat over his arm, and my secretary, right behind him, gave me signals to cut it short. I hurried out the door, putting my coat on while reaching for a box from her hands, like an object in a relay race, packed with papers to sign and reports to read. "Great, thanks, Karen, I'll do these in the car," and into the elevator, and down to Springfield.

*   *   *

ON FEBRUARY 28, 1986, the drinking-age bill passed the Senate. Victory! Sixteen to fourteen—close, but so what? We did it. The next day the press overstated this success. Be warned, I said to myself. One or two votes were the difference between being labeled either "leader" or "failure."

So my staff and I lived in two realities: the one that we personally experienced, and the other that we read about in the newspaper, heard on the radio, or watched on the evening television news. Both dictated the sped-up tempo of the executive office. If an event was covered by the press, it mattered; if not, it was forgotten. Each morning's staff meeting began with a review of what had been in the news. I suspect the same is true in any political staff meeting in the country: the discussion revolves around what the press did, might do, and should have done. But what about events that were not covered by the press? Did they have no validity? The small, seemingly insignificant one-to-one encounters that could make a profound difference in one person's life, but never became public, had their special sense of reward.

In the spring of 1990 I was asked to speak at a lunch in honor of graduates from the Reach Up Program, a welfare-reform program I had initiated five years before with the help of my two newly appointed commissioners: Sallie Soule and Gretchen Morse. The goal was to get families off welfare and into good jobs by providing education, training, child care, and other support services. As I looked at the crowd of expectant women and men, I knew that these could have been the faces that I had seen on the tenement porch when I had marched in the Brandon parade on the Fourth of July—tired and hopeless. Now I saw them seated in this paneled room, dressed in their very best.

No press. Just the graduates, staff, and myself. For the press, this event was not a story because there was no possibility of conflict. Only the graduates knew the stories they had to tell about their triumphs.

"Hi, Governor. I made it," a woman in a blue rayon dress yelled to me from across the room. "I kept climbing that ladder."

Who is she? I wondered. And then I remembered. I had been the commencement speaker at her graduation from the Adult Diploma Program, a high-school-equivalency program for dropouts, two years ago at Vermont Technical College in Randolph Center. She had been one of the five students who had given a five-minute address to the audience, and I, seated directly behind her on stage, had been mesmerized by her trembling knees. How could she keep her balance on those white high heels drilling themselves into the floor? Yet her voice had betrayed nothing. In a rousing conclusion, she had told the crowd: "This degree is the first rung on the ladder for me. Thanks for the boost. I'm going to keep right on climbing!"

I remembered the others who had spoken that day. One woman had placed her diploma in a heavy leather case. "This is so important to me," she said softly and then began to cry.

She was followed by an older woman who limped heavily across the stage to the podium. "Well, I grew up on the farm, with four brothers and two sisters," she began. "I was the oldest. And when my mother died, I left school to take care of my brothers and sisters. Brought 'em up, you might say. I made sure that they all stayed in school.

"Then I got married to a farmer, helped with chores, and took care of my children, made sure they finished school. Last year my husband passed away. Now, it's my turn."

Their turn. That is what the ceremony was about.

"It's great to see you again," I said to the woman in blue who greeted me from across the room. "I'm so glad you kept right on going. I just knew you would. What are you going to do now?"

"I got a job."

Four perfunctory words, but she said them as if she expected cymbals to clash.

The pictures taken that day by families and friends did not appear in any newspapers. But they were placed in frames and set on mantels.

"What was hardest for you?" I asked a woman after the ceremony was over.

"The courage to do it in the first place, that was the hardest."

"Yes," I answered, "I know what you mean."

What she had not known was that she had just given me new courage. Perhaps that's why I accepted the invitation to speak at the commencement cermonies of the Adult Diploma graduation every year. It reminded me why I had sought public office.

I received several thousand letters during my years in public life, but occasionally I received one that I wanted to keep for a while and reread. One such letter was enclosed with a photograph and arrived on December 30, 1992, two years after I left the governorship.

> Dear Mrs. Kunin,
>   Several years ago I had the great pleasure and honor of meeting you not once, but twice.
>   The first time I met you was at my graduation of the Adult High

School Diploma Program. You told me then that there wasn't anything I couldn't do if I really wanted to.

That statement gave me the courage to be one of the first twelve
Community Scholars at Trinity College. At the news announcement of the first twelve is when I got to see you again. When you
recognized me you gave me a hug and told me how proud you were
of me. I have cherished that day and that moment for years.

Enclosed you will find the picture of that hug. I would be honored if you would please sign it for me.

Mrs. Kunin, thanks to you I have my own daycare, a wonderful
husband, and two fine sons, and all with the knowledge that you
can do anything you want if you only try.

Thank you for your time and support when I really needed it.

A very grateful admirer
Mrs. Becky Rutkowski (Wilkins)

As I LOOK BACK, the greatest power conferred on me by the governorship was the power to set the agenda and frame the debate. Soon I discovered that great as this power was, it was also easy to squander. In my
effort to be a good governor in my first term, I was eager to prove that I
could respond to every challenge and meet every crisis. If I failed in the
day-to-day tasks of governing, I feared I would be considered incompetent. When I was illuminated under the public spotlight, there would be
no tolerance for error. I concentrated on breadth, feeling the need to
immerse myself in areas with which I was less familiar, but for which I felt
a keen sense of responsibility, such as corrections and law enforcement.
The specifics of programs, how they worked and how they did not, had to
be mastered. And immediate crises had to be addressed, whether it was
the need for a new prison because of overcrowding or the sudden closing
of a factory, putting one hundred people out of work. Throughout my
governorship, I perceived a tension between the necessity to focus on
present problems and the desire to address long-term underlying solutions that were more complicated, less well understood, and more politically risky. On a daily basis, it was increasingly difficult to think, plan,
and focus on solutions, rather than to react to outside pressures. But if the
immediate crises were not addressed, the credibility I needed to win public support for long-term solutions would be lost. However, if all I did
was react each day, I would never succeed in shaping my own agenda. To
do so, I found that I had to wrench myself away from the constant demands of governing by taking deliberate actions and carving out the time

and energy necessary to achieve depth as well as breadth. I had discovered that in my eagerness to prove I could do everything, I was accomplishing little. Over time, I realized that I could not choose between performing the daily housekeeping tasks of governing and defining the larger, future vision that reflected my priorities. I had to do both. I had to fix problems as they happened and simultaneously focus on a long-term agenda if I did not want to compromise the passionate sense of mission that had attracted me to the political life in the first place. Finding the time, energy, and perspective to carry out a dual strategy was to be the physical and mental challenge of governing. Doing so while facing an election every two years, at which time my successes and failures, both large and small, would be meticulously measured, made the task all the more formidable. I had to move in and out like a zoom lens, focusing in closely when necessary to make sure that the fine details of governing were in place and then stepping back to catch a wide angle—only then could I frame my own agenda.

Early in my political life I had learned that the art of governing was to understand the public as if it were a person who harbored unarticulated hopes and fears. The first step was to give voice and vision to what the people widely sense but infrequently express or know how to fix. Once the problem is defined, solutions can begin to emerge. The formula sounds simple; in actuality, of course, it is far more complex. Political success is often dependent on the ability to be heard above the din of controversy and debate and to set a course with one's own compass. The bully pulpit provides the greatest political mouthpiece, and it is almost always within reach of any politician, but there are select times in the political calendar when it commands extraordinary attention. The day I gave my State of the State speech before a joint session of the General Assembly each January provided such an occasion. This is when all 180 members of the General Assembly, as well as many of the citizens of the state of Vermont, focused on each word. As I look back on these speeches, they provide an index of how my agenda expanded and then narrowed in my three terms as governor.

In my first speech on January 10, 1985, I spelled out a large menu from which each constituency could pick and choose. I stated that I wanted to achieve four goals: build a strong economy, create a first-rate educational system, provide property-tax relief, and assure a clean and healthy environment. I defined the connections that were to shape my future agenda: "Our human-service programs depend on the success of our economic-development programs, and they, in turn, depend on the quality of our education. The best way to get off welfare is to get a job, and the best way to get a job is through education.

"Neither can we delude ourselves into believing that there is a choice between economic growth and a clean and healthy environment. The two are inseparable."

It developed into a good year—a bill that enabled all Vermont children to attend kindergarten was passed, and a string of victories was won on the environmental front—groundwater protection, a mini-Superfund, and a right-to-know-in-the-workplace law.

By 1986 Vermont was enjoying the benefits of a rapidly growing economy. Unemployment had dropped to 3.4 percent and 7,500 jobs had been created in the last year. Nevertheless, that year I stressed the necessity to retire the deficit and reduce taxes. I added a new theme: early intervention and prevention by focusing on unwanted teenage pregnancies, and welfare reform. I asked for an eleven-million-dollar increase in education to equalize educational spending throughout the state, to begin a process of evaluating the quality of education, and to start an early childhood program. "With each passing day, I am increasingly convinced that for Vermonters to compete for jobs, we have to have a highly skilled, well-educated labor force," I told the joint session of the legislature.

In my second term, I realized that if I were to succeed in forging fundamental changes in the lives of Vermonters, I could have the greatest impact on the largest number of people by improving the quality of public education. Every family's life would be touched. I decided to concentrate on the funding of education because this is where the greatest inequalities were to be found. The poorest communities in Vermont had the highest unemployment rates as well as the lowest capacity to finance their children's education. If we devised and funded a new state-aid-to-education distribution formula, they would be given the opportunity to bring their schools up to state standards. To succeed, I knew I would have to give this effort my total attention. On January 8, 1987, I delivered my third State of the State and budget address:

> Today I depart from the tradition of thematic inaugural addresses and ask you to rivet your attention on a single subject: education. I view this as the most important issue this legislature has to resolve. Some one hundred years after the state of Vermont first struggled to resolve the inequities of education financing, I believe we are about to break new ground and begin a historic session. . . .

The problem is simple: today in Vermont, the quality of education a child receives depends on where he or she resides. That is
neither fair nor good for the future of our state.

After describing my strategy to change the funding formula, I appealed
directly to my audience.

For a moment, I ask you to personalize the principle of educational
opportunity into the specifics of your own life. What has education
or, in some cases, the lack of it, meant to you? What do you wish
for your children and grandchildren?

I know from my personal experience what education has meant
to me. When I came to this country as an immigrant with my brother
and mother, not speaking English, it was the educational system of
this nation which opened every important door to us. Without it, we
would have deprived ourselves of the upward mobility which gave
every immigrant and every American, no matter how humble his or
her beginnings, the genuine hope for a better life.

Without access to education, the dream would have died. What
was true for my brother and me is true for the next generation of
Vermonters.

When I took the risk of narrowing my agenda, I had the greatest influence on the outcome. A new education-funding formula was passed,
and the poorest school districts in Vermont benefited the most. Some
signs of success are measurable, many are not, and some are disappoint-
ingly slow to respond. What we could measure was that teachers' salaries
in Vermont moved from forty-ninth place in 1984 to twenty-sixth in
1990. An innovative public-school assessment program was started that
tested students on a portfolio of writing and mathematics, rather than
standardized test scores, but it was too early to judge its success. Perhaps
the most significant impact I had as governor is that I made schools central to my agenda, thereby making it easier for the local communities to
win public support for educational change and encouraging parents as
well as the business community to become involved. Whenever there was
an opportunity to celebrate the opening of a new school, to present
awards, or to participate in any kind of school celebration, I was eager to
be there. These were my favorite ribbon cuttings.

The following year, 1988, I edited my agenda once again. This time, I
concentrated on winning passage of a comprehensive planning law that
would provide guidelines for growth and would be called Act 200.

Protecting the environment became integral to my sense of stewardship
as governor; it was fundamental to my belief that I had a responsibility to
future generations, both as an elected official and as a private person.

Throughout the administration, the environmental agenda was highly visible and sometimes controversial. A record number of environmental bills had recently been passed—reducing the production and disposal of hazardous waste, protecting both ground and surface water, banning the use of ozone-depleting chlorofluorocarbons in automobile air conditioners, protecting significant wetlands, enacting a plan for solid-waste disposal, creating a comprehensive energy plan, and forging an agreement with New York and Quebec to protect Lake Champlain. The result was that Vermont was ranked the number-one environmental state in the nation by the Institute for Southern Studies, an environmental think tank.

But the passage of separate laws was not enough to assure that Vermont would retain its way of life, which is intricately tied to the land. The idea for a new law that would enable us to keep our sense of community, shaped in large part by our small size and respect for the land, had occupied me for some time. All the specific laws could not protect us from haphazard changes if we did not have the capacity to plan for our future. I decided to take time to give the idea shape at a two-day staff retreat in the summer of 1987, midway in my second term. The time to think, to plan, to explore new ideas had to be carved out of the normal schedule to envision the major undertaking I had in mind. At that two-day meeting in a ramshackle house located in a Vermont state park, we sketched out the rough shape of a process that would enable Vermonters to exercise more control over the growth of their communities. The first step was to appoint a blue-ribbon commission, representing both environmentalists and developers, to provide "an overview of growth patterns . . . and a statement of goals and principles for the preservation of Vermont's character." I took great care to assure that a wide spectrum of viewpoints would be fully represented, because I feared polarization might set in at the end. But by starting at the grass roots, I hoped to avoid pitting developers against environmentalists. More than 2,500 Vermonters participated in the public hearings and offered their opinions on how to preserve what is best, while encouraging appropriate growth. Many voices were heard.

"There is something in Vermont which we have that once it is gone, it will be lost forever," one person testified.

A tenth-generation Vermonter said, "Anyone who has ever farmed knows that the land you work becomes your lifeblood, a part of yourself. Trading it for a fat paycheck from someone who will chop it into ten-acre plots and plant houses where alfalfa and clover have thrived is an act of bitter defeat."

And "Balancing the reality of living in a changing Vermont with the

part of Vermont we don't want changed is a formidable task, and one
that will have an impact for years to come. . . . Please save a little time to
discuss how we want the next generation to grow up."

The commission's findings became the focus for my State of the State
speech on January 12, 1988:

> The question we pose to one another is: How do we exercise con-
> trol over our future in a democratic society where planning has
> usually been a laissez-faire process, permitting economic forces to
> drive change? I believe Vermonters are ready to answer that ques-
> tion, to enter a new planning era, taking more direct responsibility
> for decision making in order to assure greater control over our
> destiny.
>   The movement is toward a system of planning which invites and
> respects public participation at all levels of government, but it is
> planning which will be uniform in standard, specific in require-
> ments, and tough on delinquents.

I was optimistic that if the process was participatory, the results would
be accepted.

> It is my belief that to plan effectively—to make the words on paper
> result in contours on the landscape—two ingredients are necessary:
> political will and adequate resources. Despite some of the ambi-
> tious and difficult budget goals mentioned in the commission's re-
> port, I believe it may be easier to create the financial resources to
> make this process work than it will be to galvanize political con-
> sensus, and to maintain that consensus, in good times and bad.

Giving the speech that shaped Act 200 left me with extraordinary exhilaration. It had been both a physical and a spiritual effort; I had tried to
lift my audience to another plane of thought, feeling, and, I hoped, action. At that moment, I knew absolutely what the purpose of governing
was: to create change. I had been given a great opportunity, and whatever
the consequences, it had been worth the effort. I had experienced the
thrill of articulating a vision, and now I had the chance to make it happen.
This reverie was not hidden in my private thoughts; it took place in the
public arena, where my voice was heard and often understood. Nothing
else could compare.

When the report was first issued, consensus held firm, and business
groups, developers, and environmentalists applauded the results. But as
the generalities of the report were refined into the specifics of legislation,
support began to ebb. How much of a role should the state and the counties play in approving local planning? What were the necessary resources

to achieve success? The devil, as the saying goes, was in the details. One section of the bill, however, was hugely popular—the Vermont Housing and Land Conservation Trust Fund, which enabled the state to preserve open space and protect affordable housing. Before the bill was passed, a partisan legislative battle ensued. We won, but the victory was not final. As I had anticipated when giving my State of the State address, political will was difficult to sustain once the Vermont economy began to wane. The law, however, has survived numerous efforts to weaken and repeal it, and it has continued to retain the support of both Republican and Democratic leaders.

In hindsight, Act 200 was an ambitious undertaking that required the expenditure of a large sum of my political capital, but I have no regrets. Politics is a debate about the future, and that was what we ignited.

THE PARAMETERS of a governor's responsibility are wide, I discovered. Nothing was out-of-bounds. Anything could become a political issue. One summer I came under attack because of an unusual infestation of mosquitoes. It had been a wet spring in the swampy area surrounding Brandon, a community that depended heavily on its summer tourist trade, which flocked to nearby Lake Dunmore. Several species of mosquitoes had multiplied in record numbers that year and descended on the populace like an invading army. A flurry of letters arrived on my desk, demanding reinforcements from the state. At first, I tried to ignore the problem, claiming that mosquito control was a local responsibility, but like a persistent itch, it wouldn't go away. The governor's toll-free Citizen Action Line provided the first indicator of trouble. In the daily tabulation of calls, that subject dominated all others, 2 to 1. The mosquito mail began to mount; no form letters, all handwritten—a bad sign.

Something would have to be done. "We need help!" The chairman of an ad hoc antimosquito brigade demanded over the phone that I "see this problem for myself."

After several weeks of vain hope for a dry spell, I relented. I would go to Brandon. I would leave directly from the New England Governors and Eastern Canadian Premiers meeting in Quebec and charter a plane to a small, seldom-used airport in nearby Middlebury. There I would hand the leader of the mosquito group a check. We had managed to find some funds that could be transferred from one department to another to pay for additional spraying. It would be a good photo opportunity.

As the tiny chartered plane shook violently on its approach into Middlebury, I began to question the wisdom of my decision. Sudden high winds pushed us precariously close to the mountain on our left. The runway looked like a broken shoelace left in the grass. When we bounced to the ground, I was happy to be alive. I descended the rickety stairs and swayed for a moment, trying to bring the shimmering gas-fumed scene into focus. There in front of me, in the rain, was a good-sized crowd. For a moment I felt like Amelia Earhart. But no one was the least bit interested in the details of my account of our heroic landing.

Mosquitoes. And more mosquitoes.

A microphone was stuck in my face. I saw the letters: CBS.

"CBS national news?" I asked with trepidation.

"Yes."

"Oh."

"What are you going to do, Governor, about this infestation of mosquitoes?"

"We take this situation very seriously and have developed a plan for . . ."

For five days, it had been raining. Drizzle had thickened the air to stirring consistency. I was pleased that I had thought to put on a sensible shiny black raincoat. But it became an instant magnet for a Genghis Khan–sized horde of mosquitoes. The crowd backed off to watch. I was the human sacrifice, bound to a stake on the tarmac.

"More wood." Is that what someone said?

Was I mistaken, or did I detect a look of satisfaction on everybody's face as they watched the mosquitoes feast on my flesh?

"Now she knows what we've been talking about," the self-declared spokesman for the group pronounced. Everything had worked as he had planned. The mosquito army seemed at his command.

I did my best to be gubernatorial while swatting right and left. I looked at the airplane longingly. Which would I prefer, bleeding to death now or smashing against the mountain later?

Duty first. I signaled Chad, the trooper, to hand me the check. He slipped some insect repellent along with it.

"Chad, you've saved my life," I whispered.

Someone handed me a pith helmet draped with mosquito netting. "It'd make a great picture," a voice volunteered. (That night, when I saw the television coverage, I thanked the Lord that I had the good instinct to refuse.)

As the check was handed over, the word "grateful" appeared in the script, but grudgingly, as if I had given the man his own ball back.

Just the same, it should be a good photo. I envisioned the headline: "Governor Rescues Brandon."

Instead, I turned on the TV, and there I was, slapping my wrists, arms, and forehead, a wan smile appearing briefly for the camera, but not to be maintained.

"Whoops, there they go again."

This time, around my ankles.

"Even the governor was called for help with the unusual plague of mosquitoes which has infested the state of Vermont . . ."

The camera focused on a face in the crowd. "I say bring out the National Guard!" the man shouted straight into the lens, waving his fist in the air, ready to charge.

That summer in Brandon, I caught sight of a mimeographed poster tacked to a telephone post: a drawing of a mosquito that had metamorphosed into a likeness of me. I felt like Kafka's cockroach. I could not pause long enough to read the words, but the message was clear: if you're being bitten by mosquitoes, blame the governor.

The presence or absence of the governor at an event could, in itself, send a strong message. On June 14, 1985, I was the only political leader present at a gay and lesbian pride rally, assembled before the group would march through the main street of downtown Burlington. I accepted the invitation with some trepidation, not certain how I would feel and how the press might report my appearance. But I had decided to declare openly my support for gay and lesbian rights. As I joined the assembled crowd now occupying the front lawn of the Unitarian church, the state trooper who had accompanied me looked nervously at his watch. A podium had been set up near the church steps. Overhead a large banner was strung: GAY AND LESBIAN PRIDE DAY.

I spoke to the audience about the importance of guaranteeing civil rights for all Vermonters, regardless of sexual orientation. Mingling with the crowd before the start of the parade, I detected more than the usual excitement typical of pre-parade gatherings. Theirs was nervous laughter. Suddenly, I felt ashamed of my inconsequential show of courage. These people were coming out. The men and women putting their arms around one another's shoulders were risking their employment, their friends, their safe place in Vermont society. Some of the people were straight, there to support their friends in public. It was hard to tell who was gay and who was not. Hugs were exchanged like talismans of mutual protection, as if to say, "I am with you; you are not alone."

I recalled the chant from the lesbians in the balcony in Houston at the

National Women's Conference: "We were here for you, now be here for us." I was glad I was there, now.

The trooper again pointed to his wristwatch. Time to get on the road and get to the Flag Day ceremony in St. Albans sponsored by the American Legion. One hour later, as I stood by my folding chair in City Hall Park, holding my right hand over my heart, watching the American flag being pulled up the flagpole, and listening to the "Star-Spangled Banner," I wondered, What will *these* people think when they see me on the six o'clock news at the gay rally? Will they be shocked? Will they never vote for me again?

On the way back to my car, I chatted with a woman legionnaire, dressed in royal blue.

"You must have a busy schedule," she said, to make conversation.

"Yes," I told her, and then I mentioned where I had been.

The look of disapproval I expected to see on her face did not materialize. "It seems everybody knows somebody these days who's gay."

I agreed.

But the owner of the mom-and-pop store in the small town of Groton in the Northeast Kingdom was less benign. When I stopped there to buy a soda a few weeks later, I noticed that he had taped a picture from the *Burlington Free Press* on the customer side of his cash register, with a big X marked across it. There I was. The photo was a long-focus shot of the rally, and my figure was quite small, but the banner behind me was large enough to be clearly legible: GAY AND LESBIAN PRIDE DAY.

The following year, a number of Vermont politicians attended the same rally. And in 1992 the Democratic platform and its candidate for president took a firm position on gay and lesbian rights and promised to lift the ban on homosexuals in the military. More recently, Vermont passed legislation guaranteeing gay and lesbian Vermonters the protection of civil rights. A show of support that once was considered either brave or reprehensible was now applauded, although not without controversy (as evidenced by the reaction President Clinton received when he moved to fulfill his campaign promise). But one of the great powers given to a political leader is to extend his or her own credibility to others who have less, and thereby enable them to move from outside the circle of social justice into its protective confines.

THE REWARDS of public life are usually handed over on solid, wooden plaques that are presented in stiff ceremonies to the honoree, and everybody claps. That is when such things are scheduled to occur. The real happiness that came my way while governor, however, was more serendipitous.

A huge banner, green letters on gold, WELCOME GOVERNOR, had been hung across the front entry of the Richmond Elementary School, some ten miles from Burlington. I was escorted to the library by an entourage of fifth-graders, and there in the corner of the room was a rocking chair, with a vase of golden flowers on each side. I tried not to feel like a queen.

"Please sit down."

"Yes, thank you."

A little girl threw her arms around my waist before I could do so.

The children sang, recited, and showed me their drawings. The parents took pictures. The teachers could not stop grinning. I am there for a perfect moment, when the picture and the reality were one. I loved visiting schools; they were happy places, and my presence often provided an affirmation of their value. Not only did the children thrive on praise, but so did the teachers, principals, and parents. Each such visit helped restore my sense of purpose—this is how we would change the world.

The spring of 1990 had been difficult. I had increasingly been on the firing line over Act 200 as several towns voted not to comply with the planning process. The fact that all but eight towns had agreed to participate in Act 200 was largely ignored by the press. And as revenues continued to fall, and joblessness increased, I had to grapple with larger budget cuts, which had begun to anger some of my supporters.

One evening, at a Democratic meeting, after I had given a feisty speech in defense of Act 200, Representative Don Hooper looked at me and said, "All this rolls off you like water, doesn't it? You were terrific!"

I had put on a terrific act. In fact, I was on a roller coaster, managing criticism and conquering anxiety one moment, and feeling devastated the next.

One morning I woke up in pain; I had dreamed that I had been burned by an explosion. I had walked home and looked down to see the charred parts of my body. I felt like a burnt offering.

The next day I rebounded. "Once again, I triumph over depression, defeatism, and despair by confronting the enemy," I wrote in my notes after my speech to the St. Johnsbury Rotary Club. I had come home exhilarated. St. Johnsbury was strong Republican territory, and I had survived my trip into the lion's den. When I had walked into the meeting room in the Lincoln Inn, a Democratic friend pulled me aside and warned me, "John Poole is here."

John Poole's name was familiar. With assiduous regularity he wrote scathing letters against me to the editor of the *Caledonian-Record* and the *Burlington Free Press*. An astonishing, deep hatred emanated from the pen of this man whom I had never met. I would never know what had prompted this steady ooze of venom. The *Caledonian-Record* once carried an editorial saying his letter was too vitriolic to print. The editor seemed to be unmindful that he had done Poole a service by quoting liberally from its text.

I decided to talk to the Rotary Club about Act 200—a vote was scheduled on the question for the following day. John Poole was also up for reelection as selectman. At the conclusion of my speech, I was satisfied that I had made a good case for Act 200. As I read the body language in the room, I focused on those who were less hostile. A few signaled friendliness. John Poole, who had been pointed out to me, never once looked in my direction while I spoke. He seemed fixated by the opposite wall. I had looked in his direction furtively from time to time. He was small, bald, and did have beady little eyes as I had imagined he would!

Just as the president of the Rotary was about to bring the meeting to a close at precisely one-thirty, John Poole stood up. The hatred in his voice spewed toward me like spittle. I ran my hand across my cheek.

It was his tone that was more vicious than his words. It seemed he was grappling for something terrible to say, and all he could find was that I had appointed as chairman for the Blue Ribbon Growth Commission a person who had lived in Vermont for only five months and then bought a house in Woodstock for $350,000.

I replied, "You look much nicer than your letters." Just as I intended, laughter threw him off guard. I felt I had successfully launched a hand grenade.

I accused him of bigotry against out-of-staters. "We don't give people who live in Vermont a litmus test, whether or not they are natives, what their nationality is, income is, or their religion." I managed to rise to a level of righteous indignation. The audience seemed thrilled. Someone was taking John Poole on. Shazam!

Poole sat down. The wizard disappeared.

I was Wonder Woman.

Who says this job can't be fun?

One of my delights two days later was to learn that John Poole had been defeated in his bid for reelection.

That night I went to the pre–town meeting in Bolton, where some fifty people had gathered in the school. Town Meeting Day is a long-standing, if somewhat waning, tradition in Vermont that takes place on the first Tuesday after the first Monday in March, when the voters of a town assemble to decide on municipal and school budgets and other local matters, which might include the purchase of a fire truck or the repair of a stretch of blacktop. I had attended a number of such meetings in years past to get a better sense of local concerns and briefly introduce myself to the crowd. Always, I had been warmly welcomed, and the homemade pies and potluck casserole lunches brought me back to a comforting reality. This was the case at the Bolton meeting held that night in the elementary school, where we all squeezed into third-grade chairs, drank coffee, and munched on brownies. My explanation of Act 200 was followed by an excellent discussion. The effort had been worthwhile, I concluded.

Nothing had prepared me for the following day. My first stop was in Duxbury, a rural bedroom town near Waterbury. When I got to the town hall, I saw a sign tacked up on each of the green double doors addressed to GOVERNOR KUNIN AND HER CRONIES. I didn't record the words, but the message was clear: If the town complied with Act 200, no person in Vermont would be allowed to either hunt or fish. On the lampposts leading up to the building, the message was more simple. The hand-scrawled words read: ACT 200 IS A BAD LAW.

I had come early so that I would make all three meetings I hoped to attend that day in nearby towns. The trooper just dropped me off this time and left to run an errand. "Be right back. Think you'll be here about half an hour?"

"About that," I said, and sat down in the front row.

I spotted two newspaper reporters on the other side of the room. Had they been told that something might happen?

The moderator called the meeting to order. He was ready to ask me to come up and say a few words when a man in the back row raised his hand.

"Mr. Moderator, I believe we should take a vote on whether or not the governor should be allowed to speak."

Take a vote? This could be trouble. I peered anxiously around the room, waiting for another voice to speak on my behalf.

"Well, we've never had to take a vote on things like this before," the moderator protested, but not with great conviction.

"Mr. Moderator, this is a town meeting, and that's for us to decide. I demand that we put this to a vote."

Murmurs rattled the room. The ordinary had become extraordinary.

This could be a more interesting town meeting than the good citizens of Duxbury had anticipated.

I scanned the room. Wasn't there anyone out there? Some brave soul to stand up and talk about the respect due to the governor of the state of Vermont?

Silence.

The moderator banged the gavel. "It is agreed, we will put the matter to a vote."

"What's the question?" a voice asked.

"I guess the question is, Shall the governor be allowed to address the meeting? The clerks will now distribute the ballots."

I turned beet red and headed for the only retreat: the ladies' room. It seemed obscene to be present at a public hanging. Through the flimsy ladies' room door, I thought I heard rabble noises outside. When I stepped back out, a few people came up to me, embarrassed. "We're sorry such a thing happened. It's not right."

I nodded appreciatively. Balloting would take time. I couldn't stand here while they counted. I went out into the parking lot and paced. I wished I had my car. Where was the trooper? Should I just leave? That would be worse. It would show I couldn't take it. This was just a test, and I would pass it. I wondered, Why do people think that those of us in public office have no feelings? Why on earth did I do this to myself?

Ten minutes later, the vote was in my favor. It took me a moment to gain self-control. I vowed to suppress my anger and humiliation by being more conciliatory and polite than I had ever been in my life. I did, however, with firm conviction applaud freedom of speech and commended the town for upholding it. It seemed the only way to begin.

MY POLITICAL FEARS were like my fear of flying. I would take my seat in the plane, fasten my seat belt, and listen to the tone of the voice that came over the loudspeaker. If the copilot or steward sounded warm and confident, I tended to relax. If nothing was said, I panicked. If the tone of voice was curt, I was anxious.

I scanned the sky. Clouds? Rain? Turbulence? I had to concentrate as we took off, or else we couldn't stay aloft. I arched my spine like a bird as we left the ground, responding to some primeval instinct. My body felt each lift and fall, each sway and lurch, as if I had no outer skin, no inner sense of balance. Perhaps if I didn't listen to the changing murmur of the engine, getting louder and softer from one moment to the next, I could "relax and enjoy the flight," as the flight attendants cheerfully urged us all to do. I could not believe that they did this each day for money and pleasure.

Once I listened attentively to the noise, I raised the expectation that it might stop. That is what I waited for most noises to do. The mere possibility that it might stop made me fear it would. I created a vivid image of stalled engines, plugged gas lines, and the plane plunging down, nose first, at terrifying speed.

Accidents do not happen that way, I told myself. Most occur during takeoff or landing. Planes do not fall out of the sky.

I didn't believe it. Anything that shakes so much must be vulnerable. My body told me so. Yet when there was no turbulence, and I lost the sensation of movement, it was *too* still. We were simply floating precariously, and at any moment . . .

Each time I flew, I previewed my own death. Each time I landed, I felt reborn, quick to laugh at my sweaty palms. Part of me had believed I would die, and part of me had known I wouldn't. My political anxiety followed the same pattern. I could envision either defeat or victory: life or death.

The emotional drain of public life is extraordinary. I learned to put criticism in perspective; I learned to fight back and rebound; and I learned about resilience. That is why I got on the plane, again and again. But I never lost my fear or developed a thick skin. Perhaps one shouldn't. Or perhaps I couldn't. The right balance between taking risks and protecting oneself is difficult to achieve for anyone. One difference for politicians is that all the learning takes place in public, an arena that is not devoid of private pain.

Or pleasure.

One Saturday in May of my last year in office I was invited to take a tour of the Galick farm in West Haven, two thousand acres of open farmland abutting the lower end of Lake Champlain that had been cultivated since the eighteenth century by only one family. The farm had recently been saved from development by a consortium of forces that included the state of Vermont. The purchase was made possible by Act 200, which included a provision to start the new Housing and Land Conservation Trust Fund.

Unique species of plants and animals had found natural protection there, including a rare lizard and timber rattlers on a mountaintop. The tractor took us through the fields and then stopped at the base of a hillside where a small group of us, including my son Daniel, got out and walked up the mountain, keeping our eyes out for the sunning rattlers. Every once in a while we would pause, while one member of our party, an experienced birdcaller, called in the birds. I felt he was Francis of Assisi.

"Stop, there's one," our guide said.

There, in warm comfort in the cleft of a rock, was a loosely coiled rattler. So beautiful and so deadly.

We gave him a wide berth and moved on. When we reached the top and scanned the view of lake and pasture and forest, I felt I was looking down on the Garden of Eden. This land was as close to nature undisturbed as I had ever seen. Hardly a dwelling was visible, except for a few tiny houses set on the rim of the horizon.

Human life had also been extraordinarily protected here. The two Galick brothers, now in their eighties, had been the only ones to live here. They themselves built the only road out with shovels, laying down the stones by hand. When each child in the family had been born, the midwife arrived only the morning after, to tie the umbilical cord.

I took in the view with one deep breath, wanting it to stay inside my head so that later on I could bring it out. There was the end of Lake Champlain lazily meandering into the river, bounded by wide swaths of bird-filled marshes; there were the hay fields, the herd of cattle, and the woods we had just climbed through. This was the land that others now could walk, whenever they wanted to. It would be theirs.

"This makes it all worth it." I sighed as I turned to my son. "This land will be here, for you, forever."

A Note About the Author

MADELEINE MAY KUNIN is the Deputy Secretary of the United States Department of Education and the former three-term Governor of Vermont. Born in Switzerland, Kunin immigrated to the United States in 1940 with her family. She graduated from the University of Massachusetts and holds graduate degrees from Columbia University and the University of Vermont. After serving three terms in the Vermont General Assembly, she was elected lieutenant governor in 1978, reelected in 1980, and in 1984 was elected governor. She completed her last term in 1991 and held several distinguished visiting academic positions at Dartmouth and Harvard and founded the Institute for Sustainable Communities at the Vermont Law School. She served on the three-person committee that advised President Bill Clinton on the vice presidency and on the Presidential Transition Board of Directors. She has four grown children and lives in Washington, D.C., and Shelburne, Vermont.

A Note on the Type

The text of this book was set in Sabon, a type face designed by Jan Tschichold (1902–1974), the well-known German typographer. Based loosely on the original designs of Claude Garamond (c. 1480–1561), Sabon is unique in that it was explicitly designed for hot-metal composition on both the Monotype and Linotype machines as well as for film setting. Designed in Frankfurt, Sabon was named for the famous Lyon punchcutter Jaques Sabon, who is thought to have brought some of Garamond's matrices to Frankfurt.

Composed by American-Stratford Graphic Services,
Brattleboro, Vermont
Printed and bound by R.R. Donnelley & Sons Company
Harrisonburg, Virginia
Designed by Anthea Lingeman